The Legacy of Yugoslavia

The Legacy of Yugoslavia

Politics, Economics and Society
in the Modern Balkans

Edited by

Othon Anastasakis, Adam Bennett, David Madden

and Adis Merdzanovic

I.B. TAURIS

LONDON • NEW YORK • OXFORD • NEW DELHI • SYDNEY

I.B. TAURIS
Bloomsbury Publishing Plc
50 Bedford Square, London, WC1B 3DP, UK
1385 Broadway, New York, NY 10018, USA
29 Earlsfort Terrace, Dublin 2, Ireland

BLOOMSBURY, I.B. TAURIS and the I.B. Tauris logo are trademarks of
Bloomsbury Publishing Plc

First published in Great Britain 2020
This paperback edition published in 2022

Series design by Adriana Brioso
Cover image: A flag honouring Tito hangs down the side of a building, 1948.
(© Walter Sanders/The LIFE Picture Collection via Getty Images)

A catalogue record for this book is available from the British Library.

A catalogue record for this book is available from the Library of Congress.

ISBN: HB: 978-1-7883-1796-2
        PB: 978-0-7556-3752-2
      ePDF: 978-1-7883-1799-3
     eBook: 978-1-7883-1797-9

Typeset by RefineCatch Limited, Bungay, Suffolk

To find out more about our authors and books visit www.bloomsbury.com
and sign up for our newsletters.

Contents

Foreword and Acknowledgements   vii

Maps of Yugoslavia and the Successor States   ix

Introduction: Revisiting the Yugoslav Past and its Impact on the Present
Othon Anastasakis, Adam Bennett, David Madden
and Adis Merdzanovic   1

Part One   Politics and Society

1   Liberalism in Yugoslavia: Before and after the Disintegration
Adis Merdzanovic   15

2   Civil Society in Post-Yugoslav Space: The Test of Discontinuity
and Democratization   *Ivor Sokolić, Denisa Kostovicova and*
Adam Fagan   39

3   Music, Media and Culture One Generation after Yugoslavia:
Do we Still Need 'Nostalgia'?   *Catherine Baker*   59

Part Two   International Affairs

4   Transformations of Global Citizenship in the Former Yugoslavia:
The Legacies of Yugoslav Non-aligned Multilateralism
Ljubica Spaskovska   81

5   Between a Borderless Yugoslavia and a Europe without Borders:
The Legacy of Territorial Disputes in the Western Balkans
James Ker-Lindsay   99

6   Parallel Trajectories and Legacies of the Past: Russia and Turkey
in the Western Balkans   *Othon Anastasakis*   117

Part Three   Economics

7   Macroeconomic Stability and Enterprise Self-Management
in Yugoslavia: An Impossible Marriage   *Adam Bennett*   141

8   What Happened to the Yugoslav Economic Model?   *Milica Uvalic*   169

9   Are Yugoslav Successor States on the Path to Sustainable Market
    Economies?   *Jakov Milatović and Peter Sanfey*   191

10 Conclusion: Yugoslavia, Lost in Transition?   *Othon Anastasakis,
    Adam Bennett, David Madden and Adis Merdzanovic*   209

Index   217

Foreword and Acknowledgements

The current volume is one of the most important outputs of years of work at SEESOX (South East European Studies at Oxford) on developments in the former Yugoslav/ Western Balkan space, which we as editors conducted through a series of lectures, articles, reports, workshops, travel in the region and engagement with scholars and policy makers. During the course of our work at SEESOX we were confronted by the degree of rupture between the previous state of Yugoslavia and the current Western Balkan situation: the former a solid recognizable country with global impact and the latter a rather flexible group of states whose categorization seems to depend on progress in their accession to the European Union.

We therefore decided to look at the degree of continuity between Yugoslavia and the Western Balkans or, to put it differently, to examine the Western Balkans through the prism of Yugoslavia. In an interdisciplinary exercise, we worked together with other scholars from social sciences and humanities on a number of indicative topics. The high point of this joint work was the organization of a public conference co-convened by the four editors. It took place on 23 November 2017 at St Antony's College, University of Oxford, under the title 'Revisiting Yugoslavia in the shadow of the present: Continuities and Discontinuities'. It brought together a wide mix of experts on Yugoslavia and the Western Balkans stemming from different disciplines (history, politics, international relations, economics). All the papers included in this volume were presented at this conference and are a product of the panels' interaction and the feedback from the audience too.

The story of Yugoslavia's collapse has been told many times and by many authors. The approach in this book is new and different. It uses the analytical framework of legacies, continuities and discontinuities to develop an understanding of how the past affects the present, and how the present reflects the past. During the course of our project and the editing of this volume, it became clear how important the Yugoslav past still is for the present-day region, and how the prolonged internal wars and external interferences have obscured many important historical trends and Yugoslav trademarks, which, however, continue to affect the present, directly or indirectly. Our general idea, and intention, is to encourage scholars working on the contemporary post-conflict environment to acknowledge a historical pre-conflict perspective and inform the present through a better understanding of the past.

The editors wish to express their profound gratitude to Julie Adams for her skilful administrative help at SEESOX and the organisation of the conference, all the contributors to this volume for their excellent conference papers which became chapters in the book, and the SEESOX team of colleagues for their invaluable comments and support. Furthermore, we want to thank Tomasz Hoskins, Nayiri

Kendir and the entire team at IB Tauris for their support during the editorial and publishing stages.

We hope that this book will provide readers with insights on a region which never ceases to excite our intellectual curiosity.

The Editors
Oxford, October 2019

Maps of Yugoslavia and the Successor States

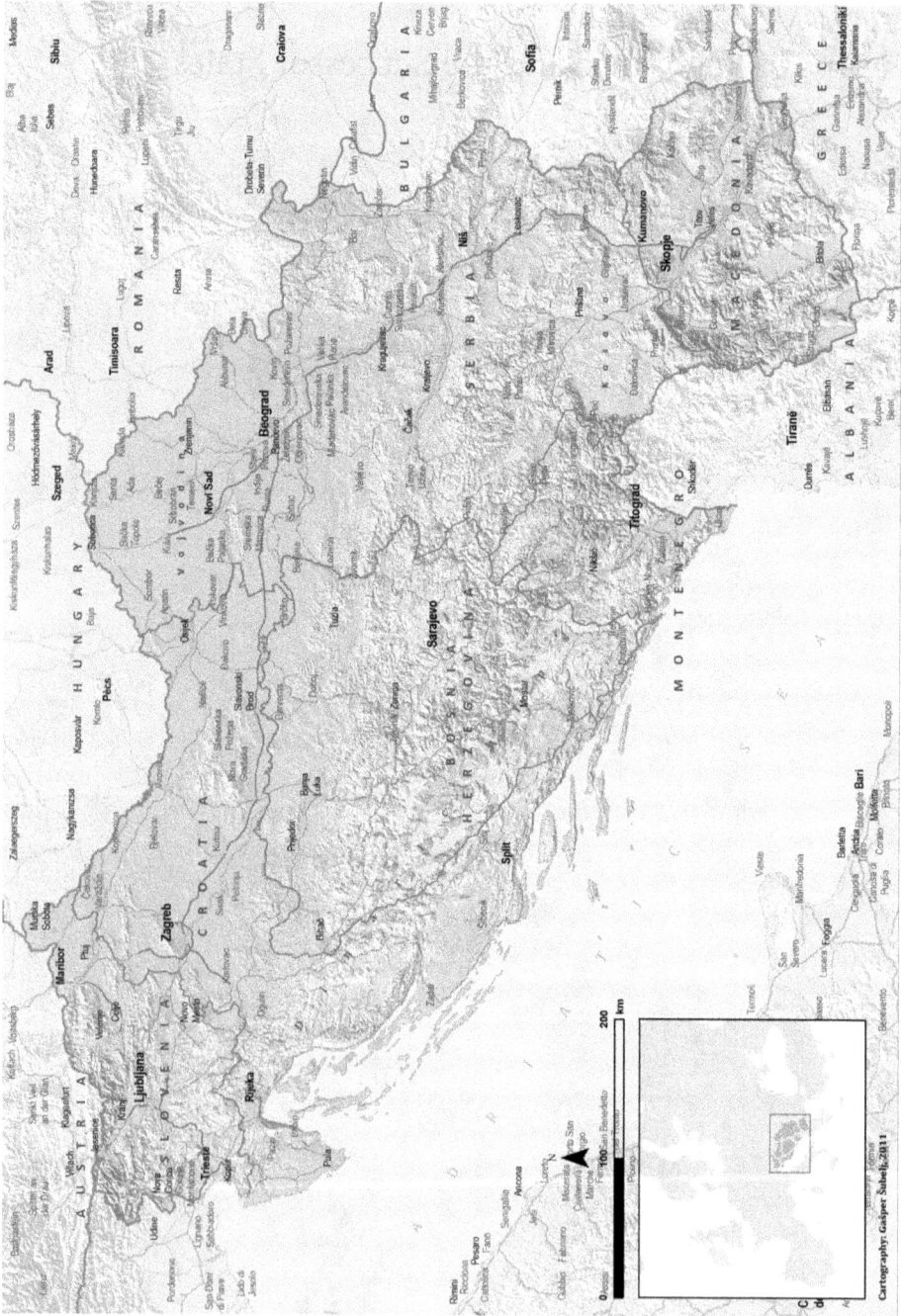

Map 1 Political and administrative map of Yugoslavia. Note: This map refers to Yugoslavia in the time period between 1946 and 1991. Source: Wikipedia, Copyright: CC BY-SA 3.0.

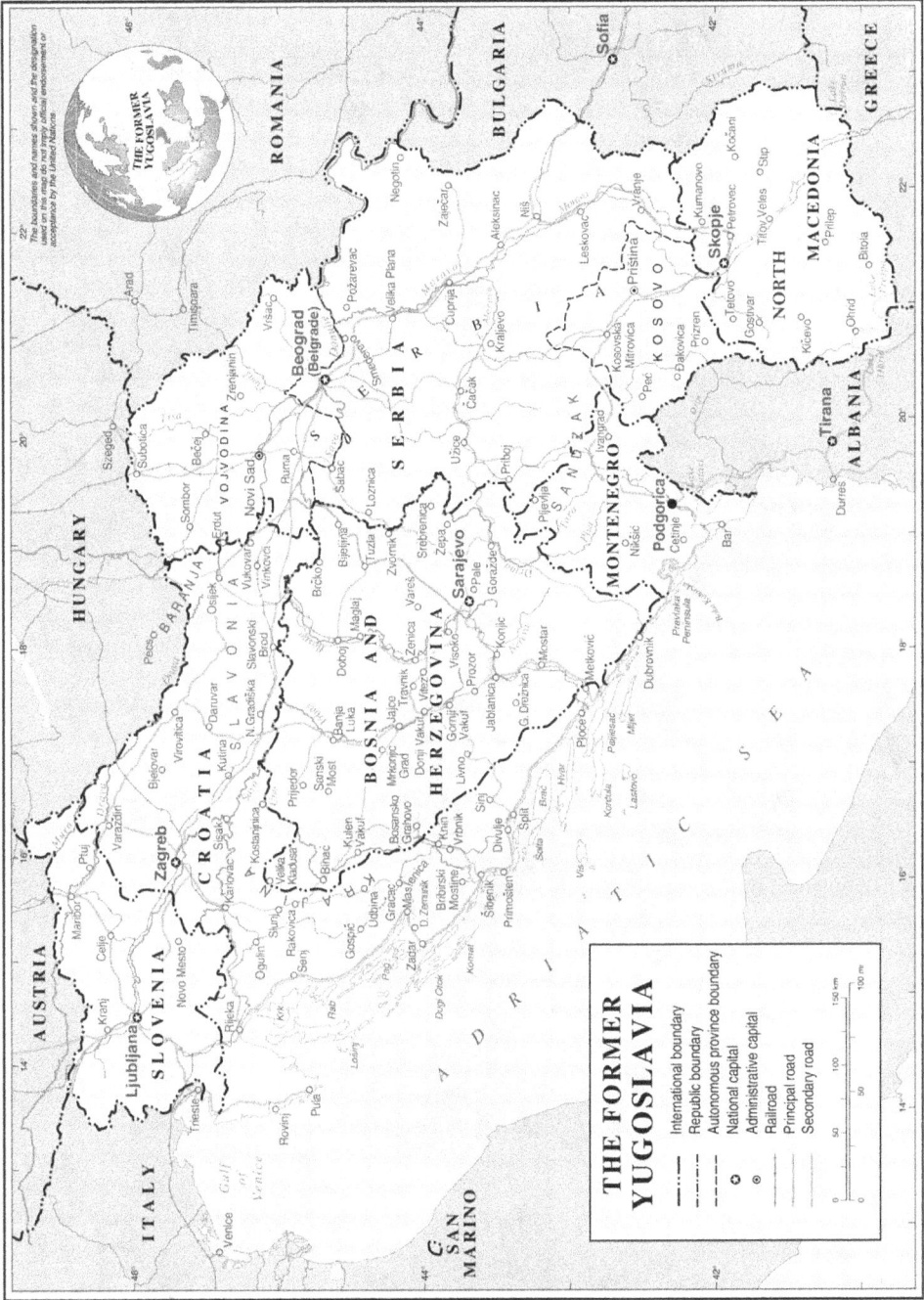

Map 2 The Western Balkans in 2019. Source: The Cartographic Section of the United Nations (adapted). Copyright: public domain.

Revisiting the Yugoslav Past and its Impact on the Present

Othon Anastasakis, Adam Bennett, David Madden and
Adis Merdzanovic
University of Oxford/Zurich University of Applied Sciences

I Introduction

Some three decades after the violent disintegration of Yugoslavia began, the Western Balkans seems like a totally different regional environment from what it was during the Yugoslav times. New states, new issues, new challenges point to a region that has nothing to do with its own past. But is this truly the case?

As Yugoslavia collapsed, what had once been one country of six republics (Slovenia, Croatia, Bosnia and Herzegovina, Serbia, Montenegro and Macedonia), six constituent nationalities (Slovenian, Croatian, Serbian, Montenegrin, Muslim and Macedonian), four religions (Catholics, Orthodox Christians, Muslims and Jews), three official languages (Slovenian, Serbo-Croatian and Macedonian), and two autonomous provinces (Kosovo and Vojvodina), has now become six internationally recognized countries, and one which still does not yet enjoy membership of the United Nations.[1] Seeking to establish themselves as firm holders of statehood, the new states embarked on the creation of new national and political projects and narratives. This meant that all of them, to a greater or lesser extent, sought to disengage their present and future completely from their shared Yugoslav past.

Some new states did better than others in this regard and the region as a whole has witnessed some political and economic successes on its path to democracy and market economy; but it is still better known for its failures and drawbacks in this process. Without wanting to reproduce the well-known negativities and stereotypes about the region, the reality today, some 30 years after the collapse of Yugoslavia began, is that

---

[1] At the beginning of January 2019, 113 out of 193 UN members had recognized Kosovo as an independent state, even if the numbers are contested (see James Ker-Lindsay's chapter in this volume). While Kosovo does not have a UN seat due to lack of Security Council unanimity, it is a full member of both the World Bank and the International Monetary Fund.

there are indeed important problems of stateness, tendencies towards illiberalism and authoritarianism fostered by self-interested political elites, regional and geopolitical (in)security challenges, and a general stagnation in terms of political, economic, and social reforms dominate the newspaper headlines dedicated to the former Yugoslav space. Some of these issues are wider European, other are explicitly Balkan and have to do with the actual post-communist transition.

These challenges need to be taken seriously, as Europe has a vested interest in keeping the region stable, prosperous, and democratic. Economically, the European Union (EU) is by far the biggest investor in the region as well as its largest trading partner. Geopolitically, its security depends on the absence of conflict and other instabilities in the Balkan Peninsula. And since the outbreak of the war, the region has become a prestigious, ideological project for Europe. It is here that the durability and transformative power of European values, norms, and principles is tested and the EU's capacity as an international actor ascertained. A deeper understanding of the region and its contemporary challenges is therefore of paramount importance, not only for the region itself, but also for Western Europe.

But one should not assume that these challenges are exclusively a contemporary, post-Yugoslav phenomenon, for some of them have root causes reaching further back in history than the conflicts of the 1990s. While the break-up of multi-ethnic Yugoslavia was unique, especially in how the different nationalities, which had formed part of one and the same country, fought each other in order to eradicate any vestiges of the past federated state and create new homogeneous nation states, today it is almost forgotten that the Western Balkan states – with the notable exception of Albania – were once part of one single country which lasted for no fewer than seven decades. Moreover, during socialist Yugoslavia, the country enjoyed over four decades of relative political stability and peaceful coexistence and, compared to its communist neighbours in Eastern Europe, some three decades of relative economic prosperity. Perhaps in part because of that lengthy experience of living together, its disintegration was the more tormented and prolonged and lasted for seventeen years – starting with the declaration of independence by Slovenia in 1991 and finishing only with Kosovo's formal independence in 2008.

Most political elites in the Western Balkan region want the world to believe that, while their ethnonational groups may have long and deep historical foundations, their nation state was deemed to be born in the year when their countries left Yugoslavia. By radically breaking with the past, this moment of national birth was supposed to represent a whole new beginning. The purpose of this book is to re-examine and test this notion of a 'new beginning'. It explores the continuities and ruptures between the Yugoslav past and the contemporary political, social and economic realities in the successor states. While Yugoslavia may have ceased to exist as a country and has been replaced by seven new state entities, there is evidence that some dimensions of its legacy have lingered, not just in certain institutions and practices, but through inter-generational memory which strongly affects the present. In other respects, there have been profound changes – some in ways which distinguish the new nation states from each other, and some collectively from their common past.

II The Yugoslav story in brief

Yugoslavia was created as part of the process of redrawing the map of Europe in the wake of The Great War. It was formed from elements of the Empire of Austria-Hungary (including Slovenia, Croatia with Slavonia and Dalmatia, Bosnia and Herzegovina, and Vojvodina) and independent Balkan states which had already evolved out of the Ottoman Empire (Serbia, with its southern province which would later become Macedonia, and Montenegro). The newly formed country was initially called the Kingdom of Serbs, Croats and Slovenes. With the support of the British and French, it was conceived as part of the Corfu Declaration in 1917, which was signed by the Serbian government in exile as well as by members of the Yugoslav Committee as representatives of Bosnians, Croats and Slovenes. It came into being in 1918 and was subsequently known as the 'Versailles State', after the conclusion of the eponymous treaty in 1919. It did not assume the name of Yugoslavia – the land of the South Slavs – until 1929. Although a union of South Slavs, as indicated above, it shared three major religions and very diverse national and cultural identities. Ironically, the assumption of the name Yugoslavia was the result of the suspension of the existing constitution by King Alexander Karađorđević, himself of Serb origin, due to the rise of inter-ethnic tensions between Croats and Serbs, culminating in the murder of Croat politician Stjepan Radić in the National Assembly. The new constitution revised the internal boundaries of the country and sought to break the historical pattern, which was partly based on nationally designated territories.

In 1941, the Kingdom of Yugoslavia was invaded by Nazi Germany and its territory largely divided into German- and Italian-controlled areas, with the Independent State of Croatia (*Nezavisna Država Hrvatska*) as a newly established Nazi-puppet state (there were also Hungarian and Bulgarian areas of control). Both the Partisans, meaning the communist movement under the leadership of Josip Broz Tito, and the Četniks, a Serb-dominated militia committed to the restoration of the monarchy under Serb leadership, resisted the Nazi occupation. Ultimately, the Partisans emerged by far the stronger of the two groups, not least because they had significant international backing.

After the Second World War, the monarchy was ended and a socialist state established; the country became the Federal People's Republic of Yugoslavia, which in 1963 was renamed the Socialist Federal Republic of Yugoslavia (SFRY). Administratively, the SFRY was reformed into six republics and two autonomous provinces. The nascent ethnic tensions, which had surfaced most visibly in 1928 and had also played a significant role in the alliances and resistance movements of the Second World War, were largely quiescent under the rule of Marshal Tito, whose partisan army had been explicitly pan-Yugoslav and whose government insisted on the idea of unity among all nations and nationalities in Yugoslavia. Since Tito was determined not to allow his country to become a mere Soviet satellite, there was a decisive break with Stalin and the Warsaw Pact in 1948 when Yugoslavia was excluded from the Cominform. It was after this break that Yugoslavia developed the policies which it pioneered and which will always be associated with its name: externally, together with Egypt and India, Yugoslavia established the Non-Aligned Movement, while internally, it developed its own version of socialism based on the system of worker self-management. When Tito died in 1980, inter-ethnic tensions began to grow, and had, by the end of the decade, become more and more visible. The socialist system gradually collapsed, while the power of nationalistically minded elites within the Republics grew stronger and stronger. With the armed conflicts in 1991, the seventeen-year disintegration of Yugoslavia began. It was only in 2003 with the establishment of the State Union of Serbia and Montenegro that the Federal Republic of Yugoslavia, the last remnant of the SFRY, ceased to exist. By the year 2019, only Macedonia still bore the term 'Yugoslav' in its name as the 'Former Yugoslav Republic of Macedonia'; however, Greece and Macedonia have now implemented the Prespa agreement establishing the name of 'The Republic of North Macedonia' for the independent state thus putting to rest this very last use of Yugoslavia in the name of a country.

For the most part, socialist Yugoslavia, which is the focus of this volume, disappeared in a welter of prolonged fighting, ethnic cleansing, and other atrocities visited upon largely defenceless civilians. The constituent Republics picked up the pieces and emerged as successor states, turning their backs on their Yugoslav past and focusing on their distinct national trajectories. The very violence of the break-up proved particularly effective in creating separations and polarizations, which help to support new post-Yugoslav identities.

Yet as a common state of the South Slavs, Yugoslavia existed for seventy years, survived many existential crises, played a considerable role in the history of the twentieth century and is not easily consigned to history. And if we look at Yugoslavia's successor states today, it is still possible to discern, as through a glass darkly, the presence of the former Yugoslavia, looming behind them. Our purpose is to examine this phenomenon face to face, showing how the past affects the present, and the present reflects the past.

III The legacies of Yugoslavia

Some of the successor states of Yugoslavia have a tendency to forget their common Yugoslav past. Indeed, to a greater or lesser degree, this has been intentional, in that the new post-Yugoslav elites adopted a nation-building mentality which opted to eradicate their Yugoslav past, in some cases even connecting directly with a pre-Yugoslav past, when such an approach seemed more convenient for the new national projects. They were now states in their own right, rather than the constituent peoples of former Yugoslavia. And the new states adopted new institutions, new market-orientated economic paradigms, new national symbols, and even renamed and manipulated the common language by emphasizing some dialectical differences; what was commonly known as Serbo-Croatian became Croatian, Serbian, Bosnian, and Montenegrin.

To view the end of socialist Yugoslavia as a complete rupture would, however, risk overlooking the fact that countries are more than just their physical and institutional setups. They comprise ideas, experiences, cultures and above all peoples with historical experiences and personal memories, all of which survive through time and provide for some continuity. And, while new ideologies and political systems may emerge, they do not necessarily fully break with the past; rather they may keep certain institutional, procedural, cultural, and economic features, which they might seek to adapt to the new circumstances, doctrines, and political power configurations. For these reasons, it is worth asking what happened to the Yugoslav legacies and what continuities exist between Yugoslavia and the successor states. What are the consequences of Yugoslavia's existence for the present? What vestiges did it leave behind? What role does its existence play in terms of contemporary developments and challenges? These are the main questions that this present book addresses.

Legacies may refer to historical *periods* or historical *developments* or historical *personalities*.[2] Our book therefore looks at the legacy of Yugoslavia, in terms of (i) its historical era as a country which existed for seventy years; (ii) its historical developments, which shaped and defined the country on the international stage such as (during the Socialist period) non-alignment, self-management, third way politics in the Cold War, and its unique federation of socialist republics; and (iii) its historical personalities such as Marshall Tito, whose long leadership provided a unifying force over different republics, languages, religions and political elites and whose death heralded the country's eventual economic and political disintegration.

Legacies can also refer to *breaking points*, which delineate the boundaries of the period whose impact we are discussing. For Yugoslavia, the early 1990s comprised such a breaking point, presaging the country's disintegration. Legacies exist and persist through time, and last *long after the breaking point*. To determine its impact and explanatory value, one must establish that the legacy in question has *some kind of continuity* with the period before and after the breaking point, in that it stays the same or keeps some characteristics which persist through change and then persist for more than one generation

In this respect, Arthur Stinchcombe[3] distinguishes between *survivals*, meaning phenomena that continue even after the conditions that originally produced them have disappeared, and *replications*, which recur because their underlying conditions continue to produce the same outcome over time. They can also act as *reactions with the past* in adopting new projects often in order to create a radical break.

It is important to note here that historical legacies, in the form of continuities or ruptures, are never uniformly perceived and have *different expressions* in different *settings*. The post-Yugoslav space is a setting of different interpretations of the past; the collective memory of Yugoslavia varies from state to state, from community to community, and from generation to generation, and it differs also at the individual

---

[2] For an interesting account of historical legacies, see Jason Wittenberg, 'What Is a Historical Legacy', 2011. Available at: https://politicalscience.ceu.edu/sites/politicalscience.ceu.hu/files/attachment/basicpage/62/05-wittenberg-legacies.pdf.

[3] Arthur L Stinchcombe, *Constructing Social Theories*, Reprint edition, original 1968 (Chicago: University of Chicago Press, 1987).

level of the people. It ranges from aversion, rejection, indifference, rediscovery or even nostalgia for the past; all these expressions have been visible in the current post-Yugoslav space.

As a snapshot of the present, or rather a connected series of snapshots, this volume traces what remains and what has disappeared for good some three decades after the beginning of the end of Yugoslavia. It deals with the questions of how Yugoslav historical facts, past practices, institutions, and cultural and social themes are remembered and seeks to explore their impact on the present. What makes Yugoslavia so special in the European context is the multiplicity and plurality of structures, agents and ideas which originated from this country and eventually made its dissolution so difficult and violent. The contributions in this volume all address these questions from different perspectives and disciplines, ranging from history and political science to sociology and economics. While this inter-disciplinarity does not allow for a strict and standardized common analytical framework, the different chapters nevertheless all address the same questions connected to the legacies of Yugoslavia and the role they or their absence played in the region's transition to what is nowadays referred to as the Western Balkans. When taken together, these different contributions offer a unique picture of the state of play and how we came to where we are today.

There is a vast literature tackling the history, reasons and consequences of Yugoslavia's collapse. For example, there are many books and articles which have dealt with the fall of Yugoslavia and the causes and the experience of disintegration.[4] Others have discussed the implications of the disintegration for the new states and their peoples, in abstract and more practical terms.[5] There are also books emphasizing the political, institutional and external reasons for the downfall of the Yugoslav state in a longer historical perspective;[6] and numerous accounts of the actual wars and the international

[4]   See, for example, Sabrina Petra Ramet, *Balkan Babel: The Disintegration of Yugoslavia from the Death of Tito to the Fall of Milosevic*, 4th edn (London: Westview Press, 2002); Laura Silber and Allan Little, *Yugoslavia: Death of a Nation*, Revised (New York: Penguin Books, 1997); Catherine Baker, *The Yugoslav Wars of the 1990s* (New York, NY: Red Globe Press, 2015).

[5]   Florian Bieber, 'Power Sharing after Yugoslavia: Functionality and Dysfunctionality of Power-Sharing Institutions in Post-War Bosnia, Macedonia, Kosovo' in Sid Noel, ed. *From Power Sharing to Democracy. Post-Conflict Institutions in Ethnically Divided Societies* (Montreal/Kingston: McGill-Queen's University Press, 2005), 85–103; Srecko Horvat and Igor Štiks, eds, *Welcome to the Desert of Post-Socialism. Radical Politics After Yugoslavia* (London: Verso, 2015); Jasmin Mujanović, *Hunger and Fury: The Crisis of Democracy in the Balkans* (London: C Hurst & Co Publishers Ltd, 2018); Damir Arsenijević, ed, *Unbribable Bosnia and Herzegovina: The Fight for the Commons* (Baden Baden: Nomos Verlagsgesellschaft, 2015).

[6]   John Lampe, *Balkans into Southeastern Europe, 1914–2014: A Century of War and Transition* (London: Palgrave Macmillan, 2015); Dejan Jovic, *Yugoslavia: A State That Withered Away* (West Lafayette, Indiana: Purdue Univerity Press, 2008); Sabrina P Ramet, *The Three Yugoslavias: State-Building and Legitimation, 1918–2004* (Washington, DC: Woodrow Wilson Press, 2006); Dejan Djokić and James Ker-Lindsay, eds, *New Perspectives on Yugoslavia. Key Issues and Controversies* (London and New York: Routledge, 2011), Milica Uvalic, *Investment and Property Rights in Yugoslavia: The Long Transition to a Market Economy* (Cambridge: Cambridge University Press, 1992).

administrations, which intervened to bring peace and contribute to state building.[7] Lastly, there are books which look at the new states separately.[8]

The approach in this book, however, is new and different. It uses the analytical approach of continuities and discontinuities to, first, encourage scholars working on the contemporary situation in the region, particularly political and social scientists as well as economists, to take a historical perspective; and secondly, to remind historians of Yugoslavia to connect their analyses with the post-Yugoslav present. It is not repeating the same questions about the deeper reasons behind Yugoslavia's demise, but rather putting the focus on the *connections between past and present*, thus putting forward a more holistic narrative which transcends periods and academic disciplines. Such an approach is of paramount importance to understanding the region's contemporary challenges. The volume also considers how engagement with Yugoslavia and the successor states by outside international bodies, such as the EU and the International Monetary Fund, and other countries, in particular, former Empires Russia and Turkey, has both evolved and fostered change. As such, we hope that our book may also provide practitioners with the detailed and rounded knowledge necessary to devise well-grounded strategies for engagement with the Western Balkans.

IV Structure of the book

This book covers the three main dimensions of Yugoslavia's existence and its legacies: politics and society; international relations; and economics. It discusses many of the distinctive features so closely associated with Yugoslavia, including the unique experiment of worker self-management; the policy and structure of non-alignment during the Cold War; the combination of liberalism and communism in Yugoslav ideology and everyday identity; and the identity of Yugoslavia itself. It asks what has happened to these legacies under the new dispensation.

This edited volume therefore presents the work of well-qualified scholars on the region. The individual chapters examine issues such as the transition from Yugoslav liberalism to EU-inspired liberalism; social transformations in civil society in general,

---

[7] Roberto Belloni, *State Building and International Intervention in Bosnia* (London and New York: Routledge, 2007); Lenard J Cohen and John R Lampe, *Embracing Democracy in the Western Balkans: From Postconflict Struggles Toward European Integration* (Washington, DC; Baltimore: Johns Hopkins University Press, 2011); Josip Glaurdic, *The Hour of Europe: Western Powers and the Breakup of Yugoslavia* (Yale University Press, 2011); Cvete Koneska, *After Ethnic Conflict: Policy-making in Post-conflict Bosnia and Herzegovina and Macedonia* (Abingdon, UK ; Burlington, VT: Routledge, 2014).

[8] Florian Bieber, *Post-War Bosnia. Ethnicity, Inequality and Public Sector Governance* (Hampshire and New York: Palgrave Macmillen, 2006); James Ker-Lindsay, *Kosovo: The Path to Contested Statehood in the Balkans* (London: IBTauris, 2011); Adis Merdzanovic, *Democracy by Decree. Prospects and Limits of Imposed Consociational Democracy in Bosnia and Herzegovina* (Stuttgart: Ibidem, 2015); Kenneth Morrison, *Nationalism, Identity and Statehood in Post-Yugoslav Montenegro* (London, Oxford, New York: Bloomsbury Academic, 2018); Sabrina P Ramet and Vjeran Pavlakovic, eds, *Serbia Since 1989: Politics and Society under Milosevic and After* (Seattle: University of Washington Press, 2005); Sabrina P Ramet and Reneo Lukic, eds, *Croatia since Independence* (München: Oldenbourg Wissenschaftsverlag, 2008).

but also with respect to distinct phenomena such as popular music, which transcend the new state boundaries; the effect of Yugoslavia's trademark form of worker self-management socialism — as an ideology, an economic model, and a form of social coexistence; the vestiges of the Non-Aligned Movement and Yugoslav multilateralism; global and regional geopolitics and the role of Russia, Turkey, and the EU in the region, both historically and today; and, last but not least, the questions of what happened to the Yugoslav economic model, how it disintegrated, and whether the successor states have become sustainable market economies as a result of the economic transition.

Section one: Politics and society

In Chapter 1, Adis Merdzanovic challenges the idea that the liberalization project in the successor states had to start from zero. As he claims, the Yugoslav system exhibited certain liberal elements, which could have been used as anchor points for the consolidation of liberalism. However, the system's disintegration made such continuity highly improbable from a domestic point of view, which meant that any new liberalization impulses had to come from the outside. That the liberal elements of the past still exerted much influence in how political rule and legitimacy was perceived became apparent when the EU's liberalization approach failed to connect to these past experiences and instead offered a radical new template. The discussion of liberalism before and after the disintegration of Yugoslavia thus shows some remarkable continuity within a general framework of discontinuity.

Chapter 2 by Ivor Sokolić, Denisa Kostovicova and Adam Fagan discusses the disordered and ambiguous nature of civil society, which has acted both for and against processes of democratization. On the one hand, it is marked by pluralism, which represents a discontinuity from Yugoslavia; but on the other, it has also challenged democracy and aided nationalist efforts. The case studies of Croatia and Serbia both point to legacies of conflict and a slow transition to liberal democracy, which has produced mixed effects on governance and transitional justice processes.

Focusing on music, media, and culture, Catherine Baker considers in Chapter 3 the concept of 'Yugonostalgia' which, since the break-up of Yugoslavia, has come to stand for almost any cultural phenomenon having something to do with the cultural legacies and everyday life of Yugoslavia as a common state. She suggests both that everyday cultural exchange between post-Yugoslav states is, if anything, more frequent and more normalized than it was during the years of violent disintegration, maybe even before; and that the politics of nostalgia operate most intensively today within ethnicized nationalisms.

Section two: International affairs

The second section of the book is dedicated to Yugoslav and post-Yugoslav international affairs. In Chapter 4, Ljubica Spaskovska examines the legacies of Yugoslav non-aligned multilateralism. As she explains, the largely selective appropriation of socialist Yugoslavia's legacies of global engagement reveals the contradictory relationship which the post-Yugoslav states and societies have with their socialist past: there is both an attempt to acknowledge the positive side of that legacy and thus use it for pragmatic political gains in international forums; but at the same time, and especially at individual level, there exists a sense of loss.

In Chapter 5, James Ker-Lindsay looks at the diverse map of contested territorial issues, which arose when Yugoslavia disintegrated: between Serbia and Kosovo over status, between Slovenia and Croatia over the Bay of Piran, and between Kosovo and Montenegro as well as between Kosovo and North Macedonia over border delimitation. They are all legacies of a Yugoslav time when boundaries meant less, and harbingers of a time when boundaries equally become less important under the EU's border elimination. But for the time being, they are important, raise questions about EU obligations, and complicate the process of EU accession. The EU has a role to play, in various ways; the question is whether it contributes to solutions or exacerbates disputes further.

In Chapter 6, Othon Anastasakis assesses the influence of the former Empires, Russia and Turkey and argues that they have been guided all along by their own strategic interests and the compatibility or incompatibility with Western ones. Despite claims of historical and cultural affinity and continuity (Orthodox/Slav influence from Russia, Muslim/neo-Ottoman influence from Turkey), the reality is that these two countries went through a long period of diplomatic and cultural disengagement during the Yugoslav times before they re-entered the post-Yugoslav scene, as influential external actors. Here is a case of pre-Yugoslav legacies becoming more dominant in some of the Western Balkan states and ethnic communities: a rupture with the recent communist past and a reconnection with the distant imperial past. For their part, the current post-Yugoslav states, despite their declared transatlantic orientation, have also espoused a 'neo-Titoist' strategy of keeping relations and options open with third external players, an interesting legacy of the Yugoslav past.

Section three: Economics

Chapters 7–9 are dedicated to continuities and discontinuities in the economic sector. In the opening chapter of this section, Adam Bennett argues that microeconomic self-management fatally undermined optimal macroeconomic management during the last decade of the Socialist Federal Republic of Yugoslavia. He covers attempts by the IMF to support Yugoslavia's stability programmes, including through the use of so-called 'real exchange rate rules' devised, in part, to correct biases inherent under self-management; and he explains the failure of these programmes and the hyperinflation and then recession which resulted. Bennett compares macroeconomic performance in the successor states, especially in light of the reforms which replaced enterprise self-management with joint stock incorporation.

In Chapter 8, Milica Uvalic recalls the main features of the mixed Yugoslav economic system (socialist, market-orientated, self-managed) and some of the controversies regarding the self-managed market economy. After Yugoslavia's break-up, the speed and direction of systemic change has been very different across the successor states. While pursuing the common objective of multi-party democracy and market economy, some countries have dismantled key elements of the old system much faster than others, as the chapter shows. These divergent paths illustrate both continuities and discontinuities with respect to the pre-1991 economic model.

Jakov Milatović and Peter Sanfey state in the ninth and final chapter of the volume that at the beginning of transition, Yugoslavia appeared to be well placed to make a rapid transition to a sustainable market economy. But the violent break-up of the country and subsequent conflicts prevented such a smooth transition. The successor countries are still characterized by a large state and resistance to private ownership, weak governance, corruption and widespread tax evasion and informality.

In the concluding remarks of this volume we, as editors, seek to re-think the disintegration of Yugoslavia in light of the substantial new insights the chapters in the previous three sections have provided. Our goal is to reflect on how the past influences the present and to what degree we need a deeper understanding of the legacies of Yugoslavia to understand the contemporary social, political and economic configuration of the modern Balkans. While the contributors in their individual chapters shed new light on continuities with the past, but also on significant breaks with it in their respective areas of expertise, our ambition in the conclusion is to take a birds-eye perspective on their arguments by applying the framework of legacy, continuity and discontinuity to their findings. The result of such a process, and indeed of such an edited volume, will undoubtedly bring up new ideas and suggestions for further research, to which we hope to have provided a first impetus. For while Yugoslavia may be gone, its legacies still linger.

References

Arsenijević, Damir, ed, *Unbribable Bosnia and Herzegovina: The Fight for the Commons.* (Baden Baden: Nomos Verlagsgesellschaft, 2015).

Baker, Catherine. *The Yugoslav Wars of the 1990s.* (New York, NY: Red Globe Press, 2015).

Belloni, Roberto. *State Building and International Intervention in Bosnia.* (London and New York: Routledge, 2007).

Bieber, Florian. *Post-War Bosnia. Ethnicity, Inequality and Public Sector Governance.* (Hampshire and New York: Palgrave Macmillan, 2006).

Bieber, Florian. 'Power Sharing after Yugoslavia: Functionality and Dysfunctionality of Power-Sharing Institutions in Post-War Bosnia, Macedonia, Kosovo'. In Sid Noel, ed. *From Power Sharing to Democracy. Post-Conflict Institutions in Ethnically Divided Societies,* 85–103. (Montreal/Kingston: McGill-Queen's University Press, 2005).

Cohen, Lenard J., and John R. Lampe. *Embracing Democracy in the Western Balkans: From Postconflict Struggles Toward European Integration.* (Washington, DC; Baltimore: Johns Hopkins University Press, 2011).

Djokić, Dejan, and James Ker-Lindsay, eds, *New Perspectives on Yugoslavia. Key Issues and Controversies.* (London and New York: Routledge, 2011).

Glaurdic, Josip. *The Hour of Europe: Western Powers and the Breakup of Yugoslavia.* (Yale University Press, 2011).

Horvat, Srecko, and Igor Štiks, eds, *Welcome to the Desert of Post-Socialism. Radical Politics After Yugoslavia.* (London: Verso, 2015).

Jovic, Dejan. *Yugoslavia: A State That Withered Away.* (West Lafayette, Indiana: Purdue Univerity Press, 2008).

Ker-Lindsay, James. *Kosovo: The Path to Contested Statehood in the Balkans*. (London: IB Tauris, 2011).

Koneska, Cvete. *After Ethnic Conflict: Policy-making in Post-conflict Bosnia and Herzegovina and Macedonia*. (Abingdon, UK ; Burlington, VT: Routledge, 2014).

Lampe, John. *Balkans into Southeastern Europe, 1914–2014: A Century of War and Transition*. (London: Palgrave Macmillan, 2015).

Merdzanovic, Adis. *Democracy by Decree. Prospects and Limits of Imposed Consociational Democracy in Bosnia and Herzegovina*. (Stuttgart: Ibidem, 2015).

Morrison, Kenneth. *Nationalism, Identity and Statehood in Post-Yugoslav Montenegro*. (London and New York: Bloomsbury Academic, 2018).

Mujanović, Jasmin. *Hunger and Fury: The Crisis of Democracy in the Balkans*. (London: C Hurst & Co Publishers Ltd, 2018).

Ramet, Sabrina P. *The Three Yugoslavias: State-Building and Legitimation, 1918–2004*. (Washington, DC: Woodrow Wilson Press, 2006).

Ramet, Sabrina P. and Reneo Lukic, eds, *Croatia since Independence*. (München: Oldenbourg Wissenschaftsverlag, 2008).

Ramet, Sabrina P. and Vjeran Pavlakovic, eds, *Serbia Since 1989: Politics and Society under Milosevic and After*. (Seattle: University of Washington Press, 2005).

Ramet, Sabrina Petra. *Balkan Babel: The Disintegration Of Yugoslavia from the Death of Tito to the Fall of Milosevic*. 4th edn (London: Westview Press, 2002).

Silber, Laura, and Allan Little. *Yugoslavia: Death of a Nation*. Revised edn. (New York: Penguin Books, 1997).

Stinchcombe, Arthur L. *Constructing Social Theories*. Reprint, Original 1968. (Chicago: University of Chicago Press, 1987).

Uvalic, Milica. *Investment and Property Rights in Yugoslavia: The Long Transition to a Market Economy*. (Cambridge: Cambridge University Press, 1992).

Wittenberg, Jason. 'What is a Historical Legacy?', 2011. Available at: https://politicalscience.ceu.edu/sites/politicalscience.ceu.hu/files/attachment/basicpage/62/05-wittenberg-legacies.pdf.

Part One

Politics and Society

1

Liberalism in Yugoslavia: Before and after the Disintegration

Adis Merdzanovic
Zurich University of Applied Sciences

I Introduction

When dealing with the Western Balkans' integration into the European Union (EU), we are usually confronted with a two-fold conceptualization of historical development, focusing on the before and after.[1] *Before*, there was the Yugoslav[2] socialist system with an authoritarian one-party rule and a strangely collectivized economic system which, throughout its existence, grappled with the problems of nationalism and centralism vs federalism, as well as strong internal economic disparities. When this system collapsed, Yugoslavia disintegrated and violent wars began. *After*, the post-Yugoslav successor states embarked on a decades-long transition aimed at transforming their political, social, and economic systems in accordance with the principles of liberal democracy and a free-market economy. Membership of the EU, the biggest promoter of these principles in the region, became a teleological fixture in Western Balkans politics.

Successful transition more or less meant having replaced the socialist institutions of politics, economics, and society with a liberal democratic framework, which ensured compliance with the European system of values and beliefs. Yet, due to the specificities of the Yugoslav socialist experience and especially the fact that disintegration happened by means of violent conflict, this transition itself was not only delayed in the Western Balkans context when compared to the Central and Eastern European (CEE) countries, but it also operated within a distinctly different framework. In fact, starting only in the *late* 1990s, the Western Balkans countries embarked on two different transformations, both of which were supported by outside actors in one form or another. As Cohen and

[1] The author wishes to thank Josette Baer, Sevan Pearson, David Madden, and Yaprak Gürsoy for their comments on earlier drafts. A version of this chapter was presented at the European Studies Centre of St Antony's College, University of Oxford in March 2016 and the ASN World Conference in New York in April 2016. This research was supported by the Swiss National Science Foundation under Grants P2ZHP1_158607 and P300P1_167673.
[2] I use the terms 'Yugoslavia' and 'Yugoslav' to refer to the state in existence between the end of the Second World War and the beginning of the 1990s.

Lampe explain, the first one was inherent in the EU membership perspective awarded to the Western Balkan states in the early 2000s, which emphasized 'a full framework for the rule of law under reformed public administrations and regulated private enterprise'. This meant moving beyond 'the political transition from one-party rule and the maxims of the neoliberal Washington Consensus of the early 1990s'. It also included 'new constitutions, immediate multi-party elections, and rapid privatizations', in return for which the 'West', i.e. the EU and the US and their associated institutions, offered 'financial support only to stabilize newly established currencies and discourage inflationary state budgets'. The second transition, according to Cohen and Lampe, followed the conflicts of the 1990s and may be termed a 'liberal democratic consensus'; it emphasized 'public and private institution building rather than simply financial stability and military security' and relied 'on a broader definition of liberal democracy and a market economy, one whose legitimacy rested on public institutions'.[3]

Cohen and Lampe's distinction clearly shows that the external understanding of the region and its engagement within it, at least as far as it formed part of a larger international consensus or narrative, was aimed at a *deep transformation* of the formerly communist polities into what may be called liberal democracies *à l'Européenne*. This went further than the generally employed models of mere 'post-conflict state building',[4] for the latter usually limit their scope of engagement to ending the armed conflict and providing a political and economic system fit to sustain the fragile peace. In the Western Balkans, the process of 'Europeanization', i.e. the establishment of a system compatible with European values and capable of potentially being integrated into the EU, was not only closely connected with the transformation from socialism to democracy which was ongoing all over the eastern bloc after the fall of the Berlin Wall, but also with the specific process of *conflict transformation*. This is the reason why the transition paradigm, at least in its most radical manifestation, permitted deeper intrusions into the system and necessarily contained the implicit notion that the outcome of transition had to be *normatively* better than the old order, for the simple reason that the old order had descended into chaos and war. Ultimately, in a truly Hegelian fashion, peace should not only triumph over war but a liberal democracy, society, and economy should triumph over authoritarianism, collectivization and managed economies.

Such an explanation rests on the argument that the process of liberalization in the Western Balkans was introduced after Yugoslavia disintegrated; or, to be more precise, after the wars surrounding its disintegration had ended. Geopolitically, it is the new international liberal order, and regionally the framework of EU association and membership that made the process of a liberal transformation of politics, economics,

---

[3] Lenard J Cohen and John R Lampe, *Embracing Democracy in the Western Balkans: From Postconflict Struggles Toward European Integration* (Washington, DC; Baltimore: Johns Hopkins University Press, 2011), 16–17.

[4] For a deeper discussion, see, for example, Francis Fukuyama, 'Nation-Building and the Failure of Institutional Memory', in *Nation-Building. Beyond Afghanistan and Iraq*, ed Francis Fukuyama (Baltimore: The Johns Hopkins University Press, 2006), 1–16; Thorsten Gromes, 'Democratisation of Post-War Societies: A Mission Impossible?' (2009) 5 *European Journal of Political Science and Theory* 418–41; Thorsten Gromes, *Ohne Staat und Nation ist keine Demokratie zu machen: Bosnien und Herzegowina, Kosovo und Makedonien nach den Bürgerkriegen* (Baden-Baden: Nomos, 2012).

and society in the Western Balkans possible. The aim of this chapter is to challenge this conventional view. While the Yugoslav system was not liberal, the chapter argues, it nevertheless exhibited some liberal elements, even if these occurred within a socialist framework. In the Western Balkans, liberalism is thus not an external invention of the late 1990s and early 2000s, but existed in certain aspects of daily life well before Yugoslavia's disintegration. However, by the time the country disintegrated, the domestic elements of liberalism had fallen victim to the state's general loss of legitimacy and its usurpation by the different nationalist ideologies and leaderships. That is the reason why a continuity of liberalism was hard to achieve, particularly because the 1990s saw almost a decade of wars and nationalist political elites uninterested in creating truly liberal societies, ultimately leading to stagnation in terms of a liberal transition. When the EU association and membership process sought to offer a new momentum for liberalization, its concept of liberalism emphasized aspects that, naturally, were distinctly different to the previous Yugoslav model. As will be shown, they focused on political and economic liberalism, while putting almost no emphasis on social liberalism, which had precisely been the foundation for Yugoslavia's political, social, and economic legitimacy. Thus, the EU's template for transition, association, and eventual membership of the Union did not allow for any kind of continuity with the past, not even with its liberal elements. Yugoslavia's liberal legacy withered away.

The chapter begins by clarifying the term 'liberalism', both in a general analytical and a Yugoslav-specific context (section 2). It then moves on to the discussion of the liberal elements within Yugoslavia's socialist system (section 3) before showing how these elements evaporated as the country's political system started to loose legitimacy and its violent disintegration became a reality (section 4). After this kind of 'domestic liberalism' had disappeared and nationalism had taken over, the new impetus for liberalization came from external actors, chief among them the EU with its association and membership processes. Section 5 therefore discusses the EU's liberalization approach and explains how its structural and ideological shortcomings prevented the establishment of continuity with the old system. Section 6 concludes the chapter by, *inter alia*, asking the question whether the main characteristics inherited by the successor states from Yugoslavia are not precisely its historical ambiguities.

II Theoretical approaches to liberalism in the Yugoslav context

1 Three analytical forms of liberalism

'Liberalism' is a difficult term to define as it relies on many conceptually connected yet distinct ideas which most often do not fit neatly together. At the same time, the notion of 'liberal democracy' has entrenched an all-encompassing *conception* of how liberalism is to be understood, which definitively falls short of capturing the many nuances within the *concept* of liberalism.[5] As my analysis focuses on the practical consequences of

---

[5] Michael Freeden, *Liberal Languages: Ideological Imaginations and Twentieth-Century Progressive Thought* (Princeton, NJ: Princeton University Press, 2004).

liberalism when applied to the most significant areas of everyday interaction, I distinguish three different forms of liberalism: political, economic, and social (Table 1). The distinctions between the three forms are *analytical*, not normative or epistemological in nature, they are not without mutual friction, nor are they fully distinct in reality. This was precisely the case in Yugoslavia where, as we shall see, the economic and social component of liberalism mixed in a particular way to form a liberal version of socialism which excluded to a large degree the political component, which in turn had an economic and social foundation.

The cornerstone of liberal thought is the notion that authority must be legitimized towards the individual, who is endowed with certain rights which can be infringed only to protect the freedoms of others.[6] All authority in a state has to be exercised solely in the individual's best interest and may not violate a basic set of inalienable rights. This restriction not only applies to governmental, but also to democratic action. In fact, this is the condition under which liberals originally agreed to 'democracy', a concept they used to equate with the tyrannical notion of majority rule.[7] The principles of the state's neutrality towards individual life choices and a rigorous system of the rule of law, which protects the individual from arbitrary use of the state's monopoly of power, are

Table 1.1 Analytical distinction of three forms of liberalism and their operationalization

Form	Thinkers (*inter alia*)	Core tenets	Operationalization
Political Liberalism	John Locke, American Founding Fathers, John Stuart Mill, Thomas Hobbes, Baron de Montesquieu, John Rawls, Isaiah Berlin	Individual as the source of political legitimation; Realm free from state interference; Individual rights, including the right to participate in the state rule; Liberal neutrality; Rule of law.	Individual rights, Democracy, Rule of law, Checks and balances, Minority rights
Economic Liberalism	John Locke, Adam Smith, David Ricardo, FA v Hayek, Milton Friedman	Property rights; Individual aspiration as foundation of societal progress; Competitive advantage theories.	Deregulation of market; Liberalization (opening up) of trade and industry; Privatization of state-owned companies
Social Liberalism	John Rawls, Ronald Dworkin, JM Keynes, Karl Polanyi	Compensation of non-deserved advantages; Social justice and fairness; a particular role for the state in the economy.	Social welfare schemes and benefits (directly paid); Governmental intervention; Curtailing of market functions in specific areas

Source: Author.

---

[6] John Stuart Mill, 'On Liberty', in *On Liberty and Other Essays*, Oxford World's Classics (Oxford: Oxford University Press, 1869), 1–128.
[7] Michael Freeden, *Liberalism. A Very Short Introduction* (Oxford: Oxford University Press, 2015), 26.

the direct consequences of this notion. As the basic proposition of liberalism, political liberalism stands in a 'lexical order'[8] when compared to the other two liberalisms discussed here.

In its classical form, economic liberalism takes up the idea of state neutrality to argue that state intervention into markets established by individuals to exercise their right to freely trade goods should be limited to ensuring compliance; individual aspiration is seen as the best foundation for societal progress. However, economic liberals from the 'neoliberal' school[9] go a step further by postulating that the market itself is the best ordering mechanism for wealth production, seen as a universal good for a society.[10] For this reason, they argue for the deregulation of markets, the opening up of trade and industry, and the privatization of state-owned enterprises.[11]

Social liberals come to a different conclusion. Starting with the Kantian notion that commends treating human beings as ends in themselves rather than mere means to a particular goal, they argue that undeserved advantages in a society need to be compensated.[12] In other words, a just society is under the obligation to care for the least well off,[13] which in practice justifies not only state involvement in the economy so as to remedy some of the dysfunctionalities markets create, but also the practical notion to do so through direct intervention and the establishment of state-led social welfare schemes. Needless to say, this is an area where social and economic liberals often disagree; just as some economic liberals express reservations towards the egalitarianism inherent in political liberalism.[14]

2 'Liberalism' in the Yugoslav context

A term of everyday and academic usage, 'liberalism' has a particular historical connotation in the Yugoslav context. As Sabrina Ramet[15] explains, the economic reforms upon which Yugoslavia embarked in the early 1960s soon acquired an ideological character, with some party ideologues going even as far as citing Adam Smith in support of their argument for further decentralization. The term 'liberalism' applied to the republican elites between the late 1960s and early 1970s, particularly in Serbia.[16]

---

[8]   John Rawls, *Eine Theorie der Gerechtigkeit* (Frankfurt am Main: Suhrkamp, 1975), 82.
[9]   For a critical discussion of the term 'neoliberalism', see C Boas and J Gans-Morse 'Neoliberalism: From New Liberal Philosophy to Anti-Liberal Slogan' (2009) 44(2) *Studies in Comparative International Development* 137–61.
[10]   Milton Friedman, *Capitalism and Freedom: Fortieth Anniversary Edition* (Chicago: University of Chicago Press, 2002); Friedrich August von Hayek, *The Road to Serfdom* (Chicago: University of Chicago Press, 1994).
[11]   Manfred B Steger and Ravi K Roy, *Neoliberalism. A Very Short Introduction.* (Oxford: Oxford University Press, 2010).
[12]   Ronald Dworkin, *Justice for Hedgehogs* (Cambridge MA: Harvard University Press, 2013).
[13]   Rawls, *Eine Theorie der Gerechtigkeit.*
[14]   George Monbiot, 'Neoliberalism – the Ideology at the Root of All Our Problems', *The Guardian*, 04 2016. Available at: www.theguardian.com/books/2016/apr/15/neoliberalism-ideology-problem-george-monbiot.
[15]   Sabrina P Ramet, *The Three Yugoslavias: State-Building and Legitimation, 1918–2004* (Washington, DC: Woodrow Wilson Press, 2006), 210–11.
[16]   I thank the anonymous reviewer for this insight.

As Ramet writes, while the devolution of economic and political power to lower administrative levels signified a victory for the 'liberal wing of the party', the 'conservative wing', which took over after 1971 put the emphasis on stronger centralization and tighter party control and would soon conflate 'liberalism' with 'anarchism', 'condemn 'anarcho-liberals' for right-wing deviationism', and accuse them of being in favour of a multi-party system and hostile to self-management. In this period, 'liberalism' had a negative connotation — but this was not to last either; by 1982, 'liberalism had once again become a respectable, even fashionable epithet'.[17]

There was thus an intrinsic fluidity to the conceptual meaning of 'liberalism', with the 'liberal'- 'conservative' antagonism referring to a somewhat convoluted version of the centralism-federalism debate, which occupied Yugoslav politics ever since the foundation of the kingdom in 1919. This historical usage is distinctly different from the analytical distinction of 'liberalism' I sought to develop in this section, which relies on the individual being the source of political power and legitimacy.

But has Yugoslavia seen this second kind of liberalism? Indeed, there have been genuinely 'liberal' moments and forces in Yugoslav history. In an influential article,[18] the economist Vladimir Gligorov specifically mentioned a strong influence of liberal ideas within Serbian intellectual circles by the end of the nineteenth century and within Croatia, until the general collapse of liberalism in the 1930s, presumably after the establishment of the absolutist regime and the Kingdom of Yugoslavia. But Gligorov nevertheless maintained that such liberal parties or thinkers never had much support and, in any case, were gradually eradicated by radical, nationalist, or socialist movements. In his opinion, it is the essence of 'the national state' that stood in liberalism's way,[19] as the historical evolution of Yugoslavia made impossible the idea of liberal equality within the state, as in the United States, or a historic liberal state narrative, as in France. In his view, liberalism in Yugoslavia had to emerge as a counter-reaction to the prevailing social and political conditions; in other words, liberalism had 'to be discovered anew, because continuity has been impossible'.[20]

Gligorov thus presents a particular kind of path dependency explanation which almost completely excludes 'liberalism' from the Yugoslav political spectrum between the 1930s and the 1980s. For this to be true, however, one would have to show that *liberal principles*, not just parties with liberal ideologies, were indeed largely absent. This was not the case, as the next section will show. It is indeed true that the events after 1930 made a continuation of organized liberal thought within the political system improbable; continuity of the ideas from the older liberal elites may have been unfeasible, as Gligorov argued. But even though a coherent liberal ideology was absent and had no political space to flourish, liberal ideas were nevertheless present in socialist Yugoslavia, and at times even supported by prominent members within the leadership, or represented in the actuality of the political system.

[17] Ramet, *The Three Yugoslavias*, 210–11.
[18] Vladimir Gligorov, 'The Discovery of Liberalism in Yugoslavia' (1991) 5(1) *European Politics and Societies* 5–25.
[19] Ibid, fn. 6.
[20] Ibid, 5.

The argument I wish to put forward is that the contours of Yugoslavia's political, economic, and social system allowed different degrees of citizen involvement and offered particular benefits to the citizenry at large. While we are obviously not talking about *a liberal system*, as we have defined it, Yugoslav citizens enjoyed certain freedoms that are not necessarily associated with socialist rule.

III Liberal Elements in Yugoslav Socialism

This section discusses the complex picture of political, social, and economic realities in socialist Yugoslavia in greater detail, especially focusing on liberal elements of the existing socialist system. As mentioned in the theoretical section, the *analytical* distinction between political, social, and economic liberalism is somewhat hard to follow when presenting the actual case of Yugoslavia, as these three distinct areas intersect quite heavily. Not shying away from these challenges, the section discusses the connecting elements between these concepts within the three-fold analytical framework.

1 Political liberalism

The ideological foundation of the Yugoslav state was the partisans' victory in the Second World War, which also meant that the wartime People's Liberation Front (PLF) and its communist leadership around Josip Broz Tito became the state's primary principle of legitimacy. Tito believed that the communist movement established around the PLF, by virtue of being a product of a successful war effort, included all 'the people', making political pluralism unnecessary as it already had all the democratic legitimacy it needed.[21] Consequently, Yugoslavia's 1946 constitution institutionalized the principle of 'rule by the people' (*narodna vlast*) with hundreds of people's councils in urban and rural areas. Actual political power, however, firmly lay within the party leadership under Tito, whose first post-war goal was the consolidation of power, which was done with ardent zeal.[22] The Stalinist interpretation of Marxism and the functionalities of government which characterized the early period of socialist Yugoslavia would soon disappear, as the Yugoslav leadership was not ready to accept a mere satellite country position under Stalin's leadership. The divergent views[23] between Belgrade and Moscow eventually culminated in the country's expulsion from the Cominform[24] in June 1948 (see Othon Anastasakis' chapter in this volume for a discussion of the Tito-Stalin break).

---

[21] Ramet, *The Three Yugoslavias*, 167.
[22] Marie-Janine Calic, *Geschichte Jugoslawiens im 20. Jahrhundert* (München: Beck, 2010), 177; Ramet, *The Three Yugoslavias*, chap. 5.
[23] On the causes of the Soviet-Yugoslav split in 1948, see Ramet *The Three Yugoslavias*, 175–76. or J Perović 'The Tito-Stalin Split. A Reassessment in Light of New Evidence' (2007) 9(2) *Journal of Cold War Studies* 32–63.
[24] Established in 1947, the Communist Information Bureau sought to coordinate and dictate the activities of Communist parties of the Eastern Block, i.e. the countries under control of the Soviet Union.

This presented a window of opportunity for the Yugoslav regime and gave party ideologues the task of developing a new kind of legitimising strategy for the country. Trying 'very hard to show that it was the Soviets and not they who had deviated from Marxism',[25] the Yugoslav ideologues sought to develop a variant of socialism which was in line with the wider Marxist ideology as well as the interests of party leadership, i.e. one-party monopoly and wartime justification for authority. In other words, they conceived of a system which did not generally question the socialist revolution and was in no way associated with the Western liberal ideal,[26] but at the same time was distinctly different to Stalinism. The new 'legitimising triad' consisted of three elements: (a) brotherhood and unity, (b) worker self-management, and (c) non-alignment.[27] These elements were connected to particular policies which shaped the realities in Yugoslavia until the death of Tito and the economic crisis of the 1980s, when the system began to disintegrate.

The re-affirmation of Yugoslavia's revolutionary genealogy served as the legitimising principle for the rule of the communist elites. As Edvard Kardelj, Yugoslavia's chief ideologue, outlined in a speech in 1951: 'In the course of a revolution, the people's will can find its full expression and that is the reason why democracy and revolutionary dictatorship mean the same thing'.[28] For the Partisan leadership, the People's Liberation Struggle in the Second World War 'had not only been a triumph of anti-fascist resistance' but had 'also borne witness to inter-ethnic cooperation, or, as the Partisans would have it, the brotherhood and unity of Yugoslav peoples under a communist banner'.[29]

It is important to untangle the dual purpose of this legitimising strategy. First, there is the clearly revolutionary notion, which the Yugoslav socialists wanted to preserve especially after the break with Stalin. It firmly anchors the absolute rule of the *communist* leadership in the governmental, social, and economic structures, thereby excluding any possibility for the establishment of a pluralist system. The Communist Party – since 1952 the League of Communists of Yugoslavia (LCY)[30] – soon became somewhat mythical, almost trans-humanist, the 'vanguard' (*avantgarda*) with its members being 'morally and politically suited (*moralno-politički podobni*) to educate others and guide society toward Communism'.[31] More practically, party membership was beneficial as the Party and its four official organizations — the Socialist Alliance of Working People; the Alliance of Socialist Youth; the Union of Fighters of the National-Liberation Struggle; and the Alliance of Trade Unions — were considered the 'subjective force' of society, making their members active elements of societal development.[32]

---

[25] Dejan Jovic, *Yugoslavia: A State That Withered Away* (West Lafayette, Indiana: Purdue Univerity Press, 2008), 59.
[26] Calic, *Geschichte Jugoslawiens*, 192–96.
[27] Ramet, *The Three Yugoslavias*, 185.
[28] Quoted in Ramet, 185.
[29] Ibid, 185.
[30] Jovic, *Yugoslavia*, 60.
[31] Ibid, 8.
[32] Jovic, 8.

The political spectrum and the extent of political engagement began and ended with the party and subsequent changes in the constitutional makeup of Yugoslavia, its gradual decentralization and the strengthening of the republics, perhaps most notably in the 1974 constitution, did not dramatically change this fact. The communist leadership still kept the reins within the different republics and autonomous provinces. However, federalism and decentralization also created a particular kind of *political pluralism*, as the communist parties of the different republics did not always see eye to eye with the central party leadership, or indeed with each other, especially in the 1970s and 1980s.[33] The devolution of power to the republics naturally strengthened the respective communist leagues and led to a plurality of opinion in different policy areas.

Even though *political* engagement was the prerogative of party members, the party nevertheless allowed for limited policy discussions and inputs from lower echelons, especially in matters of local politics. Importantly, citizen involvement was limited to enterprises, local councils and associations, meaning that it did not include political dissent with the party.[34] In general, the regime's treatment of political dissidents was, in practice, calibrated, as the authorities operated with a 'mixture of oppression and cooperation'.[35] They allowed *soft* criticism of prevailing practices but were also able to dispense harsh punishment if someone stepped over the invisible line.

However, while the communist regime, especially in the first decades of its rule, firmly engaged against its critics, it could not curb the evolution of society at large. Due to its economic system and its position in the Non-Aligned Movement (see also Ljubica Spaskovska's chapter in this volume), Yugoslavia was an inherently, even if partially, open country. As a consequence, the authorities could hardly contain societal development, which meant that they allowed society to expand more or less freely. Chief among the privileges the population enjoyed was an almost free access to information.[36] Not only could they freely receive foreign TV stations, but the leadership also abandoned any kind of advance censorship, meaning that transgressions could only be punished after the fact. While the practice of 'self-censorship' existed, Yugoslavia's publishing landscape was diverse and even foreign publications could be bought. Given the comparative openness of Yugoslav borders, ideological containment must have been impossible. Soon, critical social movements developed, challenging the existing situation through publications (e.g. the 'Praxis' group[37]), cultural manifestations

[33] Archie Brown, *The Rise and Fall of Communism* (London: Vintage, 2010), 546.
[34] Calic, *Geschichte Jugoslawiens*, 228.
[35] Ibid, 195.
[36] See the description in Marie-Janine Calic, *Krieg und Frieden in Bosnien-Hercegovina*, Erweiterte Neuausgabe (Frankfurt: Suhrkamp Verlag, 1996), 212–15.
[37] The 'Praxis' group was a movement of Yugoslav philosophers presenting an 'anti-dogmatic alternative to Soviet Marxism', (see Mira Bogdanović, 'The Rift in the Praxis Group: Between Nationalism and Liberalism' *Critique* (2015) 45, (3–4), 461) by emphasizing Marxism's humanist aspects: (Christian Fuchs, 'The Praxis School's Marxist Humanism and Mihailo Marković's Theory of Communication' (2017) 45 (1–2) *Critique* 4 159–82.) Apart from the journal *Praxis*, published in the 1960s and 1970s, the group also maintained a regular summer school on the island of Korčula in which many Western philosophers participated. When Yugoslavia disintegrated, members of the group split into liberal and nationalist camps, see Bogdanović, 'The Rift in the Praxis Group'.

in theatres and movies (e.g. the 'Black Wave'), or actual protests (e.g. the 1968 student uprisings,[38] or subsequent nationalist manifestations such as the 1971 Croatian Spring[39]). While the communist leadership reacted differently to such activities, they all stood for diverse ideological and political currents within Yugoslavia's society; and they demonstrate the prevalence of a kind of social pluralism.

This peculiar kind of pluralism was also inherent in the notion of 'brotherhood and unity' (*bratstvo i jedinstvo*) as an ordering principle for political rule. 'Brotherhood and unity' acknowledged the cultural specificities of the peoples and sought to unite them in this kind of diversity. The communists believed this to be a practical way of dealing with the realities, while they also perceived national differences to be secondary to class differences and, arguably, one of the problems which would be solved once the state structures and the class system had withered away.[40] While publicly condemning nationalism in society and acting against the promoters of such ideas with the full force of the legal and security systems, rather than discrediting national ideologies or narratives themselves, the communist leadership practically sought to integrate these narratives by striving towards 'absolute' equality between the different groups within state structures.[41] The system of 'brotherhood and unity' in no way destroyed the concept of the nation, but kept the national substrate and its idiosyncrasies alive. Since the party — be it on the federal or the republic level — controlled all organs of state and the rule of law mostly served party interests, we can hardly claim that any kind of political liberalism existed in Yugoslavia. But neither can we interpret the situation as a pure totalitarian dictatorship, for there were spaces for citizen activism and involvement. Instead, we need to understand the prevailing system as a de-politicization of society, a decoupling of the political from the practical. The political, as I understand it, concerns itself with the legitimacy of a prevailing set of commonly binding rules and laws. As such, it offers a lens through which the practical is evaluated and, ultimately, judged. Yet, this is exactly what the rule of the communist party did not allow its citizens to do. They were not treated as politically conscious subjects, and it is in this sense that the Yugoslav communist regime was indeed authoritarian (despite all the qualifications

---

[38] Calic describes the June 1968 protests, in which students occupied universities in Belgrade, Ljubljana, Zagreb, and Sarajevo and demanded democracy, social justice and better studying conditions as a 'milestone in the political development of Yugoslavia', see *Geschichte Jugoslawiens*, 235. In his response to these first open protests against the regime, Tito acknowledged that the students' anger was justified and a result of the regime's own mistakes. He also promised change. Without any further-reaching democratic reforms, his statements ended the protests, which Calic sees as a sign that the students' anger focused more on concrete minority privileges in universities rather than being a general criticism of regime and society. For a deeper discussion of the student protests, "see Calic, *Geschichte Jugoslawiens*, 234.

[39] The 'Croatian spring' of 1971 is largely credited to have been one of the major expressions of nationalism in Yugoslavia. Protesting centralism from Belgrade and demanding more rights for Croats, the leadership of the local Communist party, representatives of the national-cultural organization *Matica Hrvatske*, and students took to the streets in what became known as the MASPOK (*masovni pokret*, mass mobilization). While there was a nationalist overtone to the protest, the reasons for many protesters to participate and their demands differed and included social and economic policy changes as well, see Adis Merdzanovic, *Democracy by Decree*, 69–70.

[40] Ibid, 65–69.

[41] Sevan Pearson, 'Muslims' Nation-Building Process in Socialist Bosnia and Herzegovina in the 1960s' (2018) 24(2) *Nations and Nationalism* 432–52.

indicated above). That the curtailing of citizens' involvement in daily politics appeared tolerable to the population at large has to do with another aspect of Yugoslav socialist rule, namely the principle of worker self-management (see below). It is also intrinsically connected with the economic boom which industrialization brought about in the 1960s and 1970s, which in turn pushed aside concerns over the regime's legitimacy. However, once the economic situation started deteriorating, the disintegration of the entire system began, and it did so along predictable lines, not least due to the ideology of brotherhood and unity (see next section).

Political liberalism, as I have defined it, rests on the claim of individual rights and democracy, the rule of law, and the system of checks and balances. These elements were clearly not present in Yugoslavia, even if the citizenry was afforded a larger degree of freedom than in other socialist countries. As a result of the special geopolitical position as a non-aligned country, and in combination with its less repressive variety of its communism, Yugoslavia's society was in a sense rather open, which, of course, gave this variety of communism not only a distinct quality but also had an effect on how it was perceived within and outside the country. But while the one-party system was not totalitarian and even included some forms of pluralism, it was very far away from the democratic ideal of political liberalism. There was no real legacy of political liberalism on which the idea of liberal democracy could have been based.

2 Economic liberalism

As a socialist country which had broken with Stalin, Yugoslavia became a rather interesting partner for the West, and this had social, political, and above all, economic implications. Because the United States sought to create a wall of allied countries around the Soviet Union, it made advances to Yugoslavia. Between 1948 and 1960, the US is estimated to have given between US$ 1.4 and 2.5 billion to Belgrade.[42] Tito, however, did not want to align himself unequivocally with the West, and Stalin's death in 1953 provided him with the opportunity to normalize Yugoslavia's relations with the Soviet Union. Henceforth, Yugoslavia would occupy a geopolitical position somewhere between the blocs, committed to a status of ambiguity, which was institutionalized in 1961 with the creation of the Non-Aligned Movement (NAM). This equidistance, maintained though delicate diplomacy, allowed Yugoslavia to immerse itself into the West, without becoming part of it. It could enjoy the fruits of a Western alliance without having to sacrifice its major legitimising structures. Yugoslavia's enterprises produced for, and exported to, the West. At the same time, the non-aligned position strengthened its ties to the 'Third World' and secured access to new markets. In the 1960s and 1970s, these markets generated an estimated 1.5 billion US dollars for the Yugoslav economy.[43] At the same time, Yugoslavia's economic interconnectedness with the European Economic Community (EEC) grew larger. Different trade agreements between the two partners were signed in the 1970s, including a far-reaching Joint Declaration in

---

[42] Calic, *Geschichte Jugoslawiens*, 200.
[43] Ibid, 202.

December 1976.[44] In 1978, Yugoslavia was the eleventh largest consumer of EEC goods, while it ranked twenty-sixth among EEC suppliers; and already in the year before, 'more than 26.5% of Yugoslav exports went to the Community and 39.5% of its imports were of EEC origin'.[45] On a socio-economic level, through its laissez-faire approach in the field of tourism, the Yugoslav state allowed for some private entrepreneurism (and direct interaction) connected to the West, exemplified in its tolerance of the 'Zimmer frei' ('Rooms available') schemes on the Adriatic coast catering primarily to German-speaking tourists.

The major characteristic of Yugoslavia's economic system was, of course, the notion of worker self-management. While self-management has strong political and especially social connotations, it of course offered first and foremost a different kind of economic model, which was not in line with an economically liberal understanding of market forces and functionalities. Even though the factories were still owned by the state, their day-to-day operations were not handled directly by the communist party but either by the workers themselves, or, in enterprises with more than seventy employees, by elected workers' councils. The workers thus had the authority to decide what, when, and how to produce. This approach was innovative in that it reintroduced choice into the mix of a socialist economy and, as Milton Friedman writes in his memoirs, for a time, 'the new system was much admired by Western intellectuals as a feasible alternative to a property-owning capitalist system'.[46] The system presented a third way between a socialist command economy and free-market capitalism, which is why, given the ambiguous track records of both systems, it remains positively evaluated to this day, not only in the former Yugoslav spaces.

The Yugoslav ideologues believed that leaders of enterprises would exhibit an entrepreneurial spirit and, consequently, use the profits for re-investments. Unfortunately, they often decided to invest such profits rather in personal consumption.[47] For neoliberals, such behaviour was caused by the lack of private ownership: since the workers shared in the profits but did not own the enterprises, their incentives to re-invest profits and hire more workers were counterbalanced by an urge to raise their own salaries and provide benefits.[48] Together with Yugoslavia's inability to adapt to a changing global economic environment, the natural results of this kind of system were trade deficits, inflation, and unemployment. This was particularly true since the system itself was not bullet proof and provided ample opportunities for abuse. As Neven Andjelic writes, in 1985 'the Yugoslav economy lost 149 billion dinars in 131,014 cases of financial misconduct. Political leaderships were always solving problems by ordering someone to help out or by giving money from the budget to cover deficits'.[49]

---

[44] Commission of the European Communities, 'Yugoslavia and the European Community', July 1979. Available at: http://aei.pitt.edu/8241/1/31735055282218_1.pdf.

[45] Ibid, 7.

[46] Milton Friedman and Rose D Friedman, *Two Lucky People: Memoirs* (Chicago: University of Chicago Press, 1999), 293.

[47] Calic, *Geschichte Jugoslawiens*, 227.

[48] Friedman and Friedman, *Two Lucky People*, 615.

[49] Neven Andjelic, *Bosnia-Herzegovina. The End of a Legacy* (London; Portland, OR: Frank Cass, 2003), 59.

The evolution of the worker self-management system has to be seen in close connection to the economic situation. Furthered by the industrial revolution in the 1950s, post-war Yugoslavia's economy boomed. But when economic growth stagnated in the 1960s, the state decided to open up the economic sphere to smaller enterprises and give up control over production, prices, and salaries, together with state-run investment and subvention funds; the Yugoslav economic system was henceforth to function 'according to capitalist' rules.[50] Yugoslavia also undertook a reform of its foreign exchange system, aimed at permitting its accession to General Agreement on Tariffs and Trade and its fuller integration into the world market.[51] Economically, however, these reforms did not help much and, especially after the oil crisis in 1973, Yugoslavia's state debt rose, leading to high inflation. The situation was aggravated by the fact that the enterprises chose to cover their rising deficits by taking up foreign loans, thus worsening Yugoslavia's general economic problems in the 1980s.[52]

Yugoslavia's economic system thus relied on socialism, but included elements of capitalism, as the central state had handed over much of its control — though never ownership — over the means of production to *loyal* workers' councils, while it relied politically on devolution of powers to the constituent republics, which were also run by loyal communists (see also Milica Uvalić's chapter in this volume). Yet when the economic crisis hit, such loyalties lay with the republics rather than with the central state, since the inter-republic differences in economic terms had become staggering. Naturally, the new rise of nationalist ideology, arguably starting with the Croatian Spring in the 1970s, furthered the idea of loyalty to the republic since most republics were nationally defined. In the multi-national republic of Bosnia and Herzegovina and the autonomous provinces in Serbia, this loyalty of course lay with the local, ethno-national community.

In terms of my definition of economic liberalism, Yugoslavia shows severe shortcomings. Its economy did not rely on the deregulation of markets; trade and industry sectors were by no means open, even if significant external relations existed and Yugoslavia was part of the general international financial infrastructure; and the factories remained state-owned, which led to severe problems of mismanagement. Yet, at the same time, Yugoslavia was not immune to the capitalist logic, meaning that the genuine instruments of a free market economy were present, even if they were tightly controlled.

3 Social liberalism

While the economy was at the forefront of the state's concerns, the main contributions of worker self-management to Yugoslav socialism were political and social. For the dissident Milovan Djilas, worker self-management, once proclaimed as a 'far-reaching democratic measure' in the fight against Soviet imperialism, as well as decentralization,

---

[50] Calic, *Krieg und Frieden in Bosnien-Hercegovina*, 228.
[51] Ramet, *The Three Yugoslavias*, 209.
[52] Personal information from a former IMF expert on Yugoslavia.

were 'concessions to the masses', designed to conceal the power monopoly of the elites. This was particularly true for worker self-management, which had become a 'domain of party activity'; without political freedom the notion of worker self-management was deemed impossible.[53]

While communism or socialism generally seek to *politicize the economical*, the Yugoslav model of worker self-management socialism tried to *economize the political*. Under the rhetorical cover of a continued 'federalization' – or, at times, even 'democratization'–, it delegated some political power to the lower levels thus allowing the lower party echelons to actually engage with minor demands for systemic adaptation. Furthermore, by giving the workers a say in how their enterprises were run, the party strengthened the impression of popular involvement in the state through the exercise of immediate control over the means of production.

These two elements – involvement in factories and more or less responsive local authorities – had social implications, as they produced some kind of job security, as part of a larger net of social welfare and security. The factory was 'often the place of primary on-site health care, nutrition (eating meals at the canteen and acquiring foodstuffs through the trade union), political participation (in the institutions of self-management at the level of the enterprise) and a way to take holidays and engage in leisure pursuits (through the workplace holiday camp exchanges with other factories)'.[54] It acquired an all-encompassing quality and formed the foundation of the state's power. Coupled with the limited political freedoms the citizen's enjoyed – chief among which was certainly the possibility to freely travel to the West – , multiparty rule, democracy, and individual rights and freedoms were not necessary to secure the system's *legitimacy*. When such demands for democratization or more political rights were raised, they were either suppressed or addressed through further federalization and/or by granting the different nations and nationalities more *group-based* rights in a political manoeuvre that Grandits has termed 'nationalization' instead of 'democratization'.[55] Challenges of political liberalism were thus met with communitarian means.

In terms of social liberalism, Yugoslavia seemingly fulfilled the requirements of our definition quite well. Far-reaching and expensive social welfare schemes existed and were controlled locally and job security was connected to working in the factory. The government curtailed significant market functions and intervened in the market regularly. However, such qualifications should be made with some caution, as two caveats need to be borne in mind. Firstly, one may doubt the extent to which social security was practically provided through the factory system. Particularly in the area of public housing, one can detect severe shortcomings, which might also be connected to

[53] Milovan Djilas, *Die neue Klasse. Eine Analyse des kommunistischen Systems* (München: Kindler Verlag, 1957), 100.
[54] Rory Archer and Goran Musić, 'Approaching the Socialist Factory and Its Workforce: Considerations from Fieldwork in (Former) Yugoslavia' (2017) 58(1) *Labor History* 47–48. Available at: https://doi.org/10.1080/0023656X.2017.1244331.
[55] Hannes Grandits, 'Dynamics of Socialist Nation-Building: The Short Lived Programme of Promoting a Yugoslav National Identity and Some Comparative Perspectives' (2008) 27 *Two Homelands Migration Studies* 26.

the fact that home ownership was (and still is) quite common in the Yugoslav space. Secondly, social security in itself is not precisely the same as social liberalism; rather, it has to be seen as an operationalization of the theoretical concept of social liberalism, which has quite different philosophical foundations to those present in Yugoslavia. Having said that, one can hardly deny the importance of this particular form of social liberalism for large parts of the population and, resulting from this perception of some form of 'social justice', its system-sustaining effect. Precisely because the political system's legitimacy relied on social peace and security, the principles of social liberalism became a strong pillar of Yugoslav political order.

4 The end of Yugoslav socialism

It is not surprising that, once the economic system started crumbling, it directly put the state's legitimacy into question, precisely because its foundation was social and economic rather than political. Yugoslavia's debt rose to about US$ 20 billion during the 1980s, and the 'state managed to repay some of the debts but the standard of living was sacrificed and some voices were raised against the system'.[56] According to Andjelic, the 'unemployment rate in Yugoslavia was rising constantly while prices increased even faster, thus producing poverty'.[57] Unsurprisingly, this led to social unrest and protests, while Prime Minister Branko Mikulić's policy of 'programmed inflation', whose 'main characteristic was the reduction of interest rates with the aim of combating inflation' did not prevent prises from going up.[58] The economic situation further deteriorated, even after the government concluded an agreement with the International Monetary Fund in 1988 (see Adam Bennett's chapter in this volume). The austerity measures introduced to curb inflation engendered widespread unpopularity for the government, as Andjelic writes, particularly because of the restrictions on the rise of salaries, which due to the constantly rising inflation rate meant that the people were becoming poorer. When Mikulić resigned by the end of 1988, prices had gone up by 10 to 20 per cent every month during the last quarter of the year, the annual inflation rate was predicted to be between 200 and 700 per cent, and the Yugoslav dinar had lost 270 per cent of its value compared to the German mark and some 300 per cent compared to the British pound and the US dollar.[59]

Yugoslavia was thus challenged on two fronts, socially and economically, and the political leadership proved incapable of appropriately handling the challenges at hand, which effectively led to the rise of alternative legitimization concepts, i.e. political nationalism. After all, by presenting nationalism as the great societal evil destroying the very foundation of the state, the leadership had inadvertently created a natural alternative.[60] With its concentration on the nation which was echoed in the federal structure of the state, nationalism was in a much better position to be adopted than any

---

[56] Andjelic, *Bosnia-Herzegovina. The End of a Legacy*, 52.
[57] Ibid, 52.
[58] Ibid, 53.
[59] Ibid, 55.
[60] Stevan K Pavlowitch, *Serbia: The History Behind the Name* (London: C Hurst & Co Publishers, 2002).

liberal alternatives, especially since the communists furthered nationalist sentiments through vilification and, simultaneously and paradoxically, through the granting of group-based rights. Yet the people subscribing to nationalism did not seem to realize that nationalism could not so easily be paired with the kind of economic influence and social security to which they were used, especially in a changing geopolitical and economic global climate. Elite-led nationalism followed completely different rules from worker self-management socialism.

While worker self-management might have been a smokescreen for other forms of control, and effectively excluded large parts of the population from having a say in how the country was run, it nevertheless created a basis on which the citizens and the state could interact. What is more, it strengthened the perception of a sphere in which the rulers and the ruled appeared on equal terms. It was not political freedoms that formed the foundation of this system, as in Western societies, but social cohesion and marginal economic control by the citizens. Lacking large-scale totalitarian practices, the de-legitimization of the system which occurred in the 1980s did not lead to a complete discrediting of the political, social, and economic basis of worker-run socialism, but rather to its temporary, even if powerful, suspension. When the economic foundations broke away, nationalism took over because of the federal structure and the economic discrepancies between the republics. The ruling elites realized that the nationalist tide was about to emerge, took control over it and presented its emergence in a democratic cover. Unsurprisingly, the first free elections brought nationalistic elites to power — and ultimately led to war.[61]

At this point, the liberal elements of Yugoslav socialism ceased to exert any kind of societal pressure, precisely because they were so closely coupled with the now-discredited legitimization strategy of the old regime. A genuine continuity of liberalism – in other words, a liberalism that would develop out of the liberal elements within the old system – became impossible. Any kind of legacy liberalism might have produced eroded as a result of the nationalist ideology that swept the region in the late 1980s, and especially the 1990s. The wars that accompanied Yugoslavia's disintegration produced a true stagnation in any kind of political development; liberalism in particular was so antithetical to the ruling elite's visions of their new states that any kind of liberal transition from within was impossible. Indeed, a new impetus for liberalism had to come from the outside.

IV The EU accession process and the external introduction of liberalism

Yugoslavia's disintegration and the declaration of independence by Slovenia and Croatia forced the European Community (EC) — soon to become the European

---

[61] An exception worth mentioning is Macedonia. It managed to gain independence without engaging in the larger war or producing any spill-over effects with respect to Greece and Bulgaria. For a detailed discussion of Macedonia's transition, see Nada Boškovska, 'Im Zentrum des Balkans und am Rande des europäischen Interesses: Makedoniens schwierige Lage in den 1990er Jahren', in *Tranformation und historisches Erbe in den Staaten des europäischen Ostens*, eds Carsten Goehrke and Seraina Gilly (Bern: Peter Lang, 2000), 441–74.

Union — to adopt common rules on how to engage with the situation.[62] A first step was finding common guidelines for the eventual recognition of the newly created states. To be recognized, the latter not only had to subscribe to the principal international and regional human rights treaties and conventions, but also to 'specific human rights guarantees' including 'the right to life, freedom of expression, the right to a fair hearing, freedom from torture and slavery', as well as specific national and minority rights like 'the right to identity, culture, religion and the use of one's own language both in public and private, and [the] protection of equal participation in public affairs'.[63] These political rights and guarantees are inherently liberal; to be part of the European system, the EC demanded that the former Yugoslav republics became *politically* liberal democracies.

The profile for new Member States became clearer at the summit in Copenhagen in 1993, when the European Union refined its accession criteria. First among these was a reiteration of the politically liberal recognition principles, meaning that states wishing to join the Union had to possess 'stable institutions guaranteeing democracy, the rule of law, human rights and respect for and protection of national minorities'.[64] But the EU now attached a further condition, which can be characterized as economically liberal, namely a 'functioning market economy and the capacity to cope with competition and market forces in the EU'. By putting the emphasis on 'competition' and 'market forces', the EU clearly asked the new Member States to subscribe to the liberal ideology of free markets and competitive advantages that swept the globe after the fall of the Iron Curtain[65] which became known as 'shock therapy'.[66] The third condition, the 'ability to take on and implement effectively the obligations of membership, including adherence to the aims of political, economic and monetary union', is of lesser importance in the present context as it basically refers to functioning state structures. Yet it is perhaps noteworthy because of the lack of any social component to the EU project. For the Western Balkans, with its history of strong social liberalism within Yugoslavia's socialist system, therefore, it seems evident that the attraction of EU membership lay less in the persuasive power of its politically and economically liberal ideology and more in the general prestige attached to being part of the European family of nations, as well as the inherent sense of safety and security that EU membership promised.

While the Copenhagen criteria represented a general set of one-size-fits-all standards for post-communist countries, the EU also formulated specific criteria for

[62] Josip Glaurdic, *The Hour of Europe: Western Powers and the Breakup of Yugoslavia* (New Haven: Yale University Press, 2011).

[63] Richard Caplan, *Europe and the Recognition of New States in Yugoslavia* (Cambridge: Cambridge University Press, 2005), 29–30.

[64] All quotations referring to the Copenhagen criteria are taken from the following European Union website: http://ec.europa.eu/enlargement/policy/conditions-membership/index_en.htm (last accessed 25 March 2016).

[65] Rachel A Epstein, *In Pursuit of Liberalism: International Institutions in Postcommunist Europe* (Baltimore: Johns Hopkins University Press, 2008); Francis Fukuyama, 'The End of History?' (1989) 16 *The National Interest* 3–18.

[66] Jeffrey Sachs, *Understanding Shock Therapy* (London: Social Market Foundation, 1994).

all the individual countries, especially those from the Western Balkans in light of their past conflicts. Its regional approach of 1996 sought to create political stability and economic prosperity in the region by establishing and maintaining democracy and the rule of law, ensuring respect for national minorities and human rights and reviving economic activity; its major instrument was 'political and economic conditionality'.[67] In 1999, this approach was formalized in the Stabilization and Association Process (SAP), which focused on securing political and economic stability by offering the Western Balkan states a clear path towards EU membership as well as financial support on the journey. Apart from the Copenhagen-related criteria, the SAP emphasized the development of economic and trade relations, political dialogue, as well as judicial and police cooperation *in the region*,[68] thus binding all the Western Balkan states together.

The EU reiterated the Western Balkans' membership perspective at its Thessaloniki Summit in 2003, and again at further summits in 2006 and in 2018.[69] All three documents emphasize a fundamentally liberal view of European principles. On the one hand, they refer to political liberalism by focusing on liberty, democracy, rule of law, human and minority rights; on the other, they put forward an economically liberal agenda concentrating on market economy as the foundation for prosperity and competitiveness. Most importantly, questions of social liberalism, i.e. agenda items connected to social welfare and justice are conspicuously absent from the enlargement agenda. Neither the Copenhagen criteria, nor the accession documents, nor indeed the 35 chapters of the accession negotiation package, attach any kind of *practical* significance to social justice within the EU accession framework, even if the rhetorical commitment to the value of social justice is indeed present. This is not truly surprising as the EU concerns itself with harmonising national legislations in the respective fields only insofar it seeks to assure the major principle of preventing discrimination against EU citizens, as well as ensuring certain minimal standards to be followed by all Member States. This is completely in line with the union's commitment to 'social justice' mentioned in article 3.3 of the Treaty on European Union.

While of course defensible in its own right, this strategy seemed ill-fitted for the Western Balkan states, particularly those that were less-developed. Once the immediate danger of war was removed and the reconstruction efforts finished to such a degree as to allow actual engagement with EU policies, its consequences became evident. In the early 1990s, the introduction of what was generally referred to as 'democracy', i.e.

---

[67] Commission of the European Communities, 'Communication from the Commission to the Council and the European Parliament on the Stabilisation and Association Process for Countries of South-Eastern Europe (COM (1999) 235 Final)', 1999, 2. Available at: http://eur-lex.europa.eu/legal-content/EN/TXT/HTML/?uri=URISERV:r18003&from=EN.

[68] Ibid, 3.

[69] Council of the European Union, 'Presidency Conclusions, Brussels European Council 14/15 December 2006', 2007. Available at: www.consilium.europa.eu/ueDocs/cms_Data/docs/pressData/en/ec/92202.pdf; Joint Declaration EU and Western Balkans States, 'Declaration of the EU-Western Balkans Summit (Thessaloniki, 21 June 2003)', 2003. Available at: www.consilium.europa.eu/ueDocs/cms_Data/docs/pressdata/en/misc/76291.pdf; European Union, 'EU-Western Balkans Summit, Sofia Declaration, 17 May 2018', 17 May 2018. Available at: www.consilium.europa.eu/media/34776/sofia-declaration_en.pdf.

political liberalism in the minimal form of the political freedom of elections, had resulted in war which is why 'politics' as such is not truly well-perceived in the region.[70] Self-centred political elites had captured the state and, in the name of the people, excluded the latter from actual participation in politics. This is particularly true in Bosnia and Herzegovina (BiH), where the difficult post-war situation prevented large parts of the population from questioning the strategies of the elites, as such criticism would necessarily have been perceived as directed against the interests of the ethnic group. But it also applies to Croatia and Serbia, both of which did not truly start their transitions until the early 2000s, when the death of Tuđman in Croatia and the ousting of Milošević in Serbia opened up the political space. It took both countries years to overcome this legacy, which was not so much rooted in the difficult post-war situation that prevented social engagement but in the existence of authoritarian regimes. The notion of political liberalism, to which all new governments subscribed, must have felt empty under these conditions.

At the same time, the EU's insistence on economic liberalism meant that enterprises were privatized after the war thus depriving the people of the only kind of political influence that they knew from socialist times. As Kurtović writes in relation to post-war BiH, for many ordinary Bosnians, the establishment of state institutions 'went hand in hand with perceived withdrawal and fragmentation of various forms of socialized care, often because the remaining models of social distribution were privatized, politicized, and transformed into clientelist tools by dominant political parties'.[71] Any sense of social justice was lost, while neoliberalism took hold of the processes and produced many losers. That this socially volatile situation would, in due course, create a backlash against the political elites was perhaps evident; and indeed, we live in times of ample evidence for this trend.[72]

V Conclusion

The aim of this chapter was to showcase the political, social, and economic liberal realities in socialist Yugoslavia. While the existing system was not liberal, it nevertheless incorporated certain principles that are more closely associated with the notion of liberalism than with totalitarian socialism. The political was reserved for the party structures. However, because of the powers of the individual republics and the differences between them, this also ensured some form of political pluralism within the socialist system. To a certain degree, the regime also allowed for criticism and open

---

[70] Torsten Kolind, *Post-War Identification. Everyday Muslim Counterdiscourse in Bosnia Herzegovina* (London: Verso, 2008).

[71] Larisa Kurtović, '"Who Sows Hunger, Reaps Rage": On Protest, Indignation and Redistributive Justice in Post-Dayton Bosnia-Herzegovina' (2015) 15(4) *Southeast European and Black Sea Studies* 642. Available at: https://doi.org/10.1080/14683857.2015.1126095.

[72] Damir Arsenijevic, ed, *Unbribable Bosnia. The Fight for the Commons* (Baden-Baden: Nomos, 2015); Srecko Horvat and Igor Štiks, eds, *Welcome to the Desert of Post-Socialism. Radical Politics After Yugoslavia* (London: Verso, 2015).

access to information, including that coming from the West. The societal debate was delegated to a lower level through the system of worker self-management which operated both as a substitute for political liberties and as a space to ensure social inclusion and provide for social welfare. It formed the foundation of the system's legitimization and may explain why the system is still regarded rather favourably.

However, by the late 1980s, Yugoslavia's political system was crumbling. Precisely because its legitimacy was based on certain liberal elements within Yugoslavia's worker self-management socialism, this crisis meant that a domestic continuity of these elements became far less likely, and a genuine evolution of them into a fully-fledged liberal system quite impossible. Ideologically, nationalism took over, while strategically, the new domestic elites – all of whom were nationalist in character, even if not always in name – used the most violent means imaginable to forge new states concurrent with their interests. For them, liberalism with its focus on good governance and the rule of law was indeed not an appealing choice.

The end of the wars and the beginning of infrastructural reconstruction and political, social, and economic transition provided a new impetus for the liberalization of the Western Balkans, this time from external actors. Chief among them was the European Union which offered the most comprehensive approach towards creating liberally democratic states capable one day of joining the EU. While its Copenhagen criteria provided the minimal standards of political and economic liberalism and were applicable to the entirety of potential new Member States, its Western Balkans agenda was very much influenced by the experiences of violent conflict and thus centred on security and stability. Unfortunately, it did not take into account the fact that Yugoslavia was quite different to the CEE countries not only in this respect, but also with regard to its socialist history. In CEE, the end of socialism signified a kind of liberation from an almost totalitarian yoke and the dawn of a new age of freedom. In Yugoslavia, it was precisely the *disintegration* of socialism which led to catastrophe, even if it was the federalist structure and the ideology of brotherhood and unity which ultimately created the opportunities for the rise and acceptance of nationalism. This nationalism would soon prove destructive, but EU-advocated liberalism proved a poor alternative — precisely because it lacked any kind of social component, which was so important in the old regime. The EU's approach of liberal transition thus did not fit neatly onto the pre-war experiences of the general population, which meant that the transition process itself could not have benefitted from any kind of legacies that may still have been prevalent. Moreover, the narrative of the necessity to introduce liberalism to the region from abroad after the wars of the 1990s made any suggestions of liberal continuities that could have been revived quite impossible.

While a genuine transition was necessary in the areas of political and, to a perhaps lesser structural than ideological degree, economic liberalism, the elements of social liberalism could have formed a solid foundation for the establishment of the new system. After all, they were the real source of legitimacy in the old system, not only through their social components of welfare and job security, but also through their ideological component of exercising political control where it mattered most immanently. Incorporating this legacy and explaining it to be part of liberalism could have provided the transition paradigm with a genuine argument of continuity and might have succeeded in making liberal values more prevalent in society. To what degree the citizenry as a whole has to accept liberal values for liberal democracy to succeed is an open question;[73] but it seems clear that the EU's liberalization approach might have benefitted from better taking the liberal elements of Yugoslav socialism into account.

There is, however, a particular legacy of Yugoslavia, which becomes evident from the above analysis. While one is usually quick to ascribe certain qualities to the Yugoslav system, the central characteristic of the state seems to have been ambiguity. It was not a fully liberal state, nor was it a fully socialist one. It was neither a fully centralized federation, nor was it a wholly decentralized one. It had neither a socialist command nor a free-market economy. And its citizens were neither fully free, nor were they fully oppressed. The entire system was fluid, a combination of different elements, forms, and ideologies. Looking at the successor states, one may wonder whether their current characteristics – neither fully democratic nor wholly authoritarian, neither fully committed to the rule of law nor fully lawless, neither providing good governance for the citizens nor totally disconnected from citizen's interest – might not be the contemporary forms of precisely these historical ambiguities.

References

Andjelic, Neven. *Bosnia-Herzegovina. The End of a Legacy*. London; Portland, OR: Frank Cass, 2003.

Archer, Rory, and Goran Musić. 'Approaching the Socialist Factory and its Workforce: Considerations from Fieldwork in (Former) Yugoslavia' (2017) 58(1) *Labor History* 44–66. Available at: https://doi.org/10.1080/0023656X.2017.1244331.

Arendt, Hannah. *The Origins of Totalitarism*. New York: Harcourt, Brace & Co, 1951.

Arsenijevic, Damir, ed, *Unbribable Bosnia. The Fight for the Commons*. Baden-Baden: Nomos, 2015.

Boas, Taylor C., and Jordan Gans-Morse. 'Neoliberalism: From New Liberal Philosophy to Anti-Liberal Slogan' (2009) 44(2) *Studies in Comparative International Development* 137–61.

Bogdanović, Mira. 'The Rift in the Praxis Group: Between Nationalism and Liberalism'. (2015) 43(3–4) *Critique* 461–83. Available at: https://doi.org/10.1080/03017605.2015.10 99850.

Boškovska, Nada. 'Im Zentrum des Balkans und am Rande des europäischen Interesses: Makedoniens schwierige Lage in den 1990er Jahren'. In *Tranformation und historisches Erbe in den Staaten des europäischen Ostens*, eds Carsten Goehrke and Seraina Gilly, 441–74. Bern: Peter Lang, 2000.

Brown, Archie. *The Rise and Fall of Communism*. London: Vintage, 2010.

Calic, Marie-Janine. *Geschichte Jugoslawiens im 20. Jahrhundert*. München: Beck, 2010.

Calic, Marie-Janine. *Krieg und Frieden in Bosnien-Hercegovina*. Erweiterte Neuausgabe. Frankfurt: Suhrkamp Verlag, 1996.

---

[73] See the debate between James Dawson and Sean Hanley, 'The Fading Mirage of the "Liberal Consensus"' (2016) 27(1) *Journal of Democracy* 20–34; and Ivan Krastev, 'What's Wrong with East-Central Europe? Liberalism's Failure to Deliver' 27(1) *Journal of Democracy* 35–39.

Caplan, Richard. *Europe and the Recognition of New States in Yugoslavia*. Cambridge: Cambridge University Press, 2005.

Cohen, Lenard J., and John R. Lampe. *Embracing Democracy in the Western Balkans: From Postconflict Struggles Toward European Integration*. Washington, DC; Baltimore: Johns Hopkins University Press, 2011.

Commission of the European Communities. 'Communication from the Commission to the Council and the European Parliament on the Stabilisation and Association Process for Countries of South-Eastern Europe (COM (1999) 235 Final)', 1999. Available at: http://eur-lex.europa.eu/legal-content/EN/TXT/HTML/?uri=URISERV:r18003&from=EN.

Commission of the European Communities. 'Yugoslavia and the European Community', July 1979. Available at: http://aei.pitt.edu/8241/1/31735055282218_1.pdf.

Council of the European Union. 'Presidency Conclusions, Brussels European Council 14/15 December 2006', 2007. Available at: www.consilium.europa.eu/ueDocs/cms_Data/docs/pressData/en/ec/92202.pdf.

Dawson, James, and Sean Hanley. 'The Fading Mirage of the "Liberal Consensus"'. *Journal of Democracy* 27, no. 1 (2016): 20–34.

Djilas, Milovan. *Die neue Klasse. Eine Analyse des kommunistischen Systems*. München: Kindler Verlag, 1957.

Dworkin, Ronald. *Justice for Hedgehogs*. Cambridge MA: Harvard University Press, 2013.

Epstein, Rachel A. *In Pursuit of Liberalism: International Institutions in Postcommunist Europe*. Baltimore: Johns Hopkins University Press, 2008.

European Union. 'EU-Western Balkans Summit, Sofia Declaration, 17 May 2018', 17 May 2018. Available at: www.consilium.europa.eu/media/34776/sofia-declaration_en.pdf.

Freeden, Michael. *Liberal Languages: Ideological Imaginations and Twentieth-Century Progressive Thought*. Princeton, NJ: Princeton University Press, 2004.

Freeden, Michael. *Liberalism. A Very Short Introduction*. Oxford: Oxford University Press, 2015.

Friedman, Milton. *Capitalism and Freedom: Fortieth Anniversary Edition.*. Chicago: University of Chicago Press, 2002.

Friedman, Milton, and Rose D. Friedman. *Two Lucky People: Memoirs*. Chicago: University of Chicago Press, 1999.

Fuchs, Christian. 'The Praxis School's Marxist Humanism and Mihailo Marković's Theory of Communication' (2017) 45(1–2) *Critique* 159–82.

Fukuyama, Francis. 'Nation-Building and the Failure of Institutional Memory'. In *Nation-Building. Beyond Afghanistan and Iraq* (ed) Francis Fukuyama, 1–16. Baltimore: The Johns Hopkins University Press, 2006.

Fukuyama, Francis. 'The End of History?' (1989) 16 *The National Interest* 3–18.

Glaurdic, Josip. *The Hour of Europe: Western Powers and the Breakup of Yugoslavia*. Yale University Press, 2011.

Gligorov, Vladimir. 'The Discovery of Liberalism in Yugoslavia' (1991) 5(1) *European Politics and Societies* 5–25.

Grandits, Hannes. 'Dynamics of Socialist Nation-Building: The Short Lived Programme of Promoting a Yugoslav National Identity and Some Comparative Perspectives' (2008) 27 *Two Homelands Migration Studies* 15–28.

Gromes, Thorsten. 'Democratisation of Post-War Societies: A Mission Impossible?' (2009) 5 *European Journal of Political Science and Theory* 418–41.

Gromes, Thorsten. *Ohne Staat und Nation ist keine Demokratie zu machen: Bosnien und Herzegowina, Kosovo und Makedonien nach den Bürgerkriegen*. Baden-Baden: Nomos, 2012.

Hayek, Friedrich August von. *The Road to Serfdom*. Chicago: University of Chicago Press, 1994.

Horvat, Srecko, and Igor Štiks, eds *Welcome to the Desert of Post-Socialism. Radical Politics After Yugoslavia*. London: Verso, 2015.

Joint Declaration EU and Western Balkans States. 'Declaration of the EU-Western Balkans Summit (Thessaloniki, 21 June 2003)'. Available at: www.consilium.europa.eu/ueDocs/cms_Data/docs/pressdata/en/misc/76291.pdf.

Jovic, Dejan. *Yugoslavia: A State That Withered Away*. West Lafayette, Indiana: Purdue Univerity Press, 2008.

Kolind, Torsten. *Post-War Identification. Everyday Muslim Counterdiscourse in Bosnia Herzegovina*. London: Verso, 2008.

Krastev, Ivan. 'What's Wrong with East-Central Europe? Liberalism's Failure to Deliver'. (2016) 27(1) *Journal of Democracy* 35–39.

Kurtović, Larisa. '"Who Sows Hunger, Reaps Rage": On Protest, Indignation and Redistributive Justice in Post-Dayton Bosnia-Herzegovina' (2015) 15(4) *Southeast European and Black Sea Studies* 639–59. Available at: https://doi.org/10.1080/14683857. 2015.1126095.

Merdzanovic, Adis. *Democracy by Decree. Prospects and Limits of Imposed Consociational Democracy in Bosnia and Herzegovina*. Stuttgart: Ibidem, 2015.

Mill, John Stuart. 'On Liberty' in *On Liberty and Other Essays*, 1–128. Oxford World's Classics. Oxford: Oxford University Press, 1869.

Monbiot, George. 'Neoliberalism – the Ideology at the Root of All Our Problems'. *The Guardian*, 04 2016. Available at: www.theguardian.com/books/2016/apr/15/neoliberalism-ideology-problem-george-monbiot.

Pavlowitch, Stevan K. *Serbia: The History Behind the Name*. London: C Hurst & Co Publishers, 2002.

Pearson, Sevan. 'Muslims' Nation-Building Process in Socialist Bosnia and Herzegovina in the 1960s' (2018) 24(2) *Nations and Nationalism* 432–52,

Perović, Jeronim. 'The Tito-Stalin Split. A Reassessment in Light of New Evidence' (2007) 9(2) *Journal of Cold War Studies* 32–63.

Ramet, Sabrina P. *The Three Yugoslavias: State-building and Legitimation, 1918–2004*. Washington, DC: Woodrow Wilson Press, 2006.

Rawls, John. *Eine Theorie der Gerechtigkeit*. Frankfurt am Main: Suhrkamp, 1975.

Sachs, Jeffrey. *Understanding Shock Therapy*. London: Social Market Foundation, 1994.

Steger, Manfred B., and Ravi K Roy. *Neoliberalism. A Very Short Introduction*. Oxford: Oxford University Press, 2010.

2

Civil Society in Post-Yugoslav Space: The Test of Discontinuity and Democratization

Ivor Sokolić
London School of Economics and Political Science

Denisa Kostovicova
London School of Economics and Political Science

Adam Fagan
King's College London

I Introduction

The end of Communism is generally understood by scholars as a moment of rupture that denotes the end of the illiberal regime and the beginning of democratic transition. The liberalization of the political sphere in the wake of Communism entailed both the creation of the democratic state and civil society. The role of civil society in the process of post-Communist democratization has been deemed to be two-fold. On the one hand, civil society provides checks and balances on the nascent democratic state and its institutions. On the other hand, as an advocate of human rights and freedoms it also contributes to the deepening of democracy. By doing so, the process of democratization is expected to unfold along the ideal-typical pathway: from the first multi-party elections to democratic consolidation. Ultimately, during the process of democratic transition, civil society offers reassurance that democratization should not end as a form of 'electrocracy' or 'façade democracy',[1] where the formal trappings of a democratic regime, such as democratic elections or institutions, are not accompanied by the incremental extension of social, political and economic rights.[2] While civil society represents an important means by which democracy is fostered, its development should also be viewed as an end in itself, because civil society is an embodiment of

---

[1] Larry Diamond, 'Is the Third Wave Over' (1996) 7(3) *Journal of Democracy* 20–37.
[2] John T. Ishiyama, 'Review Essay: Democratization and Democratic Consolidation in Post-Communist Politics' (2003) 40 *International Politics* 433–43.

political pluralism and a bedrock of liberal values.[3] In sum, the flourishing of civil society is not only indicative of the break with the previous regime, but it is also a litmus test of the political transition in post-Communist settings.

In the context of examining continuities and discontinuities between the politics, economics and culture in the former Yugoslavia, and in its successor states, civil society as a theoretical perspective offers a unique insight. The emergence and existence of liberal civil society provides a valuable test of discontinuity between the two regimes, because civil society is antithetical to the essence of the Communist rule that is premised on the obliteration of any type of social organization outside state control. While we recognize that there were some forms of civic action, both clandestine and overt, in former Yugoslavia, we take discontinuity to be premised on our understanding of civil society as a source of liberal progressive politics whose activism is protected and encouraged by a democratic (or a democratizing) state; neither the autonomy of civil society nor a benevolent state supportive of civil society existed in former Yugoslavia.[4] The test of discontinuity is operationalized along three dimensions drawn from the work of Ekiert and Kubik: the relationship that civil society has with the state; the form of organization and institutionalization of civil society; and how civil society gets involved in political and public life.[5]

The relationship that civil society has with the state is dependent on how much access it has to policy-making processes.[6] This is determined by how the state defines the public space according to its laws, institutions, protection of rights and implementation of policies.[7] All of these can be used to limit or bolster civil society. The action, or inaction, of states create the diversity of outcomes across post-Communist countries. For example, NGOs can become marginalized due to a lack of funding, while others receive preferential treatment or state funding and, thereby, manage to impact policy. Alternatively, if co-opted by the state, civil society itself can be complicit in consolidation of 'illiberal democracy'.[8]

Form of organization is dependent on what kind of rights civil society receives from the state and what type of environment the state provides for civil society to work in.[9] This relationship can be pluralist; meaning civil society actors are interest-based, diverse and not associated with the state or the legacy of the state (which can include religious or nationalist organizations). The relationship can, alternatively, be corporatist; meaning actors are centralized and associated to varying degrees with the state (often as a remnant of a state-controlled trade union or professional body). Whether civil

---

[3]   Jude Howell and Jenny Pearce, *Civil Society and Development: A Critical Exploration* (Boulder, Colorado Lynne Rienner, 2001).

[4]   Krishan Kumar 'Civil Society: An Inquiry into the Usefulness of an Historical Term' (1993) 44(3) *The British Journal of Sociology* 375–95, 386.

[5]   Grzegorz Ekiert and Jan Kubik 'The Legacies of 1989: Myths and Realities of Civil Society' (2014) 25(1) *Journal of Democracy* 46–58.

[6]   Ibid, 49.

[7]   Ibid.

[8]   Steven Levitsky and Lucan Way 'The Rise of Competitive Authoritarianism' (2002) 13(2) *Journal of Democracy* 51–65 at 62.

[9]   Ekiert and Kubik 'The Legacies of 1989: Myths and Realities of Civil Society' at 50.

society is pluralist or corporatist influences how organizations develop and what organizations are privileged.[10] This is also closely linked to the level of institutionalization of civil society. In post-Communist democracies, organizations are predominantly formal (such as NGOs and unions), but also decentralized organizationally and in how they behave.[11] In the context of ethnic and identity-based conflicts, collective identity can come to play a prominent role in how civil society is organized. Groups can then become organized along ethnic and identity lines, and participation in civil society may follow ethnic divisions.

Finally, civil society involvement in political life can be contentious, accommodating or a mixture of the two.[12] This is dependent on how civil society gets involved in political life, what links it has to other actors in the political sphere and how effective these links are. When contentious, this is characterized by challenges to the state and oppositional behaviour. When accommodating, it features extensive, often institutionalized, cooperation between civil society and the state. Shifts from one type of involvement to the other are determined by regime types and specific features of party systems. Declining and unstable parties are often replaced by contentious civil society groups advocating particular policies.[13] These three dimensions are historically contingent and influenced by the regimes that preceded them. Moreover, they show a high degree of variation across post-Communist, Eastern European and former Yugoslav cases. The continuities and discontinuities are often complex and constantly shifting.

The development of civil societies in post-Yugoslav states as well as their impact on the transition has been moulded by their different contexts. While the similarity of all post-Yugoslav states should not be overstated, their development was defined by the common political legacies of the former Yugoslavia. In addition, and, unlike the trajectory of civil society development in Eastern and Central Europe, civil societies in post-Yugoslav states have been impacted by former Yugoslavia's violent disintegration and conflicts. In fact, the war was formative not only for the development of civil society, but also for the development of the post-Yugoslav states, which, according to the liberal theory of civil society, are tasked with enabling the civil society sphere to flourish.

II Civil society in Communist Yugoslavia

The brief historical overview of the fate of civil society as a form of political organization independent of the state and of the advocacy of politics and policies that challenge the state reveals dynamics that are crucial for understanding the role of civil society after the fall of Communism in the former Yugoslavia. Although the Yugoslav brand of Communism is understood to be more liberal than the dogmatic implementation of

---

[10] Ibid, 51.
[11] Ibid.
[12] Ibid, 52.
[13] Ibid, 53.

the Communist ideology in the former Soviet Union and its satellites in Eastern and Central Europe, the regime's lenience extended to the spheres of economics and culture, and only up to a point. On the one hand, the Communist experience left an organizationally barren terrain, and civil society organizations had to be created anew. While popular mobilizations against the Communist regime can be viewed as expressions of a nascent or imminent civil society, such activism became increasingly bound up with ethnic nationalism and the wars of Yugoslavia's dissolution rather than with liberal democratic politics.

As a form of a totalitarian regime, Communist rule was underpinned by a totalizing logic that removed the possibility of autonomous societal organization, which would provide a limit to state power and define whether the state should be considered legitimate. But, this does not imply that the societal sphere was void of any organizations; quite the contrary. Besides duplication of institutions of the state,[14] a key feature of totalitarianism was a proliferation of societal organizations, such as various youth groups (the pioneers), women's groups, workers' clubs, neighbourhood associations, etc.[15] The organizational landscape of Communist countries thus resembled, at least superficially, the associational life that is characteristic of democratic regimes. However, their form was meaningless in the Communist context, as societal associations merely provided an additional avenue for surveillance of subjects by secret police, and assertion of state control on any free expression of political alternatives.[16] Consequently, the end of the Communist regimes in the former Yugoslavia marked the point when civil society had to be created anew, normatively and organizationally.

Although a totalitarian regime, the rule of Yugoslav communists did not go unchallenged. The instances of the Croatian Spring, and of the Albanian demonstrations in Kosovo in 1981, demonstrated that people power can be a vehicle for the expression of political alternatives, and a means by which to challenge the illiberal regime. The Croatian Spring in the late 1960s and early 1970s denoted 'the process of democratization, liberalization and nationalist enthusiasm'.[17] The demonstrations of 1971 brought into the open not only the conflict between reformists, who demanded greater control of republican funds, and conservatives in the Croatian Communist Party, but also revealed broad popular support for reforms (including the reclaiming of the Croatian language) among intelligentsia and university students, leading to its labelling as MASPOK (short for *masovni pokret*, i.e. mass movement). In the spring of 1981, a wave of demonstrations swept Kosovo, as Albanians took to the streets expressing their dissatisfaction with the Communist regime. People voiced a medley of concerns, making socio-economic demands, expressing opposition to the Communist ideology, and requesting the upgrading of Kosovo's status as an autonomous province

[14] Hannah Arendt, *The Origins of Totalitarianism* (New York, Harcourt, Brace and World, Inc, 1951).

[15] Claude Lefort, *The Political Forms of Modern Society: Bureaucracy, Democracy, Totalitarianism*, (Cambridge, Polity Press, 1986).

[16] Ilan Berman and Michael J. Waller, 'Introduction: The Centrality of the Secret Police' in Ilan Berman and Michael J. Waller (eds), *Dismantling Tyranny: Transitioning Beyond Totalitarian Regimes* (Lanham, Rowman & Littlefield Publishers, Inc, 2006), xv–xxii.

[17] Marko Zubak 'The Croatian Spring: Interpreting the Communist Heritage in Post-Communist Croatia' (2010) 32(1) *East Central Europe*, 191–225.

into a fully fledged republic (even unification with Albania).[18] In both cases, the Communist party was quick to repress dissent uncompromisingly, targeting not only the state universities, in Zagreb and Prishtina, respectively, but also 'disloyal' members of the party and people at large. Although ten years apart, the two events demonstrated that the Communist ideology and regime was breeding resistance and dissent. However, they also showed that the articulation of opposition to the Communist regime was likely to be conflated with the expression of nationalism.[19]

Alternatives were tolerated under the guise of, however limited, civil society. For example, Slovenian academic Tomaž Mastnak produced a book entitled *Socialist Civil Society* in 1985, which allowed for a discussion about alternative civic engagement.[20] Feminist organizations emerged in the 1970s and debated socialist theory and practice, as well as disputed established theoretical and empirical aspects of the women's emancipation project.[21] They took to the streets to protest and proposed legislative changes. Intellectuals organized into semi-official state agencies (e.g. writers' associations, enjoyed limited autonomy that enabled them to critique the state).[22] These alternative voices were not only present, but they also translated into political engagement. Janez Janša, a youth leader in Yugoslavia and a vocal critic of the Yugoslav People's Army, became Slovenia's Prime Minister.[23] This is one of the most striking continuities of Yugoslav civil society: its historical personalities[24] have changed little over time. The same individuals have been promoting tolerance, democracy, peace and heterogeneity through several regimes and over several decades.[25] These individuals have commanded and in some cases continue to have an authoritative hold over a range of issues, from transitional justice, to the environment to economics and so on.

These organizations, groups and individuals presented an oppositional stance to the Communist authorities, testifying to the emergence of a non-state sphere that nonetheless remained controlled and, when it came to articulation of political alternatives, proscribed. Furthermore, these organizations were not permanent, which partly helps explain the lack of research into Yugoslav civil society. Traditional Western research into democratization and civic engagement has focused on permanent organizations that manage to withstand regime pressures, at the expense of short-lived efforts.[26] The reliance

---

[18] Shkelzen Maliqi, *Kosova: Separate Worlds* (Prishtina, Dukagjini PH and MM, 1998).
[19] Denisa Kostovicova, *Kosovo: The Politics of Identity and Space* (London and New York, Routledge, 2005).
[20] Tomaž Mastnak (ed.) *Socijalistična civilna družba [Socialist Civil Society]* (Ljubljana, Knjižnica revolucionarne teorije, 1985).
[21] Dubravka Žarkov 'Feminism and the Disintegration of Yugoslavia: On the Politics of Gender and Ethnicity' (2003) 24(3) *Social Development Issues* 59–68 at 60.
[22] Jasna, Dragović-Soso 'Rethinking Yugoslavia: Serbian Intellectuals and the National Question in Historical Perspective' (2004) 13(2) *Contemporary European History* 170–84.
[23] Bojan Bilić 'A Concept that is Everything and Nothing: Why Not to Study (Post-)Yugoslav Anti-war and Pacifist Contention from a Civil Society Perspective'(2011) 53(3) *Sociologija* 297–322, 306.
[24] Jason Wittenberg, 'What is a Historical Legacy?' *APSA 2013 Annual Meeting Paper; American Political Science Association 2013 Annual Meeting*, (2013). Available at SSRN: https://ssrn.com/ abstract=2303391.
[25] Ibid.
[26] Bojan Bilić, *We Were Gasping for Air: [Post-] Yugoslav Anti-war Activism and its Legacy* (Baden-Baden, Nomos, 2012); Mary Kaldor, *Global Civil Society* (Oxford, Oxford University Press, 2003).

on individuals and leaders is emblematic of the poor civic culture in Yugoslav civil society, which struggled to overcome the 'leader discourse'.[27]

Describing the latter stage of the totalitarian regimes (i.e. post-totalitarianism), when some of the stringent ideological and repressive controls of the Communist regime begin to let up, democratic theorists point to the existence of dissident structures of second culture and parallel society, *albeit* in the context of a flattened polity where all the power is still claimed by the party state.[28] The dissidents in the former Yugoslav space reflected the normative fractionalization of civil society in liberal groups supporting democratization as a universal human rights value, and civil society groups supporting democratization defined in exclusively ethnic terms as empowerment of one ethnic group, combined with the 'deadly' ideology of ethnic territorialization of exclusive identities. Consequently, scholars have dissected the contribution of intellectuals and cultural associations to the outbreak of war in Yugoslavia, as exemplified by the Serbian Association of Writers.[29] Nevertheless, ethnic fragmentation has continued to test and weaken civil societies in the post-Communist period. For example, divisions defined by ethnically defined interests have also managed to divide the region's feminists.[30]

Besides being shaped by the Communist legacy, the development of civil society in the former Yugoslav states was also profoundly impacted by external dynamics. Post-Communist waves of democratization differed from other historical waves of democratization, such as post-World War Two democratization, because of the 'salience of the international environment'.[31] External promotion of democracy took place both beneath and beyond the nation-state, as illustrated by the involvement of international organizations, human rights groups, foundations, media, transnational firms and dissidents.[32] While the focus on civil society in post-Yugoslav states and its agency to marshal democratic change would not have been distinct from those in other Central European counterparts, the wars of Yugoslavia's dissolution in the 1990s have put additional burden of expectations on civil societies to instigate and deliver democratic change. External funding that poured into the civil society sector on the territory of former Yugoslavia was a response to the conflict and its legacy that came to overlay the post-totalitarian legacy. On the one hand, civil society was to help address the

---

[27] Théodora Vetta '"Democracy building" in Serbia: The NGO Effect' (2009) 33 *Southeastern Europe* 26–47.

[28] Juan J. Linz and Alfred Stepan, *Problems of Democratic Transition and Consolidation: Southern Europe, South America, and Post-Communist Europe* (Baltimore and London, The Johns Hopkins University Press, 1996).

[29] Jasna Dragovic-Soso, *Saviours of the Nation Serbia's Intellectual Opposition and the Revival of Nationalism* (London, C Hurst & Co Publishers, 2002).

[30] Ana Miškovska Kajevska, *Feminist Activism at War: Belgrade and Zagreb Feminists in the 1990s* (Abingdon and New York, Routledge, 2017).

[31] Jan Zielonka and Alex Pravda (eds) *Democratic Consolidation in Eastern Europe: Volume 2 International and Transnational Actors* (Oxford, Oxford University Press, 2001).

[32] Philippe Schmitter, 'Twenty-five Years, Fifteen Findings' (2010) 21(1) *Journal of Democracy* 17–28 at 19; Laurence Whitehead (ed) *The International Dimensions of Democratization: Europe and the Americas* (Oxford, Oxford University Press, 1996).

dysfunction of the post-conflict state, whose transformation mainly through war economy resulted in the entrenchment of partial interests in the institutions and the mode of governance (such as pervasive informal economy and corruption). On the other hand, civil society, or more specifically, liberal civil society was to address the emergence of exclusive ethnic identities and exclusive nationalist ideologies, which instilled deep-seated mistrust among communities and obstructed democratization.[33]

Assessing democratization after 25 years, Schmitter has remarked that democratization may have been easier than he had anticipated, but it has also been 'less consequential'.[34] A part of the reason why democratic consolidation has stagnated lies in the role played by civil society. According to Schmitter, civil society may be a 'mixed blessing': while robust civil society is 'vital for the success of transition and consolidation', the case of former Yugoslavia made it clear that society can play an 'ambiguous and even malign' role, and directly incite divisive mobilization that leads to violence.[35] Consequently, the assessment of its contribution to democratization cannot be carried out without taking into account often contradictory normative aims, dynamics and impacts of a range of organizationally diverse forms of civil society throughout the post-Yugoslav period.

This chapter proceeds by offering a comparative assessment of the emergence and strength of civil society in Croatia and Serbia. The analysis draws on empirical data from particular sectors within civil society in both countries: environmental organizations in Serbia, and transitional justice and veterans' organizations in Croatia. The focus on these particular sectors allows us to capture the diversity of organizational forms, the variation in empowerment and efficacy, and the developmental trajectory of post-Yugoslav civil society. While environmental organizations lack the political resonance of other iterations of post-Yugoslav civil society, the perspective illustrates the impact of institutionalization and Europeanization. By contrast, veterans' and victims' associations, and organizations focusing on aspects of transitional justice have particular political status and connotations within the successor states; their interaction with elites and citizens remains fluid and acts as a litmus test of liberal reforms and democratic consolidation. These groups are all inextricably linked to both the totalitarian and conflict legacies of Yugoslavia. They highlight that 'not all forms of civil society mobilization under nondemocratic regimes help the rise of democracy, particularly if racist or radically nationalist activism is at the forefront (as in the former Yugoslavia)'.[36]

These two examples shine light on the strengths and weaknesses of civil society, as well as on domestic and external constraints the civil society faces in shaping the

[33] Christoph Zürcher 'Building Democracy while Building Peace' (2011) 22(1) *Journal of Democracy* 81–95 at 82.
[34] Philippe Schmitter, 'Twenty-Five Years, Fifteen Findings' at 19.
[35] Ibid, 24; Denisa Kostovicova and Vesna Bojicic-Dzelilovic, 'Introduction: Civil Society and Multiple Transitions – Actors, Meanings and Effects' in Vesna Bojicic-Dzelilovic, Denisa Kostovicova and James Ker-Lindsay (eds) *Civil Society and Transitions in the Western Balkans* (Basingstoke, Palgrave Macmillan, 2013).
[36] Ekiert and Kubik, 'The Legacies of 1989: Myths and Realities of Civil Society' at 55.

politics and policies of post-Yugoslav state. Bermeo warns that 'building a "strong" civil society is not as desirable as building a civil society that is tolerant and non-violent and thus supportive of democracy'.[37] In conclusion, we reflect on reasons why the growth of civil society organizations does not necessarily coincide with its unequivocal contribution to democratization, including peace-building,[38] and consider complex ways in which the agency of civil society in the context of democratic transition marks political discontinuity with the politics and policies of the Communist Yugoslavia.

III Civil society in Croatia

Croatian civil society has provided pressure for democratization and, for the most part, functions without significant institutional impediments. Its impact becomes limited when and if it attempts to challenge the key identity narrative of the nation- and state-building projects: that of a Roman Catholic nation borne out of a heroic defence against Serbian aggression. Three types of civil society groups best exemplify this: war veterans' associations, fact-finding organizations and language institutions. These show the legally protected position that Croatian civil society groups have, but that funding is used to give some more opportunity to impact policy than others; that civil society is pluralist, with some corporatist elements, but that ethnic identity of groups is key; and that civil society is contentious within the context of a weak party system, but this contention is dependent on which party is in power.

Civil society's relationship with the state in Croatia is protected by laws and rights that follow EU frameworks. These allow civil society to influence policy-making processes. Underpinning this relationship is a democratic framework in a system defined by the institutional dominance of one ethnic group, the Croats.[39] Civil society is generally well-resourced, as long as it does not challenge the dominant political narrative. Organizations that criticize this narrative can have their funds slashed, and therefore rely on private or EU donations, or they can lose state protection against threats and dangerous behaviours.[40] All three types of civil society group exemplify this relationship.

Since the 1990s and even after the 2000 regime change, war veterans' associations have had nearly exclusive access to state funding as they have been closely aligned with the nation- and state-building projects in Croatia, especially those of the right-wing Croatian Democratic Union (*HDZ – Hrvatska demokratska zajednica*). Because the war narrative, one of defence against a larger Serbian aggressor, has proven to be so

---

[37] Nancy Bermeo 'What the Democratization Literature Says – or Doesn't Say – about Post-war Democratization' (2013) 9(2) *Global Governance* 159–77.

[38] Thania Paffenholz, 'Civil Society and Peacebuilding' in Thania Paffenholz (ed) *Civil Society & Peacebuilding: A Critical Assessment* (Boulder, Colorado, Lynne Rienner Publishers, 2010), 43–64.

[39] Referred to as an ethnic democracy. See Dejan Jović, *Rat i Mit: Politika Identiteta u Suvremenoj Hrvatskoj* (War and Myth: The Politics of Identity in Contemporary Croatia), (Zaprešić, Fraktura, 2017).

[40] See the 2018 Freedom House Report. Available at: https://freedomhouse.org/report/nations-transit/2018/croatia

enduringly influential in society, war veterans' associations have been able to exploit related symbols to more effectively further their political, at times ideological, aims not specifically related to war veterans' direct interests. These associations are often vehemently opposed to any move that can be interpreted as a delegitimization of the Croatian state. This was further supported by the media, who provided associations with prominent coverage to boost sales.[41] Human rights non-governmental organizations (NGOs) are comparatively weak. They suffer from fragmentation and personality conflicts; a lack of funding in comparison to state-funded veterans' and victims' associations; and, they are branded as 'anti-Croatian' by the HDZ, which leads to negative perceptions among the public.[42] Moreover, due to the nearly complete expulsion of the Krajina Serb community in 1995, many victims of human rights abuses are no longer part of the Croatian political community.[43] War veterans' associations highlight how, in order to access policy making, organizations have to be aligned with the dominant war narrative, which forms a key part of modern Croat identity.

Much the same can be seen among fact-finding organizations related to the 1991–1995 conflict. The *Documenta – Centre for Dealing with the Past* is a typical human rights NGO concerned with fact-finding and transitional justice issues. It was established by several other human rights NGOs – the *Centre for Peace, Non-Violence and Human Rights Osijek*, the *Centre for Peace Studies*, the *Civic Committee for Human Rights* and the *Croatian Helsinki Committee* – with the aim of fostering dialogue that focuses on interpretations, rather than dispute, of facts. Other key aims are: fostering public dialogue and judicial processes (including regional truth commissions and teaching of history); documentation of human losses; and, improvement of judicial standards through monitoring.[44] They receive funding from the Croatian government, including the Ministry of Culture, as well as a broad range of international foundations, organizations and embassies. They work with war veterans and victims, as well as other associations, but remain deeply unpopular with much of this community and relatively unknown to most of the public.

Such a peripheral role can be partly explained by how the media portrays it: ignored at best and deemed anti-Croatian at worst. The public is, therefore, not familiar with the work of *Documenta* and often they hear about such NGOs through war veterans' and victims' associations, who feel threatened by them due to the relative success human rights NGOs have had in attracting international funding. Their connections to international donors have helped feed conspiracy theories about *Documenta* and their support of the International Criminal Tribunal for the former Yugoslavia (ICTY) meant that they, too, were accused of attempting to 'equalize war crimes' and criminalize Croatia's role in the war.[45] Its criticism of the dominant

[41] Sharon Fisher, 'Contentious Politics in Croatia: The War Veterans' Movement' in Petr Kopecký and Cas Mudde (eds) *Uncivil Society? Contentious Politics in Post-communist Europe.* (London, Routledge, 2003), pp 74–92.

[42] Ibid.; Christopher K Lamont, *International Criminal Justice and the Politics of Compliance* (Farnham, Ashgate, 2010).

[43] Lamont, *International Criminal Justice and the Politics of Compliance.*

[44] A detailed overview is available at: www.documenta.hr/en/programme.html.

[45] Ivor Sokolić 'Sources of Information on Transitional Justice in Croatia' (2017) 53(4) *Croatian Political Science Review* 77–104.

narrative resulted in the loss of government funding in 2018, while groups such as *U ime obitelji* (In the Name of the Family), that advocate the limitation of LGBT and women's rights, were granted government funding.[46]

Language institutions best highlight how affinity to the nation-building project results in greater influence over policy making. The Croatian language planning project, used to differentiate Croatian from Serbian, was generally not promoted by the government, but by non-governmental organizations with similar goals.[47] Most notable were the Croatian Academy of Sciences and Arts (*Hrvatska akademija znanosti i umjetnosti* or HAZU), the Council for the Norms of the Croatian Standard Language (*Vijeće za normu hrvatskog standardnog jezika*), the Institute for the Croatian Language and Linguistics (*Institut za hrvatski jezik i jezikoslovlje* or IHJJ) and *Matica Hrvatska*. Croatian governments rarely introduced legislation or regulations to control language policies, instead these civil society organizations encouraged an exclusive view of the Croatian standard language that actively eliminated anything related to the 'East'.[48] This defined Croatian language as Croatian, not Serbian, and its alphabet as strictly not Serbian Cyrillic. Not only did these organizations succeed in directly influencing policy making, they also lobbied international bodies. HAZU complained to the ICTY in 2007 about reports intended for Croatia being written in Serbian, alongside a range of other complaints to the EU and Western European universities.[49]

The form of organization in Croatian civil society is pluralist, with elements of corporatism. Civil society actors are diverse, interest-based, predominantly formal and highly decentralized. Additionally, the legacy of ethnic conflict has resulted in collective identity playing a large role in how civil society is organized. This is best exemplified by the high number of formally registered war veterans' associations (over 6,300) and their privileged position in Croatian society.[50] The multiplication and fragmentation of war veterans' associations, as well as their close association with the nation-building project, has made it easy for political parties, most notably the HDZ, to manipulate them. Their shared priorities regarding the 1991–1995 conflict have often resulted in special benefits for associations, who may see the HDZ not only as a way to protect the Croatian nation, but also as a way to access more funds and powers. The implication is that these associations no longer focus on their rehabilitating function and instead prioritize political aims, often to the detriment of other ethnic groups and democratization.

Fact-finding organizations, on the other hand, highlight both pluralist and corporatist elements of civil society. While *Documenta* is a typical example of pluralism (e.g. it was formed by a number of separate organizations), the *Croatian Memorial and Documentation Centre for the Homeland War* is essentially an arm of the government. It is run by Croatian historian Ante Nazor and shares similar aims to *Documenta*, those

[46] Freedom House, 2018.
[47] Keith Langston and Anita Peti-Stantić, *Language Planning and National Identity in Croatia* (London, Palgrave Macmillan, 2014).
[48] Ibid., 277.
[49] HAZU. *HAZU o Hrvatskom Jeziku u Europskim Integracijama (HAZU on Croatian in European integration)*, (2007), Available at: www.hkv.hr/kultura/jezik/962-hazu-o-hrvatskom-jeziku-u-europskim-integracijama.html. Accessed: 11 April 2016.
[50] See: https://registri.uprava.hr/#!udruge.

of collecting and documenting material about the 1991–1995 conflict. Their publications, however, have overt political messages and use loaded terms extensively, thereby connecting them to the dominant ethnic narrative. Titles include 'Greater Serbian Aggression'[51] and 'The Assassination of Croatia'.[52] The centre was founded and is funded by the Croatian state; it portrays itself as an independent, but state-funded, research centre. Parliamentary discourse attached to the centre is representative of its attachment to the state- and nation-building projects in Croatia: in a 2016 parliamentary progress report and debate, Members of Parliament stressed the 'independent and objective work of the centre' in 'protecting the memory of the legitimate and just, liberating Homeland War'.[53]

The centre and Ante Nazor are popular, since they tap into the Croatian zeitgeist: Ante Nazor is a recognizable historian; a war veteran; and, the centre makes a great show of publicly collecting documents. War veterans find Nazor credible due to their shared experiences and his focus on collection of documents.[54] They do not dispute the interpretations due to the acceptable manner of data collection. The centre's reach and impact on policy goes far beyond that: it presents its work in Croatian schools and involves itself in the development of school curricula on the conflict. If Croatian civil society is a zero-sum, competitive arena, then the *Memorial and Documentation Centre* belongs among the clear winners.

More corporatist and institutionalized in comparison are the various language organizations, discussed above. These are not strictly government institutions, but they all have extensive links to the state, be they institutional or financial. The extent of the corporatist relationship is that language change in Croatia occurred through sponsorship of these organizations, rather than by formal changes to Croatian law.

Civil society in Croatia gets involved in political and public life in a generally contentious manner, but this is dependent on who is in power. This is due to the dominance of war veterans' associations in civil society and their use of the narrative surrounding the 1991–1995 conflict to legitimize their actions. Political parties in Croatia are weak and most governments prioritize appeasing war veterans, because of the potential they have to disrupt and challenge the government. The power of such associations is evidenced by the scale of veteran-organized demonstrations over the years: from protesting the extradition of generals to the more recent protests in Vukovar against bilingual signs, they have consistently managed to draw thousands to the streets. This has two key implications. First, it allows political parties to manipulate these groups for their own purposes, by calling on them to protect the nation against perceived threats to the government. It also means that associations can use parties to guarantee their own existence. Often, these occur at the expense of minority and

[51] Ante Nazor, *Greater-Serbian Aggression Against Croatia in the 1990s* (Zagreb, Croatian Homeland War Memorial and Documentation Centre, 2011).
[52] Josipa M. Kraljević and Ilija Vučura, *The Assassination of Croatia: The Attack of the Pro-Serbian JNA on the Banski Dvori and the Historic Centre of Zagreb, 7 October 1991* (Zagreb, Croatian Homeland War Memorial and Documentation Centre, 2016).
[53] See http://edoc.sabor.hr/Views/FonogramView.aspx?tdrid=2012764.
[54] Sokolić, 'Sources of Information on Transitional Justice in Croatia'.

human rights, which are not pursued. Second, this diverts attention from the humanitarian aims of these groups. These highlight the need for social justice in the aftermath of conflict, which if neglected, can create social divisions.[55] War veterans' associations, however, divert attention away from this.

Fact-finding efforts are equally contentious. *Documenta* spends much of its time challenging the state, but the *Memorial and Documentation Centre* is also happy to do so. These two groups do hold some form of dialogue and they share many of the same institutional obstacles. For example, they jointly take part in discussions on how best to approach recent history and Vesna Teršelič has admitted that Ante Nazor is open to cooperation between all types of organizations, but they disagree over who is most qualified to determine facts.[56] Slaven Rašković, formerly Research Coordinator at *Documenta*, has also complained about their shared struggle to gain access to government documents in Croatia.[57] This highlights the power that civil society can hold over government in the context of an ethnic democracy with weak parties. Whoever is seen as best defending the war narrative and, therefore the Croatian nation, is given the most legitimacy. Civil society organizations can, in this way, come to replace political parties or at least challenge their legitimacy. Language institutions are an exception to this, as they are accommodating. They are highly institutionalized and their cooperation with the state is so close that they occupy a grey area between civil society and formal government institutions. They have successfully replaced the state in some areas, where they are more efficient, but they also remained guided by the government and not quite independent of it.

Since the break-up of Yugoslavia, Croatian civil society has been broadly pluralist and contentious, with elements of both corporatism and accommodation. It holds a legally protected position with opportunities to impact on policy. This position is, however, contingent on groups belonging to the dominant group identity and adhering to the dominant war narrative. Any challenges to these also challenge the Croatian state- and nation-building projects. Groups who do so see their opportunities for action limited by the government, usually through cuts in funding. This highlights that civil society in Croatia is both varied and still changing and that 'there is no convergence on a single model. On the contrary, post-Communist civil societies are becoming more divergent.'[58] The key insight from the Croatian case study is the role that the legacy of ethnic conflict plays in leading to these diverging outcomes.

---

[55] Fred P Cocozzelli, *War and Social Welfare: Reconstruction After Conflict* (Basingstoke, Palgrave Macmillan, 2009); Isabel Ströhle, 'Kosovo Liberation Army Veterans' Politics and Contentious Citizenship in Post-war Kosovo' in Srdja Pavlović and Marko Živković (eds) *Transcending Fratricide: Political Mythologies, Reconciliations, and the Uncertain Future in the Former Yugoslavia* (Baden-Baden, Nomos, 2013), 243–64.
[56] Vesna Teršelič speaking at the Fifth Regional Forum on Transitional Justice, Bečići, Montenegro, 2009.
[57] Slaven Rašković speaking at the 'Local Consultations with the Local Community about the RECOM Initiative', Knin, Croatia, 2009.
[58] Ekiert and Kubik, 'The Legacies of 1989: Myths and Realities of Civil Society', at 54.

IV Civil society and governance in Serbia

The attitude of Serbia's political elites towards engaging civil society in political life has arguably been the key political and ideological battleground since the violent collapse of Yugoslavia. Indeed, since the early 1990s, civil society has stood as the frontier between reform and stagnation, between a further descent into semi-authoritarianism and genuine liberal regime change. Despite recent progress towards EU accession, the intent expressed by Prime Minister Aleksandar Vučić to deal with corruption and organized crime and to secure Serbia on a liberal democratic path, the nexus of state/civil society relations is no less a barometer of the country's post-Milošević politics. In terms of continuities or discontinuities with the Communist past, the polymorphous civil society that exists today would seem to have an obvious link to the anti-authoritarian and pro-liberal dissident movement of the Communist era, rather than to the nationalist activism of the late Yugoslav period.

Indeed, on the surface at least, Serbian civil society today appears to resemble that which exists across Central and Eastern Europe. Such 'normalization' is characterized by four (very) broad and by no means rigidly defined categories: (i) a formal tier of apolitical semi-institutionalized non-governmental organizations and think tanks, largely dependent on international donors, but gradually gaining some access to political and public life, and acquiring domestic support and supporters; (ii) a long-established network of politically engaged human rights advocacy groups (HRGs) whose focus on war crimes and transitional justice (but increasingly also LGBTQ, race, gender and identity politics) still make them prime targets for nationalist attacks and uneasy partners for reformist elites; (iii) a small tier of community-situated civil society organizations (CSOs) who campaign on local issues and increasingly venture, albeit tentatively, into the political arena; and, (iv) emerging radical, grass-roots protest politics, most notably, the *Ne da(vi)mo Beograd* ('Let's not drown Belgrade') movement.

The fact that all four broad categories of 'civil society' are weaker, more ephemeral and far less politically discernible than their Central and Central and Eastern European counterparts reflects the particular recent history of Serbia: the way Yugoslavia collapsed and the lack of a liberal democratic revolutionary 'moment' at the end of the 1980s; the legacy of Slobodan Milošević and the subsequent delayed or interrupted transition, and the particular path of Europeanization on which Serbia has embarked. Each iteration of civil society reflects a particular aspect of Serbia's political transition: the partially institutionalized NGOs which function at the periphery of decision making and policy reform are gradually being brought in from the cold because of the increase in EU pressure since 2013 and the granting of candidacy; the HRGs, more tolerated, perhaps, than in the recent past, stand as a continued reminder of the illiberal semi-authoritarian dimension to the country's post-Yugoslav politics, but also the unresolved and still deeply fractured nature of contemporary Serbian politics. The more community-focused civil society organizations are, in part, a legacy of the 1990s and vestiges of liberal dissent amidst the nationalism of that era; and the more radical activism is perhaps best interpreted as part of a pan-European, if not global, political mobilization that has gained momentum since the financial crisis and the ensuing austerity, critiquing corrupt and unresponsive elites.

Each category of civil society is discussed below, drawing out the specificity of the Serbian context, but offering some insight as to why and how particular organizations and networks function as they do, failing to deliver the beneficial effects on transition. The primary intention is to draw out how Serbia differs from other post-Communist states in terms of its civil society. Space does not permit the opportunity to contemplate what predictive power, if any, there is in developments happening in Poland, where a far more politically active civil society is challenging the illiberal agenda of the government, or whether the experience of *Zagreb je NAŠ!* in Croatia, where a civil society network directly contested local elections to unseat incumbents, is likely or possible in Serbia. However, these questions are incipient and implicit in what is discussed below.

The professional NGO, with no overt political affiliation or obvious ideological compass, operating as close as possible to the policy process, is no less ubiquitous in Serbia than elsewhere in post-Communist Europe. Successive rounds of donor project calls have shaped the issue agendas and focus of these organizations, who have gradually acquired project management capacities and built up technical expertise. At best, they are now key players within the epistemic communities that are building up around particular policy issues and areas (e.g. environmental protection and governance). At worst, they are empty vessels and unanchored project machines with rather superficial knowledge and expertise. As already noted, the NGOs of Serbia are less institutionalized and lack access to policy elites in large part because of the complex relationship between Belgrade and Brussels, and the prevalence of the Kosovo issue. In other words, the process of opening and closing chapters of the *acquis* has only recently begun in earnest, therefore the imperative to bring NGOs to the negotiating table is still in its early stages. However, recent research on the impact of Europeanization on domestic actors in Serbia suggests that while NGOs initially benefit in terms of access, they lose influence once the detailed negotiation process begins in earnest, due to a lack of detailed knowledge and the pace of the reform process.

The dividing line between the professional NGOs and what we identified above as CSOs is quite thin and porous. We gain a good sense of the interaction between the two types of organization from the perspective of environmental activism and politics. Most of the registered environmental CSOs, like the larger NGOs, exist as formal entities due to the availability of international donor funding, invariably, but not exclusively, from the EU. They emerged as part of the wide-ranging *Otpor!* coalition of the late 1990s against the Milošević regime, which culminated in the 5 October 2000 revolution. In terms of number, there are currently about 1,000 CSOs working broadly on environmental issues across Serbia.[59] The vast majority of these are very small organizations. While a small number have the capacity to engage local communities from across the entire country, the majority are confined to operating at the local level. Of the 12 such organizations interviewed recently by the author,[60] most work on

---

[59] Interview with REC Serbia, 23 May 2017.
[60] The following organizations were interviewed during May/June 2017: Regional Environmental Center (REC); Centar za ekologiju i održivi razvoj (CEKOR); Mladi istraživači Srbije; inženjeri zaštite životne sredine; Pokret Gorana Vojvodine; Timočki klub; Ekološki centar Stanište; Ekološki pokret Vrbasa; Fractal; RES Foundation; Arhus Centar Kragujevac; European Movement in Serbia; Belgrade Open School; European Policy Centre (CEP).

environmental issues as part of broader issue and campaign portfolios. However, they have all received EU assistance or other specific assistance initiatives, to pursue an environment-related project.[61]

With a few exceptions, it is hard to contest the assertion that the NGOs and CSOs either have no political clout, or are able to exert very little influence at elite or societal levels. In this sense, they are typical of the kind of civil society iterations that flourished across post-Communist Europe in the 1990s and 2000s seeking a voice and influence within the established order. The two final categories of Serbian civil society, HRGs and radical protest movement, are overtly political in intent and focus. The former, essentially composed of Belgrade-based intellectuals, were established in the beginning of the 1990s as anti-war movements. Despite the political changes initiated in October 2000, the activities of human rights organizations remained highly contentious and unwelcome to the authorities. The HRGs took up the transitional justice agenda and this pitched them in direct opposition to successive governments, none of which sought to directly address the human rights violations of the previous regime. Today, the outright threats of violence towards these individuals and their organizations may well have dissipated, but the hostility and deep suspicion remains. In a certain sense, despite the recent progress Serbia has made towards EU accession, the HRGs represent a liberal opposition and consciousness still in waiting; more a nascent *political* society than civil society. The development of liberal civil society has not only been constrained by the state, but also by illiberal groups that have mushroomed, purveying a 'new' Serbian nationalism.[62] A variety of groups, often with a purportedly pure religious outlook, included groups such as Patriotic Movement Dignity (*Otačastveni pokret Obraz*), Association of Students 'St Justin the Philosopher' (*Udruženje studenata 'Sveti Justin Filozof'*), or the Serbian Assembly 'Doorway' (*Srpski sabor 'Dveri'*).[63] These groups were emboldened by the tacit support of the state as well as the Serbian Orthodox Church, which speaks to the lack of separation between these segments of 'uncivil' society and the state.

Perhaps the most surprising development over the past couple of years has been the *Ne da(vi)mo Beograd* ('Let's not drown Belgrade') protest movement that has emerged to protest against the highly contentious plan to transform the city's waterfront. The campaign, established in 2015 to contest what is perceived to be corruption and illegality surrounding the ongoing re-development of the city, has become one of the most successful and prominent in Serbia, if not the region. The yellow duck carried by the activists has become a powerful symbol of broader resistance. Although individuals from within the NGO sector are involved and participate in the actions, the established organizations, particularly the environmental NGOs, are not represented nor involved.

---

[61] Usually as part of Instrument for Pre-accession Assistance 2 (IPA2). Available at: www.welcomeurope. com/european-funds/ipa-ii-instrument-pre-accession-assistance-2014-2020-838+738.html#tab=onglet_details.

[62] Denisa Kostovicova 'Civil Society and Post-Communist Democratization: Facing a Double Challenge in Post-Milošević Serbia' (2006) 1(2) *Journal of Civil Society* 21–37.

[63] In 2000, Dveri became transformed from a right-wing youth group to a fully-fledged political party, elected to the Serbian Parliament. See Jovan Byford 'Christian right-wing organizations and the Spreading of Anti-Semitic prejudice in Post-Milošević Serbia: The Case of the Dignity Patriotic Movement' (2002) 32(2) *East European Jewish Affairs* 43–60.

The activism – the strategies used and the nature of the critique – are immediately reminiscent of the anti-austerity mobilizations across southern Europe and Turkey (Gezi Park), but also of contemporary civil society activism in Poland and Hungary. However, while it is easy to interpret *Ne da(vi)mo Beograd* as Serbia's version of what has swept the rest of Europe, the activism in Belgrade does not stem from an almost sudden realization of the failings of liberal democratic processes and institutions post crisis, or (as in Poland and Hungary), the deliberate dismantling and erosion of liberal politics by elected politicians. If the ongoing activism at the Belgrade waterfront is to be put in any historical context, it is perhaps a re-awakening of October 2000 and the *Otpor!* coalition and the *Narodni pokret* initiative that helped topple Milošević.

While the radicalism spearheaded by civil society over the last couple of years suggests a continuity with the rest of Europe – a response to austerity and the crisis of liberal democracy – the interaction between the government and civil society organizations in Serbia remains bound to the immediate post-Yugoslav period. The illiberal politics of the Milošević period and the overt rejection and marginalization of those within civil society wishing to contest or critique the political elites continues to frame the interaction between the sectors, regardless of the particular policy, issue or type of organization involved. Whereas in Poland and Hungary the recent politicization of civil society is arguably a regulating mechanism to try to restore liberal democratic politics; in Serbia, apart from a very brief period in early 2002 under the reformist government of Zoran Djindjić, there is no sustained period of liberal democratic politics to be 'restored'.

V Conclusion

The case studies of Croatia and Serbia capture the ambiguous state of civil society in the post-Yugoslav space. Croatia and Serbia, although different in many aspects, shared two crucial components that have affected the development of civil society: the legacy of conflict and a slow transition to liberal democracy, as neither regime turned 'liberal' overnight. At times, civil society has aided the processes of democratization, but it often exerted pressure in the opposite direction, undermining the liberal transition. The effects of the legacies of Yugoslav Communism, nationalism and conflict are all inextricably linked. This also highlights that no one model can capture the diverging paths of post-Communist civil societies.

In Croatia, parts of civil society hold a close connection to government – it is debatable if they can even be referred to as civil society. Civil society is in a legally protected position and can effectively impact on policy, but this is dependent on adherence to the dominant group identity and ideology. Any challenges to this are seen as threats to the Croatian state- and nation-building projects, which can result in funding cuts. The situation is, however, not binary: civil society organizations often face similar structural obstacles, regardless of government support. The key factor underpinning this state of affairs is the legacy of ethnic conflict in the country.

Similarly, in Serbia, each segment or component of civil society is weaker than it should otherwise be. In this sense, the particular legacies of the past three decades are as prevalent today as they were a decade ago: low levels of NGO institutionalization reflect the disrupted transition and the stalled Europeanization process; the tier of highly politicized human rights groups that are not fully part of civil society and exist as an imminent political society reflecting the legacies of war and the unfinished business of transitional justice; weak CSOs reflect the lack of a liberal democratic epoch at the end of Communism and the colonization of dissent by nationalists.

What can this analysis tell us about the continuities and discontinuities from the former Yugoslavia? The civil society perspective provides a prism of challenges and openings for democracy after the fall of Communism and after Yugoslavia's violent disintegration. The post-Yugoslav political space in successor states is no longer under the omnipresent control of the totalitarian state. However, neither do new post-Communist civil societies play an entirely benevolent role in the process of democratization. Both normatively and organizationally the civil society space is a space of pluralism. However, civil societies are often purveyors of nationalism as well as challengers and, as a type of actor, often hold the state to account, but can also act as extensions of the state. In this respect, the discontinuity with the former Yugoslavia is evident; however, so is the long shadow of its legacy that shapes the role and the form of civic activity.

Acknowledgements

Ivor Sokolić and Denisa Kostovicova gratefully acknowledge the support of the Arts and Humanities Research Council 'Art and Reconciliation: Culture, Community and Conflict' (AH/P005365/1) project grant awarded under the Conflict Theme of the Partnership for Conflict, Crime and Security Research (PaCCS) and through the Global Challenges Research Fund (GCRF).

References

Arendt, Hannah. *The Origins of Totalitarianism* (Harcourt, Brace and World, Inc, New York, 1951).

Berman, Ilan and Michael J. Waller. 'Introduction: The Centrality of the Secret Police' in Ilan Berman and Michael J Waller (eds) *Dismantling Tyranny: Transitioning Beyond Totalitarian Regimes* (Lanham, Rowman & Littlefield Publishers, Inc 2006), pp xv–xxii.

Bermeo, Nancy. 'What the Democratization Literature Says – or Doesn't Say-about Post-war Democratization' (2013) 9(2) *Global Governance*, pp. 159–77.

Bilić, Bojan. 'A Concept that is Everything and Nothing: Why not to Study (post-)Yugoslav Anti-war and Pacifist Contention from a Civil Society Perspective' (2011) 53(3) *Sociologija*, pp. 297–322.

Bilić, Bojan. *We Were Gasping for Air: [Post-] Yugoslav Anti-war Activism and its Legacy* (Baden-Baden, Nomos, 2012).

Byford, Jovan. 'Christian Right-wing Organizations and the Spreading of anti-Semitic Prejudice in Post-Milošević Serbia: The Case of the Dignity Patriotic Movement' (2002) 32(2) *East European Jewish Affairs*, pp. 43–60.

Cocozzelli, Fred P. *War and Social Welfare: Reconstruction After Conflict* (Basingstoke, Palgrave Macmillan, 2009).

Diamond, Larry. 'Is the Third Wave Over' (1996) 7(3) *Journal of Democracy*, pp. 20–37.

Dragović-Soso, Jasna. *Saviours of the Nation Serbia's Intellectual Opposition and the Revival of Nationalism* (London, C Hurst and Co Publishers, 2002).

Dragović-Soso, Jasna. 'Rethinking Yugoslavia: Serbian Intellectuals and the National Question in Historical Perspective' (2004) 13(2) *Contemporary European History*, pp. 170–84.

Ekiert, Grzegorz and Jan Kubik. 'The Legacies of 1989: Myths and Realities of Civil Society' (2014) 25(1) *Journal of Democracy*, pp. 46–58.

Fisher, Sharon. 'Contentious Politics in Croatia: The War Veterans' Movement' in Petr Kopecký and Cas Mudde (eds) *Uncivil Society? Contentious Politics in Post-Communist Europe.* (London, Routledge, 2003), pp. 74–92.

Freedom House. (2018) *Nations in Transit: Croatia Country Profile.* Available at: https://freedomhouse.org/report/nations-transit/2018/croatia.

HAZU. *HAZU o Hrvatskom Jeziku u Europskim Integracijama (HAZU on Croatian in European Integration),* (2007), Available at: www.hkv.hr/kultura/jezik/962-hazu-o-hrvatskom-jeziku-u-europskim-integracijama.html. Accessed: 11 April 2016.

Howell, Jude and Jenny Pearce. *Civil Society and Development: A Critical Exploration* (Lynne Rienner, Boulder, Colorado, 2001).

Ishiyama, John T. 'Review Essay: Democratization and Democratic Consolidation in Post-Communist Politics' (2003) 40 *International Politics*, pp. 433–43.

Jović, Dejan. *Rat i Mit: Politika Identiteta u Suvremenoj Hrvatskoj* (War and Myth: The Politics of Identity in Contemporary Croatia), (Zaprešić, Fraktura, 2017).

Kaldor, Mary. *Global Civil Society* (Oxford, Oxford University Press, 2003).

Kostovicova, Denisa. *Kosovo: The Politics of Identity and Space* (London and New York, Routledge, 2005).

Kostovicova, Denisa. 'Civil Society and Post-Communist Democratization: Facing a Double Challenge in Post-Milošević Serbia' (2006) 1(2) *Journal of Civil Society*, pp. 21–37.

Kostovicova, Denisa and Vesna Bojicic-Dzelilovic. 'Introduction: Civil Society and Multiple Transitions – Actors, Meanings and Effects' in Vesna Bojicic-Dzelilovic, Denisa Kostovicova and James Ker-Lindsay (eds) *Civil Society and Transitions in the Western Balkans* (Basingstoke, Palgrave Macmillan, 2013).

Kraljević, Josipa M. and Ilija Vučura. *The Assassination of Croatia: The Attack of the Pro-Serbian JNA on the Banski Dvori and the Historic Centre of Zagreb, 7 October 1991,* (Zagreb, Croatian Homeland War Memorial and Documentation Centre, 2016).

Kumar, Krishan. 'Civil Society: An Inquiry into the Usefulness of an Historical Term' (1993) 44(3) *The British Journal of Sociology*, pp. 375–95.

Lamont, Christopher, K. *International Criminal Justice and the Politics of Compliance,* (Ashford, Ashgate, 2010).

Langston, Keith and Anita Peti-Stantić. *Language Planning and National Identity in Croatia,* (London, Palgrave Macmillan, 2014).

Lefort, Claude. *The Political Forms of Modern Society: Bureaucracy, Democracy, Totalitarianism* (Cambridge, Polity Press, 1986).

Levitsky, Steven and Lucan Way. 'The Rise of Competitive Authoritarianism' (2002) 13(2) *Journal of Democracy*, pp. 51–65.

Linz, Juan J. and Alfred Stepan. *Problems of Democratic Transition and Consolidation: Southern Europe, South America, and Post-Communist Europe* (Baltimore and London, The Johns Hopkins University Press, 1996).

Maliqi, Shkelzen. *Kosova: Separate Worlds* (Prishtina, Dukagjini PH and MM, 1998).

Mastnak, Tomaž. (ed) *Socijalistična civilna družba [Socialist Civil Society]* (Ljubljana, Knjižnica revolucionarne teorije, 1985).

Miškovska Kajevska, Ana. *Feminist Activism at War: Belgrade and Zagreb Feminists in the 1990s* (Abingdon and New York, Routledge, 2017).

Nazor, Ante. *Greater-Serbian Aggression Against Croatia in the* 1990s, (Zagreb, Croatian Homeland War Memorial and Documentation Centre, 2011).

Paffenholz, Thania. 'Civil Society and Peacebuilding' in Thania Paffenholz (ed) *Civil Society & Peacebuilding: A Critical Assessment* (Boulder, Colorado, Lynne Rienner Publishers, 2010), pp 43–64.

Schmitter, Philippe. 'Twenty-five Years, Fifteen Findings' (2010) 21(1) *Journal of Democracy*, pp. 17–28.

Sokolić, Ivor. 'Sources of Information on Transitional Justice in Croatia' (2017) 53(4) *Croatian Political Science Review*, pp. 77–104.

Ströhle, Isabel. 'Kosovo Liberation Army Veterans' Politics and Contentious Citizenship in Post-war Kosovo' in Srda Pavlović and Marko Živković (eds) *Transcending Fratricide: Political Mythologies, Reconciliations, and the Uncertain Future in the Former Yugoslavia* (Baden-Baden, Nomos, 2013), pp. 243–64.

Vetta, Théodora. '"Democracy Building" in Serbia: The NGO Effect' (2009) 33 *Southeastern Europe*, pp. 26–47.

Whitehead, Laurence. (ed) *The International Dimensions of Democratization: Europe and the Americas* (Oxford, Oxford University Press, 1996).

Wittenberg, Jason. 'What is a Historical Legacy?' *APSA 2013 Annual Meeting Paper; American Political Science Association 2013 Annual Meeting*, (2013). Available at: SSRN: https://ssrn.com/abstract=2303391.

Zielonka, Jan and Alex Pravda, (eds) *Democratic Consolidation in Eastern Europe: Volume 2 International and Transnational Actors* (Oxford, Oxford University Press, 2001).

Zubak, Marko. 'The Croatian Spring: Interpreting the Communist Heritage in Post-Communist Croatia' (2010) 32(1) *East Central Europe*, pp. 191–225.

Zürcher, Christoph. 'Building Democracy While Building Peace' (2011) 22(1) *Journal of Democracy*, pp. 81–95 at 82.

Žarkov, Dubravka. 'Feminism and the Disintegration of Yugoslavia: On the Politics of Gender and Ethnicity' (2003) 24(3) *Social Development Issues*, pp. 59–68.

3

Music, Media and Culture One Generation after Yugoslavia: Do we Still Need 'Nostalgia'?

Catherine Baker
University of Hull

I Introduction

Almost 30 years after the Yugoslav wars began, popular culture travels across post-Yugoslav borders much more vibrantly than outside observers often expect. The continuities, or what seem like continuities, between Yugoslavia's common cultural space and a post-Yugoslav cultural space which even transcends former front lines frequently seem to be signs of 'nostalgia', a complicated set of longings for the Yugoslav past which sociologists of culture have been trying to explain since the 1990s. And yet, apparent continuities on the surface of the so-called 'Yugosphere' may be misleading.[1] While they depend on legacies, networks, social identities and tastes formed during Yugoslavia or earlier, they have actually been *re*constructed in wartime and post-war political contexts, and are always being contested and renegotiated. Examining post-Yugoslav media and culture from today's perspective, however, suggests two striking things. One is that how far a text, performer or genre can be 'marked' or 'unmarked' as politicized or 'nostalgic' is socially constructed, not predetermined; the other is that today – unlike the 1990s – these apparent continuities are often produced without evoking any remembering of Yugoslavia at all. Meanwhile, enough time has passed since the wars that the wartime past itself can exhibit more political strength than nostalgia for Yugoslavia has ever held. While some scholars have begun questioning whether 'nostalgia' is still even useful in understanding post-Yugoslav media and culture,[2] this juxtaposition shows that 'nostalgia' is still a relevant concept for post-Yugoslav cultural politics today – as long as it points to the active experiences and emotions of remembering, not just to everything which happens within the borders of where Yugoslavia used to be.

---

[1] See Tim Judah, 'Yugoslavia is Dead, Long Live the Yugosphere', LSEE Research on South-Eastern Europe Working Papers 1 (London, 2009). Available at: http://eprints.lse.ac.uk/48041/1/__Libfile_repository_Content_LSEE_Papers%20on%20South%20Eastern%20Europe_Yugoslavia%20is%20Dead(author).pdf (accessed 19 November 2017).

[2] Dalibor Mišina, 'Beyond Nostalgia: "Extrospective Introspections" of the Post-Yugoslav Memory of Socialism' (2016) 1 *Canadian–American Slavic Studies* 332–54.

Ever since commentators began noticing apparent signs of 'nostalgia' for Yugoslavia, while the 1990s wars were still at their height, many 'continuities' they noticed involved popular music. The underground popularity of Serbian as well as Bosnian 'newly-composed folk songs' or 'narodnjaci' in Croatia during the 1991–95 'Homeland War' contradicted the clear cultural boundaries between Croats and Serbs which President Franjo Tuđman's interpretation of the Croatian independence project had needed to establish, arguably at the expense of much personal memory and ambiguity.[3] Croatian journalists were surprised to see some of the same troops who were fighting the Yugoslav People's Army (JNA) and the paramilitaries who had declared a 'Republic of Serb Krajina' (RSK) listening to 'eastern'-sounding 'narodnjaci' in Croatian nightclubs or tuning into Serbian radio stations to listen to Serbian music as well as monitor 'enemy' news.[4] The root of their surprise was the idea that members of a nation involved in ethnopolitical conflict would willingly admit music or other cultural forms from the 'aggressor' nation into their own cultural worlds. Today, ethnicized processes of separation and distancing have had two more decades to harden – yet the region's sociocultural connectedness is stronger than during the 1990s. And observers are often still surprised.

Moreover, post-Yugoslav sociocultural connectivities have strengthened even though more and more viewers and listeners and fans do not remember Yugoslavia themselves. By the time Judah popularized the 'Yugosphere' term to describe everyday patterns of post-Yugoslav cultural exchange, the region (and its diasporas) contained a generation with no lived experience of a country called 'Yugoslavia' – or of the everyday popular culture which Tito's Yugoslavia deliberately cultivated for Yugoslavs from different ethnic groups to enjoy together. The proportion of people in any post-Yugoslav country who remember Yugoslavia through *their* participation in 'Yugoslav' everyday life, rather than through media representation and intergenerational 'postmemory', will only decrease.[5] Private media companies often address the whole Yugoslav region, or at least the area where Bosnian, Croatian, Montenegrin and Serbian are mutually understood, even when aiming at youth audiences: indeed, satellite and digital media (which were less constrained by state telecommunications infrastructure and national media distribution systems, i.e. the networks which fragmented when Yugoslavia broke up) have created ever more possibilities for ongoing everyday cultural exchange. If sociocultural 'nostalgia' for Yugoslavia is still a talking point, it must still be surprising. Yet is it such a surprise? Does cultural nostalgia have any political currency? Is it even nostalgia at all? Is nostalgia for the *Yugoslav* past the only significant nostalgia in the region's cultural politics? While the well-rehearsed framework of 'Yugonostalgia' may offer few fresh insights into understanding how far today's sociocultural connectivities are 'continuities' from Yugoslavia, appreciating the politics of emotion behind 'nostalgia' can.

---

[3]   See Alex J Bellamy, *The Formation of Croatian National Identity: A Centuries-old Dream?* (Manchester, 2003); Dubravka Ugrešić, *The Culture of Lies: Anti-Political Essays* (London, 1998).

[4]   Ines Sabalić, "Washingtonski sporazumi dramatično su izmijenili hrvatsku estradnu scenu: u Zagrebu je otvoreno petnaest lokala s novokomponiranom glazbom!" *Globus*, 31 March 1995.

[5]   Dijana Jelača, 'Youth after Yugoslavia: Subcultures and Phantom Pain' (2014) *Studies in East European Cinema* v/2 139–54 at 139.

II Post-socialist 'nostalgia' and the meanings of Yugoslavia

Throughout post-socialist Europe, not just the Yugoslav region, post-socialist 'nostalgia' for everyday personal and cultural memories of Communist regimes has fascinated cultural commentators.[6] Scholars and critics have wondered particularly at *Ostalgie* (nostalgia for aspects of life under the German Democratic Republic (GDR)) in reunified Germany, and the 'nostalgia' for a lost multinational federation as well as a state socialist regime that drives many forms of post-Soviet, as well as post-Yugoslav, nostalgia. Indeed, the fact that the USSR and Yugoslavia both fragmented along state socialist internal boundaries has continued to invite comparisons between their aftermaths, even though in the 1990s, immediate ethnopolitical conflict had less impact on post-Soviet nostalgia outside the Caucasus.[7] Ethnicized *historical* memories of national victimhood (such as Stalin's subjection of Ukrainians to a forced famine which Ukrainian national memory considers genocidal, and his wartime deportation of border minorities such as the Crimean Tatars) nevertheless made the Soviet past ethnopolitically contentious even when republics had separated peacefully. Moreover, Russia's annexation of Crimea in 2014 and its support for RSK-like separatist entities in eastern Ukraine has reconfigured the politics of Russian/Ukrainian nostalgia and cultural exchange into a situation closer to Croatian–Serbian cultural relations in the 1990s.[8]

Commentators on the politics – and political economy – of post-Yugoslav 'nostalgia' have emphasized that the simple term 'nostalgia' conceals many possible reference points and emotions.[9] 'Nostalgia' could involve expressions and symbols of the fact that many people, even in countries which had fought for independence against the JNA, wondered retrospectively if their lives would have been more prosperous and fulfilling if Yugoslavia had stayed together or if there had not been a war. And it could involve other aspects: regret that there had been more inter-ethnic coexistence and geographical mobility in Yugoslavia than during or after the wars, when national publics came under growing pressure to identify with narrowly defined notions of ethnicity and culture which might not match the social reality they had experienced; young people's desire to provoke their elders, which *could* explain why a Croatian teenager who did not remember Tito would wear a Tito t-shirt or sing along with a punk version of a Partisan song, but should not be taken as the only reason why; the acts of digital archiving and

---

[6] See Svetlana Boym, *The Future of Nostalgia* (New York, 2001); Maria Todorova and Zsuzsa Gille (eds), *Post-Communist Nostalgia* (New York, 2010).

[7] See Rogers Brubaker, *Nationalism Reframed: Nationhood and the National Question in the New Europe* (Cambridge, 1996); Veljko Vujačić, *Nationalism, Myth and the State in Russia and Serbia: Russian and East European Government Politics and Policy* (Cambridge, 2015).

[8] E.g. Ukrainian security services have banned more than 140 Russian entertainers who have visited Crimea from entering Ukraine, constraining the everyday presence current Russian popular music had had in Ukraine until 2014: 'Ukraine may ban Russian entrant from Eurovision over Crimea visit', *RFE/RL*, 14 March 2017. Available at: www.rferl.org/a/ukraine-may-ban-russian-entrant-samoylova-eurovision-contest-over-crimea-visit/28368002.html (accessed 9 November 2017). In 2017, when Kiev hosted the Eurovision Song Contest (following Ukraine's win in 2016 with a song commemorating the Tatars' deportation and, implicitly, Russia's annexation of Crimea), this extended to Russia's Eurovision representative, Yulia Samoilova.

[9] See Vjekoslav Perica and Mitja Velikonja, *Nebeska Jugoslavija: interakcije političkih mitologija i pop-kulture* (Belgrade, 2012).

curating with which internet users have assembled 'micro-archives' of the Yugoslav past since the 1990s;[10] and ways of expressing as-yet-unrealized 'vision[s] for the future' by ostensibly representing the past.[11]

In the mid-2000s, the media scholar Zala Volčič discerned three aspects of nostalgia for Yugoslavia as follows:[12] a political or 'revisionist' nostalgia which did look to the unified South Slav state (or, she might have added, state socialism) as a more desirable model than its individual ethnonational (and increasingly neoliberalized) successors; an 'aesthetic' nostalgia which called for 'the preservation of an authentic Yugoslav past'; and a commercialized 'escapist' or 'utopian' nostalgia, with largely decontextualized visual, audiovisual, sonic and material signifiers, which she saw as increasingly on the rise – emblematically when reunion concerts by Bijelo Dugme, the 1970s–80s Sarajevo rock band who had themselves experimented with an alternative pluralistic, emotional and 'trans-ethnic' Yugoslavism,[13] were sponsored by the very symbol of globalized US cultural hegemony, Coca-Cola. Volčič was writing just before the post-Yugoslav 'New Left' would seek to reaffirm the radical potential behind Yugoslav ideas of economic management and sociality, including the mobilization of Partisan and Communist women, to open social dialogues about alternatives to neoliberalism after the global financial crisis hit south-east Europe in 2007–08.[14] The contrast between the visions of the future available even during late state socialist Yugoslavia's 'crisis' years, and futures which appear far more limited from today's positions of stagnation and 'stuckness' – when, often, two decades later nothing perceptible seems to have changed – blends complex emotions about the present, the future and the past.

Yet 'Yugonostalgia' first came to scholars' attention as more than just a cultural phenomenon. In early 1990s Croatia, 'Yugonostalgia' was also a political accusation used to tighten the limits of what could be said in the public sphere, with serious professional consequences for cultural workers who depended on patronage from state media and official cultural institutions. 'Yugonostalgia' then, in effect, meant any public commentary which dissented from the new Croatian intellectual establishment's ethnicized project of cultural and linguistic separation from Yugoslavia.[15] Allegations of 'Yugonostalgia' brought about public hounding and death threats on writers which intimidated women, in particular, from criticizing the new regime and its patriarchal, clericalist ideology – a form of pre-emptive silencing with which feminist and marginalized writers confronting white supremacist and anti-feminist digital harassment

[10] Martin Pogačar, *Media Archaeologies, Micro-Archives and Storytelling: Re-Presencing the Past* (London, 2016).
[11] Monika Palmberger, *How Generations Remember: Conflicting Histories and Shared Memories in Post-War Bosnia and Herzegovina* (London, 2016), p. 14.
[12] Zala Volčič, "'Yugo-nostalgia: cultural memory and media in the former Yugoslavia' (2007) *Critical Studies in Media Communication* xxiv/1 21–38 at 27.
[13] Dalibor Mišina, "'Spit and Sing, My Yugoslavia'": New Partisans, Social Critique and Bosnian Poetics of the Patriotic' (2010) *Nationalities Papers* xxxviii/2 265–89 at 271.
[14] See Srećko Horvat and Igor Štiks (eds), *Welcome to the Desert of Post-Socialism: Radical Politics after Yugoslavia* (London, 2015); Ana Hofman, *Novi život partizanskih pesama* (Belgrade, 2016).
[15] This separation included sweeping changes to language policy that distanced Croatian further from Serbian, removing books in Serbian language or Cyrillic script from public libraries, and dropping Serbian or 'eastern'-sounding popular music from radio archives.

are all too familiar today, even though the policing of their political speech has been crowd sourced not state-driven.[16] Against this background, it is not hard to understand why nostalgic regard for Yugoslavia and its everyday culture should often have been interpreted as political resistance. And yet – even as Tuđman's ideology continues to structure hegemonic public discourse in Croatia almost two decades after his death[17] – is nostalgia *always* a political expression, in every post-Yugoslav context? Indeed, is every reverberation of the Yugoslav cultural past, and every common cultural space reproduced within former Yugoslavia's borders, even nostalgia at all?

The Yugoslav successor societies, moreover, each re-mediated the memory of Yugoslavia differently. Tuđman's Croatia rejected it most intensely. Slovenia's ruling liberals immediately distanced Slovenia from Yugoslavia politically, and applied citizenship laws which 'erased' more than 18,000 residents born in other Yugoslav republics (predominantly Bosnians, Albanians and Roma) from the residency register.[18] Culturally, meanwhile, some young Slovenes in the 2000s took nostalgia to practically parodic levels with their enjoyment of 'Balkan parties' and consumption of Partisan kitsch. Popular culture from the Yugoslav region acquired a curious not-quite-foreign or 'ex-home' status in Slovenia,[19] and the country became a semi-neutral venue for Croatian *and* Serbian rock bands and folk stars to perform for fans from both countries (if they could afford to travel). In Bosnia-Herzegovina (BiH), the Yugoslav Partisan tradition was reappropriated to stand for a multi-ethnic vision of citizenship and a linked socio-economic critique of privatization by people seeking a 'civic' or multi-ethnic identity for BiH. The 1992–95 war hollowed out any political platform for this 'civic' vision, while the consociational Dayton Peace Agreement enshrined the country's three largest ethnopolitical identities (Bosniak, Croat and Serb) in constitutional politics to the exclusion of all others. Macedonia, which seceded peacefully in September 1991, had arguably the fewest reasons to resent the memory of Yugoslavia, and mid-2000s Skopje boasted a minor cottage industry of Tito mementoes.[20] The country's international designation as 'the Former Yugoslav Republic of Macedonia' until 2019 was not, however, a longing expression of geopolitical nostalgia, but a condition imposed by a Greek state which feared the new country could make irredentist claims to Macedonia in northern Greece.

'Yugoslavia' had yet more meanings in Serbia and Montenegro. Milošević's regime had departed from most understandings of Yugoslavism – certainly those held by Yugoslavia's non-Serb citizens, or the Serbian democratic opposition – while retaining the name. Milošević had played the single largest role in undermining the Yugoslavia which had institutionalized Albanians' cultural and linguistic rights in Kosovo (without

[16] Stine Eckert, 'Fighting for Recognition: Online Abuse of Women Bloggers in Germany, Switzerland, the United Kingdom, and the United States' (2018) *New Media and Society* xx/4 1282–302.
[17] See Dejan Jović, *Rat i mit: politika identiteta u suvremenoj Hrvatskoj* (Zagreb, 2017).
[18] Jelka Zorn, 'A case for Slovene Nationalism: Initial Citizenship Rules and the Erasure' (2009) *Nations and Nationalism* xv/2 280–98, 281.
[19] Mitja Velikonja, '"Ex-home": "Balkan culture" in Slovenia after 1991' in Barbara Törnquist-Plewa and Sanimir Resić (eds), *The Balkans in Focus: Cultural Boundaries in Europe* (Lund, 2002).
[20] Volčič, 'Yugo-nostalgia', pp 29–30.

granting them equal constitutional status to South Slav peoples) and strengthened the
ethnonational consciousness of Bosnian Muslims, Montenegrins and Macedonians;
and he had broken from a Yugoslavia where 'worker' had once been a dignified social
identity, by persuading his Serb addressees to think of themselves as Serbs not workers
first (thus eroding their solidarity with other republics' disadvantaged workers, and
weakening the audience for trans-republican political appeals). He had played on
historical mythology of Serbs' persecution under the Ottoman Empire, and the
genocide Serbs suffered in 1941–45 under the Independent State of Croatia (NDH), in
persuading Serbs that Bosniaks, Albanians and Croats were historic enemies and
present threats. Nevertheless, Milošević still needed to be able to claim his state had
inherited Yugoslavia's sovereignty: Serbia and Montenegro thus took the name 'the
Federal Republic of Yugoslavia' in April 1992, even as forces under Milošević's control
were committing atrocities in BiH and destroying yet more of what Yugoslavia had
meant. It was officially still the Army of Yugoslavia (VJ), not Serbia, which Milošević
deployed against the Kosovo Liberation Army (KLA) during the Kosovo War. It is little
wonder, in view of Albanians' history in all three Yugoslavias, that Kosovo consistently
registered even less political nostalgia than Croatia in sociological surveys,[21] and that
Kosovo's Albanian-language cultural scene belonged to a transnational 'Albanosphere'
(which also extended into Macedonia) not the 'Yugosphere' structured around the
languages formerly known as Serbo-Croatian.

Even in the 1990s, informal economies and alternative radio stations sustained
cross-border musical connections for listeners who sought them out. The wars'
denormalization of cultural exchange across the most politicized ex-Yugoslav borders,
and the emotional associations with 'the aggressor' that people's wartime experiences
might make them project on to popular culture from the 'wrong' sides of symbolic
cultural boundaries, nevertheless made it both contested and noteworthy when cross-
border performances and legitimate music releases across the most 'problematic'
borders (Croatia–Serbia and BiH–Serbia) started to resume.[22] Visa and customs
regulations meant that states could more effectively restrict border-crossings by
musicians' bodies and equipment than their sounds, so that live performance was
nearly always the most contentious issue during the partial restitching of the
'Yugosphere' in 1998–2006. Today, even though direct memory of Yugoslav everyday
life is far more distant, post-Yugoslav societies still have more shared cultural
connections among themselves than with other adjacent states, and passing references
to 'neighbouring states' invariably connote the other post-Yugoslav republics, not a
country's actual geographical neighbours. This is not only the case for people who did
experience Yugoslavia themselves, but also in youth culture, where broadcasters and
music promoters organizing talent shows and tours are often addressing youth
audiences in several post-Yugoslav states simultaneously. Yet – as studies of

[21] Pål Kolstø, 'Identifying with the Old or the New State: Nation-building vs Yugonostalgia in the
Yugoslav Successor States', *Nations and Nationalism* xx/4 (2014), pp 760–81.
[22] See Catherine Baker, 'The Politics of Performance: Transnationalism and its Limits in Former
Yugoslav Popular Music, 1999–2004', *Ethnopolitics* v/3 (2006), pp 275–93; Ana Petrov, *Jugoslovenska
muzika bez Jugoslavije* (Belgrade, 2016).

'Yugonostalgia' already accept – how far these manifestations of a common *cultural* space acknowledge, let alone celebrate, Yugoslavia as a *political* entity, let alone Yugoslav Communism as a distinctive socio-economic ideology – vary widely. The wars thus fragmented, but did not destroy, the region's cultural connections.

III Post-Yugoslav cultural spaces with and without Yugoslavia

The term 'Yugonostalgia' is often loosely applied to many more sociocultural connectivities than just those which directly evoke Tito and his federation. Even those, however, take many forms, from the gatherings celebrating Tito's birthday in his home town of Kumrovec, Croatia, to Tito's face in left-wing or anti-nationalist political graffiti, to the badges, t-shirts and trinkets vendors sell tourists from their stalls.[23] Some such connectivities, indeed, do not even include 'Yugo' in their names, but use apparently depoliticized names which audiences still tacitly understand to mean the region. The label 'Adria', which some entertainment television franchises have used in youth-orientated music programming, alludes both to the pleasures of summer tourism on the Adriatic (which used to be another experience of everyday Yugoslavism for inland Yugoslavs, including many Serbs[24]) and to the Adriatic region which, with its Italianate history, ancient Roman heritage and famously Mediterranean way of life, represents an opposite pole to 'the Balkans' in ex-Yugoslav 'symbolic geography'.[25] It can thus connote an aspirational, brand-ready transnationalism, free from the ideological struggles of the Yugoslav and immediate post-Yugoslav past. MTV capitalized on this first when it launched its 'MTV Adria' franchise for Slovenia, Croatia and Bosnia-Herzegovina in 2005,[26] and a post-Yugoslav *X Factor* franchise also took the 'Adria' name in 2013–15.[27] This did not get a third season, though a similar show on TV Pink called *Zvezde Granda* (*Stars of Grand* – with contestants competing for a record deal with the pop-folk label Grand) which has run since 2004, is also shown on BiH's Open Broadcasting Network (OBN), and attracts competitors from Serbia, Montenegro, Macedonia, BiH plus, occasionally, Croatia.[28]

Another alternative to 'Yugo' nomenclature was 'Balkan', which could even connect musical production (especially pop-folk) in the post-Yugoslav region *and*

---

[23] Mitja Velikonja, *Titostalgija: a Study of Nostalgia for Josip Broz* (Ljubljana, 2008). In Serbia, and the Republika Srpska entity of BiH, Tito merchandise may even be beside equivalent merchandise for Radovan Karadžić.

[24] Stef Jansen, *Antinacionalizam: etnografija otpora u Zagrebu i Beogradu* (Belgrade, 2005), p 229.

[25] See Milica Bakić-Hayden and Robert M Hayden, 'Orientalist Variations on the Theme 'Balkans': Symbolic Geography in Recent Yugoslav Cultural Politics'(1992) 51(1) *Slavic Review* 1–15; Dunja Rihtman-Auguštin, 'A Croatian Controversy: Mediterranean–Danube–Balkans' (1999) xxxvi/1 *Narodna umjetnost* 103–19.

[26] Baker, 'Politics', p 278.

[27] Produced in Serbia, its first series also involved Bosnian, Macedonian and Montenegrin contestants and judges; the Croatian broadcaster RTL joined the following year.

[28] 'Nova zvijezda: Zagrepčanka krenula u osvajanje folk scene', *Dnevnik.hr*, 5 January 2017, Available at: https://dnevnik.hr/showbuzz/mladi_i_neizbjezni/hana-masic-nastupila-u-zvezdama-granda---462623.html (accessed 25 January 2018).

other south-east European countries into a transnational space. The satellite channel Balkanika, founded by two Bulgarian TV entrepreneurs in 2005, was accessible to subscribers in all post-Yugoslav states (including Slovenia and Croatia) and Bulgaria, Romania, Albania and Turkey, plus markets such as Germany, Austria and Switzerland with large combined diaspora populations.[29] South-east Europe's similar-sounding, yet still nationally distinguishable, pop-folk traditions have often been recognized as part of a wider 'Ottoman ecumene' of musical culture, evidence (unwelcome as it might be to nationalist cultural purists) that south-east European musical and cultural traditions do not reduce easily to hard national boundaries.[30] While this was already evident to any listeners who heard music in more than one regional language, Balkanika used satellite technology to bypass state-level media markets and give this music a novel transnational infrastructure on top of the many networks which musicians and cassette/CD pirates created for themselves. The channel also began hosting the annual 'Balkan Media Awards' in 2010, with winners attending from across the space it had defined as the Balkan region.

The Balkan Music Awards, addressing a cultural region defined by a private company rather than a nation-state, depicted – the ethnomusicologist Ana Hofman argues – a 'modern', 'cosmopolitan' Balkans, where local cultural specificities could run with the global mainstream.[31] Assisting this were turns in Western pop towards 'oriental' sounds and electronic dance music which now let south-east European pop producers sound global *as well as* local.[32] The resultant 'post-national' Balkan sound would not even reveal which country a singer came from unless the listener knew their celebrity background, though the language issue remained: the 'ekavica' variant of the ex-Serbo-Croatian languages was symbolically marked as Serbian (though it was also spoken in eastern Bosnia) and would be treated as such in Croatia, though Montenegrins and Bosnians who sang in the other main variant, 'ijekavica' (also the basis of Croatian), faced no such difficulty. If 2010's 'Balkan' popular music carried a post-national sound, the memory of coexistence it brought with it could sometimes be no memory at all: a typical example from 2013, 'Hotel Jugoslavija' by the Serbian pop-folk singer Saša Kapor (a 2008–09 *Zvezde Granda* finalist), uses the name of the former country and the just-reopened Belgrade hotel almost in passing, telling the story of a romantic encounter with a European female tourist (who might be called Maria, Elena or Marina and come from Paris, London or Rome) asking him for directions on Slavija Square.

Kapor and his songwriters, indeed, were far from alone among young people in no longer automatically reproducing the hotel (a landmark of the socialist redevelopment of New Belgrade) as a site of Yugoslav memory by the mid-2010s. The anthropologist Ana Petrov, interviewing a 26-year-old woman in 2014 at a Dalmatian- and Mediterranean-themed club beside the Hotel Jugoslavija which often booked

---

[29] Ana Hofman, 'Balkanske glasbe industrije med evropeizacijo in regionalizacijo: *Balkanske glasbene nagrade*' (2014) 50(1) *Muzikološki zbornik* 157–74 at 162.
[30] See Donna A. Buchanan, *Balkan Popular Culture and the Ottoman Ecumene: Music, Image, and Regional Political Discourse* (Lanham, MD, 2007); Rory Archer, 'Assessing Turbofolk Controversies: Popular Music between the Nation and the Balkans' (2012) xxxvi/1 *Southeastern Europe* 178–207.
[31] Hofman, 'Balkanske glasbe industrije' 171.
[32] Ibid, p 171.

Dalmatian (i.e. Croatian) singers to perform, was surprised the woman did not understand why Petrov, only six years older, was intrigued by 'a new clubbing space opening in front of some old hotel that just happened to be there'.[33] Petrov's observations of the atmosphere at the concert she was attending (a performance by Petar Grašo, a Dalmatian romantic ballad singer who debuted in the late 1990s so did not belong to the pre-war common musical past) complicates the idea that sociocultural connectedness between former Yugoslav states is automatically nostalgic. In fact, neither this Dalmatian club in Belgrade, nor the wider industry, offer Dalmatian popular music to young people in Belgrade as if it should have nostalgic value, nor as music which would have been culturally closer in their parents' youth: it does not come with the invitation to actively *remember*, as part of the 'affective atmosphere' of watching and hearing a singer, which did surround musicians' first contested 'return performances'.[34] Instead, the audience in their teens and twenties:

> were unfamiliar with the symbolic value of the place where the garden was located, and even with the existence of Dalmatian music as such. They seemed reluctant to acknowledge any connections between this music and contested historical events. Instead, they claimed and behaved not only as if nothing (bad) had happened in the past, but also as if the music they were listening to that evening did not signify anything beyond itself. In other words, this event, even though connected with the sea and with Dalmatia, represents an example of the new post-Yugoslav atmosphere that rejects any potential connections with either socialist Yugoslavia or with the wars that broke up the country.[35]

This is far from a setting where we could assume that expressions and manifestations of sociocultural connectedness between post-Yugoslav states were nostalgic: if anything, they might *dis*courage remembering the past. And this forgetting is, in many ways, convenient: if the young woman Petrov met was twenty-six in 2014 and had lived in Belgrade all her life, she would have been eleven when the old Hotel Jugoslavija was destroyed by the NATO bombing of Serbia and Montenegro in May 1999 during the Kosovo War; alternatively, she, or her friends, might have fled to Belgrade from Croatia or Bosnia-Herzegovina during the wars of 1991/2–95, or from Kosovo in 1999 after Milošević agreed to NATO's demands; and she would have lived much of her life amid an atmosphere of societal forgetting over Serb forces' and leaders' accountability for war crimes. Remembering the material and symbolic history of the Hotel Jugoslavija is not conducive to most people's idea of a good night out. The 'Yugosphere', examples such as Kapor's 'Hotel Jugoslavija' might suggest, is not a sphere *of* Yugoslav memory

[33] Ana Petrov, '"My Beautiful Dalmatian Song": (Re)connecting Serbia and Dalmatia at Concerts of Dalmatian Performers in Belgrade' (2015) 4(1–2) *TheMA: Open Access Research Journal for Theatre, Music, Arts*. Available at: www.thema-journal.eu/index.php/thema/article/view/38/90 (accessed 6 November 2017).

[34] Ibid, p 11.

[35] Ibid, pp 16–17.

but, increasingly, a space *without* one.[36] It is thus more than *just* an inevitability of time, perhaps, which helps to explain why many instances of everyday sociocultural connectivity between post-Yugoslav states seem less apparently political. The entertainment industry often exploits these connectivities without trying to evoke the emotions of remembering Yugoslavia at all.

IV 'Return performances': from nostalgia to routine

Another phenomenon, which once seemed self-evidently nostalgic, the 'return performances' of musicians performing across a politicized boundary for the first time since Yugoslavia collapsed, has also become less so over time. Musicians and (more mobile) fans travelled between republics everyday in Yugoslavia, but this became more difficult during the collapse and then were cut off where front lines intervened.[37] After the wars, these border-crossings met frequent interference from governments fearing they would undermine ethnicized nation-building projects. By the late 2000s, some routes had withered because of their audiences' weakened purchasing power, but other routes had become almost as routine as they once were. For the musicians' part, many actions, songs and performances which the media would have politicized as transgressing boundaries of national cultural identity in the early 2000s were far less likely to be framed as scandalous in the 2010s. Most Croatian musicians who had once publicly vowed never to perform in Serbia or Montenegro, stating that it would disrespect Croat war victims' memory if they went to entertain an audience from the 'aggressor' nation, had quietly set this aside by the 2010s. Lepa Brena, the pop-folk star who had personified Yugoslavia and Yugoslavism as a celebrity in the 1980s, received protests and death threats from Zagreb and Sarajevo veterans' groups on her first comeback tour in 2009, but returned to both cities with diminishing levels of abuse. Brena herself largely avoided contentious expressions of nostalgia during the tour, only singing her famous hit 'Jugoslovenka' ('Yugoslav woman') in Sarajevo once the crowd had requested it for ten minutes, and not performing 'Jugoslovenka' (or her two breakthrough hits, which mentioned Šumadija and Čačak in southern Serbia) in Zagreb at all.[38]

For Brena and other returning singers, the first return was always the most emotional, with more routine and smaller-scale performances likely to follow (in

---

[36] And yet, at least some internet users still have strong enough identifications with 'Yugoslav' identity to complain songs and videos like these are not Yugoslav enough: Ana Petrov (2017) 'Yugonostalgia in the Market: Popular Music and Consumerism in post-Yugoslav Space' (2017) 53(1) *Muzikološki zbornik* 203–15 at 208–9.

[37] See Ljubica Spaskovska, 'Stairway to Hell: The Yugoslav Rock Scene and Youth during the Crisis Decade of 1981–1991' (2011) 38(2) *East Central Europe* 355–72. A well-known Croatian rock song from the war's first winter, 'E, moj druže beogradski' ('Oh, my friend from Belgrade') by Jura Stublić (frontman of the Zagreb 'new wave' band Film), turned this reality into a song about Stublić, imagining fighting on the front line and having to shoot back at a Serb friend who had travelled between Zagreb and Belgrade with him all the time.

[38] Ana Hofman, 'Lepa Brena: Repolitization of Musical Memories on Yugoslavia' (2012) 61(1) *Glasnik Etnografskog instituta SANU* 21–32 at 25.

October 2017, for instance, Brena was booked to sing at the Diamond Palace Casino in Zagreb to launch a new model of Volkswagen – hardly a controversy-courting or even spectacular event[39]). The pattern was similar with a well-publicized Croatian 'return' to Serbia, that of Tereza Kesovija, whose home town of Konavle near Dubrovnik had been ransacked by Montenegrin troops during the JNA siege of Dubrovnik which began in October 1991. Kesovija's wartime music and interviews had symbolized feminine grief by calling on Dubrovnik's patron saint (in songs dedicated to the city) and Tuđman (in her interviews) to help the city and win the war.[40] In January 2011, Kesovija performed in Belgrade for the first time since the break-up of Yugoslavia.

While Serbian tabloids responded in the familiar pattern of inviting other celebrities and political or cultural figures to comment on the insult to national memory (since Kesovija, by refusing to perform in Serbia for so long, had been constructed by the same tabloids as a figure symbolising hatred towards Serbs), everyday public reactions were closer to a collective 'love and nostalgia' for Kesovija as well as Yugoslavia, and her visit and performance created a sentimental atmosphere where the past could be retold without having to dwell on the division and violence which had brought about this cultural separation.[41] Her future performances in Belgrade were less politically charged and more relaxed, though still charged with sentiment, this being the trademark of her stardom anyway. Reactions to Kesovija returning to Serbia were far from the vilification which Doris Dragović, another Dalmatian singer who had had a demonstratively patriotic (and in this case patriotically maternal) persona in the 1990s, had received after agreeing to perform in Igalo, Montenegro for New Year's Eve 1999.[42] The organized way in which Hajduk Split's fan club performatively rejected Dragović a few months later when she next sang to them at Hajduk's stadium left other Croatian pop musicians apprehensive of receiving the same treatment. Nothing of the sort happened to Kesovija, and indeed she returned to Belgrade for further performances in the following years.

Croatian musicians also had less to lose in the 2010s from musical transgressions which threatened the intensively-patrolled symbolic boundary between Croatian and Serbian culture, 'Europe' and the 'Balkans', Habsburg/Venetian heritage and Ottoman heritage, 'West' and 'East'. It had not helped Dragović retain her credentials of patriotic loyalty that her albums in 1999 and 2000 were both prime examples of the adaptation of Serbian pop-folk trends into Croatian *zabavna* (light-entertainment) music

---

[39] 'Lepa Brena ponovo stiže u Zagreb: idući petak sprema se spektakularni koncert velike regionalne zvijezde u Diamond Palace Casinu!', *Jutarnji list*, 29 September 2017. Available at: www.jutarnji.hr/ spektakli/strane-zvijezde/lepa-brena-ponovno-stize-u-zagreb-iduci-petak-sprema-se-spektakularni-koncert-velike-regionalne-zvijezde-u-diamond-palace-casinu/6599172/ (accessed 9 November 2017). The showbusiness section of *Jutarnji list*'s website still, however, filed this story under 'foreign' stars.

[40] One or two Croatian stars with similar profiles to Kesovija, such as Oliver Dragojević from Split and Mišo Kovač from Šibenik, have still not performed in Serbia since the war – but it is refusal rather than travel that seems more newsworthy.

[41] Ana Petrov, 'The Songs we Love to Sing and the History We Like to Remember: Tereza Kesovija's Comeback in Serbia' (2015) 39(2) *Southeastern Europe* 192–214 at 201.

[42] Amid rumours that the concert had been paid for by the Montenegrin president Milo Đukanović or members of the Montenegrin criminal elite, whereas Dragović stated it had been organized by a local Catholic priest.

arrangements which had been popularized (though not invented) by her composer and manager Tonči Huljić, with critics likening several songs very closely to recent hits by Serbia's most notorious pop-folk singer, Ceca Ražnatović.[43] In 2006, Severina Vučković had made Croatian headlines for several weeks after winning the right to represent Croatia at the Eurovision Song Contest with a suspiciously 'Balkan'-sounding song, but in the long run the scandal enabled her to promote herself as a pan-regional star. An explicitly 'Balkan' song by a more minor Croatian singer in this ambiguous zone between *zabavna* music and pop-folk, Maja Šuput, released in 2015, had a contrasting fate. Šuput's 'Hej, Balkano' performed the old Yugoslav lyrical device of listing place-names from 'Vardar' to the Adriatic (one end of the (former) country to another), wrapped up in a package of musical and visual clichés from 'Balkan' film,[44] but the release seemed not to generate any scandal at all – even though it took one transgressive step past Severina's song by directly incorporating Serbia itself into the collective it was addressing (one line mentioned the Belgrade landmark of Kalemegdan).

Much like Lepa Brena's early songs (and many pop-folk numbers since), 'Hej Balkano' nodded to the glamour and romance of European and global metropoles (now including Dubai), but offered 'the Balkans' (identical with the space of former Yugoslavia) as the place where her song's character, her imagined male love-interest, and her listeners could be authentically themselves ('nemoj da se lažemo kad balkanski to radimo'[45]). Its expression of what Alexander Kiossev has termed a 'Balkan popular (counter) culture', rejecting high-cultural aspirations to Western modernity, was nothing new at all for south-east Europe, but unusually unambiguous for Croatia.[46] Even accounting for its self-mockery about Croatian uptightness towards the Balkans – Šuput's different outfits in the video suggest a city girl whipped up by brass-band music going wild in the mountain hut's Balkan atmosphere[47] – such a performance would have been impossible in the 1990s Croatian entertainment industry, and deeply professionally risky in the 2000s. Neither was there what would once have been the predictable outcry in 2016 when Vesna Pisarović, a pop singer from the early 2000s who had represented Croatia at Eurovision in 2002 then retrained in jazz and moved to Berlin, released a jazz album with the bilingual title of *Naša velika pjesmarica: The Great Yugoslav Songbook* (*Our Great Songbook: The Great Yugoslav Songbook*). Croatian media discourse by 2015 could hardly have been described as markedly less nationalistic in a year when the 20th anniversary of victory in the Homeland War was looming (indeed, the tone of the anniversary commemorations made clear how much the 1990s

---

[43] Ceca married the paramilitary commander Željko Ražnatović-Arkan in 1995.

[44] See Dina Iordanova, 'Balkan Film Representations since 1989: The Quest for Admissibility' (1998) 18(2) *Historical Journal of Film, Radio and Television* 263–80.

[45] 'Let's not lie to ourselves when we do it Balkan-style.'

[46] Alexander Kiossev, 'The Dark Intimacy: Maps, Identities, Acts of Identifications', in Dušan I Bjelić and Obrad Savić (eds), *Balkan as Metaphor: Between Globalization and Fragmentation* (Cambridge, MA, 2002), 184.

[47] In fact, the semi-alpine effect of the video's winter snow might suggest it was also aimed at Slovenia, where Šuput is popular and where the mountain hut is a common video locale in Slovenia's own pop-folk, 'turbo-polka'. The song also appeared less than a year after the Polish 2014 Eurovision entry 'Mi Słowanie (We Are Slavic)', which had hypersexualized Polish village customs to create an effect not unlike Severina's in 2006.

hegemonic public narrative about Croatian participation in the war *still* structured the Croatian public sphere[48]): but the likelihood of a furore over Croatian female pop stars 'flirting with the Balkans' was not what it had been.

The knowledge that pop-folk itself had openly sought to shed the associations with the Milošević regime which critics, rockers and liberals projected on to Serbian 'turbo-folk' also helps to explain why 'Balkan'-tinged popular music became less controversial in Croatia. The 2000s' new Serbian stars had not been politically exposed as celebrities under Milošević; moreover, strategically minded turbo-folk entrepreneurs (including some of the genre's most famous stars like Lepa Brena and Dragana Mirković, who both owned record labels and in Mirković's case a satellite pop-folk music video channel, founded in December 2005) might have recognized that strong associations between pop-folk and Serbian nationalism would have limited the music's appeal to non-Serbs. Marko Dumančič and Krešimir Krolo have argued, therefore, that the region's contemporary pop-folk musicians largely 'brand themselves as *Balkan* performers, self-consciously emphasizing a general Balkan, rather than an ethno-specific, orientation':[49] most of its stars, in creating what Petrov termed 'affective atmospheres' around themselves, are not tapping their audiences' identification with *ethnonational* collectives.

Dumančič and Krolo's observation helps explain why young people in Croatia who enjoy dancing to recorded or live 'narodnjaci' in nightclubs do not consider their nights out (where many songs they hear will be by younger or older singers from Serbia, Montenegro and BiH) to be acts of nostalgia for Yugoslavia, even though wider culture continues to problematize the question of why young Croats like to listen to turbo-folk.[50] This might be an 'unintentional' revival of a common Yugoslav cultural space,[51] yet if it is a force for cultural integration, it is disconnected from any political entity. If music can cross ex-Yugoslav borders without playing on nostalgia at all, then, is nostalgia no longer a necessary or significant theme for understanding the politics of sociocultural relations in former Yugoslavia? Most musical border-crossings are certainly far less politically charged today.

V Beyond Yugonostalgia: nostalgia for the Yugoslav wars in popular culture

As an interpretation of post-Yugoslav cultural continuities, Yugonostalgia may have had its day. The sociologist Dalibor Mišina, for one, has recently argued that post-Yugoslav cultural studies must go 'beyond nostalgia', or at least 'free itself from the 'nostalgia presumption': the frame of nostalgia is not sufficient for understanding cultural production about the Yugoslav *past*, let alone cultural production with the sole time-frame of the post-Yugoslav present.[52] The 'Yugonostalgia' paradigm, which has

---

[48] Jović, *Rat i mit.*

[49] Marko Dumančič and Krešimir Krolo. 'Dehexing Postwar West Balkan Masculinities: The Case of Bosnia, Croatia, and Serbia, 1998 to 2015' (2017) 20(2) *Men and Masculinities* 154–80 at 160 (my emphasis).

[50] Aleksej Gotthardi Pavlovsky, *Narodnjaci i turbofolk u Hrvatskoj: zašto ih (ne) volimo?* (Zagreb, 2014).

[51] Dumančič and Krolo, 'Dehexing', 160.

[52] Mišina, 'Beyond nostalgia', 332.

often been applied to apparent continuities in popular music and other cultural
production between the mid-1990s and the mid-2000s, may have become part of
received wisdom about post-Yugoslav cultural politics, but has far less purchase if
music and musicians cannot be said to be engaging listeners, viewers and fans in
processes of active remembering (contrast the more direct remembering in which
bands who play songs from their own home region involve their diasporic audiences
from the same places).[53] Audiences are instead largely offered a cultural space which is
transnational, in relation to where state borders lie, and which takes coherence from a
mutually-intelligible set of language variants, cultural references, and regional–national
place-myths (Vardar and the Adriatic are intelligible as external boundaries;
Montenegro is a place young people aspire to go for a beach holiday; Croatian women
supposedly have an active sexual appetite once they have shed their bourgeois morality
and Catholic qualms) without communicating or even requiring any historical or
political sense of how this space came about. It could almost be detached from the
knowledge that, during or just before the early childhoods of today's young people, the
country where their parents lived broke up through war.

Yet this is not the only nostalgia at work in post-Yugoslav popular culture and media.
Ethnicized and mononational forms of nostalgia, which harden rather than weaken
ethnopolitical divisions, also reverberate through the region's cultural politics,
remediating historical memory in ways which observers had already started witnessing
before Yugoslavia collapsed.[54] Each country's ethnonational past, as reconstructed
through older and more recent acts of myth-making, contains its own golden ages and
troubled times which intellectuals, politicians and the public can translate into myths
for making sense of contemporary politics, the conditions the nation faces today, and
the character and intentions of groups which constitute known 'others' to the national
'self'. One aspect of such historical memory is a nostalgia for an imagined, distant and
more glorious national past (the rulers, kingdoms and battles remembered in this form
existed, although the details have often been heavily mythologized; 'imagined' is how
much sentiment and glory the mass of the population likely felt). Some of these are
long-established: for example the veneration and reappropriation of Byzantine tradition
in Serbian visual art and 'etno' music (neo-traditional music packaged for a cosmopolitan
'world music' market which values authenticity and research, not for the pop-folk
circuit), which connects past and present across a bridge which bypasses the many
traces of Ottoman heritage in contemporary Serbian culture.[55] Others are newer, such
as the ethnocentric narrative of today's Macedonian nation as a symbolic continuation
of Alexander the Great's empire (minimising any Albanian past within Macedonian
national history) which Nikola Gruevski's government made to pervade the built

---

[53] See Hariz Halilović, *Places of Pain: Forced Displacement, Popular Memory and Trans-Local Identities in Bosnian War-Torn Communities* (New York, 2013), 211.

[54] See Jasna Dragović-Soso, *Saviours of the Nation: Serbia's Intellectual Opposition and the Revival of Nationalism* (London, 2002).

[55] Ivan Čolović, *Etno: priče o muzici sveta na Internetu* (Belgrade, 2006). In 2004, Serbia's Željko Joksimović came second at Eurovision with a repackaging of precisely this aesthetic. To the Croatian press's invented surprise, viewers in Croatia awarded him a maximum twelve points.

environment of Skopje through a grandiose programme of monument-building and 'antiquitization'.[56]

Because a greater length of time has now passed since the break-up of Yugoslavia and the wars, however, the earlier post-Yugoslav past is now available as a focus of monoethnic nostalgia *as well*. The most culturally and politically significant nostalgia in today's Croatia – in the sense of political communication and cultural production which *actively calls on* audiences to remember the past and feel the emotions of longing for something which that past represented but today's reality ostensibly does not – is not Yugoslavia but the Homeland War of 1991–95, which Tuđman and the 1990s Croatian state (including its media), plus intellectual allies, effectively turned into a new myth of national origin rooted in living memory. By upholding this narrative in the 2000s and 2010s, the Croatian right wing – both the party Tuđman founded (the Croatian Democratic Union (HDZ)) and further-right parties which openly celebrate the symbols and military of the NDH – reproduces the myth of the Homeland War as expressing a spirit of sacrifice and unity to which the nation needs to return. This, too, is nostalgia, and a far more politicized form.

The aesthetics of Homeland War nostalgia in contemporary Croatia, indeed, create a two-way flow between politics and cultural domains including music and sport: the same communicative codes permeate the platforms of HDZ and other right-wing politicians, patriotic popular music, and national sporting culture. An indicative example, in 2012, occurred when the controversial musician and war veteran Marko Perković Thompson released a video for the song he had written as the anthem of the Croatian men's football team's supporters club.[57] The lyrics and video of 'Uvijek vjerni tebi' ('Always faithful to you') linked playing or cheering for the national team with fighting for Vukovar and remembering the history of the Zrinskis and Frankopans, combining recent and historic examples of military heroism.[58] The video used not only archive footage of famous goals and victories by the post-Yugoslav Croatian football team, but eventually also added wartime news footage of Croatian artillery pieces firing and Croatian soldiers victoriously entering Knin in August 1995, which elided sporting and military heroism just as Croatian media had done during the war. Indeed,

---

[56] Andrew Graan, 'Counterfeiting the Nation: Skopje 2014 and the Politics of Nation-branding in Macedonia' (2013) 28(1) *Cultural Anthropology* 161–79.

[57] Thompson became a professional musician in 1992 after recording a hit song about the volunteer platoon he had joined to defend his home village, and has continuously associated himself with the veterans' movement since 1998. ('Thompson' was his front-line nickname because he carried a Thompson machine-gun.) The fact that his debut song begins with the NDH's salute 'Za dom, spremni' ('for the Home, ready') makes every performance of this canonical and much-memorialized wartime song (unless the iconic first line is dropped) reiterate the notion that the NDH can be separated from the crimes of fascism, and arguably normalizes the slogan and the memory of the NDH in Croatian society: Dario Brentin, 'Ready for the Homeland?: ritual, remembrance, and political extremism in Croatian football' (2016) 44(6) *Nationalities Papers* 860–76 at 864. For the left, the utterance 'Za dom, spremni' is equivalent to declaring sympathy for fascism; for the revanchist right, its status as a slogan with pre-NDH noble and historic origins (as an amalgamation of two earlier Croatian battle-cries) is a patriotic truth.

[58] Vukovar was besieged, then brutally captured, by the JNA and Serb paramilitaries in autumn 1991; Zrinski and Frankopan were the two greatest Croatian noble families, who produced several generations of Croatian and Habsburg military heroes in warfare against the Ottoman Empire, until the head of the two families were executed in 1691 for rebelling against Habsburg rule.

the end of the first verse, 'kada čuješ himnu, bori se za Vukovar' ('when you hear the anthem, fight for Vukovar'), was both an encouragement to the players *and an invitation for listeners to syncretically remember,* layering sport and war memory together.

Although the Homeland War was a turbulent period during which thousands of Croats died and many more were forced to flee their homes, its hegemonic depictions in contemporary Croatia can nevertheless be called nostalgic. They hark back to a time of imagined dignity for the military and for Croatian tradition which the political, cultural and religious right argues has been violated by the post-Communist left, i.e. the heirs of a Yugoslav Communist regime which they charge had always been inimical to Croatian tradition and self-determination. Indeed, this frame was already emerging in the late 1990s: the first song through which Thompson associated himself with the veterans' movement, 'Prijatelji' ('Friends') in 1998, called on the fellow veterans he addressed to 'remember the proud days' ('sjetite se na ponosne dane') when they had stood beside each other, been able to do everything they wanted, and been who they had wanted to be. The lyrics presented a post-war society that had fallen short of these imagined expectations, and the video linked these sentiments to a political matter which had dismayed veterans and the right (the Hague Tribunal's prosecution of the Croat Defence Council (HVO) colonel Tihomir Blaškić for war crimes against Bosniaks in BiH).

The promise of returning to a time of imagined dignity for the Homeland War and its veterans – the dignity which the war supposedly had under Tuđman – is thus held out by today's HDZ politicians as a solution to Croatia's ongoing socio-economic woes since the global financial crisis of 2007–08. (They have conveniently forgotten that the late 1990s veterans' movement first mobilized for greater benefits and privileges *against* HDZ, which was still in power.) Kolinda Grabar-Kitarović's presidential victory speech in January 2015, as HDZ's winning candidate, looked back to the Homeland War and Tuđman's time in power as an inspiration for national regeneration. The nostalgic references simultaneously positioned her within this national grand narrative as a symbolic daughter to the father-of-the-nation figure which Tuđman had cultivated during the 1990s[59] – someone who would fulfil what Tuđman had not been able to complete because of his death in 1999. This has included a programme of rearmament and of marketing Croatia to its NATO allies as a modern, high-quality supplier of arms, equipment and military training-grounds.

Indicative of the contemporary mode of Croatian nostalgia for the Homeland War is how another of Thompson's patriotic/nationalist songs, 'Lijepa li si' ('How beautiful you are') – a song praising the nation's different regions, which he recorded with other male singers from those areas for a video released before the parliamentary elections in January 2000 – was incorporated in the mid-2010s first into the official repertoire of the Croatian Football Association (HNS) for play before important matches, then into military commemoration. (In 2017, Grabar-Kitarović and the HDZ prime minister Andrej Plenković were among dignitaries waving flags and singing along with it during the official commemoration of Armed Forces Day.) The reason why the HNS has been

---

[59] See Reana Senjković, *Lica društva, likovi države* (Zagreb, 2002).

reported to international governing bodies for playing this song, and why the Armed Forces Day video caused adverse comment on social media in BiH, is the same: that among the Croatian regions joined together by the couplets of 'Lijepa li si' is 'Herceg-Bosna', the name of the ethnically homogenous para-state which the HVO and the Bosnian branch of HDZ had sought to create during the Bosnian conflict, with Tuđman's knowledge and support. Bosnian social media users who do not support Bosnian Croat politicians' demands to revise the Dayton constitution and create a third, Croat-identified constitutional entity (which could more easily separate and join Croatia) might well – and not unreasonably – have inferred that the president and prime minister shared Thompson's nostalgic gaze towards Herceg-Bosna. Croatia may be where ethnicized nostalgia is currently most embedded into politics: but all post-Yugoslav nationalisms and public cultures contain the ingredients to mobilize nostalgia in a similar way. The ethnic nation and its war experience is therefore now as important a focus for nostalgia as Yugoslavia.

VI Conclusion

Do we still need nostalgia to understand sociocultural relations in the Yugoslav region, and the continuities which they often appear to reveal? Nostalgia for the many things people may long for when they express 'Yugo'-nostalgia, and the ethnocentric nostalgia of phenomena such as Croatian remediation of the Homeland War (or the Republika Srpska government's contributions to the building of 'Andrićgrad', Emir Kusturica's eco-village and film set near Višegrad, one of the towns in eastern Bosnia worst affected by Serb soldiers' and paramilitaries' massacres of Bosniaks in 1992) are coexistent in today's Yugoslav region. One form of nostalgia does not exclude the other: they are both being produced at once, and ethno-nationalist nostalgia for the war years is just as significant as nostalgia for the Yugoslav period in the region's popular culture today.

Assessing the legacy of Yugoslavia, this volume argues, requires weighing up how far the successor states' post-Yugoslav elites did indeed manage to disengage their individual presents and futures from their shared Yugoslav past through the new national and political projects and narratives they created. In popular music, as in any other domain, one would therefore have to question whether there have indeed been new, non-Yugoslav beginnings in the region, and if so in what ways. Not even Slovenia and Croatia, the states where cultural policy sought most insistently to detach popular music from Yugoslav spheres of reference, have disentangled themselves in the terms that some music professionals' public statements in the early 1990s prophesied. Indeed, since popular music relies on a dialectic between the new and the familiar in order to interface with listeners' personal memories and move their emotions, it would be impossible for legacies of Yugoslavia not to have persisted, absent the kind of root-and-branch assault on evidence of everyday coexistence which even in Croatia did not fully reconfigure public consciousness. Paradoxically, though, practices of affectively harnessing memory, tradition and sentiments of territorial belonging which were once institutionalized into Yugoslav popular music have readily been translated into music that celebrates the ethnopolitical nation. These musical directions too are partly a legacy of Yugoslavia even when, as in Croatia, they overtly perform being orientated against a Yugoslav past.

References

Archer, Rory. 'Assessing Turbofolk Controversies: Popular Music between the Nation and the Balkans' (2012) 36(2) *Southeastern Europe*, pp. 178–207.

Baker, Catherine. 'The Politics of Performance: Transnationalism and its Limits in Former Yugoslav Popular Music, 1999–2004' (2006) 5(3) *Ethnopolitics*, pp. 275–93.

Bakić-Hayden, Milica, and Robert M Hayden. 'Orientalist Variations on the Theme 'Balkans': Symbolic Geography in Recent Yugoslav Cultural Politics' (1992) 51(1) *Slavic Review* 1–15.

Bellamy, Alex J. *The Formation of Croatian National Identity: a Centuries-Old Dream?* (Manchester, 2003).

Boym, Svetlana. *The Future of Nostalgia* (New York, 2001).

Brentin, Dario. 'Ready for the Homeland?: Ritual, Remembrance, and Political Extremism in Croatian Football' (2016) 44(6) *Nationalities Papers*, pp. 860–76.

Brubaker, Rogers. *Nationalism Reframed: Nationhood and the National Question in the New Europe* (Cambridge, 1996).

Buchanan, Donna A, (ed) *Balkan Popular Culture and the Ottoman Ecumene: Music, Image, and Regional Political Discourse* (Lanham, MD, 2007).

Čolović, Ivan. *Etno: priče o muzici sveta na Internetu* (Belgrade, 2006).

Dnevnik.hr. 'Nova zvijezda: Zagrepčanka krenula u osvajanje folk scene', 5 January 2017. Available at: https://dnevnik.hr/showbuzz/mladi_i_neizbjezni/hana-masic-nastupila-u-zvezdama-granda---462623.html (accessed 25 January 2018).

Dragović-Soso, Jasna. *Saviours of the Nation: Serbia's Intellectual Opposition and the Revival of Nationalism* (London, 2002).

Dumančić, Marko, and Krešimir Krolo. 'Dehexing Postwar West Balkan Masculinities: The Case of Bosnia, Croatia, and Serbia, 1998 to 2015' (2017) 20(2) *Men and Masculinities*, pp. 154–80.

Eckert, Stine. 'Fighting for Recognition: Online Abuse of Women Bloggers in Germany, Switzerland, the United Kingdom, and the United States' (2018) 20(4) *New Media and Society*, pp. 1282–302.

Gotthardi Pavlovsky. Aleksej, *Narodnjaci i turbofolk u Hrvatskoj: zašto ih (ne) volimo?* (Zagreb, 2014).

Graan, Andrew. 'Counterfeiting the Nation: Skopje 2014 and the Politics of Nation-branding in Macedonia' (2013) 28(1) *Cultural Anthropology*, pp. 161–79.

Halilović, Hariz. *Places of Pain: Forced Displacement, Popular Memory and Trans-Local Identities in Bosnian War-Torn Communities* (New York, 2013).

Hofman, Ana. 'Lepa Brena: repolitization of musical memories on Yugoslavia' (2012) 60(1) *Glasnik Etnografskog instituta SANU*, pp. 21–32.

Hofman, Ana. 'Balkanske glasbe industrije med evropeizacijo in regionalizacijo: *Balkanske glasbene nagrade*' (2014) 50 *Muzikološki zbornik* 50(1), pp. 157–74.

Hofman, Ana. *Novi život partizanskih pesama* (Belgrade, 2016).

Horvat, Srećko, and Igor Štiks, (eds), *Welcome to the Desert of Post-Socialism: Radical Politics after Yugoslavia* (London, 2015).

Iordanova, Dina. 'Balkan Film Representations since 1989: The Quest for Admissibility' (1998) 18(2) *Historical Journal of Film, Radio and Television*, pp. 263–80.

Jansen, Stef. *Antinacionalizam: etnografija otpora u Zagrebu i Beogradu* (Belgrade, 2005).

Jelača, Dijana. 'Youth after Yugoslavia: Subcultures and Phantom Pain' (2014) 5(2) *Studies in East European Cinema*, pp. 139–54.

Jović, Dejan. *Rat i mit: politika identiteta u suvremenoj Hrvatskoj* (Zagreb, 2017).

Judah, Tim. 'Yugoslavia is Dead, Long Live the Yugosphere', LSEE Research on South-Eastern Europe Working Papers 1 (London, 2009). Available at: http://eprints.lse.ac.uk/48041/1/__Libfile_repository_Content_LSEE_Papers%20on%20South%20Eastern%20Europe_Yugoslavia%20is%20Dead(author).pdf (accessed 19 August 2019).

Jutarnji list, 'Lepa Brena ponovo stiže u Zagreb: idući petak sprema se spektakularni koncert velike regionalne zvijezde u Diamond Palace Casinu!', 29 September 2017. Available at: www.jutarnji.hr/spektakli/strane-zvijezde/lepa-brena-ponovno-stize-u-zagreb-iduci-petak-sprema-se-spektakularni-koncert-velike-regionalne-zvijezde-u-diamond-palace-casinu/6599172/ (accessed 19 August 2019).

Kiossev, Alexander. 'The Dark Intimacy: Maps, Identities, Acts of Identifications', in Dušan I Bjelić and Obrad Savić (eds), *Balkan as Metaphor: Between Globalization and Fragmentation* (Cambridge, MA, 2002).

Kolstø, Pål. 'Identifying with the Old or the New State: Nation-building vs Yugonostalgia in the Yugoslav Successor States' (2014) 20(4) *Nations and Nationalism*, pp. 760–81.

Mišina, Dalibor, '"Spit and Sing, My Yugoslavia": New Partisans, Social Critique and Bosnian Poetics of the Patriotic' (2010) 38(2) *Nationalities Papers*, pp. 265–89.

Mišina, Dalibor, 'Beyond Nostalgia: "Extrospective Introspections" of the Post-Yugoslav Memory of Socialism' (2016) 50 *Canadian–American Slavic Studies*, pp. 332–54.

Palmberger, Monika, *How Generations Remember: Conflicting Histories and Shared Memories in Post-War Bosnia and Herzegovina* (London, 2016).

Perica, Vjekoslav, and Mitja Velikonja, *Nebeska Jugoslavija: interakcije političkih mitologija i pop-kulture* (Belgrade, 2012).

Petrov, Ana, '"My Beautiful Dalmatian Song": (Re)connecting Serbia and Dalmatia at Concerts of Dalmatian performers in Belgrade' (2015) 4(1–2) *TheMA: Open Access Research Journal for Theatre, Music, Arts*. Available at: www.thema-journal.eu/index.php/thema/article/view/38/90 (accessed 19 August 2019).

Petrov, Ana. 'The Songs we Love to Sing and the History we like to Remember: Tereza Kesovija's comeback in Serbia' (2015) 39(2) *Southeastern Europe*, pp. 192–214.

Petrov, Ana. *Jugoslovenska muzika bez Jugoslavije* (Belgrade, 2016).

Petrov, Ana. 'Yugonostalgia in the Market: Popular Music and Consumerism in Post-Yugoslav Space' (2017) 53(1) *Muzikološki zbornik* 203–15.

Pogačar, Martin. *Media Archaeologies, Micro-Archives and Storytelling: Re-Presencing the Past* (London, 2016).

RFE/RL. 'Ukraine may ban Russian entrant from Eurovision over Crimea visit', 14 March 2017. Available at: www.rferl.org/a/ukraine-may-ban-russian-entrant-samoylova-eurovision-contest-over-crimea-visit/28368002.html (accessed 19 August 2019).

Rihtman-Auguštin, Dunja. 'A Croatian Controversy: Mediterranean–Danube–Balkans' (1999) 36(1) *Narodna umjetnost*, pp. 103–19.

Sabalić, Ines. 'Washingtonski sporazumi dramatično su izmijenili hrvatsku estradnu scenu: u Zagrebu je otvoreno petnaest lokala s novokomponiranom glazbom!', *Globus*, 31 March 1995.

Senjković, Reana. *Lica društva, likovi države* (Zagreb, 2002).

Spaskovska, Ljubica. 'Stairway to Hell: The Yugoslav Rock Scene and Youth during the Crisis Decade of 1981–1991' (2011) 38(2) *East Central Europe*, pp. 355–72.

Todorova, Maria, and Zsuzsa Gille (eds), *Post-Communist Nostalgia* (New York, 2010).

Ugrešić, Dubravka. *The Culture of Lies: Anti-Political Essays* (London, 1998).

Velikonja, Mitja. '"Ex-home": "Balkan Culture" in Slovenia after 1991' in Barbara Törnquist-Plewa and Sanimir Resić (eds), *The Balkans in Focus: Cultural Boundaries in Europe* (Lund, 2002).

Velikonja, Mitja. *Titostalgija: A Study of Nostalgia for Josip Broz* (Ljubljanainstitute, 2008).

Volčič, Zala. 'Yugo-nostalgia: Cultural Memory and Media in the former Yugoslavia' (2007) 24(1) *Critical Studies in Media Communication*, pp. 21–38.

Volčič, Zala, and Karmen Erjavec. 'The Paradox of Ceca and the Turbo-folk Audience' (2010) 8(2) *Popular Communication*, pp. 103–19.

Vujačić, Veljko. *Nationalism, Myth and the State in Russia and Serbia: Russian and East European Government Politics and Policy* (Cambridge, 2015).

Zorn, Jelka. 'A Case for Slovene Nationalism: Initial Citizenship Rules and the Erasure' (2009) 15(2) *Nations and Nationalism*, pp. 280–98.

Part Two

International Affairs

4

Transformations of Global Citizenship in the Former Yugoslavia: The Legacies of Yugoslav Non-aligned Multilateralism

Ljubica Spaskovska
University of Exeter

I Introduction

A peculiar artefact adorns the yard of the Museum of African Art in Belgrade. A 200-year-old 'admiral' anchor found near Porto-Novo in the Gulf of Guinea was donated to the Museum collection in 1975. The plaque in front of the anchor reads: 'Over the course of three centuries, 20 million Africans were transported to America and 200 million perished during the hunt and the transports. The peoples of Yugoslavia never took part in this human trade.' Such sense of moral self-righteousness and an emphasis on a shared revolutionary, anti-colonial past underpinned socialist Yugoslavia's interactions with the Global South. Anti-imperialism and solidarity with the different liberation movements in the developing world were appropriated as defining principles in Yugoslav foreign policy and were carried forward as prominent tropes in Yugoslav public discourse. With the dissolution of the Yugoslav federation and its disappearance from the world map, the new geo-political priorities for the successor states shifted away from the Global South. However, such developments were not exclusive to Yugoslavia. With the new geo-political realignments at the end of the Cold War, the core ideas which had sustained non-alignment and guided most of the initiatives on e.g. democratization of international economic relations, began to fade away or lose relevance in a world that celebrated the triumph of Western liberal democracy and set up market-driven structural adjustment programs under what came to be known as the 'Washington consensus'.[1] Moreover, after 1992, Yugoslavia's non-aligned foreign policy became largely equated with Tito's personality, his lifestyle and travels, and in light of the new elites' Euro-Atlantic aspirations it lost relevance as a subject of academic or serious media scrutiny. Recently, however, this trend has

---

[1] See: Nils Gilman, 'The New International Economic Order: A Reintroduction' (2015) 6(1) *Humanity* 1–16.

begun to change. At the 50th anniversary of the establishment of the Non-Aligned Movement (NAM) in 2011, the Serbian President hosted around 700 representatives of more than 100 states at a summit which accentuated 'the enduring attraction of the universal principles of Non-Alignment'[2] and a sense of continuity with socialist Yugoslavia. While political re-appropriations of this legacy are often motivated by pragmatic goals – in the Serbian case, for instance, with lobbying for preventing future recognitions of Kosovo's independence - within the realm of public history there has been growing interest[3] in these largely forgotten transnational (educational, cultural, economic) encounters and in recovering the 'obsolete' memories of the actors themselves.

This chapter seeks to shed light on the third layer of Yugoslav socialist citizenship – namely, its global dimension. In addition to the two most prominent layers of late socialist Yugoslav citizenship (i.e. its 'two-tiered' nature consisting of the republican and federal pillars) this chapter utilizes the citizenship lens in order to account for the practical implications of Yugoslavia's non-aligned policy, the impressive record of economic, intellectual and cultural exchange and their legacies. Departing from the assumption that citizenship could be conceptualised through its three dimensions of status, rights and identity,[4] the chapter explores the implications of what Bhikhu Parekh termed 'globally oriented citizenship'[5] both during the socialist and the post-socialist periods. It maintains that if analyzed not only as a phenomenon associated with diplomatic/political history, but also as a broader societal project, Yugoslavia's globally orientated citizenship could be a useful prism through which to account for the shifts which occurred after 1989 in order to understand how the post-Yugoslav redefinitions of those past global imaginaries shape or reflect today a new 'sense of citizenship'.[6] The chapter argues that the recent rediscoveries of the Yugoslav internationalist, non-aligned legacy reflect different and often conflicting ways of engaging with and making sense of the past. A largely selective appropriation of socialist Yugoslavia's legacies of global engagement is revealing of an undefined and contradictory relationship the post-Yugoslav states and societies have had with their socialist past. In addition, a tendency in the political realm to reproduce the performative dimension of non-alignment demonstrates an acute lack of awareness of and knowledge about the concrete policy orientations and achievements of non-aligned multilateralism, in particular in the spheres of international economic relations, development and global

---

[2] 'Belgrade hosts 50th Non-Aligned Movement Summit', *B92*. Available at: www.b92.net/eng/news/ politics.php?yyyy=2011&mm=09&dd=05&nav_id=76239 (accessed 30 July 2018).

[3] Two widely publicized international exhibitions took place in 2017/18: *Tito in Africa: Picturing Solidarity* at the Pitt Rivers Museum in Oxford, UK and the Museum of the History of Yugoslavia in Belgrade, and *Toward a Concrete Utopia: Architecture in Yugoslavia, 1948–1980* at New York's MoMA.

[4] Christian Joppke, 'Transformation of Citizenship: Status, Rights, Identity' (2007) 11(1) *Citizenship Studies* 37–48.

[5] Bhikhu Parekh, 'Cosmopolitanism and Global Citizenship' (2003) 29(1) *Review of International Studies* 3–17.

[6] Pamela J Conover makes a distinction between the affective (identity and meaning one gives to their membership in a particular political community) and the cognitive pole (the understanding and framework of beliefs one develops about their relationship to the state and to other citizens).
See: Pamela J Conover, 'Citizen Identities and Conceptions of the Self' (1995) 3 *Journal of Political Philosophy* 133–65.

media and communications. Both at political and at societal level, there are various tensions at work which essentially demonstrate an attempt to acknowledge the positive side of that legacy and thus use it for pragmatic political gains in international forums; in the cultural realm in order to counter/deconstruct a set of received views and an entrenched anti-Yugoslav/anti-communist discourse; and at individual level often to voice a sense of loss of what Stef Jansen termed 'geopolitical dignity'[7]. From an engaged international actor that played a central role in numerous multilateral initiatives, not least the Helsinki Process/the establishment of the Conference for Security and Cooperation in Europe (CSCE) and the North–South dialogue, the post-Yugoslav region has generally retreated to a status of peripheral player in international affairs with no distinct geo-political identity and no political interest in the issues that once shaped its vibrant multilateral diplomacy within the UN system and beyond.

II Yugoslav socialist global citizenship beyond Cold War bipolarity

'The willingness to enter into a nonhegemonic dialogue', which Parekh identified as one of the aspects of a re-formulated global citizenship, was especially visible in Yugoslavia's active participation at the United Nations, in particular in the debates in the 1970s about the establishment of a 'New International Economic Order' (NIEO) and in its rich bilateral (economic, cultural, technical) cooperation with the developing countries of the Global South, all of which underpinned its disproportionate diplomatic and political prestige within the NAM and the UN-related international forums. As early as 1951, Yugoslav President Josip Broz Tito emphasized the centrality of the UN system for safeguarding world peace 'as the institution for solving of international problems'.[8] The concept of 'active neutrality' later evolved into the principle of 'active peaceful coexistence'.[9] It was precisely during this period of the early 1950s that Yugoslavia discovered new allies and a way of reinventing its role at global level after the 1948 split with the Soviet Union. Namely, in 1950–1951 both Yugoslavia and India sat on the UN Security Council (SC) as non-permanent elected members and their SC membership overlapped with Egypt's mandate during the period of 1949–1950. These early encounters drew the Yugoslav diplomats' attention to the questions raised by former colonies and gradually shaped Yugoslavia's anti-colonial stance. As has been observed, 'The emergence of a firmly anti-colonial Non-Aligned Movement and the prominence of colonial disputes within the UN General Assembly add lustre to this picture of a multi-polar international system in which rights politics played a critical role'.[10] In this context, development and the elimination of the disparities and inequality between the North and the South became one of the defining programmatic goals of

---

[7] Stef Jansen, 'The Afterlives of the Yugoslav Red Passport', *Citizenship in South East Europe*. Available at: www.citsee.eu/citsee-story/afterlives-yugoslav-red-passport (accessed 30 July 2018).

[8] Josip Broz Tito, *Jugoslavija u borbi za nezavisnost i nesvrstanost* (Sarajevo: Svjetlost, 1977), p 27.

[9] Jadranka Jovanović, *Jugoslavija u Organizaciji Ujedinjenih Nacija (1945-1953.)* (Beograd: Institut za savremenu istoriju, 1985), p 52.

[10] Martin Thomas, *Fight or Flight: Britain, France and Their Roads from Empire* (Oxford University Press, 2014), p 351.

the Non-Aligned countries as well. Although often in disagreement, the movement's members managed to carve out alternative institutional spaces and promote novel development agendas. The 'Group of 77' (G77) at the UN, a coalition of developing countries founded in 1964 as the result of the 1963 Preparatory Committee for the United Nations Conference on Trade and Development (UNCTAD) was one such space. From the very beginning, Yugoslavia played an important formative role in both the G77 and in UNCTAD, the latter being conceived as a 'forum for conciliation and reform' and 'an instrument to promote the economic development of the Third World'.[11] As Janez Stanovnik, a prominent Yugoslav diplomat and Executive Secretary of the UN Economic Commission for Europe (UNECE) recalled: 'I think that one of the great breakthroughs for the G-77 was that they imposed the trade discussion on the General Assembly and on the Economic and Social Council. And, willy-nilly, the West had to yield under the pressure of arguments based on a number of trade studies prepared within the secretariat.'[12] Indeed, often, the newly independent, non-aligned and developing states found interlocutors in the developed market economies: from individual politicians, diplomats and economists, to think-thanks such as the Club of Rome, bodies such as the Independent Commission on International Development Issues (the 'Brandt Commission')[13] and international events such as the Paris Conference on International Economic Cooperation (CIEC). Dragoslav Avramović, the Yugoslav *ex officio* member of the Brandt Commission was the World Bank's chief economist for Latin America and the Caribbean and director of the development economics department. In the debates on a Code of Conduct for Trans-National Corporations (TNCs) Yugoslavia also played a prominent role in the so-called Group of Eminent Persons.[14] Emerik Blum, the General Manager of one of the biggest Yugoslav companies Energoinvest, was among the 20 members of the Group mandated to study the impact of multinational corporations on economic development and international relations under a 1972 ECOSOC resolution. Although, after 1983, the negotiations on a corporate code of conduct slowly died down and were completely abandoned by the beginning of the 1990s, when the UN Centre on TNCs was abolished

---

[11] 'The Non-Aligned Movement and the Group of 77', *Foreign Policy Document No 91* (London: International and Commonwealth Section, 1980); Branislav Gosovic, *UNCTAD: Conflict and Compromise* (Leiden: AW Sijthoff, 1972), p x.

[12] 'Transcript of interview with Janez Stanovnik by Thomas G. Weiss', *United Nations Intellectual History Project* (New York: City University of New York, 2007), p 49.
On the pre-history of UNCTAD, the debates on trade and development and the Prebisch-Singer thesis, see: John Toye and Richard Toye, 'The Origins and Interpretation of the Prebisch-Singer Thesis'(2003) 35(3) *History of Political Economy* 437–67.

[13] The Commission was chaired by Willy Brandt, former Chancellor of West Germany. It began work in December 1977 and the Commission's members were: Abdlatif Y Al-Hamad (Kuwait), Rodrigo Botero Montoya (Columbia), Antoine Kipsa Dakoure (Upper Volta), Eduardo Frei Montalva (Chile), Katherine Graham (USA), Edward Heath (UK), Amir H. Jamal (Tanzania), Lakshmi Kant Jha (India), Khatijah Ahmad (Malaysia), Adam Malik (Indonesia), Haruki Mori (Japan), Joe Morris (Canada), Olof Palme (Sweden), Peter G. Peterson (USA), Edgard Pisani (France), Shridath Ramphal (Guyana), Layachi Yaker (Algeria). Ex officio members: Jan Pronk (Netherlands), Goran Ohlin (Sweden), Dragoslav Avramovic (Yugoslavia).

[14] Tagi Sagafi-nejad, *The UN and Transnational Corporations: From Code of Conduct to Global Compact* (Indiana University Press, 2008).

in 1992, certain aspects were revived in debates on corporate social responsibility and the UN Global Compact.

'Self-reliance' (i.e. promoting cooperation among developing nations and hence redefining existing global patterns of trade and economic cooperation) became one of the axes of the NAM and the other groupings of the developing nations.[15] If the battles for the democratization of international economic and North–South relations were waged primarily within UNCTAD, the forgotten initiatives for the democratization of the world communication and information order where Yugoslavia played a comparatively prominent role occurred within UNESCO. The 'New World Information and Communication Order' (NWICO) was seen as being part and parcel of the NIEO. Bogdan Osolnik was the Yugoslav member of the 'International Commission for the Study of Communication Problems' led by Sean MacBride, better known as the MacBride Commission, which authored the monograph-length report *Many Voices One World: Communication and Society Today and Tomorrow*.[16] The twenty-first General Assembly of UNESCO was held in Belgrade in 1980 in the year of the release of the report that, among other things, emphasized 'the harmful consequences of the concentration of ownership in media'.[17] At the initiative of non-aligned leaders, the Non-Aligned News Agencies Pool (NANAP) was established in 1975 to redress imbalances in global news flows and the Yugoslav news agency TANJUG was the first national news agency to coordinate the collection and redistribution of news among non-aligned countries.[18]

Despite a general perception of the 1980s as the 'lost decade', some of the initiatives regarding cooperation and development pioneered by the Non-Aligned Movement were taken up and upgraded throughout the period. UNCTAD VI took place in Belgrade in 1983 and reiterated some of the old claims directed at the IMF and developed states: concessions to developing countries with difficulties and repeated calls to the US government to give backing to the seven-year-old proposal for a Common Fund for Commodities. In April 1988, Yugoslavia hosted the Ministerial Meeting of the Negotiating Committee on the Establishment of a Global System of Trade Preferences (GSTP) among developing countries and the Yugoslav Government was the depositary of the ensuing Agreement on GSTP.[19] It was negotiated by 48 developing countries (including Yugoslavia and Romania), members of the G77, and

---

[15] See, e.g. 'Lusaka Declaration on Non-Alignment and Economic Progress Adopted by the Third Conference of Heads of States or Government of Non-Aligned Countries, Lusaka', as cited in Leo Mates, *Nonalignment: Theory and Current Policy* (Belgrade/New York: Institute of International Politics and Economics/Oceana Publications, 1972), pp 485–91.

[16] *Many Voices, One World: Towards a New, More Just, and More Efficient World Information and Communication Order* (Paris: UNESCO, 1980). Available at: www.un-documents.net/macbride-report.pdf (accessed 30 July 2018).

[17] Bogdan Osolnik, 'The Macbride Report – 25 Years Later' (2005) 12(3) Javnost – The Public: Journal of the European Institute for Communication and Culture 5–11 (6).

[18] Matthew Crain, 'Non-Aligned News Agencies Pool' in John DH Downing (ed), *Encyclopedia of Social Movement Media* (SAGE, 2011), pp 368–69.

[19] See: Ljubica Spaskovska, 'Building a Better World? Construction, Labour Mobility and the Pursuit of Collective Self-reliance in the 'Global South', 1950–1990'(2018) 59(3) *Labor History* 331–51.

entered into force in 1989, with the aim to promote mutual trade and enhance economic cooperation. In 1989, Belgrade was the host of the last Cold War Non-Aligned summit, the last big international event before the country's disintegration.

For more than 40 years, socialist Yugoslavia played an active role in various transnational initiatives that sought to rethink existing geopolitical hierarchies, contribute to the 'democratization of international relations'[20] and redress perceived historical wrongs. Both moral and pragmatic motives often overlapped in its efforts to 'enter into a robust and critical dialogue'[21] with a variety of interlocutors both in the developed and the developing world. Being both a European and a developing nation pursuing non-orthodox socialism, Yugoslavia was able to assume a mediating role and reflect a sense of moral victory as the Cold War was nearing its end in 1989. The 1989 Non-Aligned summit declaration conveyed the latter by stating that 'without our historic contribution [...] the emerging multi-polarity of the world would be inconceivable.'[22] Indeed, this was also noted by external observers who argued that 'With the Non-Aligned declaring a victory in the Cold War, all that is left is the North-South dialogue and with it the long-term goals of re-establishing a Palestinian state, eradicating racism, and halting economic exploitation.'[23] Janez Stanovnik's recollection provides a succinct summary:

> Within the Group of 77 and within the Non-Aligned Movement, Yugoslavia was playing a middle-road strategy and was often a mediator between more radical—predominately African with Cuba group—and more free market-oriented Latin America and parts of Asia. In retrospect I consider this was a good policy for Yugoslavia on several scores. First, it was a morally right policy on the global scale. Second, it was a peacekeeping policy, as it interpolated between the two blocs and prevented either one to prevail globally. Third, it did help—while modestly—the economic advancement of the poorer countries, and fourth—most important for Yugoslav national interest—it increased Yugoslav national prestige in the world and thus indirectly helped Yugoslavia to resist pressure from the USSR.[24]

III Continuities and ruptures: non-alignment after Yugoslavia

In 2016, on the occasion of the 17th Non-Aligned Summit, UN Secretary-General Ban Ki-moon thanked the Non-Aligned Movement for their continued commitment to global peace, for raising awareness and mobilising the international community on

[20] Ranko Petrovic, *Non-Aligned Yugoslavia and the Contemporary World: The Foreign Policy of Yugoslavia 1945–1985* (Beograd/Zagreb: Međunarodna politika/Školska knjiga, 1986), p 233.
[21] Bhikhu Parekh, 'Cosmopolitanism and Global Citizenship' (2003) 29(1) *Review of International Studies* 3–17.
[22] Bridget Green, 'The Non-Aligned Movement in Perspective', *Sheffield Papers in International Studies* No 10 (University of Sheffield, 1992), p 28.
[23] Ibid, p 40.
[24] 'Transcript of interview with Janez Stanovnik by Thomas G. Weiss', *United Nations Intellectual History Project* (New York: City University of New York, 2007), p 38.

issues ranging from the promotion of sustainable development and the fight against extreme poverty, to nuclear disarmament and inter-cultural dialogue. Although the end of the Cold War arguably diminished the role the Non-Aligned Movement played, certain continuities persisted – at domestic/national level through different forms of revival of the discourse on global solidarity and at international level through the legacy of non-alignment in the realm of multilateral development diplomacy: most notably the Sustainable Development Agenda, the UN Global Compact, and the decision of the UN Human Rights Council to start fresh negotiations for a binding code of conduct on Transnational Corporations (TNCs). The end of the Cold War dramatically redefined Yugoslavia's position within the UN system and the OSCE – from proactive actor which adopted a conciliatory approach and promoted peaceful conflict resolution and rapprochement between East and West, the country became the problem for which solutions were suddenly urgently being sought. Being one of the main protagonists in the Helsinki process within the N + N group of neutral and non-aligned countries and a host to the Helsinki CSCE follow-up meeting in 1977/78, the successor states were put on the agenda in 1991/92 as points of grave concern. The Federal Republic of Yugoslavia was suspended from the OSCE and Slovenia, Bosnia, Macedonia and Croatia had to re-apply.[25]

The Non-Aligned Movement also faced the challenge of reinventing its role in a world no longer divided into two major military and ideological blocs. Serbia and Montenegro were absent from NAM summits in the 1990s, while Croatia, Slovenia and Bosnia-Herzegovina attended as observers or guests. Although non-permanent Security Council members in the early 1990s such as India and Cuba had reservations about authorizing a peace-keeping operation in Yugoslavia, raising arguments about infringements on state sovereignty,[26] by the time of the 1995 summit in Cartagena, Colombia, Member States condemned 'the acts of aggression, genocide and ethnic cleansing against the Republic of Bosnia-Herzegovina and its population'.[27] None of the seven successor states of socialist Yugoslavia preserved its membership of the NAM and only Bosnia-Herzegovina remained member of the G77. However, at the 16th NAM summit in Tehran in 2012, Bosnia-Herzegovina, Croatia, Montenegro and Serbia participated as observers. After a fifteen-year period of conscious political distancing from the Yugoslav past, the political elites in the region had mobilized this legacy for particular diplomatic battles or gains. For instance, Croatia's candidacy for a non-permanent member on the UN Security Council in 2008–09 was successful because of the support and votes from developing/NAM states – the result of a long and successful

---

[25] Valery Perry, 'The OSCE suspension of the Federal Republic of Yugoslavia', *Helsinki Monitor*. Available at: www.cvce.eu/content/publication/2005/11/7/3766bd03-0e5c-4541-b4d6-5412e1489a76/publishable _en.pdf (accessed 30 July 2018). On the Belgrade follow-up meeting, see: Vladimir Bilandžić, Dittmar Dahlmann, Milan Kosanovic (eds), *From Helsinki to Belgrade: The First CSCE Follow-up Meeting and the Crisis of Détente* (Bonn University Press, 2012).

[26] 'Informal Consultations of the Security Council: Situation in Yugoslavia', 25 November 1991, United Nations Archive, Secretary-General Javier Perez de Cuellar (1982–1991), S-1024-0175.

[27] '11th Summit Conference of Heads of State or Government of the Non-Aligned Movement, Cartagena, Colombia, 18–20 October 1995', p 42, *Non-Aligned Movement Database*. Available at: http://cns.miis.edu/nam/documents/Official_Document/11th_Summit_FD_Cartagena_Declaration_ 1995_Whole.pdf (accessed 30 August 2019).

88 *The Legacy of Yugoslavia*

lobbying process carried out by the last Yugoslav Foreign Minister Budimir Lončar, who fifteen years later, acted as advisor to then Croatian President Stjepan Mesić.[28]

Similar voting support at the UN GA was demonstrated during the rare secret ballot for President of the 67th session of the GA in 2012. Vuk Jeremić, the Minister of Foreign Affairs of Serbia, defeated Dalius Čekuolis, the Lithuanian Ambassador to the UN, by a vote of 99 to 85. Jeremić's statement in an interview for the UN News Centre is revealing of the complex relationship with the Yugoslav past which Serbia has demonstrated in official politics and public history. In front of an international audience, Yugoslavia features as part of a 'usable past',[29] where its status as a founding member of the UN and relative diplomatic prestige serves as the background for Serbia's new image, new chapter in international relations and its self-construction as a successor of 'a country that was a founding member of the United Nations, and a proud victor over fascism'. Indeed, as Liudmilla Jordanova observed: 'If the past is usable, then history is an open field that is available to be put to very different, even conflicting ends.'[30] As Jeremić stated,

> Yugoslavia, the political predecessor of Serbia, was one of the founding members of the United Nations and a country that was very active in the international arena for a number of decades. Close to the end of the 80s and beginning of the 90s, the country became one of the last victims of the Cold War. We were torn apart by strife and now there are six countries. That process was very, very painful [...] We put forward our candidacy for the Presidency of the General Assembly to mark the end of an era; I am very grateful for the support of a vast number of countries. My tenure will mark the re-instatement on the international scene of a country that was a founding member of the United Nations, and a proud victor over fascism.[31]

A sense of continuity with the Yugoslav past has also been prominent in the establishment of a scholarship programme in 2010 financed by the Serbian government for students from Non-Aligned countries. At the commemoration of the 50th anniversary of the 1961 Belgrade Summit, the Serbian President emphasized the interrelationship between the same practice of educational cooperation with the Global South which socialist Yugoslavia implemented, with the similar course the Serbian state was pursuing today:

> We have also established a "World in Serbia" Scholarship Fund for students for Non-Aligned nationals, enabling hundreds each year to study at the University of Belgrade. This is a continuation of the tradition that was established here, in Belgrade, fifty years ago. Tens of thousands of your countrymen were educated in this city, and went on to contribute to the development of your proud nations.[32]

[28] See: Tvrtko Jakovina, *Treća strana hladnog rata* (Zagreb: Fraktura, 2011), 627–33.
[29] Liudmilla Jordanova, *History in Practice* (London: Arnold, 2000), 141–71.
[30] Ibid.
[31] 'Interview with Vuk Jeremić, President of the 67th session of the General Assembly', *UN News Centre*. Available at: www.un.org/apps/news/newsmakers.asp?NewsID=69 (accessed 30 July 2018).
[32] 'Belgrade hosts 50th Non-Aligned Movement summit', *B92*.

This builds upon the robust educational exchange programme which Yugoslavia initiated for students from the newly independent/developing countries in 1955 when it awarded the first five scholarships to Burmese students.[33] In 1961/62 that number rose to fifty-five scholarships for the 'non-liberated' territories (such as Kenya, Tanganyika, North Rhodesia, Zanzibar, Uganda) and twenty-seven for liberation movements or trade unions.[34] Training and education of students from developing nations was also provided outside the higher education framework, for instance at institutions such as the International Centre for Public Enterprises in Developing Countries (ICPE), based in Ljubljana.[35] Among other activities, the centre implemented a training programme for Namibian students within the 'Nationhood Programme' of the UN Council for Namibia, 'as a specific contribution to the struggle of the Namibian people for their independence'.[36] It focused on preparing young Namibians for management of public enterprises in independent Namibia; hence, between 1980 and 1984, 200 Namibian students attended training at ICPE. ICPE was only one of several research and policy institutes whose mandate was to study the developing world and supply expert advice to the government. Above all, their knowledge production about the developing world was firmly embedded in a progressive anticolonial paradigm and was underpinned by the debates occurring within the United Nations and its agencies. The Zagreb-based Africa Research Institute, established in 1963, captures very well both the continuities and ruptures in the region's engagement with the non-European world: in 1971 it changed its name into the Institute for Developing Countries to reflect the country's expanding multilateral engagement across what became known as the developing world. In 1989, with the onset of European integration, it changed its name to the Institute for Development and International Relations (IRMO) and in 1996 it dropped the word 'development' completely. In 2013, it changed its name back to the Institute for Development and International Relations (IRMO). ICPE also had to reinvent itself in a post-1989 world and changed its name to the International Centre for the Promotion of Enterprises. The Slovenian government in its 2015 foreign policy strategy referred to the Centre as 'an example of a regional platform for cooperation with India – as well as other non-European countries [...] which is the only intergovernmental organization with over 40 years of experience in Slovenia'.[37] The same document in the short section on Africa acknowledged the Yugoslav legacy and

---

[33] Archive of Yugoslavia, Belgrade, hereafter AY. 145 *Savez Studenata Jugoslavije*, 32–286, 'Stanje i problemi školovanja stranih studenata u Jugoslaviji', p 3.

[34] AY, 145 *Savez Studenata Jugoslavije*, 32–299, 'Pitanje materijalne i druge pomoći /stipendije/ oslobodilačkim pokretima u Africi', p 3.

[35] Yugoslavia was generally financing the Centre with assistance from the UNDP, UNIDO and the Dutch government until 1980. From 1980, it was financed by contributions from Member States. The construction of the Centre was financed by the Yugoslav authorities and the City of Ljubljana. The Yugoslav government transferred the management of the building and all of its equipment for an annual rent of 1 dinar (in 1978 approximately 6 USD cents) to ICPE.

[36] Anton Vratusa, 'Ten Years of ICPE', *Public Enterprise* (offprint), 5/1 (1984), p. 11.

[37] *SLOVENIA: SAFE, SUCCESSFUL, GLOBALLY RESPECTED. The Foreign Policy of the Republic of Slovenia* (Ljubljana: Ministry of Foreign Affairs, 2015), p. 25. Available at: www.mzz.gov.si/fileadmin/pageuploads/Zakonodaja_in_dokumenti/dokumenti/strategija_ZP_ang.pdf (accessed 30 July 2018).

stated that 'Great potential for future contacts may be found in the active cooperation established in the fields of the economy and education at the time of the former Socialist Federal Republic of Yugoslavia'.[38] International development cooperation is also listed among Slovenia's foreign policy priorities, since the country has been an official development assistance donor since 2004 and a member of the OECD Development Assistance Committee since 2013, which makes it unique in the post-Yugoslav region.[39]

Beside Slovenia, Serbia and Bosnia-Herzegovina are the only other Yugoslav successor states that embed references to their pre-independence past in their contemporary foreign policy. In the basic directions and activities of Bosnia's foreign policy, the Ministry of Foreign Affairs lists the continuation of relations and cooperation with member states of the NAM and acquiring the status of an observer for Bosnia and Herzegovina.[40] While at the last 2016 NAM Summit in Venezuela, Bosnia, Croatia, Montenegro and Serbia participated as observers,[41] Serbia is the only one to explicitly refer to the Non-Aligned Movement in its list of multilateral issues and international organizations, along the UN, the OSCE and the Council of Europe.[42] When in 2014 the Serbian ambassador to Zambia presented Kenneth Kaunda with an album of photographs from his meetings with Josip Broz Tito for his ninetieth birthday, Serbia openly assumed the role of Yugoslavia's legal successor. For Serbia, the UN and NAM also provide venues for what James Ker-Lindsey termed 'the foreign policy of counter secession'.[43] Vuk Jeremić was also the public face of Serbian diplomacy that set as its goal to prevent as many recognitions as possible in the aftermath of the unilateral declaration of independence by Kosovo. In the two years following its declaration of independence, Jeremić visited over 90 countries.[44] Indeed, many of Yugoslavia's former allies in the Non-Aligned Movement, including India, Indonesia, as well as many African states, refuse to recognize Kosovo. One could also consider as important the fact that Tanjug – once the driving force behind the Non-Aligned News Agencies Pool (NANAP), now operates as the Serbian state news agency and, despite speculation in 2015 that it would shut down due to financial difficulties, it still maintains a solid visible presence both in the region and internationally. However, the initiatives to resurrect

[38] Ibid., p. 26
[39] *International development cooperation and humanitarian assistance*, Ministry of Foreign Affairs of Republic of Slovenia. Available at: www.mzz.gov.si/en/foreign_policy_and_international_law/international_development_cooperation_and_humanitarian_assistance/ (accessed 30 July 2018).
[40] *Basic Directions of BiH Foreign Policy*, Ministry of Foreign Affairs of Bosnia-Herzegovina. Available at www.mvp.gov.ba/vanjska_politika_bih/osnovni_pravci_vanjske_politike_bih/?id=2 (accessed 30 July 2018).
[41] Observers participate in the plenary deliberations and take the floor after being authorized by the Bureau. For the Venezuela Summit. Available at: http://namvenezuela.org/.
[42] *Multilateral Issues: The Non-Aligned Movement*, Ministry of Foreign Affairs of the Republic of Serbia. Available at: www.mfa.gov.rs/en/foreign-policy/multilateral-issues/the-non-aligment-movement (accessed 30 July 2018).
[43] James Ker-Lindsay, *The Foreign Policy of Counter Secession: Preventing the Recognition of Contested States* (Oxford: Oxford University Press, 2012).
[44] Ibid. See also: Marija Krstić, 'Pokret nesvrstanih kao jugoslovensko nasleđe' in Ivan Kovačević (ed), *Ogledi o jugoslovenskom kulturnom nasleđu* (Belgrade: Filozofski fakultuet Univerziteta u Beogradu, 2012), pp 57–82.

NANAP in 2005 through the establishment of the NAM News Network (NNN) saw Bernama, the Malaysian national news agency, take the lead instead.[45]

IV Globally re-imagined citizenship

In late 2017, the Belgrade Museum of Yugoslavia hosted the first edition of the collaborative project and exhibition *Tito in Africa – Picturing Solidarity*, which used the Museum's photographic archive to capture Yugoslavia's 'outreach to the newly decolonized states of Africa from the 1950s', 'reveal a rich history of encounter' and portray Tito as 'a new kind of European whose experience of fragile sovereignty and national struggle, and whose commitment to anti-fascism and a non-racialised world order, made him a subject of great fascination across the African continent'.[46] This recent discursive shift with regard to their global, non-aligned history, however, does not necessarily imply a radical shift in the way the post-Yugoslav states have made sense of their Yugoslav past through the various forms of public history. The Yugoslav past has been 'musealised' at the intersection of post-Yugoslav academic history with public institutions such as museums and commercial/popular culture. As Tanja Petrović observed, one could detect several general trends in recent museum representations of the Yugoslav past: a trend to present a linear historical narrative; a tendency of commercialization of the socialist past; a normative approach to the Yugoslav past; and nationalization of the Yugoslav heritage.[47] The exhibition/ international project *Unfinished Modernisations: Between Utopia and Pragmatism*, the exhibition *Solidarity, an Unfinished Project?* and the exhibition/international project *Travelling Communiqué* in different ways seek to engage with Yugoslavia's role as a global player or as a space which was open for transnational encounters. While they evidently have different thematic foci and approaches – the first analysing urbanism and architecture, the second Skopje's post-earthquake reconstruction as a symbol of international solidarity and the third the founding NAM Summit in Belgrade in 1961 – all the authors deemed it necessary to emphasize that their projects are not underpinned by the spectre of 'nostalgia'. Thus, the authors of the first exhibition underline that: 'The purpose of Unfinished Modernisations – as is reflected in the title – is no idealisation of the period, nor of the system in which the architectural and urban production under discussion developed [...] Modernist architecture and urbanism in socialist Yugoslavia reveal many original and progressive models.'[48] Yet,

---

[45] 'About NAM News Network', *Non-Aligned Movement News Network*. Available at: www. namnewsnetwork.org/v3/about.php (accessed 30 July 2018).

[46] James Mark, 'Foreword', in Radina Vučetić and Paul Betts (eds), *Tito in Africa: Picturing Solidarity* (Belgrade: Museum of Yugoslavia, 2017), p 11.

[47] See: Tanja Petrović, 'Jugoslovenski socijalizam u muzeju: socijalističko nasleđe kao kulturna baština' in Maša Kolanović (ed), *Komparativni postsocijalizam, slavenska iskustva* (Zagreb: Filozofski fakultet, 2013).

[48] 'Unfinished Modernisations: between Utopia and Pragmatism', *Museum of Architecture and Design*. Available at: www.mao.si/Event/Unfinished-Modernisations-between-Utopia-and-Pragmatism. aspx (accessed 30 July 2018).

despite the evident attempt at distancing from an emotionally charged, 'nostalgic' approach and at dissociating from any potential accusations of adopting a pro-Yugoslav, hence a biased, narrative all these projects also convey a sense of acknowledgement of the positive legacies (i.e. of what they consider 'progressive models', aspects 'worth preserving' or recovering silenced voices). This is precisely where the tension lies – in an appropriated imperative to distance oneself from the stigma of nostalgia, all the while partially subverting widely held negative views about the socialist past and its internationalist dimension.

Without doubt, every piece of public history is a product of the vision of the authors, the criteria set by funders and the (assumed) preferences of the target audiences. Indeed, museums 'convey narratives and values as well as insights and information [...] they often communicate a sense of the past and its meanings ...'[49] Cases where international partners and donors have been involved – in this case some from NAM members – demonstrate a more affirmative approach to representing this particular global aspect of the socialist past. *The Travelling Communiqué* project and exhibition was funded by the German Foreign Office and the Serbian Ministry for Culture, co-produced by the Dutch Art Institute and the Netsa Art Village from Addis Ababa and supported among others by the Embassies of Algeria, Egypt and Indonesia in Serbia. The project borrowed its title from the joint public statement – communiqué – issued at the end of the 1961 NAM summit and it blends archival material (photographs from the Presidential Photo Service archive of Josip Broz Tito) with various re-interpretations of the significance of the NAM seen as 'an early example of globalization'.[50] Although the authors stressed the aim was not to paint a glorified picture, the general tone is one of approbative criticism. Moreover, the project acknowledges the contemporary relevance of the 'new kind of internationalism' conceived in 1961:

> Travelling Communiqué does not aspire to celebrate the histories and geographies of the Cold War and the NAM. Instead, it enquires into the possibilities of 'prolonging' the formation of the NAM into the social conditions of the present. The NAM can be understood as a third space of emancipation that sought to unsettle the bipolar world order through a wide variety of anti-colonial thinking. The Travelling Communiqué is an attempt to understand the process of becoming a political subject, initiated by those without names whose voices exist despite efforts to silence them [...] The Travelling Communiqué project begins with the idea that the collective statements, images and sounds announced during the first Conference of the NAM in Belgrade in 1961, as a call for a new kind of internationalism, are still travelling.[51]

Indeed, there has been a growing trend of recovering silenced voices and aspects of the Yugoslav non-aligned/global past. Three smaller-scale public events in Belgrade and

---

[49] Liudmilla Jordanova, *History in Practice*, p 145.
[50] 'Travelling Communique', *Museum of the History of Yugoslavia*, Belgrade, August 2014.
[51] Ibid.

Ljubljana reveal a departure from the self-vindication narrative. Although I would not go as far as labelling them committed or celebratory public history, the exhibitions *Historical Witnesses: Stevan Labudović and the Algerian Liberation Struggle* at the Serbian National Library, *Tito – a Yugoslav Icon* in Ljubljana and *Up Close and Personal with Tito* at the Museum of Yugoslav History in Belgrade take on an affirmative approach. The first exhibition told the story of Stevan Labudović, the young Yugoslav cinematographer and photographer who spent three years with the fighters of the Algerian National Liberation Front (FLN). As has been observed: 'Algerian nationalists found ideological inspiration in numerous foreign sources, including Nasser's call for pan-Arab solidarity, Kwame Nkrumah's vision of pan-African unity, and the socialist non-alignment perfected by the Yugoslav premier, Tito.'[52] Alongside Dutch-Canadian photojournalist Kryn Taconis and Algerian FLN fighter and famous photographer Mohamed Kouaci, Stevan Labudović was one of the few who offered an alternative, insider's perspective on the Algerian war for independence – a 'war of admittedly unequal access to dominant means of representation.'[53] As has been noted, 'figures from the international Left took an interest in documenting the Algerian cause in order to make visible the atrocities being committed by the French state'.[54] However, these trans-national links and Yugoslavia's support for the anti-colonial, liberation movements remained absent from the public realm until recently. In this case, the choice of producing this exhibition should be seen as part of Serbia's recent intensification of bilateral relations with some of the NAM member states and her new 'political strategy' to improve its international standing.[55] Hence, the Algerian ambassador's address at the opening of the exhibition in November 2014 came after Labudović's attendence at the exhibition *Les photographes de guerre: les djonouds du noir et blanc* at the Algerian Museum of Modern and Contemporary Art the previous year and his decoration with the National Medal of Merit on the occasion of the 50th anniversary of Algeria's independence.[56]

The widely held perception that the Yugoslav President who championed the cause of non-alignment was a dictator, and the one to blame for setting the scene for the bloody break-up of the country, is challenged in the above-mentioned exhibitions, which partially focus on the Non-Aligned Movement, Tito's travels and meetings with foreign dignitaries and Third World leaders. The exhibition *Up Close and Personal with Tito* at the Museum of Yugoslav History displayed an array of photographs from the Museum's collection showing Tito's meetings with foreign leaders and even used statistics to capture the breadth of his international engagements: 'Between 1945 and 1979, wanting to secure a place for Yugoslavia on the political map of the world, Tito

---

[52] Martin Thomas, *Fight or Flight: Britain, France and Their Roads from Empire* (Oxford University Press, 2014), p 306.

[53] Hannah Feldman, 'Flash Forward: Pictures at War' in Ali Behdad and Luke Gartlan (eds), *Photography's Orientalism: New Essays on Colonial Representation* (Los Angeles: Getty Research Institute, 2013), p 158.

[54] Ibid.

[55] Krstić, 'Pokret nesvrstanih kao jugoslovensko nasleđe', p 79.

[56] 'M. Stevan Labudovic honoré par Algérie', *Ambassade d' Algérie – Serbie*. Available at: www.ambalgserbia.rs/2013/06/26/m-stevan-labudovic-honore-par-laglerie/ (accessed 30 July 2018).

visited seventy countries and met 250 heads of state (monarchs and presidents) and government leaders [...] Tito's perseverant foreign policy activity contributed to an international reputation for Yugoslavia which was out of proportion to the reality of the state.'[57] Although the exhibition in Ljubljana dedicated a section to the 'Goli otok' prison camp and the issue of political prisoners, it started with Fitzroy Maclean's famous dictum – 'People like Tito or not. Some don't. People like the 20th century or not. Some don't. But they belong together, this man and this century', and openly admitted its nostalgic subtext: 'The exhibition is intended for Tito aficionados, who recall the times of his leading of the common country with nostalgia, as well as for his opponents and detractors [...] The exhibition Tito – The Face of Yugoslavia is historical, iconographic, interesting, educational and nostalgic.'[58] The section on the Non-Aligned Movement qualified Yugoslavia's foreign policy as 'extremely fruitful' and somewhat misleadingly noted that the 'non-aligned countries are today among the main promoters of equal relations in the world'.[59] The fact that the exhibition was a commercial initiative without any public institutional involvement (it was produced by a small company indicatively named 'Ti & To' from the Slovenian city of Maribor) implies that there was a larger manoeuvring ground and an additional incentive – since it was a paying exhibition – to gear it towards a larger audience including both 'nostalgic' and more neutral observers who acknowledge Tito's role as a respected statesman and whose part in establishing Yugoslavia's global prestige could hardly be questioned.

Serbia and Slovenia stand out in this context – the former because of its sense of historical continuity with both royal and socialist Yugoslavia, the latter because of its less-traumatic process of exiting the Yugoslav federation in 1991 and a more positive attitude towards its Second World War anti-fascist past. In Croatia, interest in non-alignment as a cultural, historical and political legacy has been restricted to the academic realm, although one poignant example of the amount of public interest this history attracts is the Museum on the Island of Brijuni which houses the photo exhibition 'Josip Broz Tito on Brijuni', which has not been modified since it was first opened in 1984. In the proximity of Istria, the city of Rijeka in its preparations for European Capital of Culture in 2020 acquired Tito's ship *Galeb* which came to symbolise the country's non-aligned diplomacy, with plans to turn it into a museum and a tourist attraction that 'will now speak up about the international influence of our former country'.[60]

---

[57] 'Up Close and Personal with Tito', *Museum of the History of Yugoslavia, Belgrade*, August 2014.

[58] 'Tito – a Yugoslavian Icon', *Ljubljana Exhibition and Convention Centre*. Available at: www.ljubljanafair.com/for-visitors/previous-events/2018/06/16/378-Tito-a-Yugoslavian-icon (accessed 30 July 2018).

[59] Ibid.

[60] *Galeb*, Rijeka 2020 European Capital of Culture. Available at: http://rijeka2020.eu/en/infrastructure/brod-galeb/ (accessed 30 July 2018).

V Conclusion

Socialist Yugoslavia's 'globally imagined citizenship' was a chartered foreign policy course which enabled the country to vie for influence and recognition in a divided world; nevertheless, it was also embedded in 'an active commitment to create a just world order, one in which different countries, working together under fair terms of cooperation, can attend to their common interests in a spirit of mutual concern'.[61] The particular 'sense of citizenship' those political, cultural and economic encounters engendered were significantly transformed after the fall of European state socialism and the violent break-up of Yugoslavia.

This chapter sought to offer insight into the different ways Yugoslav socialist global citizenship has been re-interpreted and re-appropriated in the realms of politics, foreign policy and culture. The various recent rediscoveries of the Yugoslav internationalist, non-aligned legacy reflect different, often conflictual ways of engaging with and making sense of the past. From strategic political thinking and diplomatic pragmatism, to public histories which reluctantly convey an affirmative assessment of this legacy, the array of initiatives which re-actualise this global past and the ideas that underpinned non-alignment – for a long time considered politically and culturally irrelevant and outdated – are testament to a gradual paradigm shift in the post-Yugoslav space, where new and old generations of decision-makers, artists and scholars are rediscovering a common global history. In some cases, these new political subjectivities that surface in public history events represent a departure from the ethno-national as the dominant frame of interpretation and reference; often, however, in the realm of politics, they are only acts of instrumentalising a usable past.

References

Primary sources

Archival collections

Archive of Yugoslavia, Belgrade: League of Socialist Youth of Yugoslavia (SSOJ); Student Union of Yugoslavia;
United Nations Archive, New York: Secretary-General Javier Perez de Cuellar (1982–1991).

Exhibitions

'Solidarity, an Unfinished Project?', *Museum of Contemporary Art,* Skopje, October 2014.
'Tito – a Yugoslavian Icon', *Ljubljana Exhibition and Convention Centre*, November 2013.
'Travelling Communique', *Museum of the History of Yugoslavia*, Belgrade, August 2014.
'Up Close and Personal with Tito', *Museum of the History of Yugoslavia*, Belgrade, August 2014.

---

[61] Parekh, 'Cosmopolitanism and Global Citizenship', p 13.

Printed documents

Broz, Josip Tito. *Jugoslavija u borbi za nezavisnost i nesvrstanost* (Sarajevo: Svjetlost, 1977).
'The Non-Aligned Movement and the Group of 77', *Foreign Policy Document No 91*
    (London: International and Commonwealth Section, April 1980).
'Transcript of interview with Janez Stanovnik by Thomas G Weiss', *United Nations
    Intellectual History Project* (New York: City University of New York, 2007).
Vratusa, Anton. 'Ten Years of ICPE', *Public Enterprise* (offprint) 5/1 (1984).

Online documents

11th Summit Conference of Heads of State or Government of the Non-Aligned Movement,
    Cartagena, Colombia, 18–20 October 1995, p 42. Non-Aligned Movement Database.
    Available at: http://cns.miis.edu/nam/documents/Official_Document/11th_Summit_
    FD_Cartagena_Declaration_1995_Whole.pdf
Basic Directions of BiH Foreign Policy, Ministry of Foreign Affairs of Bosnia-Herzegovina.
    Available at: www.mvp.gov.ba/vanjska_politika_bih/osnovni_pravci_vanjske_politike_
    bih/?id=2 (accessed 30 July 2018).
*Many Voices, One World: Towards a New, More Just, and More Efficient World Information
    and Communication Order* (Paris: UNESCO, 1980). Available at: www.un-documents.
    net/macbride-report.pdf (accessed 30 July 2018).
Multilateral Issues: The Non-Aligned Movement, Ministry of Foreign Affairs of the Republic
    of Serbia. Available at: www.mfa.gov.rs/en/foreign-policy/multilateral-issues/the-non-
    aligment-movement (accessed 30 July 2018).
*SLOVENIA: SAFE, SUCCESSFUL, GLOBALLY RESPECTED. The Foreign Policy of the
    Republic of Slovenia* (Ljubljana: Ministry of Foreign Affairs, 2015), p 25. Available at:
    www.mzz.gov.si/fileadmin/pageuploads/Zakonodaja_in_dokumenti/dokumenti/
    strategija_ZP_ang.pdf (accessed 30 July 2018).

Secondary sources

Conover, Pamela J. 'Citizen Identities and Conceptions of the Self' (1995) 3 *Journal of
    Political Philosophy*, pp. 133–65..
Crain, Matthew. 'Non-Aligned News Agencies Pool' in John DH Downing (ed),
    Encyclopedia of Social Movement Media (SAGE, 2011), pp. 368–69.
Feldman, Hannah. 'Flash Forward: Pictures at War' in Ali Behdad and Luke Gartlan (eds),
    Photography's Orientalism: New Essays on Colonial Representation (Los Angeles: Getty
    Research Institute, 2013), pp. 153–70.
Gilman, Nils. 'The New International Economic Order: A Reintroduction' (2015) 6(1)
    Humanity, pp. 1–16.
Gosovic, Branislav. *UNCTAD: Conflict and Compromise* (Leiden: AW Sijthoff, 1972).
Green, Bridget. 'The Non-Aligned Movement in Perspective', *Sheffield Papers in
    International Studies* No 10 (University of Sheffield, 1992).
Jakovina, Tvrtko. *Treća strana hladnog rata* (Zagreb: Fraktura, 2011).
Joppke, Christian. 'Transformation of Citizenship: Status, Rights, Identity' (2007) 11(1)
    Citizenship Studies, pp. 37–48.
Jordanova, Liudmilla. *History in Practice* (London: Arnold, 2000).
Jovanović, Jadranka. *Jugoslavija u Organizaciji Ujedinjenih Nacija (1945–1953)* (Beograd:
    Institut za savremenu istoriju, 1985).

Ker-Lindsay, James. *The Foreign Policy of Counter Secession: Preventing the Recognition of Contested States* (Oxford: Oxford University Press, 2012).

Krstić, Marija. 'Pokret nesvrstanig kao jugoslovensko nasleđe' in Ivan Kovačević (ed), *Ogledi o jugoslovenskom kulturnom nasleđu* (Belgrade: Filozofski fakultuet Univerziteta u Beogradu, 2012), pp 57–82.

Mark, James. 'Foreword', in Radina Vučetić and Paul Betts (eds), *Tito in Africa: Picturing Solidarity* (Belgrade: Museum of Yugoslavia, 2017), pp 10–12.

Mates, Leo. *Nonalignment: Theory and Current Policy* (Belgrade/New York: Institute of International Politics and Economics/Oceana Publications, 1972).

Osolnik, Bogdan. 'The Macbride Report – 25 Years Later', *Javnost – The Public: Journal of the European Institute for Communication and Culture* 12/3 (2005), pp 5–11.

Parekh, Bhikhu. 'Cosmopolitanism and Global Citizenship' (2003) 29(1) *Review of International Studies*, pp. 3–17.

Petrović, Ranko. *Non-Aligned Yugoslavia and the Contemporary World: The Foreign Policy of Yugoslavia 1945–1985* (Beograd/Zagreb: Međunarodna politika/Školska knjiga, 1986).

Petrović, Tanja. 'Jugoslovenski socijalizam u muzeju: socijalističko nasleđe kao kulturna baština' in Maša Kolanović (ed), *Komparativni postsocijalizam, slavenska iskustva* (Zagreb: Filozofski fakultet, 2013).

Sagafi-nejad, Tagi. *The UN and Transnational Corporations: From Code of Conduct to Global Compact* (Indiana University Press, 2008).

Thomas, Martin. *Fight or Flight: Britain, France and Their Roads from Empire* (Oxford University Press, 2014).

Online resources

'Belgrade hosts 50th Non-Aligned Movement summit', *B92*. Available at: www.b92.net/eng/news/politics.php?yyyy=2011&mm=09&dd=05&nav_id=76239 (accessed 30 July 2018).

Galeb, Rijeka 2020 European Capital of Culture. Available at: http://rijeka2020.eu/en/infrastructure/brod-galeb/ (accessed 30 July 2018).

'Interview with Vuk Jeremić, President of the 67th session of the General Assembly', *UN News Centre*. Available at www.un.org/apps/news/newsmakers.asp?NewsID=69 (accessed 30 July 2018).

Jansen, Stef. 'The Afterlives of the Yugoslav Red Passport', *Citizenship in South East Europe*. Available at: www.citsee.eu/citsee-story/afterlives-yugoslav-red-passport (accessed 30 July 2018).

'M. Stevan Labudovic honoré par Algérie', *Ambassade d'Algérie – Serbie*. Available at: www.ambalgserbia.rs/2013/06/26/m-stevan-labudovic-honore-par-laglerie/ (accessed 30 July 2018).

Perry, Valery. 'The OSCE suspension of the Federal Republic of Yugoslavia', *Helsinki Monitor*. Available at: www.cvce.eu/content/publication/2005/11/7/3766bd03-0e5c-4541-b4d6-5412e1489a76/publishable_en.pdf (accessed 30 July 2018).

'Tito – a Yugoslavian Icon', *Ljubljana Exhibition and Convention Centre*. Available at: www.ljubljanafair.com/for-visitors/previous-events/2018/06/16/378-Tito-a-Yugoslavian-icon (accessed 30 July 2018).

'Unfinished Modernisations: between Utopia and Pragmatism', *Museum of Architecture and Design*, Available at: www.mao.si/Event/Unfinished-Modernisations-between-Utopia-and-Pragmatism.aspx (accessed 30 July 2018).

5

Between a Borderless Yugoslavia and a Europe without Borders: The Legacy of Territorial Disputes in the Western Balkans

James Ker-Lindsay
London School of Economics and Political Science

I Introduction

One of the most enduring and tragic legacies of the state of Yugoslavia is the bloodshed and war that occurred when the country collapsed in the early 1990s. The break-up of the federation led to the most bitter conflict in Europe since the end of the Second World War. It is no exaggeration to say that even now the reverberations continue to be felt. To this day, the Western Balkans pose a challenge to regional and international stability. While the era of major armed confrontation between the former republics of Yugoslavia is widely believed to be over,[1] some of the territorial issues which arose when the country disintegrated still remain unresolved.[2] A few of these disputes are well known. For example, the declaration of independence by Kosovo, in 2008, still divides international opinion. Other issues, however, have received little international attention. For instance, few outside the region are aware of the ongoing territorial dispute between Slovenia and Croatia over the Bay of Piran – even though it threatened to derail Croatia's bid to join the European Union. Likewise, few paid much attention to the question of the border demarcation between Kosovo and Montenegro, even though it sparked considerable political upheaval in Pristina and became one of the factors complicating Kosovo's path towards European integration.

What makes these disputes particularly interesting is that they are all legacies of a time when boundaries meant relatively little in the Western Balkans. Within socialist Yugoslavia, the territorial divisions had little day-to-day significance. It was only with the collapse of the federation, and the emergence of the independent republics, that nominal frontiers that had existed within Yugoslavia became important – often in a profoundly existential manner. And yet, ironically, these disputes are also a prelude to a time when the boundaries of the region will again have less significance. Within the

---

[1] British official, comments to the author, April 2018.
[2] Marija Ristic, 'Boundaries Still Unresolved in ex-Yugoslav Countries', *BIRN*, 11 April 2012.

European Union – which is characterized by the free movement of people, goods, services and capital – borders take on a very different meaning. Of course, the idea that borders are wholly insignificant in the EU context, as some may suggest, is wrong. They remain obvious symbols of statehood. However, with some notable exceptions, they lose their potency. They cease to be barriers to political and economic interaction.[3] That said, in the current period of uncertainty, as the countries of the Western Balkans float temporally and politically between a united Yugoslavia and a united Europe, these border disputes have, or have had, the potential to derail the region's development and the course of EU integration. Simply put, borders complicate the transition from an existence where borders had little practical meaning to another existence where they have little practical meaning.

This chapter therefore considers several of the most significant outstanding border disputes within the former Yugoslavia and examines how they have affected the process of European integration. In doing so, it raises an important question about the degree to which the current border issues are, in fact, a legacy of Yugoslavia or a product of the break-up of the country, including the way in which the international community handled the dissolution of the federation. In truth, it would seem that both elements are at play. As will be shown, international law creates a framework on international interaction that elevates notions of sovereignty and territorial possession in a way that makes the form of shared sovereignty in place under Yugoslavia impossible to perpetuate. However, the ethno-nationalism that drove the collapse of Yugoslavia, and the extremism that was nurtured throughout the 1990s, have also served to underscore in the minds of the peoples of the region the sacrosanct nature of the borders that now exist between the entities of the former Yugoslavia. Meanwhile, the European Union has, in almost all cases, taken on a major role as an actor in the attempts to resolve the issues. However, as will be seen, it has done so in rather different ways, and with very differing results. Ultimately, as will be shown, the EU provides a way to eventually mitigate this, but only after the resolution of the disputes that arise from the imposition of the sovereign territorial aspects of statehood.

II The break-up of Yugoslavia and European integration

Yugoslavia first came into being at the end of the First World War with the creation of the Kingdom of Serbs, Croata and Slovenes; an entity combining the independent Kingdoms of Serbia and Montenegro, with lands that had formerly been under Austro-Hungarian rule. In 1929, the new country changed its name to the Kingdom of Yugoslavia. At the end of the Second World War, the monarchy was abolished and the country was reconstituted under the leadership of Tito as the People's Republic of

---

[3] While the significance of borders is certainly diminished, the idea they do not matter at all within the European Union has been challenged in recent years by the migration crisis. For example, in 2015, Hungary closed its border with neighbouring EU member, Croatia. 'Migrant crisis: Hungary closes border with Croatia', *BBC News*, 17 October 2015. In June 2018, Austria closed its border with Slovenia as part of a controversial 'anti-migrant' military exercise. 'Austria conducts anti-migrant border exercise in show of defiance against Angela Merkel', *The Telegraph*, 26 June 2018.

Yugoslavia. In 1963, the country underwent yet another name change, becoming the Socialist Federal Republic of Yugoslavia (SFRY). By this point, the country was composed of six separate republics: Bosnia and Herzegovina, Croatia, Macedonia, Montenegro, Serbia and Slovenia. With the exception of Bosnia and Herzegovina – which was explicitly recognized as being composed of Bosnian Muslims (now generally known as Bosniaks), Serbs and Croats – these were broadly understood to represent the six nations of Yugoslavia. In addition, the country also defined the existence of a number of nationalities. These were defined as ethnic communities that were either transnational in nature – such as Ruthenians, Roma and Jews – or were considered to have a separate national 'homeland'. This latter category included Italians, Hungarians, Slovaks, and Albanians.

In 1974, the constitution of the country was revised. Two key changes occurred. First, the right of secession was formally recognized. Crucially, however, it was not wholly clear as to whether this right extended to the nations or their respective republics. This would be a major point of contention when the country collapsed less than two decades later. Secondly, the largest of the six republics, Serbia, was effectively divided into three parts. The northen province of Vojvodina, one of the most multi-ethnic parts of the country, was given autonomy. So too was the predominantly Albanian-populated southern province of Serbia. Crucially, although both were granted a seat on the country's collective Federal Presidency, neither was given the right of secession. Both decisions would have major effects later on.

Notwithstanding the differences over the status of the republics and provinces, in general terms, Yugoslavia operated like other federations. As noted, 'the borders between the republics were merely administaryoive in nature'.[4] The nominal divisions on the map often meant little in terms of day-to-day life. People moved freely around the country for work, education and pleasure. Roads and railways were built with little regard for the territorial divisions. International maritime and air boundaries fell under the authority of the federal government. Indeed, these boundaries were not even determined between the republics.[5] Economic interaction occurred unimpeded. As one long-standing observer of the region noted, 'the Western Balkans had a free-trade zone before the EU: Yugoslavia'.[6]

However, in 1991, Yugoslavia began to collapse. The first two republics to break away were Slovenia and Croatia, which declared independence on 25 June 1991. The Yugoslav National Army (JNA) immediately tried to prevent both from seceding. In the case of Slovenia, this led to a short war. However, the Yugoslav Government quickly relented, and Slovenia was soon accepted as an independent state. However, Croatia's attempt to break away led to a much more brutal conflict, complicated by the efforts of the country's Serb minorities to form their own separatist states. This raised

[4]   Matej Avbelj and Jernej Letnar Černič, 'The Conundrum of the Bay of Piran: Slovenia v. Croatia: The Case of Maritime Delimitation' (2007) 5(2) *The University of Pennsylvania Journal of International Law and Policy*, 3.

[5]   Avbelj and Černič, 'The Conundrum of the Bay of Piran: Slovenia v. Croatia: The Case of Maritime Delimitation', 4.

[6]   Valerie Hopkins, 'Borders have become a barrier to a reborn Balkans', *Financial Times*, 22 November 2018.

fundamental questions about the nature of the Yugoslav constitution and whether the recognized right to secession applied to the Republics (the position of the Croatian and Slovenian administrations), or to the six constituent nations of the Federation,[7] the position of the Serbian administration.

While the internal factors that precipitated the country's disintegration are still heavily contested,[8] the break-up of Yugoslavia also raised serious questions for the international community about the sanctity of the internal boundaries of the Republics and the way in which it should respond to acts of secession. In the nineteenth century, the traditional response to independence movements was to adopt a wait and see approach. If a territory seeking statehood was able to cement its statehood to the extent that it became clear that the parent state – the state it was breaking away from – could not reasonably expect or be expected to reassert its authority, then the presumption was that the independence of the territory should be recognized.[9] However, with the end of the Second World War, this position changed. The principle of the territorial integrity of states became enshrined in the Charter of the United Nations. This meant that unilateral acts of secession became prohibited. Meanwhile, the established international legal principle of *uti possidetis juris* (literally 'as you possess') meant that the boundaries of sub-state units which became independent should be respected as their state borders. The big question was whether these principles applied to Yugoslavia given its specific circumstances.

In August 1991, the European Union referred the matter to a specially constituted commission under the former president of the French Supreme Court, Robert Badinter.[10] In a series of opinions delivered over the next two years, the Commission decided that Yugoslavia was in the process of breaking up. To this extent, the independence of the Republics could not be viewed as unilateral acts of secession. Moreover, sovereignty lay with the Republics and their internal boundaries within Yugoslavia should be their new external borders as sovereign states.[11] These findings were subsequently accepted by the EU,[12] and by extension also formed the basis of the

---

[7]   In this context, the term 'nations' refers to the six main ethno-national groups in Yugoslavia: Croats, Bosniaks (Bosnian Muslims), Macedonians, Montenegrins, Serbs, and Slovenes. The term 'nation' has a specific meaning in this context to differentiate these 'indigenous' Yugoslav peoples from the so-called nationalities of Yugoslavia, which were made up of transnational minorities (such as Roma, Jews and Ruthenians) and national minorities, such as Italians, Hungarians, Romanians, and Albanians.

[8]   See Catherine Baker, *The Yugoslav Wars of the 1990s* (London: Palgrave Macmillan, 2015).

[9]   Mikulas Fabry, *Recognizing States: International Society and the Establishment of New States Since 1776* (Oxford: Oxford University Press, 2009). See also James Ker-Lindsay and Mikulas Fabry, *Secession and State Creation: What Everyone Needs to Know* (New York: Oxford University Press, 2019).

[10] For an analysis of the Commission, see Steve Terrett, The Dissolution of Yugoslavia and the Badinter Arbitration Commission: A Contextual Study of Peace-making Efforts in the Post-Cold War World (Aldershot: Ashgate, 2000); Peter Radan, 'The Badinter arbitration commission and the partition of Yugoslavia' (1997) 27(3) *Nationalities Papers* 527–57; Michla Pomerance, 'The Badinter Commission: Then Use and Misuse of the International Court of Justice's Jurisprudence' (1998) 20(1) *Michigan Journal of International Law* 31–58.

[11] Alain Pellet, 'The Opinions of the Badinter Arbitration Committee: A Second Breath for the Self-Determination of Peoples' (1992) 3(1) *European Journal of International Law* 178–185.

[12] For a detailed analysis of EU practices see Richard Caplan, *Europe and the Recognition of New States in Yugoslavia* (Cambridge: Cambridge University Press, 2005).

rest of the international community's acceptance of the new states emerging from the break-up of Yugoslavia, and their state borders.

In the years that followed, Yugoslavia continued its disintegration. The Socialist Republic of Macedonia declared independence in September 1991. However, while this did not lead to conflict within Yugoslavia, the country was not admitted to the United Nations until 1993 as a result of a dispute with Greece over its constitutional name – an issue that was only finally resolved in 2018 when the country officially became the Republic of North Macedonia. Meanwhile, a bitter war broke out in Bosnia and Herzegovina in early 1992 following its decision to pursue independence. This came to an end in 1995 with the signing of the Dayton Peace Agreement. Soon after that, fighting broke out in the southern Serbian province of Kosovo. In 1999, NATO launched airstrikes against the Federal Republic of Yugoslavia (by that point just Serbia and Montenegro), which then saw Kosovo placed under UN administration according to the terms of Security Council Resolution 1244. In 2003, the name Yugoslavia disappeared with the creation of the State Union of Serbia and Montenegro. Three years later, in 2006, the last vestiges of Yugoslavia – as a union of six republics – disappeared when Montenegro voted to end the union with Serbia and become a fully independent state. That same year, a process was started under UN auspices to determine the final status of Kosovo. This concluded without agreement in 2007. On 17 February 2008, Kosovo declared independence.

While the battles for independence were all but over by the end of the first decade of the twenty-first century, a number of bilateral territorial disputes had emerged between the new states. As the countries of the region began their quest for European integration, these outstanding differences would come to present a major problem for the European Union.

III Slovenia and Croatia

The first major dispute to create complications for the region's European integration was one which few observers had perhaps anticipated. While attention had been focused on the legacy of the violent wars which had blighted the region, and the ongoing political problems which these had created, a seemingly insignificant territorial dispute between two republics which had not fought against each other in the 1990s came to the fore. On 1 May 2004, Slovenia became the first republic of the former Yugoslavia to join the European Union as part of the so-called 'Big Bang' enlargement. At the time, it appeared to be a relatively uncontroversial membership. It had appeared to have avoided the worst of the violence which had ravaged the region a decade earlier. However, it soon became apparent that Slovenia's membership had led to the importation of a territorial dispute which would disrupt the accession of neighbouring Croatia in a way that rather parallels the higher-profile case of Cyprus, which joined the EU at the same time as Slovenia and became an obstacle to Turkey's accession.[13]

---

[13] For more see James Ker-Lindsay, *EU Accession and UN Peacemaking in Cyprus* (Basingstoke: Palgrave Macmillan, 2005).

Since 1991, when the two countries became independent, Slovenia and Croatia had, in fact, been at odds over the delimitation of their boundary.[14] As well as differences over their land border, which stretches to 670 kilometres (415 miles), there was a major dispute over their territorial waters. In particular, the two countries were at odds over the Bay of Piran, a 19 square kilometre (7.3 square mile) gulf located close to the maritime border with Italy. While Croatia, which now calls the area the Bay of Savudrija, wanted it to be delineated on the basis of equidistance, the Slovenian Government insisted on controlling the entire the area. At the same time, the Slovenian Government also raised concerns that its territorial waters were enclosed by those of Italy and Croatia, thereby preventing it from having direct access to international waters. It therefore wanted to be given a corridor through Croatian waters. In 1993, the two countries agreed to set up a joint expert group to examine the issues. Over the next few years, the two countries held various meetings to try to resolve both the land and sea disputes and, in 2001, the parties reached an agreement on their common borders, both land and sea. Slovenia would get two-thirds of the Bay of Piran and a corridor to the sea. However, while this was accepted by Slovenia, it was rejected by the Croatian Parliament. Zagreb now called for the issue to be resolved by international arbitration.

Although Slovenia joined the EU in 2004, the question of the border did not come to the fore until 2008, when Croatia presented maps which appeared to prejudge a settlement of the border issue. In response, the Slovenian Government announced that it would block Croatia's EU accession until such time as an agreement was reached on the border. The move led to a rapid deterioration of relations between the neighbours as Zagreb accused Ljubljana of resorting to blackmail and extortion.[15] With the question of the border now threatening Croatia's European integration process, the EU intervened. On 4 November 2009, the European Commission brokered an agreement. The two countries established an Arbitration Tribunal. Crucially, Article 9 of the agreement explicitly stated that Slovenia would lift its reservations regarding the opening and closing of chapters 'where the obstacle is related to the dispute'.[16] As a result, Croatia was able to continue its EU accession path unhindered. On 9 December 2011, it signed the Treaty of Accession. This was then ratified by all EU members, including Slovenia. On 1 July 2013, Croatia became the twenty-eighth member of the EU.

Even though Croatia had joined the EU, the dispute was far from resolved. In 2012, the sides agreed that the Permanent Court of Arbitration (PCA), an international body operating in The Hague, would act as registry for the arbitration. Over the course of the next two years, the tribunal received written submissions and counter-submissions from the two sides. This included a two-week hearing in June 2014. A year later, in July 2015, the tribunal announced that it would release its findings later that year. However, just two weeks later, recordings of telephone conversations between the Slovenian

[14] Mladen Klemenčić and Anton Gosar, 'The Problems of the Italo-Croato-Slovene Border Delimitation in the Northern Adriatic' (2000) 52 *GeoJournal* 129–37; Matej Avbelj and Jernej Letnar Černič, 'The Conundrum of the Bay of Piran: Slovenia v. Croatia: The Case of Maritime Delimitation' (2007) 5(2) *The University of Pennsylvania Journal of International Law and Policy* 1–19.

[15] 'Slovenia to Block Croatia's EU Accession Talks', *EU Observer*, 18 December 2008.

[16] 'Arbitration Agreement between the Government of the Republic of Slovenia and the Government of the Republic of Croatia'. Available at: https://pcacases.com/web/sendAttach/2165.

representative and a member of the arbitration panel appointed by Slovenia emerged. In response, Croatia announced that it had decided to terminate the arbitration agreement.[17] This was rejected by Slovenia. Intervening in the dispute, the European Commission stated that there was no alternative to the arbitration process. Meanwhile, the PCA president appointed new arbitrators. The court also decided that while Slovenia had indeed violated the provisions of the arbitration agreement, these violations were 'not of such a nature as to entitle Croatia to terminate the Arbitration Agreement, nor do they affect the Tribunal's ability, in its current composition, to render a final award independently and impartially'.[18] The proceedings therefore continued, albeit with Croatia's continued absence. On 29 June 2017, the tribunal delivered its ruling.[19] It decided that Slovenia's claim to most of the Bay of Piran should be recognized. Moreover, a 10-kilometre-long corridor should be established providing the country with direct access to international waters in the Adriatic. The PCA gave the parties six months to implement the ruling.

The ruling was a clear victory for Slovenia. The decision was welcomed by the European Commission, which stated that it expected both sides to abide by it.[20] However, the Croatian prime minister announced that Zagreb would not accept the decision and told the Commission not to meddle in the matter as, 'it has no competencies for border issues'.[21] Croatia's decision to ignore the Tribunal's ruling led to considerable anger in Slovenia. Ljubljana called upon the EU to take a firmer position on the case. Miro Cerar, the Slovenian Prime Minister, stressed that the case had important wider implications. As he noted, given the border disputes elsewhere in the region, it would be difficult for the other countries of the Western Balkans to join the EU without a reliable way to resolve their outstanding issues.[22]

In the months that followed, no progress was made. A Croatian offer for new talks was rejected by Slovenia.[23] In early 2018, the Slovenian Government announced that it was planning to bring the case before the European Union using the provisions laid down in Article 259 of the Lisbon Treaty.[24] This measure allowed one EU Member State to bring a case against another before the European Court of Justice (ECJ) for infringing its obligations under EU treaties. However, before this happens, the article stipulates that the dispute should be addressed by the European Commission, which would allow both parties to present their case before it issues a 'reasoned opinion' on the matter. Needless to say, such a step would amount to a major development. It would

---

[17] 'Croatian MPs Vote to End Slovenia Arbitration', *Balkan Insight*, 29 July 2015.
[18] 'Tribunal Issues Partial Award: Arbitration between Croatia and Slovenia to Continue', Press Release, Permanent Court of Arbitration, 30 June 2016.
[19] 'In the Matter of an Arbitration under the Arbitration Agreement Between the Government of the Republic of Croatia and the Government of the Republic of Slovenian, Signed on 4 November 2009', PCA Case No 2012-04, Permanent Court of Arbitration, 29 June 2017.
[20] 'Statement by First Vice-President Timmermans on the final award made on 29 June by the Arbitration Tribunal of the Permanent Court of Arbitration in the arbitration between Croatia and Slovenia', Statement, European Commission, Strasbourg, 4 July 2017.
[21] 'Croatia tells Commission to stay away from border dispute with Slovenia', *Euractiv*, 5 July 2017.
[22] 'Slovenian PM: EU Enlargement at Risk if Croatia Border Ruling Ignored', *Politico Europe*, 29 June 2017.
[23] 'Croatia and Slovenian Fail to Move Forward in Talks on Border Issue', *Reuters*, 19 December 2017.
[24] 'Slovenia ups Stakes in Adriatic Border Dispute', *Politico Europe*, 19 February 2018.

force the Commission to take a far more direct role in the issue than has hitherto been the case.

At the time of writing, the issue remains unresolved. Croatia still refuses to honour the ruling of the Court of Arbitration. For the EU, this is a source of embarrassment on several levels. For a start, it has underlined just how important it is to resolve issues before they are imported into the European Union. Now it has joined the EU, Croatia has no reason to resolve the issue. More to the point, the issue has also reinforced just how powerless the EU is to resolve such disputes once they have been imported. For this reason, there appears to be a new determination to ensure that such problems do not arise in the future.

IV Serbia and Kosovo

While the border dispute between Slovenia and Croatia was the first significant territorial issue the EU confronted in the Western Balkans during the process of enlargement, and remains an issue of contention, the most significant outstanding border dispute in the region concerns Serbia and Kosovo. Indeed, nowhere is the EU's determination to avoid importing border issues in the Western Balkans clearer than in this example. In this case, however, the dispute is not over the delimitation of the border, but instead relates to whether a border exists at all.

Unlike the other states that emerged from the break-up of Yugoslavia, as noted earlier, Kosovo was not a republic within the SFRY. Instead, it had been an autonomous province of Serbia during Socialist Yugoslavia. In 1990, as tensions grew in Yugoslavia, Belgrade imposed direct rule. Although Kosovo organized a referendum on independence in 1990, the issue failed to gain much international attention, let alone support. Only Albania recognized it as an independent state. Indeed, Kosovo's right to statehood was initially denied by the Badinter Commission by virtue of its status as an intrinsic part of the Serbian state, rather than a republic of the Yugoslav federation. After the end of the war in Bosnia-Herzegovina, it became clear to an increasing number of ethnic Albanians in Kosovo that the quest for independence would achieve little by peaceful means. A violent guerrilla campaign was therefore launched by the Kosovo Liberation Army (KLA) which in turn led to brutal reprisals by the Serbian state. In early 1999, following a well-publicized massacre of ethnic Albanians, a peace conference was convened in the French town of Rambouillet. When this failed to reach an acceptable solution, NATO launched a military campaign against Serbia. This ended a few months later when Serbia capitulated. Kosovo was placed under United Nations administration pending a decision on its final status.

In 2006, the UN launched a process to determine the final settlement of Kosovo's status under the auspices of Martti Ahtisaari, a former president of Finland.[25] Although

---

[25] James Ker-Lindsay, *Kosovo: The Path to Contested Statehood in the Balkans* (London: IBTauris, 2009); Marc Weller, *Contested Statehood: Kosovo's Struggle for Independence* (Oxford: Oxford University Press, 2009).

Kosovo's right to independence had previously been rejected, by this point it had become clear to most Western observers that there was no alternative to statehood. However, this was strongly opposed by Serbia. Crucially, Belgrade was supported by Russia. Moscow announced that it would not authorize any settlement which had not been agreed by both sides. Understanding that this meant that the UN Security Council would not authorize independence, Kosovo and its key supporters decided to proceed with a unilateral declaration of independence. This occurred on 17 February 2008. In the months that followed, over 50 countries recognized Kosovo, including all but five Member States of the European Union.[26] However, Serbia fought a strong campaign to prevent Kosovo from being accepted internationally. After much lobbying, it successfully managed to secure a UN General Assembly resolution referring the legality of the declaration of independence to the International Court of Justice (ICJ).[27] In the end, the ICJ ruled that the declaration of independence was not contrary to general international law. However, it also stated that it was not taking any position on whether Kosovo was a state.[28] While Serbia wanted to use the ruling to relaunch its efforts to prevent Kosovo from being recognized, the EU stepped in and put a halt to these ambitions. Fearful that the issue could destabilize the Western Balkans if left to fester, and that it would also undermine Serbia and Kosovo's efforts to pursue EU integration, the EU instead proposed a process of dialogue between Belgrade and Pristina which would aim to normalize relations between the two sides. This process was subsequently endorsed by the UN General Assembly with Resolution 64/298.[29]

The dialogue process officially started in March 2011. At first, the talks were focused on a range of very technical issues aimed at facilitating direct contacts between Kosovo and Serbia; such as energy and telecommunications and managing the border/boundary between the two. In the following period, it appeared as though the past tensions were finally easing. On 19 April 2013, the two sides reached a 15-point 'First Agreement of Principles Governing the Normalization of Relations'. This laid down, amongst other things, the principles for the establishment of an Association of Serbian Municipalities in Kosovo and ensuring ethnic Serbian participation in the Kosovo police force. It also committed the two sides not to block one another's path towards EU accession.[30]

Although the agreement marked an important development in relations between Belgrade and Pristina, its implementation has been fraught with delays and problems. In part, this has been due to prolonged political instability in Kosovo, not least over the

---

[26] The five non-recognising Member States are Cyprus, Greece, Romania, Slovakia and Spain. For more on the reasons why they did not recognize Kosovo see, *Kosovo Calling: International Conference to Launch Position Papers on Kosovo's Relation with EU and Regional Non-recognising Countries* (Pristina: Kosovo Foundation for Open Society and British Council, 2012); and James Ker-Lindsay and Ioannis Armakolas (eds), *Lack of Engagement: Surveying the Spectrum of EU Member State Policies towards Kosovo* (Pristina: Kosovo Foundation for Open Society, 2017).

[27] For an analysis of the process see Marko Milanovic and Michael Wood (eds), *The Law and Politics of the Kosovo Advisory Opinion* (Oxford: Oxford University Press, 2015).

[28] 'Accordance with international law of the unilateral declaration of independence in respect of Kosovo (Request for Advisory Opinion)', International Court of Justice, 22 July 2010.

[29] 'Serbia backs compromise U.N. resolution on Kosovo', *Reuters*, 9 September 2010.

[30] For more on this see, 'Serbia/Kosovo: The Brussels Agreements and Beyond', Workshop Report, SEESOX, St Antony's College, University of Oxford, March 2014.

border demarcation with Montenegro (which will be explored below). As a result of these difficulties, relations between the two sides began to sour. While it may have appeared as though Serbia was preparing to accept Kosovo's independence, its stance has hardened considerably in recent years. For example, Belgrade launched a strong effort to prevent Kosovo from being admitted to UNESCO.[31] It has also intensified its efforts to prevent it from being recognized. Since November 2017, according to information from the Serbian Ministry of Foreign Affairs, 10 countries have withdrawn their earlier recognition.[32] While Pristina has contested a number of these claims, the reality is that Kosovo's path to international recognition is blocked. In the face of this stalemate, and aware that Kosovo's prospects of joining the UN are blocked, some officials started to consider previously unthinkable ideas. The prospect of partitioning Kosovo by ceding the northern 10 per of the country to Serbia in return for Belgrade's acceptance of Kosovo statehood, an option that was once dismissed, is increasingly being spoken about again in various circles.[33] Such thinking has even gained adherents in Pristina.[34] Indeed, it was explicitly raised by the presidents of Kosovo and Serbia, Hashim Thaci and Aleksandar Vucic, in August 2018.[35] In this instance, the ceding of the north of Kosovo to Serbia would be matched by ceding parts of the Presevo Valley, a predominantly Albanian inhabited region of Southern Serbia, to Kosovo. However, while senior officials in the United States and the EU have signalled that they are open to the idea,[36] the suggestion has been condemned across the political spectrum in both Kosovo and Serbia. As a result, public discussion of the issue has subsided.

As things stand, the situation is deadlocked. It is clear that Serbia is not prepared to accept Kosovo's independence. However, Belgrade is also aware that the issue needs to be resolved at some point. Although five EU Member States still do not recognize Kosovo – Cyprus, Greece, Romania, Slovakia and Spain – and therefore recognition cannot be a formal EU-imposed condition for membership, the European Union has repeatedly reaffirmed that the normalization of relations is a requirement for Serbia to join. While the EU is unable to require that Serbia recognizes Kosovo as a condition of membership – due to the continued non-recognition of five of its members, and the fact that it has no independent recognition mechanism – German parliamentarians have frequently suggested that they will not ratify any Treaty of Accession with Serbia unless it has recognized Kosovo. Meanwhile, the battle over recognition continues. Although Pristina states that 114 UN members had recognized Kosovo by mid-2019, Belgrade insists that 15 of those countries had withdrawn their recognition and had

---

[31] 'Kosovo's UNESCO Membership Bid Fails', *Balkan Insight*, 9 November 2015.
[32] 'Confirmed: 10th country revokes recognition of Kosovo', B92, 7 November 2018. The countries are Burundi, Dominica, Grenada, Guinea-Bissau, Lesotho, Liberia, Papua New Guinea, Sao Tome and Principe, Suriname.
[33] This has been raised by a number of officials and long-standing regional observers the author spoke to in early 2018.
[34] Senior Kosovo officials, comments to the author, September 2018.
[35] 'Serbia and Kosovo May Be Ready to End Their Feud', *Bloomberg*, 28 August 2018.
[36] 'US open to Kosovo border changes, Trump adviser says', *Politico*, 24 August 2018; 'Mogherini defends Kosovo border change talks', *Politico*, 31 August 2018.

again accepted Serbian sovereignty over Kosovo.[37] Whatever the actual figure, Kosovo's hopes of joining the UN remain remote due to ongoing opposition from Russia and China. For its part, and given its experiences elsewhere in south-east Europe, the EU remains adamant that while it is committed to further enlargement in the Western Balkans, it has no intention of importing another territorial dispute into its ranks.[38] This will make it very difficult for Serbia to join the European Union without a settlement.[39]

V Kosovo and Montenegro

Kosovo's declaration of independence did not just lead to tensions with Serbia. It also raised territorial issues with two other neighbours and erstwhile partners within Yugoslavia: Montenegro and what is now North Macedonia. In the case of North Macedonia, a problem arose because the border between Serbia and Macedonia had been defined in 2001 in an agreement that had been reached between Belgrade and Skopje without the involvement of the self-governing authorities in Pristina. Following Kosovo's declaration of independence, in February 2008, a new agreement was needed between Pristina and Skopje. In this case, the issue of the 173-kilometre boundary between the two countries was settled relatively easily. The Macedonian government set an agreement on border demarcation as a condition for recognising Kosovo.[40] With help from the International Civilian Office (ICO), the international body overseeing Kosovo's transition to statehood, Pristina and Skopje managed to reach an agreement which was ratified by the two parliaments on 17 October 2009.[41] Overall it proved relatively uncontroversial. An attempt to challenge the demarcation by the Liberal Democratic Party (LDP), which had four seats in the parliament, was rejected by the Macedonian constitutional court on the grounds that the agreement was over the demarcation of the border and was not a change to the border as such.[42]

In contrast, the question of Kosovo's border with Montenegro became a far more complex, fractious and drawn-out issue. Montenegro recognized Kosovo on 9 October 2008, the same day as North Macedonia.[43] However, diplomatic relations were not established immediately. In part, this was because Podgorica wanted to see the

---

[37] These include Burundi, Central African Republic, Comoros, Dominica, Grenada, Lesotho, Madagascar, Palau, Papua New Guinea, Soloman Islands and Suriname. The most recent was Togo, which was announced in August 2019,

[38] 'A credible enlargement perspective for and enhanced EU engagement with the Western Balkans', Communication from the Commission to the European Parliament, the Council, the European Economic and Social Committee and the Committee of the Regions, Strasbourg, 6 February 2018, p 3.

[39] For more on EU attitudes towards the dispute, see Ioannis Armakolas and James Ker-Lindsay (eds), *Lack of Engagement: Surveying the Spectrum of EU Member State Policies towards Kosovo* (Basingstoke: Palgrave Macmillan, 2020).

[40] 'Macedonia & Kosovo Set For Border Talks', *Balkan Insight*, 24 March 2008.

[41] 'Macedonia and Kosovo break the ice in border dispute', *Deutsche Welle*, 18 October 2009.

[42] 'Macedonia-Kosovo Demarcation Legal', *Balkan Insight*, 24 December 2009.

[43] 'Montenegro, Macedonia defy Serbia, recognize independent Kosovo', *Associated Press*, 9 October 2008.

Montenegrin community in Kosovo formally recognized within the constitution. However, as had been the case with North Macedonia, the border needed to be demarcated. Although a boundary had been defined between Serbia and Montenegro within Yugoslavia, the Montenegrin authorities raised questions about the exact line of demarcation after Kosovo declared independence. As a result, the two countries established national state commissions to mark and maintain the border. Over the course of the next three years, the two bodies met for sixteen two-day sessions, alternating between Kosovo and Montenegro. By the summer of 2015, they had reached an agreement. This was signed by representatives of the two governments, in Vienna, on 26 August 2015.

The agreement was hailed by all parties, and by the European Union. In Podgorica, the deal was soon ratified by the Montenegrin Parliament. However, in Kosovo, the demarcation of the border became a major political issue. Opposition parties and nationalists argued that the agreement meant that Kosovo would lose 8,200 hectares of land. This was seen as an unacceptable infringement of its sovereignty.[44] In response, on 15 March 2016, the President of Kosovo established a commission to review the border delineation. Composed of three international experts, the Commission issued its report two weeks later. It concluded that, 'based on legal and technical criteria, the Kosovo Process of delineating the border with Montenegro clearly satisfied international standards'.[45] This sparked an angry response from the opposition. In an attempt to prevent the deal from being ratified by the parliament, *Vetevendosje* (Self-Determination), one of the main opposition parties, organized rallies in Pristina and even resorted to setting off tear gas cannisters in the Assembly chamber to prevent a vote.[46] It later opted to boycott parliament altogether. Kosovo now entered a period of deep political instability.

Soon afterwards, in May 2016, the European Commission issued its latest report on visa-free travel for the people of Kosovo. This was a major issue in Kosovo inasmuch as it was by now the only country of the Western Balkans not to have a visa-free regime in place. The report noted that while Kosovo had met all the requirements in the areas of readmission, integration, document security, migration management, asylum, law enforcement cooperation, judicial cooperation in criminal matters, data protection, and fundamental rights relating to freedom of movement, there were two areas where there were shortcomings. While Pristina had fulfilled fourteen of the fifteen requirements for preventing and combating organized crime, corruption and terrorism, it had not managed to fulfil sufficient elements of the key priority of building up a track record of investigations, final court rulings and confiscations in high-profile organized crime. Most importantly, while Kosovo had also met fourteen of the fifteen requirements in

[44] Fjona Krasniqi, 'The Kosovo-Montenegro border agreement: what you need to know', *Open Democracy*, 23 February 2017.
[45] 'Final Report of the Ad Hoc Commission for Reviewing the Border Delineation Process Between the Republic of Kosovo and the Republic of Montenegro', Pristina, Kosovo, 30 March 2016. Available at: http://president-ksgov.net/repository/docs/Final_Report.pdf.
[46] 'Kosovo Opposition Releases Tear Gas in Parliament', *New York Times*, 19 February 2016.

the area of border/boundary management, the one and only outstanding issue was the ratification of the border agreement with Montenegro.[47]

Despite the clear statement from the EU that a deal would have to be agreed before Kosovo could gain visa-free travel, the opposition parties, including *Vetevendosje*, which now returned to parliament, continued to oppose the deal.[48] This led to a further year of disruption as the dispute took centre-stage in Kosovo politics. On 10 May 2017, the Kosovo government fell, in part as a result of the strong opposition to the agreement.[49] Following a snap election, a new coalition government was formed between the Democratic Party of Kosovo (PDK), which supported the agreement, and Alliance for the Future of Kosovo (AAK), led by Ramush Haradinaj, who had previously been a strong opponent of the border demarcation agreement.[50] Assuming the post of prime minister, Haradinaj remained firmly against the demarcation agreement. However, he soon appeared to be easing his opposition. In November 2017, he hinted that the agreement could be sent to the Permanent Court of Arbitration for adjudication – although this was quickly rejected by Podgorica.[51] Meanwhile, the EU held firm to the demand that any move to ease travel between Kosovo and the EU remained dependent on Kosovo ratifying the border deal with Montenegro.

By the start of 2018, Haradinaj appeared to have accepted that a settlement needed to be reached. On 16 February 2018, the two governments announced that they had at last reached an agreement on the border and that the deal would now go before the Kosovo Assembly. According to the agreement, the border arrangement would be examined by experts and that any 'mistakes' could be corrected.[52] The announcement was hailed by the European Union. Federica Mogherini, the High Representative of the Union for Foreign Affairs and Security Policy, welcomed the agreement as evidence that even 'complicated' issues can be resolved.[53] Nevertheless, even at this late stage, *Vetevendosje* continued to disrupt efforts to cement the deal, again setting off tear gas in the parliament when the crucial vote was due to be held.[54] Despite this, in March 2018, the Kosovo Assembly finally passed the legislation demarcating the border by 80 votes to 11 with no abstentions (29 members did not vote). Again, the EU immediately welcomed the news.[55] For his part, Haradinaj called on the EU to abide by its part of the agreement: 'Kosovo now waits for the EU to do its part, as it was promised, so that

---

[47] 'Report from the Commission to the European Parliament and the Council: Fourth Report on Progress by Kosovo* in Fulfilling the Requirements of the Visa Liberalisation Roadmap', Brussels, 4 May 2016. Available at: https://ec.europa.eu/home-affairs/sites/homeaffairs/files/what-we-do/policies/european-agenda-migration/proposal-implementation-package/docs/20160504/fourth_progress_report_on_kosovo_visa_liberalisation_roadmap_en.pdf)

[48] 'Kosovo's Vetevendosje Renews Opposition to Montenegro Border Deal', *Balkan Insight*, 9 June 2016.

[49] 'Snap election to follow Kosovo government collapse after no-confidence vote', Deutsche Welle, 10 May 2017.

[50] 'Haradinaj: Demarcation with Montenegro cannot be negotiated', *Gazeta Express*, 29 January 2018.

[51] 'Montenegro Snubs Kosovo's Talk of Arbitration Over Border', *Balkan Insight*, 7 November 2017.

[52] 'Kosovo and Montenegro reach deal on 2015 border agreement', *Reuters*, 16 February 2018.

[53] 'Remarks by HR/VP Federica Mogherini at the joint press conference with Ekaterina Zaharieva, Minister of Foreign Affairs of Bulgaria' European External Action Service, 16 February 2018.

[54] 'Kosovo MPs let off tear gas in parliament over controversial border deal', *Euronews*, 21 March 2018.

[55] 'Joint statement on the ratification of the Border Demarcation Agreement between Kosovo and Montenegro', European External Action Service, Brussels, 21 March 2018.

finally Kosovo citizens can freely travel to the EU as other Europeans.'[56] Although the law was challenged by opposition parties, the following month the Kosovo constitutional court ruled that the agreement had been reached legally.[57]

VI Conclusion

As a federation, Yugoslavia had operated as single sovereign state. While administrative boundaries had been created to demarcate the six republics and the two autonomous provinces of the country, these meant little. People moved around freely. It was, as noted, a single economic, political, social and geographical space. The violent break-up of the country therefore had profound consequences and led to the emergence of a number of border issues in the Western Balkans. Some of these have been extremely serious. Others have appeared rather more frivolous. In truth, all are important inasmuch as they have served as obstacles to the European integration of the countries of the region. At a wider level, these disputes – especially those between Croatia and Slovenia and between Kosovo and Montenegro – have been notable inasmuch as they have highlighted the degree to which the question of borders truly divide the region, and how the need to resolve these territorial divisions in fact hinders the process of making such boundaries all but irrelevant. The question of the border between Serbia and Kosovo is obviously far more significant. In this instance, it is not a question of where the border should be, but whether it should exist at all. In reality, though, there seems to be little doubt that what we are seeing is a process which will eventually see Serbia accept that Kosovo is no longer part of its sovereign territory. The big question in this context is whether that final agreement will also include a process of border demarcation, or even a more significant process of border adjustment. Quite apart from the barrage of criticism the suggestion of some form of territorial settlement received from international observers,[58] it is hard to see how this could be achieved. If the relatively minor demarcation of the border between Kosovo and Montenegro elicited such a strong reaction, it is hard to see how Kosovo could accept what would be a substantial revision of its territory. There are also fears that it could stoke violence in the region. However, balanced against this, such a settlement could open the way for Kosovo to join the UN, and would thus end the opposition of the five EU non-recognizers, thereby easing its future EU accession path. In any case, the discussions over Kosovo and Serbia have served to highlight just how contentious the subject of borders remain in the Balkans. Despite claims that the issue of borders has been settled in the Western Balkans, this chapter has in fact shown that this is not strictly correct.

These cases raise several important questions. One obvious issue is the extent to which the border disputes can be seen to be a legacy of Yugoslavia or a legacy of the break-up of Yugoslavia. In truth, the answer is not clear cut. As is often the case in

---

[56] 'Kosovo parliament ratifies border deal with Montenegro after stormy session', *Reuters*, 22 March 2018.
[57] 'Kosovo Constitutional Court: OK to Montenegro border deal', *Associated Press*, 30 April 2018.
[58] 'US-backed Kosovo land-swap border plan under fire from all sides', *The Guardian*, 3 September 2018.

federal type systems, territory can be manipulated for political purposes at a time when the political ramifications of such actions are limited. Some of the decisions taken to apportion territory within Yugoslavia may have been made with little consideration of the effects they could have if the state eventually collapsed, as it did. Other decisions may have been made precisely in order to minimize or mitigate forces that could cause state collapse. Whatever the reason, the true impact of such decisions only became clear at the point when the country did indeed disintegrate. As was shown the principle of *uti possidetis*, a cornerstone of international law in the context of state creation, ensured that the republican and sub-state boundaries created under specific contexts many decades earlier became effectively set in stone. This in turn created tensions of their own. The newly emerging states of the former Yugoslavia necessarily, and some would argue inevitably, saw their new borders as potent symbols of the new found sovereignty. They were to be protected and defended at all costs. Even today, these boundaries remain potent symbols of statehood, to the point that even relatively minor changes become highly contentious. To this extent, the border problems that beset the Western Balkans today are a combination of decisions made in socialist Yugoslavia, which were then given significance by the structures and strictures of international law, and then made potent and non-negotiable symbols of sovereignty by the ethno-nationalism that fed a desire to protect these newly significant boundaries. In other words, the tensions over borders are the products of an array of forces that emerged during and after Yugoslavia.

What has been particularly significant in each of the examples examined here is the role of the EU. In each case, the European Union was a key actor, albeit with very different results. The most obvious success has been the border demarcation between Kosovo and Montenegro. In this instance, political opposition in Kosovo was overcome by a very strong stand by the European Union. Without a settlement, there would be no visa liberalization, which was widely seen as a significant step towards Kosovo's further European integration. This proved to be a major incentive. As described above, eventually, in March 2018, the Kosovo Assembly passed the necessary legislation. It can therefore be regarded as a success story for the EU. At the other end of the scale, the ongoing dispute between Slovenia and Croatia has been a failure. While Ljubljana's decision to allow Croatia to accede without reaching a settlement was a reflection of European values, and so can be seen as a success of sorts, Zagreb's decision to ignore the ruling of the International Court of Arbitration reflects a disdain for the fundamental EU principle of the respect for international law and legal institutions. Looking ahead, it is unclear how the issue will be resolved. There is a very real possibility that the matter will eventually end up before the European Court of Justice as part of a procedure brought under Article 25 of the Lisbon Treaty.

Between these two cases lies Kosovo and Serbia. This has been a far trickier situation. Unlike the other two cases, which effectively amount to relatively minor boundary disputes, this has revolved around the creation of an entirely new state. In this case, the EU's leverage was hindered by the discord within its own ranks. While the vast majority of the Member Staes recognized Kosovo, five chose not to do so. This meant that it could not take a strong stand one way or another. Nevertheless, while it has been unable to definitively resolve the issue, it has been able to create a process of dialogue between

Belgrade and Pristina. This has seen the two engage with one another in a meaningful and open way, even if the tangible benefits of this engagement have been rather less than many would have hoped. In this case, the ultimate test will be whether it is able to persuade the two sides to reach a full and final agreement, whatever that may be. As things stand, the demand is for the full normalization of relations between Belgrade and Pristina prior to Serbia's accession to the European Union. In reality, most believe that Serbia will have little choice but to recognize Kosovo formally if it wants to achieve full membership. Quite apart from the possible demands to do so from individual members, such as Germany, the EU as a whole is extremely unlikely to want to take the risk of letting Serbia join, only for Belgrade to then use its veto to block Kosovo from joining. Not only that, once Serbia joins, it would also be in a position to affect the EU's other contractual interactions with Kosovo in a variety of ways.

The way in which the European Union acted in these different cases also highlights the range of ways in which it can shape conflict resolution processes. In particular, there is a clear difference between the passive and the active role in can bring to bear in situations. In the passive context, it is the much-vaunted power of attraction that acts on the parties. By virtue of their wish to pursue integration, and where the resolution of a conflict is a clear requirement for such integration, parties can engage in settlement processes. This can either be done directly between the two sides, as happened between Kosovo and Montenegro. Alternatively, this can facilitate the good offices – either by mediation or arbitration – of another external actor, as happened in the case of Slovenia and Croatia. In these cases, the EU, as an institutional actor, is usually reactive. It does not shape the formal process of dispute resolution, as such. However, the EU can also act as a formal mediator. Again, the lure of membership serves to support this process, but the EU serves as the mediating actor. This has been seen most clearly in the case of Kosovo and Serbia, where the European External Action Service has overseen the dialogue between Belgrade and Pristina. The role of the EU therefore needs to be understood according to these two 'active' and 'passive' variations.

Looking ahead, the problem of border disputes is unlikely to be limited to the three cases examined in this chapter. Further issues could well arise. In some cases, these will be fairly minor, but still have the potentially to be very disruptive. Most notably, there is the question of the demarcation of the border between Serbia and Croatia. Caused by a change in the course of the River Danube, the two countries have vowed to resolve it.[59] However, the issue could yet complicate Belgrade's hopes of joining the EU, even if the thorny issue of Kosovo has been resolved. As the countries of the former Yugoslavia move from a political existence where borders meant very little to a situation where such borders will again cease to have significance, the temporary re-imposition of hard borders is proving the be a major source of tension. And, as a final comment, as one looks at the map of the region with its various border complications, one is also looking at a map of former Yugoslavia, where such issues could lie dormant.

[59] 'Croatia, Serbia Vow to Solve Long-Standing Border Dispute', *Bloomberg*, 12 February 2018.

References

Armakolas, Ioannis and James Ker-Lindsay, (eds) *The Politics of Recognition and Engagement: EU Member State Relations with Kosovo* (London: Palgrave Macmillan, 2020)

Avbelj, Matej and Jernej Letnar Černič. 'The Conundrum of the Bay of Piran: Slovenia v. Croatia: The Case of Maritime Delimitation' (2007) 5(2) *The University of Pennsylvania Journal of International Law and Policy*, pp. 1–19.

Baker, Catherine. *The Yugoslav Wars of the 1990s* (Basingstoke: Palgrave Macmillan, 2015)

Caplan, Richard. *Europe and the Recognition of New States in Yugoslavia* (Cambridge: Cambridge University Press, 2005).

Fabry, Mikulas. *Recognizing States: International Society and the Establishment of New States Since 1776* (Oxford: Oxford University Press, 2009).

Ferrero-Turrión, Ruth. 'Spain', in Ioannis Armakolas and James Ker-Lindsay (eds), *The Politics of Recognition and Engagement*, pp 215–36

Ker-Lindsay, James, and Mikulas Fabry. *Secession and State Creation: What Everyone Needs to Know* (New York: Oxford University Press, 2019).

Ker-Lindsay, James. *EU Accession and UN Peacemaking in Cyprus* (Basingstoke: Palgrave Macmillan, 2005).

Ker-Lindsay, James. *Kosovo: The Path to Contested Statehood in the Balkans* (London: IBTauris, 2009).

Klemenčić, Mladen and Anton Gosar. 'The Problems of the Italo-Croato-Slovene Border Delimitation in the Northern Adriatic' (2000) 52 *GeoJournal*, pp. 129–37.

Milanovic, Marko and Michael Wood, (eds) *The Law and Politics of the Kosovo Advisory Opinion* (Oxford: Oxford University Press, 2015).

Pellet, Alain. 'The Opinions of the Badinter Arbitration Committee: A Second Breath for the Self-Determination of Peoples' (1992) 3(1) *European Journal of International Law*, p. 178.

Pomerance, Michla. 'The Badinter Commission: Then Use and Misuse of the International Court of Justice's Jurisprudence' (1998) 20(1) *Michigan Journal of International Law* 31.

Radan, Peter. 'The Badinter Arbitration Commission and the Partition of Yugoslavia' (1997) 27(3) *Nationalities Papers*, pp. 527–57.

Terrett, Steve. *The Dissolution of Yugoslavia and the Badinter Arbitration Commission: A Contextual Study of Peace-making Efforts in the Post-Cold War World* (Aldershot: Ashgate, 2000).

Weller, Marc. *Contested Statehood: Kosovo's Struggle for Independence* (Oxford: Oxford University Press, 2009).

6

Parallel Trajectories and Legacies of the Past: Russia and Turkey in the Western Balkans

Othon Anastasakis
St Antony's College, University of Oxford

I Introduction

As the European Union has been struggling to define a sustainable strategy in the post-Yugoslav space, it has to compete with two increasingly assertive countries from the East, Russia and Turkey, both of whom have developed strong political, economic, security and cultural links with the Western Balkan states. Both these regional powers are former Empires, Eurasian in nature, with a historical presence and a traditional influence in the region, based largely on identity politics and cultural affinities. Indeed, Russia's solidarity with the Slav and Christian Orthodox communities in the region, on the one hand, and Turkey's brotherhood with the Muslim populations, on the other, have been repeatedly invoked to explain why, on occasions, these two external actors have had such a big impact on domestic developments in the region. The following chapter discusses Russian and Turkish interests in the region and argues that, beyond their cultural and religious affinities with the people in the region, their considerations are largely determined by geopolitical factors and a balance of power with the West.[1]

The chapter looks at recent developments through the prism of a longer-term historical perspective and focuses on both the relevant structures and actors that affected past and present. It, thus, traces and compares the impact of Russian and Turkish engagements in the region from the Yugoslav times to the present, in order to pinpoint continuities and discontinuities in the way these two big countries approach this geopolitically sensitive area. It looks at the respective relationships in the context of a timeframe which includes references to the Cold War years, to the post-1989 transition and disintegration of Yugoslavia, and to the subsequent creation of new states in the post-Yugoslav space; and at how these two external actors have been engaging with, or disengaging from, the region. It argues that both states, following a long period of cautious policy towards Yugoslavia, then went through a period of

---

[1] This chapter defines 'the West' as 'Western bloc' during the Cold War and as the 'transatlantic alliance' between the EU and the US after the end of the Cold War.

multilateralism during the 1990s, before asserting their presence vis-à-vis the post-Yugoslav states. At present, both post-Soviet Russia and post-Kemalist Turkey approach the Western Balkan countries as low cost, accessible allies (potential or actual), as a means of showing their strength and ability to compete with the West. They have done this by building bridges with 'client' states' and 'client' communities, arising from the disintegration of Yugoslavia. Against what many authors and politicians in Turkey or Russia argue as the 'rightful presence' of these two countries, based on historical legacies and cultural solidarity,[2] this chapter suggests the tactical and opportunistic nature of these relationships, which are not sustained by a longer-term vision. While the Yugoslav experience for both external actors was a period of geopolitical distance, which had to do with the Cold War balance of power and Yugoslavia's neutrality, the disintegration of Yugoslavia provided both with strategic opportunities for historical revisionism and re-engagement with the local economies, politics, societies: as well as for meddling with inter-ethnic conflictual relations in the successor states. The breakdown of the country brought back the lost legacies of the past pre-Yugoslav Empires, with the Muslim Yugoslav populations rediscovering their affinities and memories with Turkey as descendants of the Ottoman Empire and the Christian Orthodox Serb populations with the Russian, pre-Soviet Empire in an often nostalgic way (the Catholic Slovenes and Croats emphasized their closeness with Central Europe and Germany accordingly). This they did by building strategic alliances, through economic, social and cultural links which started during and because of the wars in Yugoslavia and continued at an increasing pace until the present times. The Yugoslav legacies of distant relations with Turkey and frozen, often inimical, relations with Soviet Russia were downplayed and eradicated from the respective memories, the latter revisited, redefined and instrumentalized to suit the strategic interests of the in-fighting ethnic communities in post-1989 Yugoslavia.

II The Age of the Empires

The Balkans was historically a special geographical space for Russia and Turkey in the context of their own Czarist and Ottoman imperial influences. For centuries, the two competed as Empires over the control of Balkan lands, the Black Sea and the Bosporus Straits, and also for influence along ethnic and religious lines.

Without being a direct ruler, Czarist Russia found ways of intervening in Balkan political, economic and cultural internal affairs. In particular, the narratives of Pan-Slavism and Orthodox unity were both influential and durable across parts of the region, and created allegiances between elites and the peoples.[3] The Pan-Slavist ideology in the form of protection of Slavic populations gained prominence in the

---

[2] Roy Medvedev,'Brothers in the Balkans' *The Guardian* 28 April 1999; Address by Ahmet Davutoglu at the opening ceremony of the conference 'Ottoman legacy and Balkan Muslim Communities today' in Sarajevo (Friday, 16 October 2009).

[3] Barbara Jelavich, *Russia's Balkan Entanglements, 1806–1914* (Cambridge: Cambridge University Press, 1991) p 35.

second part of the nineteenth century. It created frictions between the Russians and the Ottomans and culminated in the Russian-Turkish war of 1877, when Russia came to the support of Serbia and Bulgaria. Naturally, such ties were not due purely to cultural and religious solidarity, but had other motives in the realm of high politics, including Russia's strategic interest in asserting its imperial presence in the disintegrating Ottoman Empire. Within this power game, economic interests were instrumental given Russia's long-term readiness, and indeed eagerness, to dominate the Black Sea and to have free commercial traffic through the Straits, the only route to the Mediterranean; and in that respect the Balkans were potentially useful allies in undermining Ottoman power. In the run up to the Great War when the Balkans became a central stage of great power rivalry, Russia competed with the Central Powers and sought allies in the region with Serbia a prominent ally.[4]

The Ottoman Empire, for its part, had a long-term historical presence in the region, as a direct ruler, in some parts from the fourteenth until the early twentieth century. In this multi-ethnic, multi-religious and multi-lingual environment, Ottoman rule, which exhibited some forms of religious and ethnic tolerance, ruled the Empire under the 'millet system'.[5] The rise of nationalism and the emergence of independent states affected a large number of Muslims, with many of them having to abandon the Balkans and resettle in the Anatolian lands. While a relationship between the Ottoman centre and the remaining Muslim (Turkish) people of the Balkan lands continued during the era of republican Turkey, amid an official policy of 'non-interference', such special links were rediscovered during the post-Yugoslav times and Muslim solidarity became a powerful narrative in Turkey's foreign policy in the Balkans. This narrative legitimized Turkey's links with the diverse and dispersed Muslim communities in the Balkans, most of whom were descendants of the Ottoman Balkan Muslims. Between 1878 and 1913, around 1.5 million Muslim refugees resettled in Istanbul and Anatolia, most of them victims of wartime violence and displacement.[6]

At the beginning of the twentieth century, both the Russian and the Ottoman Empires were suffering major blows to their internal stability and sustainability, and they eventually collapsed largely as a result of their massive failures during the First World War.[7] The inter-war story is one of detachment from the Balkans, focusing on the building of a communist Soviet Union and a Republican secular Turkey, respectively. At the same time, the First World War planted the seeds of a complex and distrustful relationship with the West. In the case of the Soviet Union it was deeply ideological and military in nature. In the case of Turkey, and despite its subsequent Western orientation, the so-called 'Sèvres syndrome' became a powerful narrative

---

[4] Christopher Clark, *The Sleepwalkers: How Europe Went to War in 1914*. (Penguin, 2012).
[5] In the heterogeneous Ottoman Empire, a millet was an autonomous self-governing religious community, each organized under its own laws and headed by a religious leader who was responsible to the central government for the fulfilment of millet responsibilities and duties particularly those of paying taxes and maintaining internal security.
[6] Kerem Oktem 'Between Emigration, De-Islamisation and the Nation-state: Muslim Communities in the Balkans Today' (2011) 11(2) *Southeast European and Black Sea Studies* 155–71.
[7] Othon Anastasakis, David Madden, Elizabeth Roberts (eds), *Balkan Legacies of the Great War: The Past is Never Dead* (Palgrave Macmillan, 2015).

affecting how Turks perceived Europe thereafter. According to this popular belief, the West was conspiring to weaken and carve up Turkey just as it had planned to do in the Treaty of Sèvres.[8]

III Cold War geopolitics

The Soviet Union and the fear of the 'Yugoslav spillover'

During the inter-war period, relations between the Soviet Union and the region were largely non-existent, and the kingdom of Yugoslavia, ruled by the Serbian Karadjordjevic dynasty, was seen by the West as part of the Eastern European buffer against both Germany and the Soviet Union. The Soviet Union appreciated the strategic importance of Yugoslavia in the context of the Second World War and the fight against the Nazis.[9] Marshall Josip Broz Tito, the communist leader of the Yugoslav Partisans, one of the most effective resistance movements of occupied Europe, fought on the side of the World War II 'big four' Allied powers including the USSR. After the war, the Soviet Union viewed all the Balkan states as potential ideological satellites in the fight against the West and, later on, NATO. The superpower's ideological influence in the Balkans varied across countries and time, with the states in the region developing different degrees of allegiance to the Soviet Union. While Yugoslavia was the first country after the war to adopt a Soviet-style economic model,[10] it was also the first to break with the Soviet camp and follow a more independent path towards its own brand of communism in the fields of self-management and foreign policy, becoming one of the leaders of the Non-Aligned Movement from the 1950s onwards (see Lubica Spaskovska's chapter in this volume). The initial period of ideological and political convergence between Yugoslavia and the Soviet Union was short lived and was subsequently marked mostly by tensions and some failed attempts at rapprochement.

Yugoslav independence from Soviet control and Tito's break with Stalin were made evident with the expulsion of Yugoslavia from the Cominform in 1948.[11] Tito's aim was to distance his country from the ideological grip of the Soviet Union and extract as many concessions as possible in the economic and security fields from the West,

[8] The Treaty of Sèvres signed in 1920 marked the partitioning of the Ottoman Empire between the Kurds, Armenia, Greece, France, Italy and Britain leaving a small area around Ankara under Turkish rule. While this was never implemented, due to Turkish military victories during the Turkish Wars of Independence, the hostile narrative and the defensive perceptions vis à vis the West remained.

[9] James Headley, *Russia and the Balkans: Foreign Policy from Yeltsin to Putin*, (London: Hurst & Company, 2008) p. 19.

[10] The Royal Institute of International Affairs, 'Yugoslavia's Five-year Plan: The Economic Background of the Cominform Split' (1948) 4(8) *The World Today* 331–36.

[11] In 1948 Tito challenged the right of the Communist Party of the Soviet Union (CPSU) to interfere in Yugoslavia's internal affairs demanding the removal of Soviet military and economic 'advisers' who were forcing Yugoslavia to follow the Soviet path of communism. For further reading see Ivo Banac *With Stalin against Tito, Cominformist Splits in Yugoslav Communism*, (Cornell University Press, 1988)

without being part of this either. The 1953 Balkan Pact was both a notable example of Yugoslavia's need for a more independent security framework vis-à-vis the Soviet Union, and a short-lived attempt of a security cooperation among ideological foes (Yugoslavia, on the one hand, NATO members Greece and Turkey, on the other).[12]

Following Stalin's death in 1953, the next Soviet leader Nikita Khrushchev, faced with the durability and legitimacy of the Yugoslav leader,[13] attempted to mend relations with Yugoslavia by signing a bilateral agreement guaranteeing non-interference in Yugoslavia's internal affairs and allowing for socialist states the right to interpret Marxism in a different way (the 1955 'Belgrade declaration'). This was a short-lived rapprochement which ended with the Soviet intervention in Hungary in 1956, when Yugoslavia was criticized in a Soviet campaign for having an influence on the Hungarian insurrection. With the reversion of Romania to national communism in the early 1960s, and Albania's resistance to post-Stalinist Soviet influence, there was a growing Soviet fear that the three Balkan states might form a 'Southern Alliance', which would be supported by China, and challenge Soviet supremacy in the region (Bulgaria remained the most loyal Soviet satellite).

The 1968 Soviet invasion of Czechoslovakia let to another crisis in relations, with Yugoslavia being yet again criticized for inspiring disunity in the eastern bloc.[14] During the early 1970s, Moscow tried to benefit from Yugoslavia's internal republican and ethnic divisions[15] – there was even speculation that Soviet intervention was imminent in Yugoslavia – and sought gradually to increase its influence in the Mediterranean and reduce Yugoslavia's ongoing policy influence. Yugoslavia responded by mobilising the Non-Aligned Movement in its favour, built closer relations with Beijing, thawed relations with Tirana, discussed defence plans with Bucharest and sought support from the US Nixon administration.

Through the Cold War years, the Yugoslav foreign policy machinery worked well to offset Soviet advances, and, in many ways, Marshall Tito managed to use the Soviet threat effectively to keep his country together. Having said that, it did work to his favour that both the US and the USSR had chosen not to stir the waters over Yugoslavia and instead to respect it as a European neutral ground. The Soviet leadership recognized the limits to its ability to alter the nature of the Yugoslav regime. This does not mean that the Soviet elites did not try to destabilize the system from within, by means of

---

[12] Greece and Turkey joined NATO in 1952. See Odd Arne Westad, 'The Balkans: A Cold War Mystery' in S Rajak, K Botsiou, E Karamouzi and E Chatzivassiliou (eds) *The Balkans in the Cold War,* (Palgrave Macmillan, 2017), pp 355–62

[13] 'New Evidence from the Former Yugoslav Archives introduced by Svetozar Rajak' (2001) 12/13 *Cold War International History Bulletin.* Available at: www.wilsoncenter.org/sites/default/files/CWIHPBulletin12-13_p5_0.pdf.

[14] Mirolad Lazic, 'The intervention that never happened' (Wilson Centre, 4 December 2017). Available at: www.wilsoncenter.org/blog-post/the-soviet-intervention-never-happened.

[15] In 1971 the Yugoslav authorities suppressed the Croatian spring, a cultural and political movement which called for reforms in SFR Yugoslavia and more rights for the Republic of Croatia within Yugoslavia

conspiracies.[16] It was only during the gradual de-ideologization of Soviet foreign policy and the changing discourses vis-à-vis Europe under Gorbachev,[17] who visited Belgrade in 1988, that relations between Yugoslavia and Soviet Union were normalized but by that time, Yugoslavia was disintegrating politically and economically (see Adam Bennett's chapter in this volume).

Throughout the Cold War years, the level of economic relations between the Soviet Union and Yugoslavia remained low and most of Yugoslavia's trade was with Western Europe. Similarly, cultural and identity similarities played no part in the relationship and were nowhere to be found in Soviet policy considerations in relations to the Balkans. Regarding Serbia in particular, a country which has been traditionally perceived as a natural ally of Russian interests, throughout most of the period between 1917 and 1990 relations remained rather poor.[18] A general attitude of distrust and antagonism governed Soviet-Yugoslav bilateral relations during the course of the Cold War period, with, in particular, a fear by the Soviets that the Yugoslav paradigm would be emulated by other communist countries in Eastern Europe.

Kemalist Turkey and the principle of 'non-interference'

Since the birth of the Turkish Republic in 1923, the Kemalist dogma of 'non-interference in the affairs of the former provinces of the Ottoman Empire' was fully applied in the Balkans.[19] After its own war of independence, Turkey sought to integrate the influx of Muslim refugees within the territory of Anatolia and the borders of the new independent state, and to focus on the development of a new national Turkish identity at the expense of the past imperial Ottoman legacy. In 1934, Turkey signed a non-aggression Balkan Entente with Greece, Romania and Yugoslavia, aiming at sustaining the post-Second World War geopolitical status quo. The pact helped to ensure peace between Turkey and its former Ottoman territories in the Balkans, but failed to keep the countries on the same side at the start of the Second World War.[20]

During the Cold War, Turkish foreign policy was confined within the contours of superpower bipolarity and the capitalist-communist ideological divide. Being a firm part of the NATO alliance, Turkey kept a safe distance from the Balkans which were

[16] The arrests inside Yugoslavia in 1975–1976 of a number of so-called Stalinists for trying to form an underground organization was one example of the Soviet attempt at creating underground cells to destabilise the League of Communists of Yugoslavia (LCY) leadership and an expression of Soviet frustrations at being incapable of effecting change otherwise. See Mark Cichock 'The Soviet Union and Yugoslavia in the 1980s: A Relationship in Flux' (1980) 105(1) *Political Science Quarterly* 53–74. Available at: www.jstor.org/stable/pdf/2151225.pdf?refreqid=excelsior%3A549e7b9fc626efa89efbbcd1a959617e.

[17] Samokhalov Vsevolod, 'Writing Russianness, Greatness, Europe and the Balkans in the late Soviet Discourse in the 1980s' in *Russian-European Relations in the Balkans and the Black Sea region*, (Palgrave Macmillan, 2017), pp 81–125.

[18] Dimitar Bechev, 'Russia in the Balkans-Conference report' LSEE & SEESOX, (LSE, 13 March 2015) p 13. Available at: www.lse.ac.uk/LSEE-Research-on-South-Eastern-Europe/Assets/Documents/Events/Conferences-Symposia-Programmes-and-Agendas/2015-Report-Russia-in-the-Balkans-merged-document.pdf.

[19] Sylvie Gangloff, *The Impact of the Ottoman Legacy in the Balkans (1991–1999)*, (CERI, 2005), p 17.

[20] William Hale, *Turkish Foreign Policy 1774–2000*, (Franck Cass: London 2000) p. 63 and Esra S Degerli 'Balkan Pact and Turkey' (2009) 2(6) *The Journal of International Social Research* 136–47.

seen as the 'ideological other', with a view to the security threat from the neighbouring Soviet Union. Turkey enjoyed better relations with Yugoslavia than with all the other Balkan states. The 1953 Balkan Pact and the 1954 Treaty of Alliance between Turkey, Greece and Yugoslavia was a defensive arrangement by three countries which felt threatened by the Soviet Union at the time.[21] In the following years, however, the meetings foreseen in the Treaty failed to take place and the alliance became a dead letter due to the deterioration of Greek-Turkish relations and the short-lived rapprochement between Yugoslavia and the Soviet Union in 1955.

Unlike in other countries where religious beliefs, including Islam, were undermined and suppressed by the communist regimes, Yugoslavia' religious policy was rather tolerant towards Islam, with the exception of instances of Muslim nationalism.[22] Having said that, when opportunity arose for Muslims to leave, or when the levels of suppression got high, Turkey would become the prime destination for many Yugoslav Muslims. Between 1953 and 1961 a large emigration of the Turkish nationality from Yugoslavia took place – around 80,000 according to Yugoslav data and over 150,000 according to Turkish sources.[23] Many of these emigrants did not speak Turkish but were Muslim Albanians, who fearing for their positions in Yugoslavia, claimed that they were Turks to obtain the possibility to emigrate. This 'voluntary' migratory wave was based on a Migration Treaty signed at the time between Tito and Menderes.[24]

For the greater part of the Cold War years, Turkey's main interest in the Balkans revolved around the well-being of the Turkish people living there and the migratory movements towards Turkey.[25] The orientation of the Turkish republic, without interfering in the domestic affairs of the neighbouring states, focused on the security of the Turkish populations in South East Europe, as part and parcel of its nationalist secular project at home; this gave Turkey the right to protect the Turks abroad, at times when they perceived that they were threatened by the local authorities.

IV The period of US hegemony

1990s Russian multilateralism

During the Cold War years, Yugoslavia was feared by the Soviets for the spillover effect that its alternative model could have on other East European states. Following the

[21] Baskin Oran (ed) *Turkish Foreign Policy 1919-2006: Facts and Analyses with Documents* (The University of Utah Press, 2011), p 352

[22] Pedro Ramet, 'The Dynamics of Yugoslavia Religious Policy' (1986) 6(6) *Occasional Papers on Religion in Eastern Europe* 9-10.

[23] Vladimir Ortakovski, 'Interethnic Relations and Minorities in the Republic of Macedonia' (2001) 2(1) *South East European Politics* 24-45.

[24] Similarly, in Bulgaria, in 1950-51, around 150,000 Turks were forced to migrate to Turkey, and again in 1989, more than 300,000 were forced to escape due to Zhivkov's assimilationist policies. Kerem Oktem, *New Islamic Actors after the Wahhabi Intermezzo: Turkey's Return to the Muslim Balkans*, European Studies Centre, Oxford, December 2010.

[25] One source puts the number of immigrants moving from the Balkans to Turkey between 1923 and 1995 at 1,643,058. Esra Bulut, 'Friends, Balkans, Statesmen Lend us Your Ears. The Trans-state and State in Links between Turkey and the Balkans' (2006) 5(3) *Ethnopolitics* 309-26.

collapse of communism, Yugoslavia continued to haunt Russian policy making, this time for the possible spillover that the breakdown of the country could have for the post-Soviet space. During the 1990s, the violent disintegration of Yugoslavia became the dominant story of ethnic strife and ethnic cleansing in Europe and the world. With the Soviet Union's parallel break-up and Russia at the epicentre of change, the fear was that a similar violent disintegration could happen on Russian territory, with Russian populations, remaining outside the borders of the new Russian Federation, creating similarly inflammable majority-minority situations like the Yugoslav ones.[26]

With the collapse of communism, the post-1989 era signalled the victory for the single superpower, and the hegemony of the United States was undoubted and uncontested, so much so that many rushed to predict the end of history and the triumph of liberal democracy.[27] In this nascent unipolar world,[28] the Yugoslav quagmire stood out as the most violent European conflct since the Second World War. It drew the United States and Europe into a series of military and diplomatic moves to solve the conflicts[29] and split Russia over what kind of position to adopt. Russian elites were divided between those who advocated that their country should act as a unilateral great power and those with a more cooperative approach in the new environment of increasing American hegemony. Russia's initial position claimed that these conflicts were Yugoslav internal matters and consequently should be settled peacefully, without use of force, with the help of UN or the OSCE as mediators. Along with Western states, it recognized the independence of the new post-Yugoslav states. When the wars intensified, Russia cooperated with the international peacekeeping and crisis management missions. Russian forces joined the NATO-led Implementation Force (IFOR) and the subsequent Stabilization Force (SFOR) for Bosnia-Herzegovina in 1996. There was also broader cooperation between NATO and Russia in the context of a Permanent Joint Council following the NATO-Russia Founding Act of May 1997. The two sides agreed to consult on a wide range of security issues, including peacekeeping, international terrorism, military strategy, and nuclear doctrine.[30]

This policy of multilateralism and cooperation with the West was perceived as a sign of weakness and decline by the Russian nationalists, who claimed that Russia had an obligation to support the unity of the Yugoslav state with its central authority in Belgrade. When the conflicts broke out, they formed their parallel external operational networks and took to supporting the Serbs and Bosnian Serbs and the idea of the creation of a Greater Serbia. Russian 'volunteers' fought with Serbs in Croatia, Bosnia and Kosovo during the wars of the 1990s. This joint experience and the Russian nationalist support for Serbs laid the foundations for the development of a closer relationship between Russia and Serbia, following a long period of Cold War

---

[26] See James Headley, pp 61–62.
[27] Francis Fukuyama *The End of History and the Last Man* (Penguin 1992).
[28] Charles Krauthammer, 'The Unipolar Moment' (1990/91) 70(1) *Foreign Affairs America and the World 1990* 23–33.
[29] Josip Glaurdic, *The Hour of Europe: Western Powers and the Breakup of Yugoslavia* (Yale University Press 2011)
[30] Mike Bowker, 'The Wars in Yugoslavia: Russia and the International Community' (1998) 50(7) *Europe-Asia Studies* 1245–261.

competition and even animosity under Marshall Tito. It brought back historical myths of solidarity between the Russians and the Serbs, gradually leading to a closer cooperation under Vladimir Putin, sealed by a common approach on the issue of Kosovo.

Turkey and Muslim solidarity

Following a long period of uneventful Cold War bilateral relations, Turkish elites, already from the 1980s, were trying to find ways to connect more constructively with Yugoslavia and develop commercial and trade relations, consistent with the emergence of a new business mentality in Turkey under Turgut Ozal.[31] However, it was the disintegration of the Soviet Union and the new post-communist dynamics in Eastern Europe which created the opportunities and the pressures for a more diverse Turkish foreign policy in which the Balkans gained a prominent position. At the beginning, just like Russia, Turkey supported the unity of Yugoslavia; but when the wars broke out, Turkey became entangled in the violent conflicts in its near abroad where Muslim populations were under threat. More emphatically, it was the ethnic war in Bosnia which sensitized the elites and the public in Turkey and even strengthened the influence of Islamic culture in the once secular Turkish domestic political discourse. Elites and public opinion in Turkey embraced a wider notion of the Muslim Balkan identity and came to the support of all the Muslim – not just the Turkish – people in the wars in Bosnia and Kosovo. This created a hostility towards Serbs who were regarded as the aggressors and perpetrators of crimes against humanity in war torn Yugoslavia. As in the parallel case of Russia, Turkish elites were divided between the traditional Kemalist multilateralists and the more assertive unilateralists.[32] Among the latter, the Islamists and ultra-nationalists evoked historical brotherhood with the total of four million Turks of Bosnian origin living in Turkey, seeing that the Turks in Bosnia, one of the oldest ethnic minorities, and other Muslim populations, were deemed to be under severe threat.

During the war in Bosnia, Turkey, a key destination for Bosniak refugees, was extremely critical of the West's inability to take effective measures to protect the Muslims and assigned itself a more active role in the region. Throughout the conflict, it exerted pressure on the West to intervene militarily to save the endangered Bosniak communities; it mediated diplomatically to bring together the Bosniaks and Croats who were fighting against each other;[33] and, apart from its participation in military operations in Bosnia, it assumed a major role in training the Bosnian-Croat Federation post-war army. Turkey's role was also prominent as the representative of the Islamic countries within the Steering Board of the Peace Implementation Council in Bosnia and Herzegovina. At the same time, media reports revealed clandestine military

---

[31] Philip Robins, *Suits and Uniforms: Turkish Foreign Policy since the Cold War*, (London: Hurst, 2003)
[32] Ibid, p. 364.
[33] As a broker between the Bosniaks and Croats in November 1993 Turkey contributed to the American-led Washington Agreement and participated in the monitoring of the ceasefire in Zenica.

The Legacy of Yugoslavia

support for the Muslims in Bosnia, supplying arms to Bosnia during the embargo and being involved in secret arm deals during the wars.[34]

During the Kosovo crisis, Turkish public opinion again pushed the government to take an active stance to stop Serb aggression. With Kosovo, however, considerations were more complex: on the one hand, Turkey was radically opposed to the brutality of the Milosevic regime against fellow Muslim Albanians in Kosovo and supported strongly a NATO action in Kosovo; on the other hand, it was more cautious towards Kosovo secession from Serbia which could be regarded as a precedent for Turkey's Kurds. Turkey had been at the beginning restrained regarding the creation of an independent Kosovo and had focused its attention on the protection of the rights of Kosovo Albanians within Serbia, rather than outright independence.[35]

V Global multipolarity

Russia's energy hegemony

The unipolar US hegemonic moment proved to be brief and the post-2000 international environment was marked by the rise of competing actors on the global landscape. With the end of the Kosovo military campaign and the downfall of the Milosevic regime, the US withdrew itself from the region, with the EU taking a central role in the post-conflict reconstruction and development. The post-2000 period of the Western Balkans' Europeanization has seen the strengthening of the EU as the single hegemonic actor through the adoption of a holistic strategy for enlargement and a regional commitment of the EU accession.

The 1999 NATO military campaign in Kosovo and the bombing of Serbia was a turning point in Russia's approach towards the liberal interventionist international order. It was claimed to be an illegal attack on a sovereign state in a way that the military intervention in Bosnia was not. With Chechen separatism in mind, Russia objected vehemently to the secession of Kosovo and became Serbia's closest supporter against the latter's independence. At the same time, in accordance with the West, it endorsed the UN Security Council Resolution 1244[36] (which ended the war in Kosovo and kept it within Serbia but with an international administration) and subsequently the 2001 Ohrid agreement (which ended the conflict in the Former Yugoslav Republic of Macedonia). But these were the last vestiges of Russia's multilateralism which with the advent of Putin in the leadership changed the Western-Russian relationship to what some have termed as a 'new Cold War'.[37]

Under Putin's rule, Russia sought to diversify its relationship with the Western Balkan states cultivating economic and political links with some of the most prominent

---

[34] Didem Ekinci, *Turkey and the Balkans in the post-Cold War era: Diplomatic* PhD dissertation (Bilkent University April 2009. Available at: https://core.ac.uk/download/pdf/52925878.pdf.

[35] Sylvie Gangloff, p 6.

[36] The brief confrontation between Russian and NATO forces over the Pristina Airport in June 1999, when the former occupied the airport ahead of the latter was resolved peacefully, yet illustrated both Russian unhappiness with what was taking place, and their inability to command the situation.

[37] Edward Lucas, *Putin's threat to Russia and the West*, (Bloomsbury Publishing 2014).

local elites. At the centre of the new strategy lay energy whereby Russia consolidated its position as a major Eurasian energy provider, through its state-owned gas monopoly company, *Gazprom*, and strategic control of foreign direct investment. The pinnacle of energy influence was the so-called *South Stream* project, Russia's major regional project, setting up South East Europe as the alternative to the Ukraine energy route to Europe. Through energy, Russia developed its own distinct hegemonic brand, extending the dependency of most Balkan states on Russian gas, promising to transform these countries into transit routes for oil and gas towards Europe and creating a friction with the West. Numerous contacts and basic agreements on the construction of the *South Stream* gas pipeline were signed with countries forming potential routes through Serbia and Hungary, Bulgaria and Greece, or Austria and Slovenia. Russia's energy diplomacy advocated the inclusion of as many states as possible into the gas pipeline project bypassing Ukraine.[38]

Beyond the regional energy tactics, Russia cultivated bilateral links with individual states of the region. Serbia was central in Russia's Balkan plans: on the one hand, Russian companies became majority stakeholders in Serbia's former state-owned oil companies; on the other hand, Russia rediscovered its past Soviet model of intrusion into Serbia's party politics, causing divisions between pro-European and pro-Russian political forces. The parties with a pro-Russian orientation included prominent parties such as the Radical Party of Tomislav Nikolic,[39] the Democratic Party of Serbia of Vojislav Kostunica and the Socialist party of Serbia, descendant of the Communist party and founded in 1990 by Slobodan Milosevic.

Moscow's influence became very visible in Montenegro, with substantial investment in the extractive sector, tourism and property. The acquisition of real estate was so impressive that public opinion and press often talked about the *selling off* of Montenegrin land to Russian investors.[40] In addition, Russia built exceptionally close relations with Republika Srpska by cultivating links with Bosnian Serb leader Milorad Dodik, investing in the country's oil refineries and including RS in the prospective pipeline projects. As a rule, Russia tried to build close relations with the countries with an Orthodox Christian Slavic majority in the Western Balkans as allies in its increasingly difficult relationship with the West. At the pinnacle of all this, Russia vetoed repeatedly Kosovo's ambitions to join the UN after it declared independence in 2008, thus becoming Serbia's major ally in the fight against Kosovo's recognition.

Turkey's neo-Ottomanism

Towards the end of the 1990s, allusions to the Ottoman legacy in the Balkans appeared more frequently in Turkish official discourses, and even politicians from the Kemalist

[38] See Dimitar Bechev, *Rival Power: Russian in South East Europe*, (Yale University Press 2017) for a brilliant analysis on the subject
[39] In 2012, Nikolic after being elected president and in a state visit to Russia declared that he loved only Serbia more than Russia.
[40] According to unofficial estimates, between 2005 and 2010, Russian nationals bought about 100,000 real estate properties in Montenegro.

establishment such as Bulent Ecevit, Suleyman Demirel and Ismail Cem made references to the historical Ottoman presence in the region.[41] The most emphatic neo-Ottoman claims came from the emerging and rising political class of the Justice and Development Party (AKP). One of the most flamboyant AKP ideologues and prominent politicians, Ahmet Davutoglu, openly espoused an Ottoman nostalgia, as a past Empire which promoted multi-ethnic tolerance, linkages between cities, and cultural interactions. In one of his most famous neo-Ottoman speeches in Sarajevo, Davutoglu claimed that:

> During the Ottoman state, the Balkan region became the centre of world politics in the 16th century . . . the golden age of the Balkans. . . The Ottoman centuries of the Balkans were success stories. Now we have to reinvent this.[42]

Turkey's period of assertive Balkan policy was based on Davutoglu's thesis of 'strategic depth',[43] and 'zero problems with neighbours'[44] and adopted diplomacy at three levels: (a) political diplomacy, through mediation and good neighbourly services; (b) grass roots diplomacy, through cultural policies and civil society links and a growing 'soft' Islamic presence; and (c) economic diplomacy, through trade and direct investment.

Turkish foreign policy improved bilateral relations with all the Western Balkan states, including Serbia, and assumed a very active role in mediating between the competing ethnic communities in Bosnia, in particular. As such it established trilateral consultation mechanisms between Turkey, Bosnia and Croatia, and Turkey, Bosnia and Serbia, and assumed the role of mediator in the region. It strengthened relations with the once hostile Serbia, and increased its influence on the Sandžak region by opposing demands of local activists for autonomy from Serbia and by opening an influential Cultural Centre in its capital Novi Pazar.[45]

The neo-Ottoman Turkish cultural presence in the Western Balkans became very noticeable in the restoration of mosques, in the expansion of the schools and universities of the Gülen network, and in the granting of scholarships and inviting scholars from the Western Balkans to Universities in Turkey.[46] The space was broad given the substantial number of Muslims in the Balkan countries: in Kosovo 90 per cent of the population, Albania around 60 per cent and Bosnia close to 50 per cent. Turkey's cultural engagement in the Western Balkans was welcomed by most Muslim communities, and was tolerated by the governments who did not object to a discreet assertion of Turkish influence among the Muslim minorities, seeing Turkey's brand of

[41] Sylvie Gangloff, p 17.
[42] Extracts from Speech by Ahmet Davutoglu.
[43] Ahmet Davutoglu, *Strategic depth: Turkey's International Position* (book in Turkish) and Alexander Murinson 'The Strategic Depth Doctrine of Turkish Foreign Policy' in (2006) 42(6) *Middle Eastern Studies* 945–64.
[44] Republic of Turkey, Ministry of Foreign Affairs, 'Policy of Zero Problems with Neighbours'. Available at: www.mfa.gov.tr/policy-of-zero-problems-with-our-neighbors.en.mfa.
[45] Sanja Kljajic, 'Sandzak: The Balkans Region where Turkey is the Big Brother' *Deutsche Welle*, 21 October 2016. Available at: www.dw.com/en/sandzak-the-balkans-region-where-turkey-is-the-big-brother/a-36115582.
[46] Kerem Oktem, *New Islamic Actors after the Wahhabi Intermezzo*.

Islam as more responsible, moderate and European, than most other oriental Islamic tendencies emanating from the Middle East.[47] The Turkish Cooperation and Coordination Agency (TIKA) was active in areas populated by Muslims in the Western Balkans, focusing on restoration and rebuilding of monuments of Ottoman and historical cultural significance, with a particular focus on Bosnia.[48] Turkey managed to make its benevolent presence felt in Bosnia from the bigger cultural projects to smaller everyday issues that mattered to people.[49]

Since the early 2000s, Turkey's foreign trade with the Balkan countries showed a noteworthy revival. A growing Turkish economy facilitated an advanced economic diplomacy in the region. Despite a series of earlier economic setbacks and the major financial 2001 crisis in Turkey, the country managed to recuperate quickly and record an average growth of 7% in GDP, between 2002–09. Turkey benefitted from this economic upswing and increased its investment in the Western Balkans in the context of a more dynamic economic diplomacy abroad. But whereas other regional investors, like Austria or Greece, had invested heavily in the banking sector, Turkey's economic presence came from big construction projects and old-fashioned import-export trade.[50] Turkey forged a more systematic approach towards the Balkans within the framework of the 'Strategy for Developing Trade with the Neighbouring and Peripheral Countries'.[51] Dozens of private and state-owned Turkish companies went to Bosnia, where Turkey by 2010 had become the fourth-largest investor behind Austria, Slovenia, and Germany.[52] Turkish investment in FYR Macedonia rose after the mid-2000s with important contracts in the two main airports – Skopje and Ohrid.[53] In Kosovo, Turkish companies were competing for key stakes in the privatization of two of Pristina's largest public companies: Kosovo Energy Corporation, and Post and Telecommunications of Kosovo, and there were further investments in the country's airport and highway infrastructure. Finally, Turkey became one of the biggest investors in Albania with strategic holdings in telecommunications and finance industries, public engineering contracts and higher education.

While most emphasis was laid on Muslim populated countries, the Serbian case stands out as an example of a pragmatic turn in foreign policy towards a country which was regarded by Turks as a main instigator and culprit of discrimination and war against Balkan Muslims, and a traditional ally of rival Greece. The animosity towards Serbia had reached a high point in 1999, when Turkish airplanes took an active part in

---

[47] Marcus Tanner 'Ottoman Past Haunts Turkey's Balkan Image' *Balkan Insight*, 2 December 2010. Available at: www.balkaninsight.com/en/article/ottoman-past-haunts-turkey-s-balkan-image.

[48] Alida Vrasic 'Turkey's Role in the Western Balkans', *SWP Research Paper*, (Berlin 2016).

[49] One characteristic example of Turkish activism at the societal level was in 2012 when a big snow storm hit Sarajevo and the city was literally snowed in for days. The Turkish battalion within EUFOR were by far the most visible and actually got out and helped to clear the roads.

[50] Neil MacDonald, 'Turkey's business in the Balkans', *Financial Times online*, April 26, 2011

[51] 'Turkey's trade with the Balkans', Turkish Radio Television website. Available at: www.trtdari.com/trtworld/en/newsDetail.aspx?HaberKodu=0c042a26-8141-4035-bc21-04b45f67f8ab.

[52] Aleksandra Stankovic, 'Turkey's Balkan shopping spree' in *Balkan Insight,* 7 December 2010. Available at: www.balkaninsight.com/en/article/turkey-s-balkan-shopping-spree.

[53] See Darko Duridanski, 'Macedonia-Turkey: The ties that bind', *Insight Balkans*, 10 February 2011. Available at: www.balkaninsight.com/en/article/macedonia-turkey-the-ties-that-bind.

NATO bombing of rump-Yugoslavia. Diplomatic relations were severed when Turkey became one of the first countries to recognize Kosovo's unilateral declaration of independence in February 2008. Despite the deep historical, religious and ideological differences, the two decided to embark on a process of rapprochement, and in October 2009, President Abdullah Gul visited Belgrade, the first such visit by a Turkish President since 1986. This resulted in the signing of a number of bilateral agreements on infrastructure, transport and social security. Meanwhile, Turkish diplomats became active in mediating between Serbs and Bosniaks and it was largely thanks to Turkey's mediation that the Bosniak leaders agreed with the Serbian Parliament's text which recognized for the first time since the Yugoslav wars Serbian culpability for the massacres of Muslims in Srebrenica, yet without using the term 'genocide'. This reflected Turkey's own refusal to use the term 'genocide' for the Armenian massacres during the last years of the Ottoman Empire. In July 2010 Prime Minister Recep Tayyip Erdogan, despite his vociferous criticism of the Srebrenica massacres, visited Belgrade and signed further agreements on visa, infrastructural projects and industrial plants.

Crises, illiberalism and competition with the West

The foreign policy of a country becomes more powerful and influential when there is a strong and stable government at home; but, more importantly, when there is room for regional leadership and limited competition from other powerful rivals.[54] Russian and Turkish dynamic engagement in the Balkans was sustained not only by the two regional powers' rising influential positions, stronger economies, skilful cultural diplomacy and historical familiarity, but also by an emerging environment of geopolitical competing interests, and a weakening influence from the European Union during the years of the Eurozone crisis. The dawn of the twenty-first century witnessed an intense phase of EU engagement in the region, through the stabilization and association process, the Stability Pact for South Eastern Europe and the EU's commitment set out by the 2003 Thessaloniki summit on the European perspective of the Balkans. Paradoxically, the 2007 accession of Bulgaria and Romania in the EU, a move which was designed originally to give a boost to the integration of the more difficult Balkan states, had the opposite effect. The accession of the two former communist countries, part and parcel of the wider Eastern European enlargement, led to so-called enlargement fatigue and the EU's reluctance to accept more members. The countries of the EU felt that the two Balkan states had been ill-prepared to join the European Union, in terms of reforms and economic readiness and decided to postpone any further enlargement. The 2013 EU accession of Croatia, which took place at a time of severe economic crises for both the EU and Croatia, was not the outcome of a revived enthusiasm for the process, but a sense of unfinished business in the case of a small country which was formally ticking all the boxes of the accession process. As for all the other prospective Western Balkan Member States, the EU's Stabilization and Association Process was

---

[54] Ziya Onis, 'Multiple Faces of the "New" Turkish Foreign Policy: Underlying Dynamics and a Critique' (2011) 13(1) *Insight Turkey* 47–65.

tainted by inconsistencies, problems and delays, reflecting both the EU's unwillingness to commit and the region's unwillingness to change and reform. The growing gap between the EU and the Western Balkans, at a time of crises in geopolitics, economics and migration, was a good opportunity for Russia and Turkey to increase their influence in the region and consolidate their presence even further. The new phase of more open competition between Russia and Turkey and the West was accompanied and aggravated by growing illiberalism at home under the strong and unchallenged leaderships of Putin and Erdogan, respectively, and the increasing geopolitical insecurities in their immediate neighbourhoods. Russia and Turkey intensified and diversified their own bilateral rapprochement, based largely on some commonly agreed goals in the Middle East and a common anti-Western rhetoric.

Russia's friction with the West was further exacerbated by the 2014 Ukraine crisis and NATO's competing presence in the eastern neighbourhood. Its policy towards the Western Balkans was largely guided by considerations in its own neighbourhood: in Ukraine and the occupation of Crimea. From a Western perspective, Russia was pursuing a disruptive influence in the Western Balkans, by infiltrating in the fields of security, party politics and cyber space. From then on, Russia was repeatedly accused by the West of obstructing Montenegro's NATO membership, hindering the normalization agreement between Serbia and Kosovo, fighting against the resolution of the Macedonian name dispute, developing close relations with pro-Russian elites in most Western Balkan states and stirring anti-Western feelings in the region through influential media and social media presence. Following the period of increasing economic and energy activity in the Western Balkans, Russia, affected by its own economic crisis due to EU sanctions, falling gas prices and the unstable rouble, reduced the volume of Western Balkan exports to Russia, diminished the inflow of Russian investment and put a sudden, unexpected stop to the South Stream project in December 2014. This last development in particular seems to have resulted from tensions flowing from the annexation of Crimea.

For the majority of Western scholars and policy makers, competition in the Western Balkans is a typical reflection of a 'new Cold War-like' environment between Russia and the West, with the former pursuing its disruptive policies further afield to gain points at home, and in its own immediate post-Soviet neighbourhood. From its part, Russia sees an imminent NATO threat to its western neighbourhood. It also sees the Western Balkan states, which are still not in the EU or NATO, as the soft underbelly of Europe where it can exert some influence. The region is for Russia a fitting arena for confrontation with the West, being the most vulnerable part of Europe; Russia seeks to exploit by tactical manoeuvring and manipulation any regional security uncertainties, economic dependencies and democratic backsliding, as well as the rise of nationalism and Euroscepticism, enlargement fatigue and Europe's declining normative leverage.[55]

It is an undisputable fact that Russia was deeply annoyed by Montenegro's decision to join NATO, and was at odds with Prime Minister Milo Djukanović's ruling party for taking such a course of action. What made it even more irritating was that Montenegro

---

[55] Othon Anastasakis, 'Russia, South East Europe and the "Geopolitics of Opportunism"'. Available at: https://spectator.clingendael.org/pub/2017/4/russias-involvement/

joined EU sanctions against Russia and supported the UN General Assembly resolution on Crimea. The Montenegrin allegations that, on the 16 October 2016 election day, they prevented a Kremlin-based coup aided by pro-Russian Serbs, is indicative of a climate of suspicion and animosity between two former friends.[56] Similarly, in FYR Macedonia, the June 2018 agreement with Greece to end the name dispute, and change the name of the country to 'The Republic of North Macedonia' leading to the accession of the latter to NATO and the start of accession talks with the EU, prompted Russia to interfere against a solution, through negative publicity in social media and financial support for demonstrations against the deal in both countries, a move which soured relations between the two traditional allies, Greece and Russia.[57] At the same time, relations with Serbia continued to intensify seemingly making Serbia 'Russia's Trojan horse' in the eyes of the West, the two enjoying growing relations at the political and military levels, including the sale of military equipment by Russia to Serbia and the conduct of joint military activities.[58]

Turning to Turkey, the slowing down of the country's accession talks with the EU, the centralization of power into the hands of one man, Erdogan, serving as Prime Minster between 2003 and 2014 and then moving to the Presidency, and the rise of illiberalism at home, led to the deterioration of relations with the West. From the mid-2010s, the country was faced with its own external and internal instabilities as a result of the failed Arab Spring, the collapse of the Kurdish peace process, the (then)successes of Syrian Kurds in that country's civil war and the growing numbers of refugees from Syria, causing a major blow to the previous neo-Ottoman confidence, the 'zero problem with neighbours' policy and the cultural activism which had been a joint project with the Gülen movement.[59] The failed July 2016 coup to topple Erdogan prompted an extensive purge of the once dominant Gülenists, largely seen as the instigators, which spread not just inside Turkey with zealous intensity but also beyond Turkey's borders in the Balkans and beyond.

While Turkey continued its policy of engagement with the Western Balkans, Erdogan, became personally fixated with the 'de-Gülenization' of Turkey's economic and cultural influence in the region. One after the other, the Western Balkan states faced increasing pressure from Turkey to eliminate any Gülenist presence and to close down all Gülenist educational institutions in Albania, Bosnia and Kosovo,[60] which became a condition for more cooperation and economic agreements.[61] In addition,

---

[56] Reuf Bajrovic, Vesko Gardevic and Richard Kraemer, '"Hanging by a thread" Russia's strategy of destabilisation in Montenegro' *Russia Foreign Policy Papers,* Foreign Policy Research Institute July 2018. Available at: www.fpri.org/wp-content/uploads/2018/07/kraemer-rfp5.pdf.

[57] Kurt Volker 'Don't let Russia get its way in Macedonia' *Foreign Policy,* 28 September 2018. Available at: https://foreignpolicy.com/2018/09/28/dont-let-russia-get-its-way-in-macedonia/.

[58] For an alternative view see Vuk Vuksanovic 'Serbs are not "Little Russians"' in *American Interest* 26 July 2018. Available at: www.the-american-interest.com/2018/07/26/serbs-are-not-little-russians/.

[59] See Ezgi Basaran's book *Frontline Turkey: The Conflict at the Heart of the Middle East* (IB Tauris, 2017).

[60] In March 2018, the Turkish Intelligence Agency brought six suspended Gulenists from Kosovo to Turkey – apparently without the knowledge of Kosovo's prime minister, a deportation which was seen as 'kidnapping' from Turkey with the help of the Kosovo authorities.

[61] Zia Weise 'Turkey's Balkan Comeback' *Politico* 17 May 2018. Available at: www.politico.eu/article/turkey-western-balkans-comeback-european-union-recep-tayyip-erdogan/.

Turkey threatened to create political and social disruption in the region and many EU Member States, through its control of the Syrian tides of refugees through the Aegean and the Western Balkan route. The 2016 EU-Turkey refugee agreement became the cornerstone of a controversial relationship between Turkey and the EU, the latter becoming increasingly critical of Turkey's rising illiberalism but also increasingly dependent on the latter keeping the Syrian and other refugees from coming to Europe.

VI Concluding comparative remarks: Defining the influence of the two external actors

The uniqueness of the Western Balkan region in European and international politics is evident and runs through history: from the 'Third Way' Yugoslavia, to the decline and violent disintegration of the country and the creation of new states, the former Yugoslav space has always been at the centre of superpower geopolitics and security concerns. In Yugoslavia, both Russia, as the central actor within the post-Tsarist Soviet Union, and Turkey, as a post-Ottoman Western-orientated secular state, saw the limits of their external influence during the Cold War years; the imperial legacies of past interferences in the Yugoslav territory ceased to exist and marked a radical break with the pre-Second World War past. Belgrade kept competitive relations with Moscow, and relations between Serbs and Russians were ruptured, re-defined in the context of their respective Yugoslav and Soviet identities. Turkey for its part, broke radically with the Ottoman past through the adoption of the official policy of non-interference in the affairs of its post-Ottoman neighbours. Following the end of the Cold War bipolarity and the disintegration of Yugoslavia to its pre-Yugoslav components, the two external actors supported competing nationalities and ethnic groups during the 1990s and eventually exerted a more assertive presence within the post-2000 multipolar global environment. The influence of both of them varied through time with parallel trajectories before, during and after the death of Yugoslavia. At present, the leaderships of both Eurasian powers are operating in the Western Balkans as a means to show their regional external influence and to appeal to their domestic audiences at home.[62] Both sides rediscovered long-lost imperial memories and re-engaged with the pre-Second World War past, building cultural, social and economic links. As has become clear from the previous narrative, the two states have devised their own priorities in the region, and have chosen their respective allies in their pursuit of their foreign policy interests. Having discussed these parallel trajectories, this chapter concludes that there are some interesting similarities regarding the nature of the influence of these two regional actors in the post-Yugoslav Western Balkan area and the levels of continuity or rupture with the distant and the more recent past. In both cases these former empires are

---

[62] Othon Anastasakis, 'Regional Players in the Western Balkans: The Influence of Russia and Turkey' in *Mapping the Western Balkans and the State of Democracies in Transition: A Social Democratic Perspective*, PES & European Forum for Democracy and Solidarity (Amsterdam, July 2017), pp 36–39. Available at: www.foundationmaxvanderstoel.nl/uploads/publicaties/mappingbalkans_def.pdf

'striking back' following a rupture with the more recent Yugoslav past and a continuity with the more distant pre-Yugoslav one. Below are some final remarks which define the nature of the present external influences, in the shadow of the past.

The region as wider neighbourhood of low-cost engagement

Both countries treated the Yugoslav and post-Yugoslav space as part of a wider neighbourhood, not of direct immediate concern and, hence, not as a priority zone in their foreign policy design. Both states focus their attention on their immediate neighbouring areas, Russia in the post-Soviet space (the Commonwealth of Independent States) and Turkey in its vicinity in the Eastern Mediterranean and the Middle East. The former is dynamically involved in Ukraine, Belarus, Moldova, and is worried about the Western military presence in the Baltic states, Poland and Romania. While the Western Balkan region is further afield, the fact that some countries are still outside the NATO fold allows Russia to promote its anti-NATO, anti-Western rhetoric and strategy. Turkey is deeply concerned with its own turbulent neighbourhood in the Middle East, its competition with Greece in the Aegean, and Cyprus in the Eastern Mediterranean. While the Western Balkans pose no security concern, for Turkey it is a region where it can be seen to be offering its mediating services and keep friendly relations. In the economic field, while trade and economic relations have been increasing during the last two decades, the volume is less important compared to that of the EU in the region. While Russian investors have become visible in Serbia and Montenegro, Russia is far behind Italy, Austria and Germany in terms of volume and economic presence. Similarly, for Turkey, despite the increase in the investment flows and trade, the country is far from an economic heavyweight when compared with other European states and most of its investments concentrate on some key infrastructural and cultural sectors. However, by keeping a low-cost maintenance economic presence in the region, they achieve the visibility that they require as influential regional players.

Opportunistic vs normative influence

To better understand the relationship between the Western Balkan countries and their external environment, the region can be envisaged as lying at the centre of different concentric and overlapping circles which denote varying degrees of influence and levels of engagement. Undoubtedly, the most influential circle belongs to the European influence, which is comprehensive, tied to a gradual process of internal change, Europeanization and normative influence. In this chapter we have been dealing with two former empires, part of an outer circle of engagement which overlaps and competes with the inner circle of Europe, two regional powers with an increasing presence but offering no credible alternative to Europe's overwhelming influence. The two states have a tactical interest in the region and they choose selective areas of engagement where they have strategic advantages; they perform more effectively when the West is weaker or less interested in the region. Their influence increased with the downsizing of the Western influence, be it a reduced US interest, the EU's enlargement fatigue or the crisis of the Eurozone.

The region as 'mirror image' and 'lessons learned'

For the Soviet Union and its Russian descendant, the Yugoslav experience was always a mirror image to their domestic politics and a threat to the unity and sustainability of the system. During the Cold War years, the Soviet Union saw Yugoslavia as an ideological alternative which had the potential to contaminate its satellite states in Eastern Europe and elsewhere in the world. The disintegration of Yugoslavia, and the violent wars which accompanied this, were an important global lesson which was particularly relevant to the disintegrating former Soviet space, as well as to Turkey's own secessionist fears about the Kurds. Turkey's 'Yugoslav other' was however more visible in relations to the Turks living in Yugoslavia, and, later, the Muslim populations living in the Western Balkan states, and as such the country felt the responsibility to protect when their deteriorating well being had a direct bearing on Turkey's domestic politics.

A volatile and divisive influence

The influence of these two external actors has never been consistent or continuous but always contingent upon their own internal and external developments. During the communist times, it was based on exclusively security concerns, when both tried to create unsuccessful security alliances with Yugoslavia. Already from the 1980s, both countries attempted to normalize and diversify their relations with Yugoslavia. With the disintegration of Yugoslavia, the two countries tried to build relations with the new states using different means and a more variable approach. Having said that, there is no overall consistency in the nature of the engagement which is rather tactical and varies according to circumstances. For both states their influence oscillates from security, to energy, to economy, culture or politics, with varying degrees of spatial intensity and temporal success. Because of the volatile nature of the influence, the outcome is often uncertain and ambiguous. To begin with, their respective cultural influences cater to certain groups and end up alienating others; their connections with political elites are also divisive given the primary orientation of all the Western Balkan states to integrate with the European Union; finally, their illiberal influence, while appealing to some individual leaders, are in sharp contrast to the Western models which they have espoused, at least in principle, and is antagonistic to the liberal democratic model evident in the EU.

The Titoist legacy

Despite the volatility and divisiveness of these external influences, the Western Balkan states have chosen to be practical and transactional in their engagement with Russia and Turkey; this is because they also see benefits from such opportunistic interaction, be it for their local economies, or for their negotiating power vis-à-vis the West. For Serbia, Russia's solidarity over Kosovo independence has clear benefit in the non-recognition by the UN Security Council and enhances the identity solidarity with the Orthodox Christian brothers from Russia. Yet Serbia, at the same time, chooses to cooperate with Turkey in a number of fields, despite the historical enmity and the competition over the Muslims of Kosovo and Bosnia.

This chapter, in response to the themes of this book, deals with the notions of continuity and rupture with the past from the imperial to the Yugoslav and to the post-Yugoslav context, by pointing to how legacies and memories can be manipulated to serve strategic and geopolitical interests. Having said that, it could be argued that despite the post-Yugoslav rupture with the recent Yugoslav past, the way of conducting foreign policy by all Western Balkan states has a Yugoslav reference to it. The Titoist tradition of balancing East and West, North and South is being played by all political actors in the Western Balkans from Serbia, to Bosnia, North Macedonia, Montenegro, even Croatia and Slovenia which are full members of the EU. Tito's non-aligned mentality allowed him to sustain relations with opposing camps and to create an international movement of neutrality vis-à-vis the geopolitical bipolarity. This is one notable continuity with the Yugoslav times, a legacy which all the elites in the region have retained in their foreign policy affairs: a post-Yugoslav 'neo-Titoist' strategy, aspiring to join the EU, yet keeping options open with other regional and global powers in an increasingly multipolar world.

References

Anastasakis, Othon. 'Russia, South East Europe and the "Geopolitics of Opportunism"' in *Balkans Clingendael Spectator 4* (2017) Vol 71. Available at: https://spectator.clingendael.org/pub/2017/4/russias-involvement/.

Anastasakis, Othon, David Madden, Elizabeth Roberts. (eds), *Balkan Legacies of the Great War: The Past is Never Dead* (Palgrave Macmillan, 2015).

Anastasakis, Othon. 'Regional Players in the Western Balkans: The Influence of Russia and Turkey' in *Mapping the Western Balkans and the State of Democracies in Transition: A Social Democratic Perspective*, PES & European Forum for Democracy and Solidarity (Amsterdam, July 2017), pp 36–39. Available at www.foundationmaxvanderstoel.nl/uploads/publicaties/mappingbalkans_def.pdf.

Bajrovic, Reuf, Vesko Gardevic and Richard Kraemer. 'Hanging by a Thread' Russia's strategy of destabilisation in Montenegro' *Russia Foreign Policy Papers,* Foreign Policy Research Institute July 2018. Available at: www.fpri.org/wp-content/uploads/2018/07/kraemer-rfp5.pdf.

Banac, Ivo. *With Stalin against Tito, Cominformist splits in Yugoslav Communism* (Cornell University Press, 1988).

Basaran, Ezgi. *Frontline Turkey: The Conflict at the Heart of the Middle East* (IB Tauris, 2017).

Bechev, Dimitar. 'Russia in the Balkans-Conference report' LSEE & SEESOX, (LSE, 13 March 2015). Available at: www.lse.ac.uk/LSEE-Research-on-South-Eastern-Europe/Assets/Documents/Events/Conferences-Symposia-Programmes-and-Agendas/2015-Report-Russia-in-the-Balkans-merged-document.pdf

Bechev, Dimitar. *Rival Power: Russian in South East Europe* (Yale University Press, 2017).

Bowker, Mike. 'The Wars in Yugoslavia: Russia and the International Community' (1998) 50(7) *Europe-Asia Studies*, pp. 1245–261.

Bulut, Esra. 'Friends, Balkans, Statesmen Lend us your Ears. The Trans-state and State in Links between Turkey and the Balkans' (2006) 5(3) *Ethnopolitics*, pp. 309–26.

Cichock, Mark. 'The Soviet Union and Yugoslavia in the 1980s: A Relationship in Flux' (1980) 105(1) *Political Science Quarterly*, pp. 53–74.

Clark, Christopher. *The Sleepwalkers: How Europe Went to War in 1914*. (Penguin, 2012).

Davutoglu, Ahmet. *Strategic Depth: Turkey's International Position* (book in Turkish) and Alexander Murinson 'The strategic depth doctrine of Turkish foreign policy' (2006) 42(6) *Middle Eastern Studies*, pp. 945–64.

Degerli, Esra S. 'Balkan Pact and Turkey' (2009) 2(6) *The Journal of International Social Research*, pp. 136–47.

Duridanski, Darko. 'Macedonia-Turkey: The ties that bind', *Insight Balkans*, 10 February 2011. Available at: www.balkaninsight.com/en/article/macedonia-turkey-the-ties-that-bind.

Ekinci, Didem. *Turkey and the Balkans in the post-Cold War era: Diplomatic* PhD dissertation (Bilkent University April 2009). Available at: https://core.ac.uk/download/pdf/52925878.pdf.

Fukuyama, Francis. *The End of History and the Last Man* (Penguin 1992).

Gangloff, Sylvie. *The Impact of the Ottoman legacy in the Balkans (1991–1999)* (CERI, 2005).

Glaurdic, Josip. *The Hour of Europe: Western Powers and the Breakup of Yugoslavia* (Yale University Press 2011).

Hale, William. *Turkish Foreign Policy 1774–2000* (London: Franck Cass 2000).

Headley, James. *Russia and the Balkans: Foreign Policy from Yeltsin to Putin*, (London: Hurst & Company, 2008).

Jelavich, Barbara. *Russia's Balkan Entanglements, 1806–1914* (Cambridge: Cambridge University Press, 1991).

Kljajic, Sanja. 'Sandzak: The Balkans Region where Turkey is the Big Brother' *Deutsche Welle*, 21 October 2016. Available at: www.dw.com/en/sandzak-the-balkans-region-where-turkey-is-the-big-brother/a-36115582.

Krauthammer, Charles. 'The Unipolar Moment' (1990) 70(1) *Foreign Affairs America and the World*, pp. 23–33.

Lazic, Mirolad. 'The intervention that never happened' (Wilson Centre, 4 December 2017). Available at: www.wilsoncenter.org/blog-post/the-soviet-intervention-never-happened.

Lucas, Edward. *Putin's Threat to Russia and the West*, (Bloomsbury Publishing 2014).

MacDonald, Neil. 'Turkey's business in the Balkans', *Financial Times online*, 26 April 2011.

Medvedev, Roy. 'Brothers in the Balkans', *The Guardian* 28 April 1999; Address by Ahmet Davutoglu at the opening ceremony of the conference 'Ottoman legacy and Balkan Muslim Communities today' in Sarajevo (16 October 2009).

'New Evidence from the Former Yugoslav Archives' introduced by Svetozar Rajak, (2001) 12/13 *Cold War International History Bulletin* (Wilson Centre, 2001). Available at: www.wilsoncenter.org/sites/default/files/CWIHPBulletin12-13p50.pdf.

Oktem, Kerem. *New Islamic Actors after the Wahhabi Intermezzo: Turkey's return to the Muslim Balkans*, European Studies Centre, Oxford, December 2010.

Oktem, Kerem. 'Between Emigration, De-Islamisation and the Nation-state: Muslim Communities in the Balkans Today' (2011) 11(2) *Southeast European and Black Sea Studies*, pp. 155–71.

Onis, Ziya. 'Multiple Faces of the 'New' Turkish Foreign Policy: Underlying Dynamics and a Critique' (2011) 3 *Insight Turkey*, pp. 47–65.

Oran, Baskin, (ed) *Turkish Foreign Policy 1919–2006: Facts and Analyses with Documents* (The University of Utah Press, 2011).

Ortakovski, Vladimir. 'Interethnic Relations and Minorities in the Republic of Macedonia' (2011) 2(1) *South East European Politics*, pp. 24–45.

Ramet, S. Petra. 'The Dynamics of Yugoslavia Religious Policy' (1986) 6(2) *Occasional Papers on Religion in Eastern Europe*.

Robins, Philip. *Suits and Uniforms: Turkish Foreign Policy since the Cold War*, (London: Hurst, 2003)

Royal Institute of International Affairs. 'Yugoslavia's Five-year Plan: The Economic Background of the Cominform split' (1948) 4 *The World Today*, pp. 331–36.

Stankovic, Aleksandra. 'Turkey's Balkan shopping spree' *Balkan Insight,* 7 December 2010. Available at: www.balkaninsight.com/en/article/turkey-s-balkan-shopping-spree.

Tanner, Marcus. 'Ottoman past haunts Turkey's Balkan image' *Balkan Insight*, 2 December 2010. Available at: www.balkaninsight.com/en/article/ottoman-past-haunts-turkey-s-balkan-image

'Turkey's trade with the Balkans', Turkish Radio Television website. Available at: www.trtdari.com/trtworld/en/newsDetail.aspx?HaberKodu=0c042a26-8141-4035-bc21-04b45f67f8ab.

Volker, Kurt. 'Don't let Russia get its way in Macedonia' *Foreign Policy*, 28 September 2018. Available at: https://foreignpolicy.com/2018/09/28/dont-let-russia-get-its-way-in-macedonia/

Vrasic, Alida. 'Turkey's Role in the Western Balkans', *SWP Research Paper*, (Berlin 2016)

Vsevolod, Samokhalov. 'Writing Russianness, Greatness, Europe and the Balkans in the late Soviet discourse in the 1980s' in *Russian-European Relations in the Balkans and the Black Sea Region*, (Palgrave Macmillan, 2017), pp. 81–125.

Vuksanovic, Vuk. 'Serbs are not 'Little Russians'' in *American Interest* 26 July 2018. Available at: www.the-american-interest.com/2018/07/26/serbs-are-not-little-russians/

Weise, Zia. 'Turkey's Balkan comeback' *Politico* 17 May 2018. Available at: www.politico.eu/article/turkey-western-balkans-comeback-european-union-recep-tayyip-erdogan/.

Westad, Odd Arne. 'The Balkans: A Cold War Mystery' in S Rajak, K Botsiou, E Karamouzi and E Chatzivassiliou (eds) *The Balkans in the Cold War* (Palgrave Macmillan, 2017), pp. 355–62.

Part Three

Economics

7

Macroeconomic Stability and Enterprise Self-Management in Yugoslavia: An Impossible Marriage

Adam Bennett
University of Oxford

I Introduction[1]

The political factors, and especially the ethnic tensions, that led to the dissolution of Yugoslavia in the early 1990s have been extensively analysed both in academic literature and in the media more generally.[2] Rather less has been written about the role that economics, and those political economy features peculiar to Yugoslavia, may have played in this process.[3] This chapter looks at the structure of the Yugoslav economy, especially as it existed under the socialist system post the Second World War. It argues that the microeconomics of enterprise self-management – unique to Yugoslavia during its socialist era – fatally undermined optimal macroeconomic management – a requirement for the long-term sustainability of the state as a whole. It explores the role of the International Monetary Fund (IMF) in its efforts to support Yugoslavia's stability programmes, including through the use of so-called 'real exchange rate rules' devised in part to correct biases inherent under self-management. It analyses in detail the final two IMF-supported programmes at the end of the 1980s and explains their failure and the hyperinflation and then recession that resulted. It argues that this macroeconomic trajectory – a near-inevitable consequence of the unique microeconomic self-management structure of Yugoslavia – was a significant and perhaps the determining

---

[1] An earlier version of this chapter was presented at a seminar at the European Studies Centre, St. Antony's College, Oxford University, in June 2014. This chapter draws on the experience of the author who was a junior desk economist on the IMF's Yugoslavia mission team during 1986–88, and subsequently a senior IMF advisor with oversight, inter alia, over the Yugoslav successor states during 2009–11. The chapter utilizes previously unpublished IMF documents which have been in the public domain since 2010 and available in the IMF Archives. The author would like to thank Jakov Milatović for help in the preparation of Chart 1.

[2] See references in this book's Introduction.

[3] Harold Lydall's book *Yugoslavia in Crisis* (Clarendon Press, 1989) is relatively unusual, in that it concentrates on the economic tensions of the Yugoslav system, rather than on the political tensions.

factor in the eventual break-up of the federation. Finally, it compares macroeconomic performance in the wake of transition in the successor states following the disintegration of Yugoslavia, especially in light of reforms which replaced enterprise self-management (worker control) by joint stock incorporation (shareholder control).

II The political economy of Yugoslavia – a brief history

The economy of Yugoslavia during the inter-war years of the monarchy was largely agrarian (Chart 7.1). Some 60 per cent of output was agricultural in 1923, and the share in 1939 was still more than half. The share of industrial production rose only modestly from 13 per cent in 1923 to 20 per cent in 1939. Following the hiatus of the Second World War, the new post-war Communist government launched a centrally planned economy in 1946 under the Five-Year Plan of 1946–51. This represented a conscious effort to industrialize, as reflected in other centrally planned economies at the time and following the model of the USSR in the 1930s. The share of industry rose dramatically during this period to a peak of 48 per cent of total output in 1952, at the expense of agriculture. Yugoslavia's break with Cominform (the newly formed coalition of communist powers) in 1948 presaged a change in the system of governance from a centrally planned model to a much more devolved arrangement in 1952, which was codified by a new constitution in 1974. The republics gained substantial powers from the Federal government, and within them, the worker-managed enterprises (Basic Organizations of Associated Labour, or BOALs) became key micro-power centres and decision-making bodies. The advance of industrialization (as such) stalled – having arguably overshot its natural share even for a developed economy – and was instead replaced by the expansion of services (particularly retail), construction and other non-industrial activities. The share of agriculture, however, continued its decline.

In terms of economic growth overall, pre-Second World War Yugoslavia grew at around 2½ per cent per annum on average, with industrial production growing a little faster at 4 per cent per annum (Table 7.1). With population growth of about 1½ per cent per annum during this period, output per capita grew by about 1 per cent per annum. This growth rate was quite volatile, but mainly in consequence of the dominance of agriculture and the vagaries of drought and other exogenous supply events connected to this sector. Industrial production was more robust, except during the Great Depression during 1931–32. This respectable, but modest, overall growth rate was consistent with an economy that was not developing at the pace needed to escape a pre-industrial dependence on agriculture. The advent of the post-Second World War federal republic ushered in, as has been noted, a rapid growth of industrial output, which slowed with the end of central planning but still remained strong, in line with overall output growth of around 6 per cent per annum until 1979 and the onset of the Latin American debt crisis. Yugoslavia was party to this easy over-accumulation of recycled petrodollar debt by developing countries (mostly in Latin America) and the burden of these debts slowed growth down to a near negligible rate in the remaining decade of the country's life.

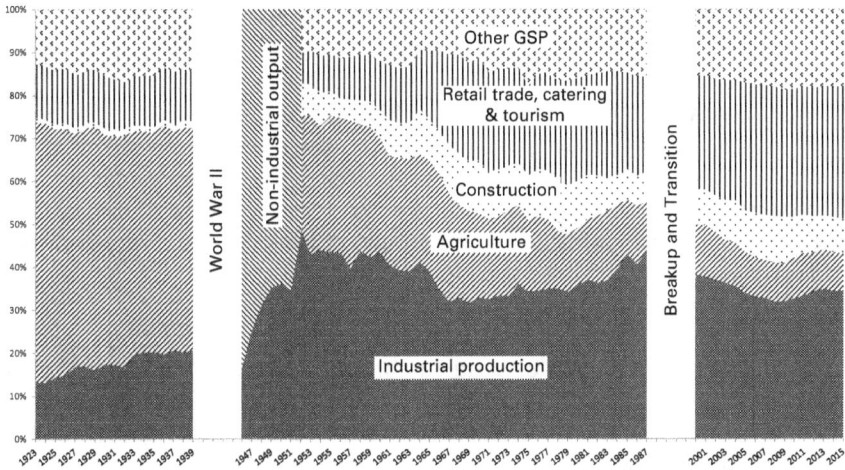

Chart 7.1 Output shares in Yugoslavia and (collective) successor states. Source: *Narodni Dohodak Jugoslavje 1923-39*, Ekonomski Institut NR Srbije, Beograd, 1959; *Jugoslavija 1918-1988*, Statisticki Godisnjak, Beograd 1999; national statistics for successor states. Gross Social Product (GSP) for sum of successor states calculated by excluding administration, defence, health care, housing and finance from GDP.

Table 7.1 Growth and Inflation in Yugoslavia and successor states

	Monarchy 1923–39	Five-Year Plan 1946–51	1952–79	1980–87	Post-transition successor states
GSP/GNP	2.6	...	6.2	0.6	2.8
Industrial prod.	4.2	17.4	8.1	2.4	...
Fiscal balance	−1.3	...	−0.5	0.1	−2.5
Inflation	0.1	14.5	10.7	60.5	3.1

Source: *Narodni Dohodak Jugoslavje 1923-39*, Ekonomski Institut NR Srbije, Beograd, 1959; *Jugoslavija 1918-1988*, Statisticki Godisnjak, Beograd 1999; IMF WEO database for successor states, 2002–16 inclusive, simple averages

The inflation rate during the pre-war monarchy was volatile, again reflecting the fortunes of agricultural prices, as well as the effects (downward) of the onset of the Great Depression, but there was no bias – the price level in 1939 was little different from the level in 1926 (when data began to be collected). Aside from the period of political upheaval in 1928–29, government fiscal operations were fairly conservative, and the average fiscal balance was a deficit of 1.3 per cent of GDP. In part, this relatively stable price level reflected the link of the Yugoslav dinar to the gold standard during 1925–32. The inflation situation was, however, very different in the post-war republic. The annual rate of inflation during the Five-Year Plan was 14½ per cent per annum on average. This slowed slightly to an average annual rate of 10½ per cent during the remainder of the Tito era, and then accelerated dramatically to an average rate of over 60 per cent per annum through 1987. What explains this divergent performance? Not fiscal extravagance, as the post-war Federal Government's fiscal stance was, if anything, even more conservative than that of the pre-war one. The answer lies rather with quasi-fiscal indiscipline on the part of worker-controlled enterprises and their links with provincial power centres outside the control of the Federal Government. This political-economic feature was unique to the Socialist Federal Republic and absent from both the pre-war monarchy and the post-dissolution successor states, so it is instructive to compare macroeconomic performance under the three regimes.

III Factors underlying the break-up of Yugoslavia

The political processes leading to the dissolution of Yugoslavia have been well documented, including in Susan Woodward's magisterial work *Balkan Tragedy*.[4] Her book is, however, distinct from others in asserting that political/economic factors – as opposed to political/ethnic ones – played the determining part in explaining the dissolution of Yugoslavia. Woodward characterizes three different interpretations of the reasons for the break-up:

(i)   Serbian aggression, initiated by Milosevic's nationalist agenda in 1988; caused by a desire to create a Greater Serbia, chiefly at the expense of Croatian and Bosnian territory.

(ii)   Revival of ethnic conflict, which had been suppressed by the authority of Tito and resurfaced after his death in 1980; manifested as a three-way war between Croats, Serbs and Bosnians.

(iii)   Collapse of central governmental authority, bringing about a breakdown of political and civil order; caused by 'the politics of transforming a socialist society to a market economy and democracy'.[5]

Woodward asserts that the third factor is the most important. This hypothesis is part right. While nationalist and ethnic tensions undoubtedly played their part, there was nothing inevitable about the result (dissolution of the Yugoslav nation), absent the third element – the collapse of central government authority. Ethnic and nationalist tensions have existed in many post-war nation states which are, for the most part, amalgams of smaller national identities. But they do not invariably lead to dissolution unless the central authority is too weak to hold them together. The hypothesis is also valid in claiming that the principal catalyst behind the erosion of central authority was

---

[4]   *Balkan Tragedy*, Susan L Woodward, Brookings Institution, 1995; see also Susan L Woodward, *Socialist Unemployment: the Political Economy of Yugoslavia 1945–90.* (Princeton University Press, 1995). The influence of economic factors in the break up is also acknowledged in Dejan Jović's book *Yugoslavia: A State that Withered Away.* (Purdue University Press, 2009) but here is it accorded a subsidiary role to the political one.
[5]   Woodward, *Balkan Tragedy*, 15.

economic. It is wrong, however, to suggest that this was caused by 'the politics of transforming a socialist society to a market economy and democracy' – because no such transformation actually took place. What destroyed central government authority (and thereby its ability to resist Nationalists like Milošević) was its systemic inability to control a high and accelerating rate of inflation which ended as a hyperinflation in 1989. When the government finally succeeded in halting the hyperinflation in 1990, what little remained of its perceived authority and competence was lost when it then failed to forestall the inevitable deep recession in 1991 – which was the other horn of the economic dilemma that was built into Yugoslavia's unique brand of socialism. With no central government glue left to hold down the lid, the nation's *Pandora's Box* of ethnic and nationalist rivalry blew the nation to pieces in 1992.

There were other economic factors that worked against the union of the republics. As in many other unions of culturally and ethnically diverse peoples, there were divergent trends in productivity and Gross Social Product (GSP) per capita, with Slovenia and Croatia in the North performing better than average, and Bosnia, Macedonia and Montenegro in the South doing worse than average (Charts 7.2 and 7.3).[6] This,

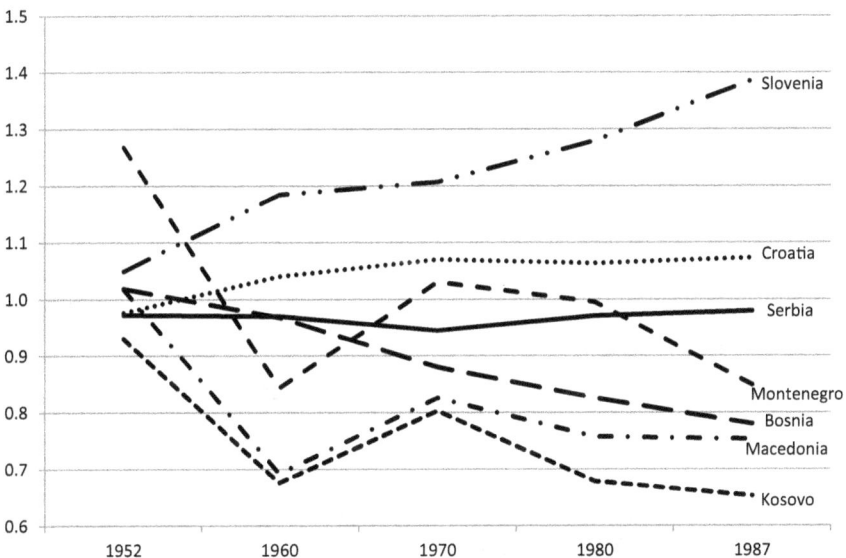

Chart 7.2 Relative republic productivity in Yugoslavia. Source: *Jugoslavija 1918–1988*, Statisticki Godisnjak, Beograd 1999.

[6] GSP was the unit of measurement of economic output preferred by the Yugoslav authorities. It corresponded to Gross Domestic Product (GDP), minus services considered non-economic such as banking and government. Most post-Second War II Yugoslav data is in this form, though attempts have been made to construct a GDP equivalent for some Yugoslav time series by the Maddison Data Project (2013).

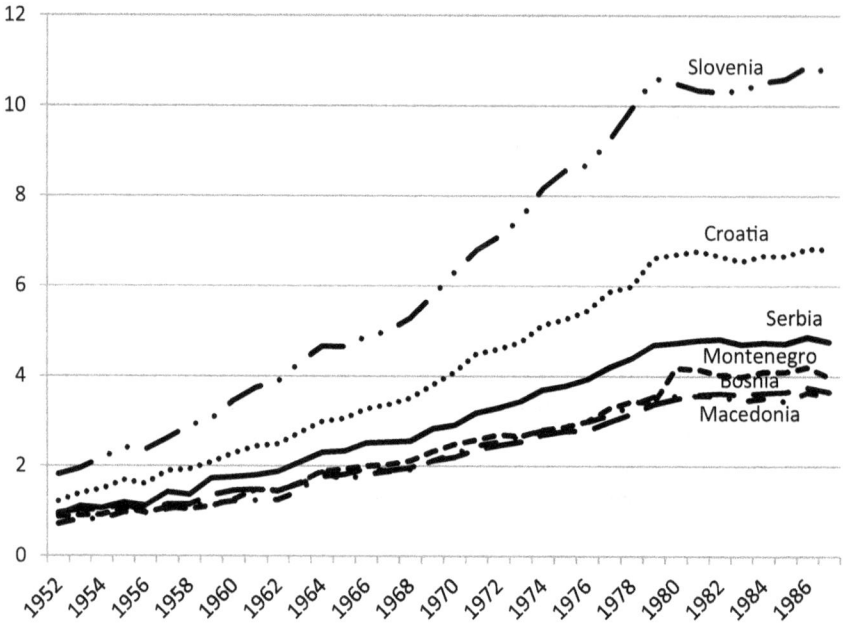

Chart 7.3 Yugoslavia – per capita GSP. Source: *Jugoslavija 1918–1988*, Statisticki Godisnjak, Beograd 1999.

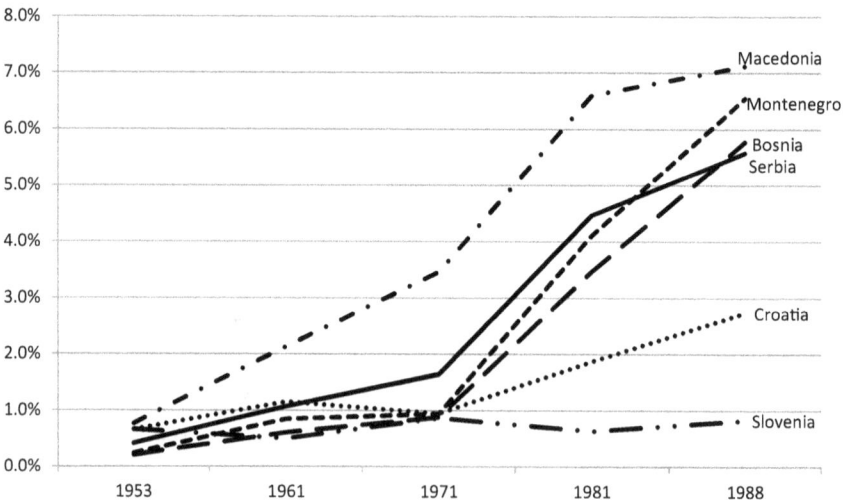

Chart 7.4 Yugoslavia – people seeking work. Source: *Jugoslavija 1918–1988*, Statisticki Godisnjak, Beograd 1999.

in turn, led to rising unemployment in the South (Chart 7.4). Since all the republics shared a common currency (the Yugoslav dinar), they were not able to offset these divergent competitive trends through inter-republic exchange rate adjustment. Such pronounced regional disparities (between North and South) have also persisted in other European countries such as the United Kingdom and Italy, and even in post-unification Germany (between East and West), but in all these cases there has been and remains a system in place for inter-regional support in the form of fiscal transfers. This is one of the reasons why none of these countries has undergone the severe stresses experienced by the Eurozone since 2010 – a clear demonstration of what happens when a group of countries with divergent productivity trends operates under a collective common currency without an adequate system of fiscal transfers (from rich to poor). Yugoslavia, by contrast, did have such a system of fiscal transfers in place (see Chart 7.5). This economic feature was not, therefore, sufficient on its own to force the dissolution of the country (although it did cause some irritation on the part of the richer transferor republics).

Another more relevant factor, however, which was not so much a long-term trend as a more specific event at the beginning of Yugoslavia's last decade, was the onset of the Latin American debt crisis at the beginning of the 1980s. This resulted from the recycling of the huge dollar surpluses accumulated by Saudi Arabia and other oil-producing states following the sharp increase in oil prices at the end of 1973. While the rise in debt by oil consuming middle-income countries was partly a consequence of the higher oil import bill, the majority was due to overinvestment prompted by what was very easy money as the banks tried to find profitable ways to on-lend the surpluses. The rate of investment in Yugoslavia climbed to nearly 35 per cent of GSP

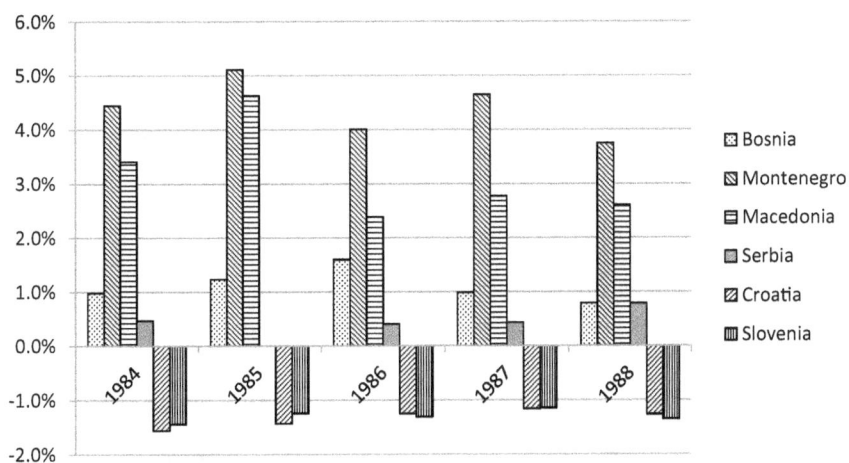

Chart 7.5 Inter-republic fiscal transfers. Source: *Statistical Pocket-Book of Yugoslavia* 1987, 1989.

during the 1970s (Chart 7.6) to a level seen only once before in the early 1960s.[7] Even for a developing country, such high rates of investment can rarely be undertaken without running into negative marginal returns, as the number of viable projects in any given year is exhausted. It is notable that the rate of growth during the 1970s was no faster than before, despite this ramping up of investment. This suggests that much of this extra investment was essentially wasted, and in no position to help service the debts that had financed it. In this regard Yugoslavia shared features similar to the Asian Crisis in the 1990s – excessive investment financed by enterprise borrowing. This resulted from what became known as 'crony-capitalism' where projects – facilitated by political contacts – were undertaken not because of their prospective returns, but for prestige reasons, or as a means of pocketing (the borrowed) resources either through extra jobs, salary payments or side-deals. In Yugoslavia, the pervasive influence of political objectives in the decision making of enterprises under self-management meant that investment decisions were similarly diverted from their optimal economic criteria, while banks (which were also part of the political nexus) provided the finance without adequate consideration of the credit-worthiness of the projects. The onset of the debt crisis, triggered by the interest rate hikes by Paul Volcker in the USA, resulted in an inability to service the now high level of external debt, and ten years (the last ten years of Yugoslavia) of near stagnant growth in

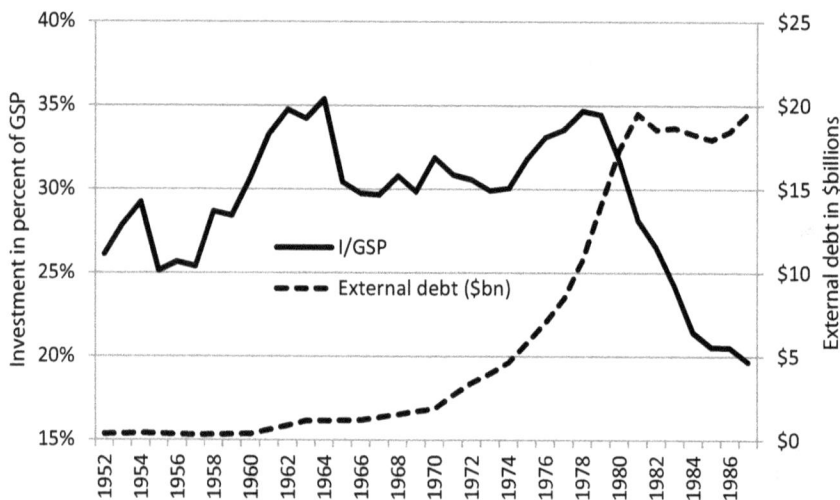

Chart 7.6 Yugoslavia investment and external debt. Source: *Jugoslavija 1918–1988*, Statisticki Godisnjak, Beograd 1999.

[7] These ratios have been calculated at constant prices to avoid misleading stock valuation effects. They are broadly comparable in level to those reported by Kucic (2017). Yugoslavia's external convertible currency debt was guaranteed by the National Bank of Yugoslavia and regularly reported in its Quarterly Bulletin.

per capita terms.[8] This, in turn, contributed to the growing political crisis and weakening of the authority of the Federal Government of Yugoslavia and thereby the weakening of the bond that was holding the country together.

IV The role of the IMF and the World Bank

The debt crisis prompted the banks (mostly based in New York) to grant Yugoslavia a Multi Year Rescheduling Agreement (MYRA) (i.e. debt relief) in 1986 subject to Yugoslavia submitting to what was known as 'Enhanced Surveillance' by the International Monetary Fund (IMF). Yugoslavia had a long relationship with the IMF, being a founder member in 1946. It was a regular user of Fund resources and also submitted to annual Article IV Consultations (visits by IMF staff) following their introduction for all IMF members in the wake of the collapse of the Bretton Woods system in 1971.[9] Contrary to what has been suggested, the IMF did not attempt to change the political economy system of Yugoslavia 'into a market economy and democracy' – which it felt was beyond its mandate – but instead tried to work with the existing system to promote 'orderly economic growth with reasonable price stability', while the use of its resources were intended to 'shorten the duration and lessen the degree of disequilibrium in the international balances of payments of members'.[10] Prior to the 1980s, World Bank lending to Yugoslavia (as elsewhere) had been focused on project finance and then on institutional strengthening (e.g. schools, health, etc.). In 1983, the bank approved a 'Structural Adjustment Loan' for Yugoslavia (the first of two).[11] Given the potential for overlap with the IMF, the 'structural' terms of such loans affecting the economy were aligned with those of the Fund. Bank conditionality was fairly weak and, other than provide additional financing on favourable terms, these loans had relatively little effect on Yugoslav structural policies.

[8] Starting in 1980, the new Chairman of the Federal Reserve Board began raising interest rates aggressively to bring down the high rates of inflation that had afflicted the USA for most of the 1970s. In this he was mostly successful, but this policy had unintended adverse effects on the debt service of governments in Latin America and elsewhere that had borrowed heavily (from recycled petro-dollars) in the wake of the 1973 oil crisis. The result was widespread default and the Latin American debt crisis of the 1980s.

[9] Yugoslavia enjoyed a close relationship with the IMF throughout its post-war history. It had Article XIV and then (from 1979) Article IV Consultations nearly every year 1949–90, outright purchases in 1949, 1963, 1974 and 1975, and Stand-by Arrangements in 1958, 1960, 1965, 1966, 1971, 1979, 1980, 1981–83, 1984, 1988 and 1990. Article XIV and Article IV Consultations were/are purely discussions, resulting in a Staff Report to the IMF's Executive Board, but otherwise involved no money or conditionality. Outright purchases are essentially short-term balance of payments loans in one single disbursement with very limited conditionality, by contrast to Stand-by Arrangements which usually involve phased disbursements and quarterly conditionality.

[10] Articles of Agreement, International Monetary Fund, Second Amendment, 1978.

[11] This 1983 loan was for a total of $275 million, to be disbursed over a period of two years. The second loan was approved in 1990, for an amount of $400 million, of which only $150 million was disbursed.

Enterprise self-management

Chief among the IMF's tasks in advising the various Yugoslav governments during this period – and it is important to point out that its interlocutor was the Federal government (not the Republican governments) – was to try to bring down the chronic double digit rate of inflation that had been a feature of Yugoslavia for much of its life. For most countries suffering such problems, the usual IMF cure (at least through the 1980s) would be to reign in the country's fiscal deficit (hence the IMF's sobriquet from that era being 'It's Mostly Fiscal'). The IMF recognized, however, that the government sector's fiscal deficit was not (usually) the problem in Yugoslavia, and its programmes did not normally involve conventional 'fiscal adjustment' for the government. While the federal government was only responsible for about 20 per cent of total public spending, with the remainder carried out at the level of the republics, neither level of government was in the habit of running large financial deficits. This high rate of Yugoslav inflation instead had its roots rather in the devolved system of enterprise self-management and the lack of financial discipline – both in investment decisions and in setting wage rates – that resulted. This process generated what is sometimes known as a 'quasi-fiscal' deficit in the enterprise sector. Yugoslavia's system of self-management has been extensively analysed in the academic literature, and it is not the intention of this chapter to summarize this material.[12] It is sufficient to say that there is a substantial (if not universal) body of opinion that the system provided the wrong incentives – in particular to worker income maximization – into the management of self-managed firms.[13] The Federal authorities tried to control the resulting inflation using incomes policies, credit limits, and price controls, but with little success. Incomes policies (agreed under 'social compacts') included a wage indexation element that undermined their effectiveness, credit controls encouraged financial disintermediation, and price controls resulted in supply distortions and shortages so that they could not be held in place for long.

The result of this indiscipline was a large enterprise sector financing requirement, and the accumulation of bank borrowing (from banks that had close political links with the enterprises to which they lent). The 'profits' of the enterprises (i.e. the balances left over after wages and other current expenditures had been paid) were insufficient to meet both

---

[12] See, e.g. James Meade 'The Theory of Labour-Managed Firms and of Profit Sharing' (1972) 82 *Economic Journal* 402–28; Andre Sapir, 'Economic Growth and Factor Substitution: What Happened to the Yugoslav Miracle?' (1980) 90 *Economic Journal* 294–313; Saul Estrin, *Self-Management: Economic Theory and Yugoslav Practice*, (1983) Cambridge University Press; and Leonard Kukic (2017) 'Socialist Growth Revisited: Insights from Yugoslavia', *Economic History Working Papers*, No 268, LSE.

[13] Self-management *per se* is not without its successful examples in Western market economies. Partnerships are widespread in such systems, but these tend to be (a) explicitly worker-owned, (b) in services (e.g. law firms, architects, etc.) where capital requirements are relatively low, and (c) free of political agenda. One of the largest such 'partnerships' is the John Lewis retail chain in the UK. Arguably, however, this company works because it operates in a setting where wages and prices are set in a competitive market that is dominated by other, joint stock, companies in the same sector. For industrial concerns where capital requirements are high, joint stock companies with a clear delineation between labour and capital have proven the more natural structure.

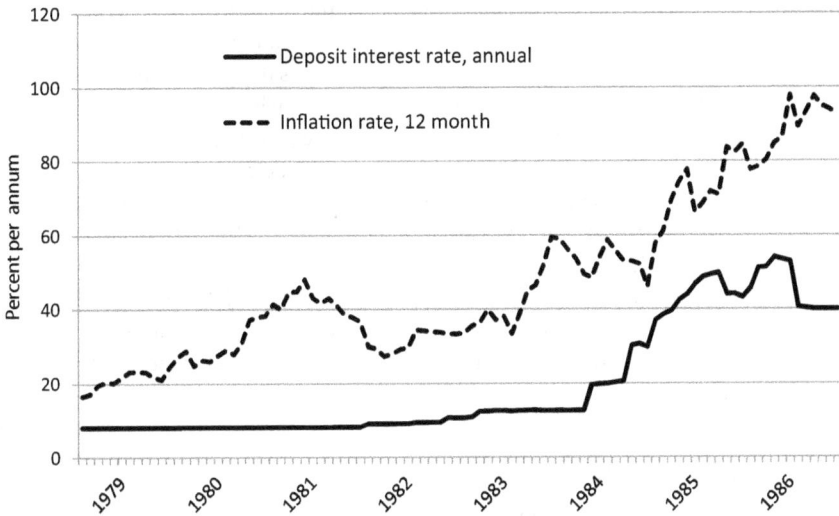

Chart 7.7 Interest rates and inflation in Yugoslavia. Source: *National Bank of Yugoslavia Quarterly Bulletin* (various issues).

the investment objectives and the servicing of debt, unless the latter was essentially subsidized. The subsidy operated via the 'inflation tax', which amounted to a real transfer from bank creditors (mainly households) to debtors (enterprises). This tax resulted from interest rates always being – ex post – less than the rate of inflation (Chart 7.7).

Interest rate policy

Attempts were made by the Yugoslav federal government – supported by the IMF – to enforce discipline and plug the inflation tax by raising interest rates. In market economies such policies usually work to dampen inflation, but in Yugoslavia, the effect went the other way because enterprises responded to higher interest rates by raising prices, rather than by cutting spending. It has been shown that, in an environment of such enterprise financial indiscipline (as defined above), raising interest rates can have a perverse effect on inflation.[14] The simplified equation below (from Bennett and Schadler, 1992) explains the drivers of inflation in such an environment:

$$\pi = \gamma i \left[1 - \left(\frac{1}{1 + \phi i} \right) \right] - \omega e^{-\beta} - \Delta lny$$

[14] See *Interest Rate Policy in Central and Eastern Europe: The Influence of Monetary Overhangs and Weak Enterprise Discipline*, Adam Bennett and Susan Schadler, IMF Working Paper 92/68, 1992. The properties of this model represent a special case of Thomas Sargent and Neil Wallace *Some Unpleasant Monetarist Arithmetic*, *FRBM Quarterly Review*, Fall 1981.

where π is the sustained rate of inflation, i the rate of interest, ω the quasi-fiscal primary balance as a proportion of output, and y an index of real output.[15] Thus, the sustained rate of inflation is positively associated with interest rates depending on the degree of indiscipline, and negatively associated with the quasi-fiscal balance (surplus) as well as to the real rate of growth. The first two terms in this equation (connected to interest rates and the quasi-fiscal balance) effectively capture monetary accommodation from borrowing. As Chart 7.7 shows, the policy of raising nominal interest rates in the mid-1980s failed to close the gap with inflation, which simply accelerated so as to keep real interest rates sufficiently negative to enable the necessary debt-subsidy resource transfer to enterprises. The underlying quasi-fiscal deficit of the enterprise sector remained persistently negative (reflecting wages pressures), while the slowdown of growth during this final decade of Yugoslavia's existence added to the upward pressure on inflation.

Real exchange rate rule

While inflation 'solved' the problem for enterprise finances, it created a new one for enterprise competitiveness vis-à-vis overseas markets. To deal with this, a policy of continuous nominal exchange rate adjustment to correct for domestic inflation – a so-called 'real exchange rate rule' – was followed by the Federal authorities in control of the National Bank of Yugoslavia. In this way, external competitiveness was maintained, but at the expense of validating the inflation rate. With the nominal exchange rate thus constantly devaluing on a monthly basis, the unique Yugoslav political economy system of self-management found a sort of macroeconomic 'equilibrium', albeit a suboptimal one with a high rate of inflation. Figure 7.1 shows the theoretical relationship between internal and external balance in terms of the real exchange rate and domestic demand. The target real exchange rate (E1) was deemed to be consistent with both the desired external position (e.g. current account balance) and full employment, at the intersection of the linear and dashed schedules.[16] In Yugoslavia there was a natural tendency (given the chronic inflation rate) for the real exchange rate to appreciate (in the direction of the arrow) for any given level of nominal rate. This would have resulted in a fall-off of exports, a trade deficit, and a recession. The rule adopted was therefore to prevent this natural tendency to appreciate by continuous nominal monthly adjustments downwards. This policy of maintaining a target (competitive) level for the real exchange rate was not unique to Yugoslavia. Many other countries (especially in Latin America) battling high inflation rates (albeit generated for different reasons) sought to preserve their external competitiveness through the use of such rules during the 1970s and

---

[15] The parameters γ, $\varnothing$, and β represent measures of financial indiscipline (from zero to unity), the interest elasticity of interest bearing money (as a share of total money), and the ratio of the total money supply to GDP (the demand for money) respectively.

[16] The upward sloping linear schedule in the diagram represents that combination of real exchange rate and domestic demand that would ensure domestic equilibrium (i.e. full employment). The downward sloping dashed schedules represent the combinations that deliver the desired current account (CA) position (surplus, balance, or deficit) in the balance of payments.

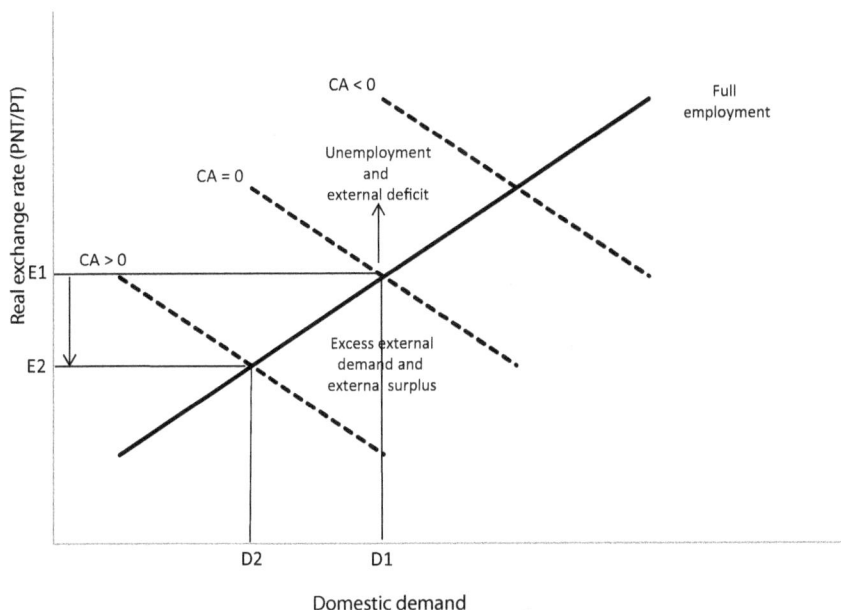

Figure 7.1 Real exchange rate and domestic demand.

1980s. However, doubts began to surface in mid-1980s about the wisdom of these rules, when it was realized that the price level becomes indeterminate (there is no nominal anchor) under such regimes, which is rather disconcerting for a macroeconomic policy maker.[17] The experience of Yugoslavia was to prove a (spectacular) case in point.

The 1988 Stand-by Arrangement

Following the onset of the debt crisis in the early 1980s, the IMF supported Yugoslavia's adjustment programmes with a series of Stand-by Arrangements in 1980, 1981, 1984, and 1985.[18] During the course of the 1985 arrangement, the commercial banks agreed a MYRA to reschedule 100 per cent of the debt owed to them by Yugoslavia, while at the Paris Club official creditors also granted debt relief on the remainder of Yugoslavia's total of US$18 billion of long-term convertible currency debt.[19] As part of this

---

[17] See, for example, Charles Adams and Daniel Gros 'The Consequences of Real Exchange Rate Rules for Inflation: Some Illustrative Examples', IMF Staff Papers, 1986.

[18] The 1980 arrangement was for one year and in the amount of SDR 339 million, the 1981 arrangement was for three years and in the amount of SDR 1,662 million, the 1984 arrangement was for one year and for SDR 370 million, and the 1985 arrangement was also for one year and for SDR 300 million. By the time of the latter arrangement, repurchases (i.e. repayments to the Fund) were exceeding purchases (new lending). One SDR (Special Drawing Right) was approximately equal to one US dollar at this time.

agreement, Yugoslavia agreed to submit to 'Enhanced Surveillance' (ES) by the IMF (essentially a twice-yearly review by IMF Staff made available to creditors). This ES was requested to run from 1986 through 1991.[20] However, by 1988, it was clear that policies to bring inflation down were failing, as were policies to get economic growth going again. The inflation rate had risen further to (a then record of) 167 per cent (per annum) by December 1987, and Gross Social Product (output) actually fell (by 0.5 per cent) in that year. The Yugoslav authorities therefore requested a new Stand-by Arrangement, not least to help finance repayments to the Fund falling due.[21] This programme that the arrangement was designed to support was similar to the earlier series of programmes, with two important differences. The first change in strategy was to make a more concerted effort to enforce enterprise financial discipline and lower inflation by raising real interest rates to positive levels. The second change in strategy was to try to kick start growth by engineering a real devaluation of the exchange rate, to a super-competitive level compared to the level that had been targeted under the preceding programmes in the 1980s. In addition, the programmes included measures to strengthen incomes policies by including overall nominal caps, impose public spending limits in cash terms, improve the commercial allocation of foreign exchange based on a flexible exchange rate, and (partially) roll-back price controls.

Nominal interest rates were hiked a number of times during 1984 through 1986, but inflation followed suit, with the result that real interest rates did not increase. The 1988 programme therefore attempted to guarantee a positive real interest rate, both on deposits as well as loans, by introducing an element of indexation.[22] The enterprise sector had already moved into an overall loss (after wage payments, but before investment) in 1987, and had doubled its bank debt to cover this and investment needs during the year (Table 7.2). It was only saved from outright bankruptcy by inflation and negative real interest rates which left outstanding bank borrowing lower in real terms than what it had been at the beginning of the year. However, the indexation of one-year loans in mid-1988 failed to instil the required discipline on borrowing, and instead the enterprise sector was plunged into an even larger (book) loss, despite

[19] The Paris Club is a forum (usually held in the French Treasury in Paris) to allow official creditors to agree terms for debt relief for governments in debt to them. It was established in 1956.

[20] ES did not involve financial support, nor did it involve explicit conditionality. But a report would not be submitted unless the IMF staff could describe the policies being pursued by the Yugoslav authorities in a positive light. It was in the government's interest for a positive report to be issued. ES therefore conferred soft conditionality and an ability for IMF staff to influence policy making in Yugoslavia.

[21] This Stand-by Arrangement was for one year and SDR 306 million. While repurchases (repayments to the Fund) exceeded this amount during the period of the Stand-by Arrangement, Yugoslavia's outstanding use of Fund resources would have exceeded the limit stipulated in the Articles of Agreement (200 per cent of quota) following the first purchase (drawing) and this therefore required a special waiver.

[22] The Letter of Intent signed by the authorities required banks to index the principal of time deposits of three months or longer maturity, and loans of longer than one year's maturity, in line with the concurrent month's retail price index. An interest rate of no less than 5 per cent (per annum) would apply to the revalued amount.

Table 7.2 Enterprise sector finances in Yugoslavia

Enterprise sector finances	1984	1985	1986	1987	1988	1989	1990[1]
Real interest rate (average monthly, percent per annum)	−8.4	−10.1	−13.8	−27.3	8.2	11.1	−5.5
Nominal interest payments (as a percentage of enterprise gross revenue)	3.7	5.6	6.2	9.2	14.0	23.8	4.0
Wage costs (percent of income before tax and wage costs)	67.5	71.6	75.0	98.2	118.0	96.6	95.3
Enterprise profit (percentage of income before tax and wage costs)	21.4	17.5	10.6	−17.6	−41.1	−21.6	−9.1
Dinar bank credit to enterprises (percentage change from previous year)	35.6	40.3	85.4	97.4	208.4	2,191	84.9

Source: IMF 1990 Article IV, Recent Economic Developments, SM/91/44; [1]First nine months

output recovering in 1989. Bank lending blew through the ceiling set for it under the IMF programme, as did the wage bill, also subject to a ceiling.

The other key feature of this programme was the decision to devalue the real exchange rate in May 1988 by 19.3 per cent (compared to its level in March 1988).[23] In principle, the exchange rate was thereafter to be determined by market forces (with the allocation of foreign exchange determined by the market). Because the new real exchange rate was significantly lower than before, the pressure was always upward. However, the programme introduced a policy which essentially reinstated the real exchange rate rule because it included the following commitment in the Letter of Intent: 'It has been decided to implement before the Board's discussion of the proposed SBA a flexible exchange rate policy, but it is also understood that the real effective exchange rate (on the basis of the retail price index and similarly on CPI indexes for partner countries) will not be allowed to appreciate from the level that will be reached at the start of the program.'[24] The effect was to push the real exchange rate down from E1 to E2 in Figure 7.1, and contain it there. The proposed devaluation was not, however, accompanied by any further tightening of domestic demand. The fiscal position was already close to balance, and it would have been politically difficult to move it into surplus. And higher real interest rates, as noted above, failed to constrain spending. Absent a shift in domestic demand from D1 to D2, the effect of the devaluation was therefore to push the economy off the 'full employment' schedule and into the zone described as 'excess demand and external surplus'. As Table 7.3 shows, the effect on the Yugoslav economy was precisely this. The external accounts moved into substantial surplus – much greater than planned – and foreign exchange reserves ballooned to

---

[23] This devaluation, and the decision to hold it at the new level in real terms, was at the request of the IMF's internal review department (ETR) who argued that the draft programme hitherto negotiated by the area department (EUR) was insufficiently ambitious, and unlikely to generate the desired recovery in economic growth.

[24] Yugoslavia Letter of Intent EBS/88/89, Annex G, IMF Document 1988.

Table 7.3 Balance of payments of Yugoslavia

Balance of payments	1987	1988		1989		1990	
	Actual	Target	Actual	Target	Actual	Target	Actual
Current account ($bn)	1.1	0.5	2.2	0.9	2.0	1.3	−0.9
Reserves (months of imports)	2.2	2.7	3.9	3.3	6.2	7.6	5.0

Source: IMF 1990 Article IV, Staff Report, SM/91/38

twice the level intended. The excess demand did not, however, deliver significantly higher output. It was instead translated into an explosion of the price level.[25]

The evolution of the real exchange rate and price inflation is shown in Chart 7.8. The effect of the real devaluation in May 1988 was an immediate acceleration of price inflation. This continued to rise until reaching 60 per cent a month (the accepted definition of hyperinflation) in December 1989. Despite breaching all their nominal targets agreed under the IMF programme – except for external reserves which was massively exceeded – the Yugoslav authorities nevertheless stuck religiously to the new real exchange rate target all the way through to December 1989. The economy, pushed into a disequilibrium of sustained excess demand, kept pushing prices higher and higher in an attempt to restore the original real exchange rate level – only to be thwarted by repeated nominal devaluations aiming at the new real exchange rate target. With credit ceilings (albeit breached) acting as a break on the domestic sources of money creation, the monetization of this inflation was achieved as much through the massive over-performance of external reserves through 1989 (Table 7.3).

In 1963, Milton Friedman famously concluded that 'inflation is always and everywhere a monetary phenomenon'.[26] However, while the Yugoslav inflation could not have been sustained without monetary accommodation, it was not monetary growth which drove inflation but rather inflation (itself generated by an undervalued real exchange rate) which drove monetary growth. See Annex 1 to this chapter for a statistical analysis of this hypothesis.

The 1990 Stand-by Arrangement

By 1989 it was obvious that the strategy underlying the 1988 programme had failed. In late 1988, the government led by Branko Mikulić passed a number of constitutional

---

[25] Efforts in Latin America to push down the real exchange rate without an accompanying fiscal tightening also achieved little but higher inflation, see Guillermo Calvo, Carmen Reinhart and Carlos Vegh 'Targeting the Real Exchange Rate' (1995) 47 *Theory and Evidence Journal of Development Economics* 97–103. This article contains an extensive list of references regarding the debate on real exchange rate rules. By the time it was published, however, such rules had fallen out of favour, and nominal exchange rate rules based on the currency board arrangement (CBA) were becoming fashionable instead, starting with Argentina's CBA in 1991.

[26] Friedman, Milton. *Inflation: Causes and Consequences.* (New York: Asia Publishing House, 1963).

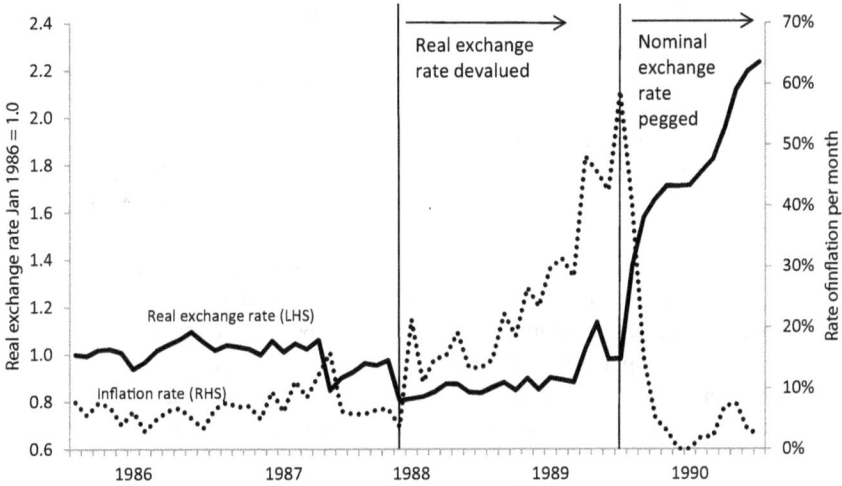

Chart 7.8 Real exchange rate and inflation in Yugoslavia.

amendments and laws (including the Enterprise Law of December 1988) designed to pave the way for the replacement of enterprise self-management by Western-style corporate models.[27] These changes were entirely at the initiative of the Mikulić government, and were not envisaged in the authorities' Letter of Intent under the 1988 Stand-by Arrangement and not thereby the result of IMF conditionality. But with the inflation rate continuing to accelerate, the Mikulić government felt compelled to resign in March 1989, and was replaced by a new administration led by Ante Marković, the last prime minister of Yugoslavia. The new administration embarked on an ambitious programme of stabilization and reform that would represent a profound break with the past. The key element of the stabilization programme was to stop the hyperinflation by abandoning the real exchange rate rule and instead pegging the dinar to the deutsche mark (on 18 December 1989).[28] This change of strategy marked the beginning of a wave of similar exchange rate based stabilizations in the 1990s.[29] In support of this policy, the government undertook to implement fundamental reforms which included (i) the transformation of banks from institutions owned by enterprises and run for the benefit of those same enterprises into fully capitalized

---

[27] See chapter by Milica Uvalic 'What Happened to the Yugoslav Economic Model?' in this volume for a detailed description of these changes.

[28] The dinar was at the same time redenominated at a rate of 10,000 old dinars to 1 new dinar.

[29] The Yugoslav 1990 experiment in 'exchange-rate based stabilisation' was in the vanguard of the later, more celebrated examples, such as Argentina's currency board arrangement (CBA) in 1991, and the Estonian CBA in 1992. As such, it was a lead example of a global trend (but distinct from the 'liberal' weltanschauung that led to the collapse of communism elsewhere). Similar schemes were also used in Lithuania and Latvia following independence from the Soviet Union (though these were not CBAs) and in Bulgaria in 1997. They fell out of favour after Argentina crashed out in 2002. The Baltic countries converted to the Euro, and as of 2019, only Bulgaria retains its CBA.

profit-motivated institutions with equity ownership; (ii) the transformation of socially owned enterprises into legal entities with proper capital and the clarification of the ownership status of those enterprises; and (iii) the removal of restrictions affecting privately owned firms and enterprises of mixed ownership. The Marković government had recognized that macroeconomic stabilization could not be achieved without root-and-branch reform of the system of enterprise self-management. This broad strategy was initiated on 1 January 1990, and supported by a new IMF Stand-by Arrangement in March 1990.

Although the new policy framework was endorsed by the Federal, Republican and Provincial Assemblies, there was resistance in some republics, especially in Serbia under the government of Milošević, to the reform of enterprise self-management. Irrespective of the support the reforms may have had, they would have taken time to implement, and Yugoslavia had run out of time. The effect of the exchange rate peg was indeed successful in controlling inflation. The hyperinflation halted almost immediately, and by May 1990 the monthly increase in prices was zero. By July, however, prices started rising again. Although the price rises thereafter were not at hyperinflation levels, they were sufficient to steadily appreciate the real exchange rate and erode competitiveness. By December 1990, the real exchange rate had appreciated by 100 per cent (Chart 7.8). Yugoslavia had merely transferred itself from one horn of the dilemma (high inflation) to the other horn (loss of competitiveness) which the real exchange rate rule was designed to avoid. The result of the real exchange rate appreciation was a huge trade deficit and a severe recession (Table 7.4). Large numbers of enterprises ran into illiquidity, and many went into bankruptcy (Table 7.5). Marković's bold gamble was too late, and failed to avert the now inevitable break-up of the country.

The thesis of this chapter is that the Yugoslav economic system, on which its political system was based, was doomed to fail – not because of pressure from IFIs to move it to a market economy, but because of its own internal economic contradictions. Centred on the self-management system, these internal contradictions were, moreover, unique to Yugoslavia, and were unrelated to the internal economic contradictions of the Communist countries of Eastern Europe and of the Soviet Union. The latter contributed coincidentally to the demise of their political systems at around the same time, because inefficiencies of central planning resulted in poor quality output – much of which was directed to supporting the Cold War – to the detriment of household consumption which failed to keep up with standards in the West where output was determined by market forces. This, combined with the political beacon of democracy and the rule of

Table 7.4 Yugoslav economic activity 1986–90: The Endgame

Real economic activity	1986	1987	1988	1989	1990
GSP (% change)	3.2	−1.1	−1.7	0.8	−7.5
o/w contribution from net foreign trade	−2.2	1.8	1.9	−1.3	−5.9
Unemployment (% of workforce)	10.7	10.6	11.0	11.5	12.1
Real income per worker (1981=100)	90.9	85.6	79.2	94.9	75.6

Source: IMF 1990 Article IV, Staff Report, SM/91/38, and Recent Economic Developments, SM/91/44

Table 7.5 Enterprise sector insolvency in Yugoslavia 1989–90

	Illiquidity		Bankruptcy proceedings	
	Number of enterprises[1]	Number of workers affected	Number of enterprises[1,2]	Number of workers affected
1989 Q2	1,114	424,824	142	54,787
1989 Q3	1,025	334,514	198	67,658
1989 Q4	949	361,890	207	94,803
1990 Q1	2,777	1,536,895	188	135,936
1990 Q2	2,382	1,325,780	516	316,433
1990 Q3	2,627	1,356,952	778	556,673
1990 October	3,902	1,622,354	979	678,049

[1]Enterprise sector only; [2]Since the beginning of the calendar year

Source: IMF 1990 Article IV, Recent Economic Developments, SM/91/44

law as manifested in the West, is what brought down communism. Yugoslav socialism had a different economic flaw. It enjoyed better living standards than under communist systems, but could not deliver macroeconomic stability. Yugoslavia's political weaknesses lay not in a poverty of democracy (as in communism), but rather in its lack of ethnic cohesion. The collapse of the economy weakened further the authority of (an already weak) Federal government and this dissolved the glue that held the country's different ethnic groups together. If Yugoslavia had been 100 per cent in the Western sphere of influence post-Second World War and adopted (or rather retained) a market economy from the start, it might have avoided its break-up and still be a country at peace with itself in the twenty-first century.

V Yugoslav successor states in transition

It is not the purpose of this chapter to analyse the economic chaos that ensued following the outbreak of conflict in Yugoslavia in 1991, and its subsequent dissolution into its successor states over the ensuing ten years.[30] Nor is it the purpose of this chapter to document all the reforms and policy initiatives undertaken subsequently.[31] Each of the external actors involved (the IMF, the European Bank for Reconstruction and Development, World Bank and European Union) provided such assistance to the region as lay in their area of expertise, for the most part in a consistent and complimentary manner with each other. The IMF tended to confine itself to reforms necessary for macroeconomic stability consistent with sustainable growth. As such,

---

[30] For an account of the country's descent into conflict, see Catherine Baker *The Yugoslav Wars of the 1990s*. (Palgrave Macmillan, 2015).

[31] For a comprehensive analysis of the transition of the Yugoslav successor sates (along with Albania, Bulgaria and Romania), see Adam Bennett, Russell Kincaid, Peter Sanfey, and Max Watson *Economic and Policy Foundations for Growth in South East Europe: Remaking the Balkan Economy*. (Palgrave Pivot, 2015).

IMF supported reforms focused on setting up central banks, reform of banking regulations, fiscal reforms, labour market reforms, liberalization of price controls, and reforms to trade arrangements.

More relevant to this chapter, however, were reforms to enterprise governance. One of the most important changes in the successor states has been the wholesale abandonment of the Yugoslav system of enterprise self-management. Here the role of the IMF was marginal, as most of the successor states followed the cue of the existing Yugoslav Law on Enterprises which was passed in late 1988 by the Mikulić government and the later laws passed by the Marković government. The task was rather to implement and build on these laws. The only country which retained a significant formal role for worker representation was Slovenia, although control (as such) still passed to shareholders.[32] In all other respects, firms in the successor states came to resemble firms in other Western countries, with partnerships, limited liability companies, and joint stock companies. IMF advice, and IMF programmes of financial support (some of which applied conditionality) focused, inter alia, on encouraging this ownership clarification, and then the privatization of the resulting structures by a variety of techniques including voucher schemes (whereby shares were distributed to citizens generally and could later be bought and sold on nascent stock markets), strategic investment (purchases) by large stakeholders, and management/worker buyouts. Voucher schemes had the advantage of speed, but conferred diffuse ownership rights that could impede effective management. Strategic investments and outright sales to third parties could – if such willing investors were available – also be speedy, but risked the charge of selling below true value given the difficulty of valuing such enterprises in the absence of a developed capital market. Management buyouts were dependent on workers being able to find the funds needed to finance such buyouts, and also raised questions about the resulting governance.

One of the consequences of this reform to corporate governance – with shareholders in charge – was intended to be a reconfiguration of incentives toward greater enterprise financial discipline. This may explain the broadly coincident achievement of a much better record of (lower) inflation from the mid-1990s onwards (Table 7.6), with the inflation rate now under the control of the central bank instead of being the by-product of income maximization by workers. Apart from the unavoidable recession (shared globally) following the global financial crisis (GFC) that unfolded in 2008 –which affected Western Europe and North America in equal measure – all the successor states enjoyed respectable growth rates (before and after the recession). So the lower inflation was not at the cost of growth which was strong and higher than in the final decade of

---

[32] Perhaps in deference to Germany's early recognition of its independence in 1991, Slovenia introduced the 'the system of co-determination' in 1993 in line with the German model of enterprise governance. Under this Slovenian system (as in Germany) workers should be represented by one-third of members on supervisory boards of small companies, and one-half in the case of large companies – but this does not include the chairman (who has the casting vote). Shareholders determine the residual membership. These supervisory boards are responsible for selecting the board of directors (the firm's management). Crucially, therefore, workers lost their controlling stake in the management of firms (compared to the old Yugoslav system). Equally important, shareholders (in place of political agents) were now represented and moreover got control.

Yugoslavia's existence. In terms of the structure of output, the shares of the successor states considered collectively continued the trends observed during the later socialist period, with modest further declines in agriculture and industry and a rise in services (Chart 7.1).[33] The changes in enterprise governance do not, therefore, seem to have profoundly altered the broad nature of the work undertaken, but rather the financial manner in which it was conducted.

The transition model adopted by the successor states undoubtedly suffered a shock to its credibility as a result of the GFC. There is little doubt that the growth rates recorded in the previous ten years – the boom years – were (ex post) unsustainable and based on drivers such as consumer spending, speculative construction, and reliance on foreign short-term capital which made the successor states very vulnerable to a downturn. In part, this reflected – as a result of an overestimation of growth potential – fiscal stances that were too loose. The underlying fiscal positions were not as secure as the headline figures suggested. A more conservative fiscal stance would therefore have been advisable, and this would have depressed growth from its observed path prior to the GFC – but perhaps to a more sustainable level that would have lessened the reliance on fickle short-term capital and the risk of capital flight. But in this, the successor states were not alone. The same policy criticism could be levied against many other transition economies elsewhere, as well as countries in Western Europe and North America at this time. The IMF, in its advice to the successor states, was equally

Table 7.6 Yugoslav successor states: growth and inflation

Real GDP growth and Inflation	Transition 1991–99	Boom 2000–08		Bust 2009–14		Recovery 2015–16	
	Growth	Growth	Inflation	Growth	Inflation	Growth	Inflation
Slovenia	1.6	4.2	5.3	−0.1	1.3	2.7	−0.3
Croatia	−2.0	4.2	3.3	−2.2	1.8	2.6	−0.8
Bosnia	2.8	4.8	3.3	0.6	1.1	2.5	−1.1
Serbia	−8.6	6.1	24.3	−0.2	7.1	1.8	1.3
Montenegro		5.0	11.3	0.4	2.2	2.9	0.6
Kosovo		4.1	3.4	3.1	2.2	3.8	−0.1
Macedonia	−1.5	3.5	3.1	1.9	1.7	3.1	−0.3

Average annual rates of change for the period of real gross domestic product and CPI

Source: Maddison Project Database (2013) for Transition, IMF WEO database for the rest. The Madison data set employed are not official data, but statistical constructs for a period (over 1991–99) when official data either did not exist or were not reliable. This data must therefore be interpreted with an element of caution

[33] The external debt of Yugoslavia was apportioned to the successor states roughly in line with their agreed quota shares. Slovenia promptly regularized its relations with creditors, and Croatia and Macedonia reached accords with official and commercial creditors in Paris and London Club agreements during 1995–97. None obtained debt reduction, but their debt burdens were deemed manageable. Following the Dayton Agreement, Bosnia renegotiated its debts with the Paris and London Clubs over 1997–98 and achieved significant debt reduction (about two thirds). Serbia and Montenegro achieved comparable terms in 2001.

slow to recognize the growing problem in the run up to the GFC.[34] The IMF did, however, respond rapidly with assistance to the region as the crisis unfolded.[35] But whatever the causes of downturn in 2008, it is not clear that the reforms to enterprise governance were to blame. Rather the problem was one of policymakers learning (by experience) how to safely ride and tame the wild stallion of a newly minted market economy once it has found its mettle.

Slovenia largely avoided military conflict (apart from a brief clash in the summer of 1991) and, being closest to the Western markets of Austria and Italy, was well placed to take advantage of the reforms that it initiated ahead of its fellow successor states. It was also traditionally the most competitive and fastest growing republic of Yugoslavia (Charts 7.2, 7.3 and 7.4) even before independence. Of all the successor states, it was the one which perhaps had the most to gain from independence – not least from ridding itself of the obligation to transfer resources to the poorer fellow provinces to its south. Reflecting these advantages, it never had to resort to an IMF programme.[36] Perhaps also reflecting this arm's-length relationship with the IMF, it implemented its reforms relatively slowly compared with the other successor states – which being an early starter it could afford to do. In 1990, Slovenia already had in place two new agencies – the Agency for Restructuring and Privatization and the Development Fund. The latter was the holding body for enterprises requiring restructuring prior to privatization. The 1988 and 1989 Yugoslav laws were made more proactive with the addition of a new Law on Ownership Transformation in 1992. By 1998, the ownership structure of 90 per cent of enterprises had been transformed in line with the modern corporate model typical in market economies, and most of these had been privatized.[37] This process, however, concerned 'socially owned capital' (former worker-controlled enterprises), and not state assets which included the banks. The Slovenian government was much slower to proceed with the privatization of the latter, and it is partly in

[34] See Bennett et al. (2015) (op cit) for a detailed analysis of this fiscal myopia.
[35] There is a common perception that IMF programmes in the region were responsible for slow or negative growth as a result of conditionality and 'austerity' programmes. A country enjoying robust growth is unlikely to seek assistance from the IMF, so that the direction of causation is more likely the other way – countries in crisis and recession seek IMF assistance. In fact, the evidence for the Western Balkans (the successor states plus Albania, Bulgaria and Romania) for the period 2003–14 is that the presence or otherwise of an IMF programme had a negligible correlation with growth. What they did correlate with were balance of payments deficits which would otherwise have been unfinanceable without IMF assistance. In other words, absent an IMF programme, the growth performance of the crisis affected country would have been worse (see 'IMF and the Balkans', paper presented by the author, European Studies Centre, St Antony's College, 30 November, 2015).
[36] Although the constituent provinces were deemed to have succeeded to shares of the IMF membership of Yugoslavia in 1992, they did so de facto at different stages: Croatia (1993), Slovenia (1993), the former Yugoslav Republic of Macedonia (1993), Bosnia and Herzegovina (1995), and the Federal Republic of Yugoslavia (2000). The Federal Republic of Yugoslavia was later renamed Serbia and Montenegro and in 2006, Serbia and Montenegro separated to become the Republic of Serbia and the Republic of Montenegro. Serbia retained its membership, while Montenegro separately became a member of the Fund in 2007, while Kosovo seceded from Serbia and became a member of the Fund in 2009.
[37] See Nancy Wagner *Privatization and Corporate Governance in Slovenia: the Shift from Comrade to Shareholder* (1998) Selected Issues, IMF Staff Country Report, No 98/20 for an account of this process.

consequence of this that the country found it more difficult to clean up the (still politicized) banking system's balance sheet in the wake of the GFC. The country grew more rapidly than most of the other Yugoslav successor states prior to the GFC and was the first to join the EU in 2004 (and the euro in 2007). However, Slovenia took much longer (than other successor states apart from Croatia) to emerge from the recession following the GFC in 2008 and this in turn can be linked to the problems in its banking system. The country eventually resumed growth in 2015.

Croatia was more extensively involved in the Yugoslav conflicts, both with Serbia and within Bosnia. Its economy was significantly affected by the war as well as by the dislocation of traditional trading arrangements within the disintegrating Yugoslavia. The legal framework for privatization in Croatia was strengthened by the Law on Transformation of Socially Owned Enterprises in 1991, which instituted the Croatian Privatization Fund on the model of the German Treuhand. This process reserved 50 per cent of shareholdings in the transformed enterprises for workers (available at a 20 per cent discount), the rest being auctioned off at fair market value. This was relatively successful in transferring smaller enterprises into private ownership, but larger ones proved more difficult to shift (in part because of the ongoing conflict and the lack of domestic financial resources to take up the equity). In support of its reform and stabilization programme, the government turned to the IMF for assistance and was the first of the successor states to avail itself of a Stand-by Arrangement in 1994. This coincided with, and perhaps helped facilitate, a turnaround in its economy. Croatia continued to have a close relationship with the Fund, with further arrangements in 1997, 2001, 2003 and 2004, each one of which aimed, inter alia, to keep the slow moving privatization process going forward. The country continued to grow rapidly until the GFC in 2008, but – like Slovenia – found it difficult to emerge from the post GFC recession. Croatia's competitiveness was not as sharp as that of Slovenia, and its wages less flexible downwards. Although it retained its own currency and the scope thereby to devalue to restore competitiveness, it chose not to do this for fear of worsening the balance sheet of its financial system which had become extensively exposed to foreign currency risk. Like Slovenia, Croatia finally returned to a respectable growth rate in 2015.

Of the other successor states, *Bosnia and Herzegovina* was the first to attract the attention of the international community, and the IMF supported its reforms toward a market economy as well as the adoption of a currency board arrangement in 1998 with a three-year Stand-by Arrangement. In addition to other reforms, this programme supported the authorities' preferred choice of a cash and voucher-based mass privatization programme for smaller enterprises, which, on the whole, proceeded satisfactorily. The privatization of larger enterprises, on the other hand, proved a more protracted process. Moreover, slow progress in introducing accompanying governance arrangements, such as bankruptcy legislation, meant that many of the newly privatized enterprises remained more incentivized by cash flow than by profit. To help maintain the momentum of its reform programme, therefore, Bosnia continued to avail itself of close IMF support in the form of successive three year Stand-by Arrangements in 2002,

2009, 2012, and 2016. Bosnia's complex political post-conflict structure, made the process of reform especially protracted, and the role of a politically independent driver of reform (such as the IMF) was therefore all the more important. Despite these difficulties, the strong support of the international community helped Bosnia make a robust recovery from the severe effects of the conflict and post the best average growth rate in the final decade of the last century, as well as a strong showing until the onset of the GFC. Bosnia was a direct beneficiary of the so-called 'Vienna Initiative', whereby the international financial institutions encouraged banks not to withdraw financing from selected countries and recapitalize their subsidiaries where needed in return for those countries agreeing to an arrangement with the IMF.

Serbia was the slowest to reform and suffered the most prolonged downturn during the 1990s. This reflected the two stages of the conflict – initially outside its borders during 1991–95 and then within with the secession of Kosovo in 1999–2000, as well as the country's isolation under international sanctions. After the end of the Kosovo conflict and the re-engagement of Serbia with the international community, Serbia entered into its first Stand-by Arrangement with the Fund in 2001, followed by an Extended Fund Arrangement for 2002–05. These programmes aimed, inter alia, to support the authorities' privatization programme. This process was actually initiated in 1997, with a Privatization law and the sale of 800 socially owned enterprises through management buyouts, and was furthered by another privatization law in 2001 which envisaged sales to strategic investors. Overall, however, privatization took longer than envisaged.[38] Nevertheless, under this reform framework, Serbia posted one of the best growth rates of the successor states through to the GFC in 2008 (which hit it quite hard). Like Bosnia, it benefitted from the Vienna Initiative and entered into a series of post-GFC Stand-by Arrangements in 2009, 2010 and 2012. Serbia joined other successor states in returning to strong growth in 2015.

Following its separation from Serbia in 2006 (with whom it had mirrored its privatization programme hitherto), *Montenegro*'s growth rate accelerated into double digits, enjoying strong foreign direct investor interest in its private sector – especially in residential construction and tourism – but it then hit the buffers with the GFC (with the third deepest recession after Croatia and Slovenia). It never availed itself of an IMF arrangement, but struggled with governance issues concerning its banks and their political connections (which persisted despite their private status). Despite these problems, Montenegro joined the other successor states in resuming strong growth in 2015. *Kosovo*, whose (violent) separation occurred earlier, enjoyed the support of the international community and was never as exposed to the GFC as the other countries because of its greater dependence on international aid than on international trade. It entered into its first IMF arrangement in 2010, mainly to provide a coherent policy framework.

---

[38] Serbia's privatization programme did not near completion for socially owned enterprises until 2009, and remained unfinished for state-owned enterprises as of 2015.

The former Yugoslav Republic of *Macedonia* was the furthest from the conflict in the 1990s, though found itself uncomfortably close in between 1999 and 2001. It was, however, always one of the weakest provinces in terms of competitiveness. Despite its economy not suffering directly from battle damage, Macedonia did nevertheless have to deal with the disruption of its traditional supply lines and trading relationships with the other successor states and with the loss of fiscal support from the richer provinces, of which it and Montenegro were the main beneficiaries. Reflecting its (marginal) low-income status, its first borrowing arrangement from the IMF was in the form of subsidized lending from the Enhanced Structural Adjustment Facility in 1997. By 2001, it was judged no longer 'low income', and resorted instead to an unsubsidized Extended Fund Arrangement, and then a series of Stand-by Arrangements in 2003 and 2005. Macedonia's privatization programme began with the passage of the Law on Transformation of Social Capital in 1993, and sales began in 1994 – mostly to insiders with generous financing terms. With little change in the actual management (or motivation) of these enterprises, their performance subsequent to their privatization was lacklustre and many remained lossmakers.[39] Because much of the privatization had been undertaken prior to IMF and World Bank involvement, most of the work of their programmes was instead to unpick the flaws resulting from the earlier insider sales by bolstering efforts to improve their performance (through strengthened bankruptcy legislation and increased participation by strategic investors). All in all, however, Macedonia's privatization programme was (initially) the least effective of the successor states. Perhaps reflecting this, Macedonia's growth rate up to the GFC was less rapid than other successor states, but unlike the others, it largely avoided the recession that followed the GFC.

VI Conclusion

The system of enterprise-self management, peculiar to Yugoslavia's unique model of democratic socialism, proved fatal to optimal macroeconomic management – despite the best efforts of the Yugoslav government and its international advisors to make this marriage work. Wage pressures and wasteful investment created a large borrowing requirement that could only be financed by a ruinous domestic inflation tax. This led to disintermediation and a chronic and unacceptably high rate of inflation. The latter ate progressively into the internal credibility of the Federal government which proved unable to control it. The hyperinflation in 1989 (itself the result of a specific well-meant but fatal policy error) merely accelerated what would have been the eventual collapse of central government authority, and exposed the other horn of the dilemma – that inflation could only be avoided in Yugoslavia with severe recession. The reforms introduced in 1988 and consolidated in 1989 toward dismantling enterprise self-management in favour of shareholder control were in the right direction, but far too late. Had they been introduced twenty years earlier, it is quite possible that the political,

---

[39] See Enterprise Restructuring and Transition: Evidence from the former Yugoslav Republic of Macedonia, Juan Zalduendo, IMF Working Paper WP/03/136, June 2003.

ethnic and economic fissures that existed in Yugoslavia (as typically exist to a greater or lesser extent in most modern nation states) would never have resulted in fracture. But Tito was still in power then, and such reforms would have likely been impossible under his watch. Reform in 1980 after he died might yet have worked, but it would have been a race against time for them to bear fruit before the forces of dissent and dissolution overwhelmed the union. Instead, the changes were implemented in the successor states. Even then, it sometimes took over ten years to achieve the critical mass of reforms to effect the necessary change. While emerging from conflict and the transition to market economies – not to mention their exposure to globalization and the GFC – was not easy, all the successor states did nevertheless eventually secure by 2015 sustainable growth and low inflation – the optimal macroeconomic management scenario that had consistently eluded them when they were part of Yugoslavia. Nevertheless, even fifteen years on from the end of the Yugoslav Federation, there remained gaps (varying from small to large) between the prosperity of the successor states and those of Western Europe, especially among those states that had yet to join the European Union – the holy grail that many hoped these reforms would bring. For some successor states, therefore, a long section of the road to transition and redemption still lay ahead.

The ending of enterprise self-management in the successor states comprises the single most important economic discontinuity from the old socialist Yugoslavia era. There undoubtedly remains a widespread nostalgia for this unique system amongst the citizens of the successor states. Yet this nostalgia arguably defies the other undeniably beneficial economic discontinuity – the absence of chronically high inflation – that many do not appreciate may have directly resulted from this reform of enterprise governance.

References

Adams, Charles and Daniel Gros. 'The Consequences of Real Exchange Rate Rules for Inflation: Some Illustrative Examples' (1986) Vol 33(3), IMF Staff Papers, pp. 439–76 Sept.

Baker, Catherine. *The Yugoslav Wars of the 1990s*. (Palgrave Macmillan, 2015).

Bennett, Adam, Russell Kincaid, Peter Sanfey, and Max Watson. *Economic and Policy Foundations for Growth in South East Europe: Remaking the Balkan Economy*. (Palgrave Pivot, 2015).

Bennett, Adam and Susan Schadler. *Interest Rate Policy in Central and Eastern Europe: The Influence of Monetary Overhangs and Weak Enterprise Discipline*, IMF Working Paper 92/68, 1992.

Calvo, Guillermo. Carmen Reinhart and Carlos Vegh (1995) 'Targeting the Real Exchange Rate: Theory and Evidence' 47 *Journal of Development Economics*.

Estrin, Saul. *Self-Management: Economic Theory and Yugoslav Practice*. (Cambridge University Press, 1983).

Friedman, Milton. *Inflation: Causes and Consequences*. (Asia Publishing House, 1963).

Jović, Dejan. *Yugoslavia: A State that Withered Away*. (Purdue University Press, 2009).

Kukic, Leonard. *Socialist Growth Revisited: Insights from Yugoslavia*, Economic History Working Papers, No 268, LSE, 2017.

Lahiri, Ashok. 'Yugoslav Inflation and Money', IMF Working Paper WP/91/50, May 1991.

Lydall, Harold. *Yugoslavia in Crisis* (Clarendon Press, 1989).

Meade, James. 'The Theory of Labour-Managed Firms and of Profit Sharing' (1972) 82 *Economic Journal*, pp. 402–28.

Sapir, Andre. 'Economic Growth and Factor Substitution: What Happened to the Yugoslav Miracle?'(1980) 90 *Economic Journal*, pp. 294–313.

Wagner, Nancy. *Privatization and Corporate Governance in Slovenia: the Shift from Comrade to Shareholder* (1998) Selected Issues, IMF Staff Country Report, No 98/20, March.

Woodward, Susan. *Balkan Tragedy.* (Brookings Institution, 1995).

Woodward, Susan. *Socialist Unemployment: the Political Economy of Yugoslavia 1945–90.* (Princeton University Press, 1995).

Zalduendo, Juan. (2003) *Enterprise Restructuring and Transition: Evidence from the Former Yugoslav Republic of Macedonia*, IMF Working Paper WP/03/136, June.

Annex 1

Statistical Analysis of Money and Inflation in Yugoslavia 1987–89

Equations 1 and 2 display the results of a Sims-style causality test, which shows that while past changes in the money supply appear to have had a negligible role in explaining inflation in Yugoslavia during this period in question (equation 2), past movements in the price level explain subsequent movements in the money supply (equation 1).[40] Equation 3 represents an effort to econometrically model the pressure on the inflation rate from changes in the real exchange rate target. Although the relevant estimated coefficients are only weakly statistically significant, they are of the correct sign and this estimated equation thereby suggests that holding the real exchange rate below its equilibrium level (represented by the estimated constant term) may have caused the inflation rate to accelerate during the period in question.

Monetary growth (money demand) was mostly driven by inflation, not the other way around:

1. $\Delta\%^{\Delta}R = 4.4 - 0.1\Delta\%^{\Delta}P_{-1} - 0.3\Delta\%^{\Delta}R_{-1} + 0.7\ln(P/R)_{-1}$ $R^2=0.51$
     (4.2) (0.5)   (1.6)   (4.2)   (t-value)

2. $\Delta\%^{\Delta}P = -0.0 - 0.5\Delta\%^{\Delta}P_{-1} + 0.2\Delta\%^{\Delta}R_{-1} - 0.0\ln(P/R)_{-1}$ $R^2=0.35$
      (0.0) (2.2)   (1.1)   (0.1)   (t-value)

Where R is dinar reserve money liabilities of NBY, P is the price level , Δ denotes 'change in' and $\%^{\Delta}$ denotes 'percent change in'; estimated over January 1987 through December 1989

---

[40] See Ashok Lahiri 'Yugoslav Inflation and Money', IMF Working Paper WP/91/50, May 1991, for a corroboration of the tendency for inflation to lead money in Yugoslavia during this period.

Inflation itself was partly driven by real exchange rate target:

3. $\Delta\%^{\Delta}P = 0.1 - 0.5\Delta\%^{\Delta}P_{-1} - 0.3(P/P^{F}.e)_{-1} + 0.2(P/P^{F}.e)_{-2}$ $R^2=0.27$
     (1.0) (2.5)   (1.4)   (1.0)   (t-value)

Where superscript F denotes 'foreign' and e is the nominal effective exchange rate; estimated over January 1987 through December 1989.

8

What Happened to the Yugoslav Economic Model?

Milica Uvalic
University of Perugia

I Introduction

The Socialist Federal Republic (SFR) of Yugoslavia (hereafter Yugoslavia) was a federation consisting of six republics – Bosnia and Herzegovina, Croatia, Macedonia, Montenegro, Serbia with its two autonomous regions (Vojvodina in the north and Kosovo in the south) and Slovenia. While retaining the main features typical of the socialist economic system operating behind the so-called 'Iron Curtain', following the break with Stalin in 1948, Yugoslavia went on to introduce elements of the market economy, parallel with substantial decentralization and the development of a system of workers' self-management. Yugoslavia's unique economic system stimulated considerable academic interest for several reasons.[1] First, the Yugoslav model appeared to offer an example of a potential 'third way' between capitalism and socialism. Second, the extension of the principles of democracy in decision making was viewed by many as an objective in its own right, combining the efficiency properties of a competitive market economy with the ethical and moral superiority derived from democratic workplace decision-making.

The aim of the present chapter is to recall the specific features of the Yugoslav economic model and to explore whether and to what extent, after the country disintegrated in 1991, there were continuities in the Yugoslav successor states with respect to the previous economic system. The countries included in our analysis are the successor states of Yugoslavia, namely Bosnia and Herzegovina, Croatia, Federal Republic (FR) of Yugoslavia (more recently represented by three countries – Kosovo, Montenegro and Serbia), the Former Yugoslav Republic of Macedonia (today, North Macedonia) and Slovenia.

The chapter will first describe the foundations of the Yugoslav economic system developed during the 1945–1991 period, deriving from its socialist, market, self-managed and international features (section 2). It will then proceed to recall some of the controversies about the labour-managed economy, developed in the rich literature

---

[1] Saul Estrin and Milica Uvalić, 'From Illyria towards Capitalism: Did Labour-Management Theory Teach Us Anything about Yugoslavia and Transition in Its Successor States?', 50th Anniversary Essay (2008) 50 *Comparative Economic Studies* 665.

on the labour-managed firm (LMF) (section 3). It will also consider the main achievements and failures of the Yugoslav economic model and the starting conditions in Yugoslavia on the eve of transition (section 4). The analysis will then shift to transition-related economic and institutional reforms implemented by the Yugoslav governments in 1988–90 and by its successor states after 1991, showing how some countries have dismantled key elements of the old system faster than others (section 5). In the last section, the most important conclusions are drawn regarding the continuities and discontinuities of the Yugoslav successor states with respect to the pre-1989 economic model (section 6).

II Main features of the Yugoslav economic model

The Yugoslav economic system was a combination of four groups of ingredients deriving from its socialist, market, self-managed and international features.

Socialist features

Throughout its post-1945 existence Yugoslavia retained some of the key features typical of the socialist economic system:[2] (i) non-private property; (ii) planning and other non-market mechanisms of allocation of resources; and (iii) party control of the economy.

The *property regime* in the bulk of the Yugoslav economy was non-private, since private property on a larger scale was considered incompatible with the socialist economic system. Enterprises in Yugoslavia were considered to be social property, or the property of the entire society. The notion of social property was first introduced in the 1953 Constitution, whereas the 1974 Constitution explicitly speaks of social property as 'no-one's property'. This system gave workers the right to use socially owned capital and to appropriate its proceeds (*usus* and *usus fructus* rights), but not full property rights, since workers were not allowed to sell their enterprise. In case of a firm's closure, whatever remained of its assets went to the state, confirming that a socially owned enterprise had effectively remained state property.[3] The expansion of the private sector, mainly in agriculture and certain crafts and services, was restricted by law.

The Yugoslav economy also relied on the *planning mechanism* and other *non-market mechanisms of allocation of resources*. Although the system of centralized planning, copied from the Soviet model, was replaced by a more flexible system of indicative planning already in the early 1950s, Yugoslavia continued to use various planning instruments. As part of the system of economic planning, there were annual plans (in the 1970s replaced by annual Economic Resolutions) and medium-term (usually five-year) plans, which defined the main priorities of economic development. The Yugoslav

---

[2] Marie Lavigne, *The Economics of Transition. From Socialist Economy to Market Economy*, 2nd edn (Basingstoke and London, 1999).
[3] Milica Uvalic, *Investment and Property Rights in Yugoslavia. The Long Transition to a Market Economy* (Cambridge, 1992); Reprinted in paperback in 2009.

government also used other non-market mechanisms in the allocation of resources, such as the General Investment Funds (until the reforms in the 1960s) or the Fund for the Development of the Less Developed Republics and Regions through which resources were transferred from the more developed towards the less-developed parts of the country.

Party control of the economy was also a constant feature of the Yugoslav economic system, since it was the political authorities who determined the most important 'rules of the game' both at the macro and the microeconomic level. Enterprises were subject to regulations regarding the distribution of earned income, such as obligatory depreciation rates necessary for the maintenance of the value of social capital, permissible wage increases or prescribed minimum rates of accumulation. Although these regulations changed continuously, enterprises were never entirely free of them.

Yugoslavia had other features in common with countries in Eastern Europe. Yugoslavia's *pattern of economic development* to a great extent resembled those of other socialist countries. Particularly during the first two decades, the priorities of Yugoslavia's development strategies were almost identical to those in other countries in Eastern Europe, including fast economic growth, rapid industrialization with emphasis on the development of heavy industry and high investment rates at the expense of consumption. With increasing problems of unemployment and inflation from the mid-1960s, Yugoslavia had to abandon some of the objectives of the traditional socialist economic system (full employment, low inflation), but it retained other socialist priorities, such as the *principle of solidarity* (as exemplified by the policies of transfer of resources to the less developed parts of the country, or of bailing out loss-making enterprises); *egalitarianism* (e.g. wage scales that were to ensure that workers with the same qualifications earned similar personal incomes);[4] and a *strong welfare state* (free education, free health care, low-cost transport, various in-kind benefits and specific housing policies for employed workers).

Reliance on the market mechanism

When Yugoslavia abandoned the centrally planned economic system in the early 1950s, it also introduced the first elements of the market mechanism, along with a unique system of self-management (see section 2.3. below). During the 1950s, a single-price structure was introduced and some price controls were relaxed. State monopoly of foreign trade was abolished, giving enterprises more freedom in conducting their foreign trade operations. The first steps were taken to decentralize the banking system by setting up sectoral banks for agriculture, investment and foreign trade. However, investment policies remained strictly centralized, as the mobilization and allocation of investment resources were undertaken by the government through the General Investment Funds.

---

[4] However, these wage scales were not very effective, since there was substantial dispersion in wage earnings in Yugoslavia, as documented in detail by Saul Estrin, *Self-management: Economic Theory and Yugoslav Practice* (Cambridge, 1983).

The economic reforms implemented in 1963–67 were much more far-reaching. Enterprises were given more freedom in deciding over the distribution of their net income and other enterprise policies. A two-tier banking system was introduced, separating the central bank's operations from those of all-purpose commercial banks. The General Investment Funds were abolished in 1963 and their resources were transferred to the banks. There was further decentralization of the economy with responsibility for some economic policies transferred to the six republics. In order to open up the Yugoslav economy to the world market, a uniform exchange rate was introduced to replace the system of multiple exchange rates and the dinar was devalued as to introduce a more realistic exchange rate. The first foreign joint ventures law was adopted in 1967, though the share of the foreign partner's capital was limited to 49 per cent.

Further institutional changes were implemented in the 1970s. Since the reforms in the 1960s had led to the concentration of power in the hands of banks and technocratic elites which was regarded ideologically unacceptable, the new reforms were meant to reinforce the planning mechanism. These reforms were implemented through the 1971 constitutional amendments and were fully enacted in the new 1974 Constitution and the 1976 Associated Labour Act. New mechanisms of policy coordination, based on the principles of self-management, were introduced (see section below). Banks were transformed into 'service' agencies of enterprises operating under their direct control. New methods of mobilizing savings were introduced, which would not necessarily require banks' intermediation – the 'pooling of labour and resources' meant to stimulate direct investment of one enterprise into another. Financial instruments were diversified, to include bonds, treasury bills and promissory notes. The 1974 Constitution introduced even greater decentralization, transferring substantial economic powers to the republics and autonomous regions. The foreign trade system was further reformed in order to give more freedom to the republics in their foreign trade operations and allowing them to retain a larger part of earned foreign exchange.

Workers' self-management

Yugoslavia's move toward workers' self-management began with a law adopted in 1950 giving workers the right to elect members of workers' councils, which were to decide on production, inputs, hiring policies, and to a limited extent on prices and income distribution. The workers' councils were also responsible for the election of members of management boards and for appointing and removing the enterprise's manager. In line with self-management, the 1953 Constitution introduced social property, specifying that enterprises were the property of the whole of society. Initially capital was given to enterprises free of charge, but after 1954 they had to pay a 6 per cent tax. The planning system now envisaged the active participation of the newly established councils of producers.

During the 1960s, the system of self-management was extended to all sectors and types of organizations. Enterprises' decision-making rights were substantially increased regarding the distribution of earned income and other specific policies. The charge for the use of social capital was first reduced and finally abolished in 1971; this was interpreted by some scholars as the introduction of 'group property', and the effective redistribution of property rights in favour of enterprises vis-à-vis the state.[5]

Reforms in the 1970s aimed to improve the system of self-management.[6] Because self-management was reported as not functioning well in very large firms, enterprises were divided into smaller units, so-called Basic Organizations of Associated Labour (BOALs), each having its own self-management organs and statutory acts. Several BOALs were to be part of an Organization of Associated Labour (OAL) and, in turn, several OALs of a Complex Organization of Associated Labour (COAL). New mechanisms of policy coordination were introduced with the aim of strengthening the planning component – social contracts, self-management agreements and self-managed communities of interest – which once concluded were legally binding. Social contracts were agreements concluded between enterprises, political representatives, trade unions, chambers of commerce and other organizations on main directions of economic policies, such as priorities of social plans, and principles regarding prices, income distribution, employment and wages. Self-management agreements were to regulate relations between firms and other organizations (including banks) in areas of mutual interest, such as the creation of firms, investment projects, transfer prices or joint transactions. Self-managed communities of interest were to regulate relations between the providers and the users of various services, initially in the areas of health, education and social insurance but later extended to foreign trade.[7] With the introduction of these various types of agreements, all economic and non-economic agents were expected to participate in the system of social planning. Yugoslavia's economy during this period was therefore often referred to as 'the contractual economy'.

During the 1980s there were no substantial changes in Yugoslavia's economic system – its socialist, market and self-managed features. As a response to the economic crisis which started developing in the early 1980s, a long-term stabilization programme was prepared in 1982 which contained a detailed list of measures meant to improve the functioning of the Yugoslav economy. However, this four-volume government document did not touch upon the foundations of the economic system. The target model in Yugoslavia was officially changed only at the end of the 1980s, when the Federal government decided to implement a series of more fundamental economic reforms which would mark the beginning of the country's transition towards a fully-fledged market economy based on private property (see section below).

Specific international relations

Unlike the Soviet Union and much of Eastern Europe, Yugoslavia was a founding member of the International Monetary Fund and the World Bank in 1945. After its expulsion from Cominform in 1948, Yugoslavia sought to balance its economic and political relations with both the East and the West. Yugoslavia was not a member of the

---

[5] Aleksandar Bajt 'Property in Capital and in the Means of Production in Socialist Economies' (1968) 11 *Journal of Law and Economics* 1–4.
[6] Uvalic, *Investment and Property Rights in Yugoslavia*.
[7] Ibid.

Council of Mutual Economic Assistance (CMEA) nor of the Warsaw Pact. It was one of the founders of the Non-alignment movement,[8] together with India and Egypt. From August 1966, when it signed the General Agreement on Tariffs and Trade (GATT), Yugoslavia regularly participated in its negotiation rounds and had observer status in the Organization for Economic Cooperation and Development (OECD). Yugoslavia also had privileged relations with the European Economic Community: it signed several trade agreements from 1970 onwards and a comprehensive Trade and Economic Cooperation Agreement in 1980 which, in addition to preferential trade, included other areas of cooperation (energy, transport, technology) and a special financial protocol.[9]

Yugoslavia's openness towards the West was not restricted to the economic sphere. Symbols of Western consumer society were allowed to 'penetrate' into the Yugoslav society early on.[10] In the 1950s Yugoslavia started producing 'Cockta', a soft drink very similar to Coca Cola; rock music posters of top Yugoslav singers were almost identical to those of Elvis Presley; and Western music festivals, such as the one in San Remo, were regularly listened to. The Yugoslav airlines JAT began direct flights to New York in the early 1970s.

III Controversies about the Yugoslav model

The specific features of Yugoslavia's economic model have inspired a large literature on the labour-managed firm (LMF) and the labour-managed economy. Benjamin Ward's seminal article on the 'Firm in Illyria'[11] (1958) stimulated increasing academic interest in self-management.[12] Ward argued that, contrary to the capitalist firm which maximizes profits, the LMF maximizes income per worker. This specific maximand of the LMF could, however, lead to various types of inefficiencies. The list of drawbacks include the inefficient allocation of labour due to the 'perverse' or at least rigid response of the LMF to changes in product price, technology and capital rental; restrictive employment policies, since increasing the number of workers would cause the reduction in income per worker; more restrictive monopolistic behaviour due to

---

[8] See Ljubica Spaskovskaja's contribution in this volume.

[9] Milica Uvalic, *Serbia's Transition – Towards a Better Future* (Basingstoke and New York, 2010), 17–18. Expanded edition in Serbian: *Tranzicija u Srbiji – Ka boljoj budućnosti* (Belgrade, 2012). In 1990, more than 50 per cent of Yugoslavia's trade was with the OECD, mainly European, countries. 46 per cent of its exports went to the twelve countries of the European Community (EC) and another 7 per cent to the EFTA countries, while 44 per cent of its imports were from the EC and another 10 per cent from the EFTA countries (data provided in Savezni zavod za statistiku, *Statistički godišnjak Jugoslavije 1991* (Belgrade, 1991)).

[10] See Branislav Dimitrijević, *Potrošeni socijalizam. Kultura, konzumerizam i društvena imaginacija u Jugoslaviji (1950–1974)* [*Consumed Socialism. Culture, Consumerism and Social Immagination in Yugoslavia (1950–1974)*], (Beograd, 2016).

[11] Benjamin Ward, 'The Firm in Illyria – Market Syndicalism'(1958) 48(4) *American Economic Review* 566–89.

[12] For a survey of the literature, see Will Bartlett and Milica Uvalić, 'Labour-managed Firms, Employee Participation and Profit-sharing: Theoretical Perspectives and European Experience' (1986) 12(4) *Management Bibliographies and Reviews* 3–66. Special Issue.

maximization of monopoly profit per man instead of total profit; and the unsuitability of the LMF outside of labour intensive sectors and for risky ventures. Regarding mid-term inefficiencies, Furubotn and Pejovich[13] suggested that the LMF will tend to underinvest. Given that the LMF is in non-private (collective) property, workers would adopt a short-term horizon and would not have an incentive to invest in the firm, as they would benefit from such investments only for the duration of their employment. When deciding whether to invest in 'non-owned assets' (the firm) or 'owned assets' (their private savings accounts), LMF workers would prefer the latter. This could lead to underinvestment by the LMF in comparison with its capitalist counterpart.

The LMF theory was developed further by Evsey Domar,[14] Jaroslav Vanek,[15] James Meade,[16] Jan Svejnar,[17] Saul Estrin,[18] Mario Nuti[19] and many others. Some scholars have argued that the above inefficiencies might not necessarily hold under alternative theoretical assumptions, or that they could be attenuated or even completely removed by introducing different institutional arrangements. Outside the context of Yugoslavia, there have been various empirical studies on workers' cooperatives (similar in some respects to Yugoslav self-managed firms) in Western market economies, which suggest that workers' participation in decision-making and in enterprise results, far from leading to inefficient behaviour, can have positive effects on incentives and labour productivity.[20] What the experience of workers' cooperatives does suggest, however, is their unsuitability outside labour-intensive sectors and for risky ventures.[21]

Among the most outspoken critics of the LMF literature was the Yugoslav economist Branko Horvat. Horvat[22] argued that Ward's 1958 model was inconsistent with actual enterprise behaviour in Yugoslavia. According to Horvat, Yugoslav worker's council targeted an 'aspiration income' (the level of personal income it wanted to achieve). Beyond that level the LMF would seek to maximize total enterprise profits above the targeted personal income payments, generating the same equilibrium conditions as for a capitalist firm.[23]

Another criticism of the LMF model was advanced by the Slovenian economist Aleksandar Bajt, in response to an article by André Sapir. Sapir[24] presented an empirical

[13] Eirik Furubotn and Steve Pejovich, 'Property Rights and the Behaviour of the Firm in a Socialist State – The Example of Yugoslavia' (1970) 30 *Zeitschrift für Nationalökonomie* 431–54.
[14] Evsey Domar, 'The Soviet Collective Farm as a Producer Co-operative' (1966) 56(4) *American Economic Review* 734–57.
[15] Jaroslav Vanek, *The General Theory of Labor-managed Market Economies.* (Ithaca, NY, 1970).
[16] James Meade, 'The Theory of Labour-managed Firms and of Profit-sharing' (1972) 82 *Economic Journal* 402–28.
[17] Jan Svejnar, 'On the Theory of a Participatory Firm' (1982) 27(2) *Journal of Economic Theory* 313–30.
[18] Saul Estrin, *Self-management: Economic Theory and Yugoslav Practice* (Cambridge, 1983).
[19] Domenico Mario Nuti (1992) 'On Traditional Cooperatives and James Meade's Labor-Capital Discriminating Partnerships' 4 *Advances in the Economic Analysis of Participatory and Labor-Managed Firms* 1–26.
[20] See, e.g. Saul Estrin, Derek Jones and Jan Svejnar, 'The Productivity Effects of Worker Participation: Producer Cooperatives in Western Economies' (1987) 11 *Journal of Comparative Economics* 40–61.
[21] Nuti, 'On Traditional Cooperatives and James Meade's Labor-Capital Discriminating Partnerships'.
[22] Branko Horvat, *The Political Economy of Socialism* (Armonk, New York, 1982).
[23] Horvat, *The Political Economy of Socialism.*
[24] André Sapir, 'Economic Growth and Factor Substitution: What Happened to the Yugoslav Miracle?' (1980) 90(358) *The Economic Journal* 294–313.

analysis of the performance of the Yugoslav economy after 1965, which led him to conclude that it was the workers' policy of maximizing income per worker which was responsible for the slowing down of economic growth, as well as for slow employment growth. Bajt[25] showed that the slowdown in Yugoslavia's economic growth was negligible and that Sapir's analysis depended essentially on which period was being considered. Bajt argued that the post-1965 economic slowdown in Yugoslavia was due to other factors, including the growing power of managerial elites, social unrest due to unemployment, and liberalist and nationalist deviations, rather than the alleged LMF maximand.

More recently, Uvalic (1992) has argued that the LMF model did not fit the Yugoslav experience well because – despite self-management and a role for the market –Yugoslavia nevertheless retained the most important overarching defining features of the socialist economy. *Social property* was a camouflaged form of state property, as workers never had full property rights over their enterprise (as explained above). Similar to firms in other socialist countries, Yugoslav enterprises also operated under *soft-budget constraints*,[26] since the cost of capital (interest on bank loans) was usually negative in real terms. Moreover, instead of closing down a loss-making enterprise, the government would more frequently help it out through the socialization of its losses. Furthermore, the Yugoslav economy was also characterized by very high investment rates (as in other socialist countries) or an 'overinvestment drive',[27] rather than by underinvestment. 'State paternalism', another term coined by Kornai,[28] to explain political tutelage over enterprises in socialist economies, was also very much present in Yugoslavia, as the political authorities set the most important regulations. The literature on the LMF was therefore based on a hypothetical labour-managed firm operating in a *free market environment* which effectively had never existed in Yugoslavia.

These socialist features of the Yugoslav economy had a number of negative implications for incentives, reproducing the inefficiency problem typical of the socialist economic system.[29] Also in Yugoslavia, there were no adequate rewards and penalties at the firm level according to market performance, which typically disciplines firms in a market economy, therefore there was no risk-bearing by the individual firm. At the macroeconomic level, in the absence of private property in the dominant part of the economy, it was the state which remained in charge of the most fundamental issues, including the coverage of losses through income redistribution from profitable to less-profitable firms, or the entry and exit of enterprises. Extensive market-orientated economic reforms in Yugoslavia therefore had a limited impact because of the essentially unchanged nature of the political system. A one-party political regime in Yugoslavia, which remained faithful to the Marxist ideology until the very end, did not

[25] Aleksandar Bajt, 'Economic Growth and Factor Substitution: What Happened to the Yugoslav Miracle? Some Comments' (1986) 96 *The Economic Journal* 1084–88.
[26] See Janos Kornai, *Economics of Shortage* (Amsterdam, 1980).
[27] Ibid.
[28] Ibid.
[29] Uvalic, *Investment and Property Rights in Yugoslavia*, 61.

permit the full affirmation of the market mechanism, the diffusion of private property on a larger scale, or the effective functioning of a labour or a capital market.[30]

Despite the strong resilience of the socialist features of the Yugoslav economy, workers' self-management still played an important social and economic role.[31] Although there were many deficiencies in its practical implementation, workers' participation in decision making was an important instrument for providing checks and balances, for example on managerial power.[32] Even more importantly, the economy-wide application of self-management produced a working class actively participating in decision making, which resulted in greater workers' satisfaction. In combination with greater individual freedoms[33] and the fact that Yugoslav 'communism' was not imposed by an outside power (the USSR) but was home grown by Second World War partisans, arguably secured greater acceptance of the economic and political regime in Yugoslavia than elsewhere in the socialist world.[34]

IV Achievements and failures of the Yugoslav model

Among the most important achievements of the Yugoslav model were rapid economic growth, which permitted fast industrialization, urbanization and a substantial increase in wellbeing and living standards of its population. The most important failures were the model's inability to avoid unemployment and inflation; increasing external imbalances; and the widening of regional economic disparities, which greatly contributed to the mounting political crisis in the 1980s and Yugoslavia's disintegration.

The Yugoslav economy developed rapidly during the first thirty five years of its existence, at an average GDP growth rate of around 6 per cent, thanks to very high investment rates which were maintained until the early 1980s.[35] Despite a slowdown after the mid-1960s, growth rates remained close to 6 per cent from 1966 to 1979. A sharp deterioration in growth performance was recorded only after 1979, when a severe economic crisis unfolded (see below). Despite this, Yugoslavia's real GDP per capita (in Purchasing Power Parities – PPP) increased from around US$ 1,200 in 1947 to over US$ 6,200 in 1989, confirming impressive long-term results in economic development.

However, Yugoslavia was confronted with unemployment and inflation which had started in the mid-1960s.[36] The official unemployment rate increased from 6 per cent

---

[30] Uvalic, *Investment and Property Rights in Yugoslavia;* Milica Uvalic, 'The Rise and Fall of Market Socialism in Yugoslavia' (Berlin: Dialogue of Civilizations (DOC) Research Institute, Special Report, 27 March 2018).
[31] See also Adis Merdzanovic's contribution in this volume.
[32] Aleksandar Bajt,'Economic Growth and Factor Substitution: What Happened to the Yugoslav Miracle?'
[33] Despite the political regime, there were more individual freedoms in Yugoslavia than in other countries in Eastern Europe. After 1965, all Yugoslav citizens had the right to a passport valid for five years which, at that time, enabled visa-free travel throughout Europe and many developing countries worldwide.
[34] Uvalic, *Investment and Property Rights in Yugoslavia.*
[35] Ibid.
[36] Ibid.

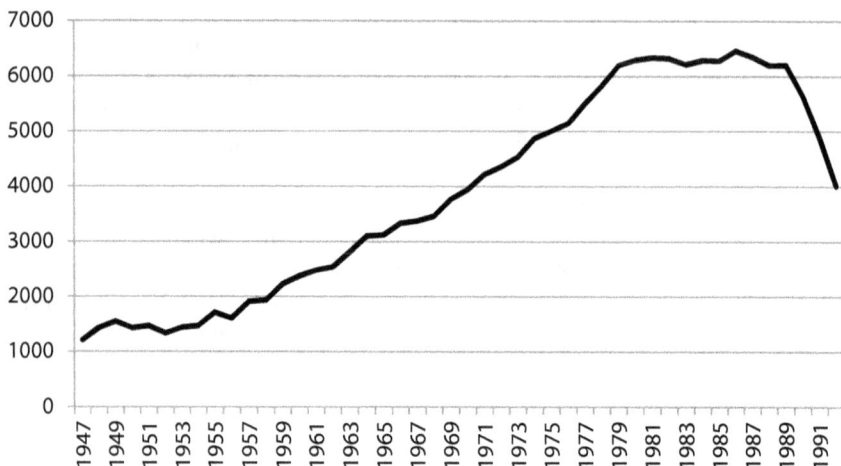

Figure 8.1 Gross domestic product per capita (US$, PPP) in Yugoslavia, 1947–1992.
Source: The Maddison-Project. Available at: www.ggdc.net/maddison/maddison-project/home.htm, 2013 version; GDP per capita is expressed in Geary-Khamis (GK) dollars, equivalent to the international 1990 dollar (in Purchasing Power Parities).

in 1965 to 7.7 per cent in 1970, to 12 per cent in 1980 and further to 16.4 per cent in 1990; but whereas Slovenia had practically full employment, Macedonia and Kosovo already had very high unemployment rates. There were also rising inflationary pressures, particularly after the mid-1960s. Due to the inadequate instruments of monetary control by the National Bank of Yugoslavia, especially after the adoption of the 1974 Constitution which gave greater monetary autonomy to its constituent parts, there was excessive monetary emission. Inflation was also fuelled by the uncontrolled growth in inter-enterprise credit through the issuing of promissory notes by enterprises. The average annual inflation rate increased to around 20 per cent in the 1970s, reaching particularly high levels in the 1980s – increasing from 30 per cent in 1980 to three-digit figures in 1987–88 and to 1,252 per cent (hyperinflation) in 1989.[37]

Yugoslavia was also facing increasing external imbalances from the late 1960s – a widening trade and current account deficit – which were initially offset by workers' remittances and revenues from tourism.[38] The Yugoslav government did not react to the 1973–74 oil shock by lowering domestic spending but continued with an unbalanced economic growth strategy, relying heavily on imports and particularly on external borrowing. Yugoslavia's external debt (net of lending) increased from less than US$2 billion in 1970 to US$14 billion in 1979 and, following the second oil shock, to US$18 billion in 1980. Structural imbalances emerged due to insufficient investment in crucial sectors (energy, raw materials) and rising dependence on imported inputs, while there was excess capacity in other sectors and the duplication of plants of

[37] Uvalic, *Serbia's Transition – Towards a Better Future.*
[38] Uvalic, *Investment and Property Rights in Yugoslavia*, 10-1.

suboptimal size across regions. After a record trade and current account deficit in 1979, Yugoslavia was no longer able to service its external debt, forcing the government to implement stabilization policies which, after 1981, were supported by the IMF. A severe economic crisis brought stagnating or declining GDP growth, negative rates of investment growth, falling real net wages, modest growth of employment, rising unemployment and inflation.[39] Restrictive income policies in the presence of rising inflation led to declining living standards: between 1980 and 1984 alone there was a 34 per cent drop in real net wages.

Another major failure of the Yugoslav model was the widening regional disparities in economic development. The regional policies aimed at bridging the gap between the more- and the less-developed parts of the country were unsuccessful. Despite transfers secured through the Federal Development Fund to help the less-developed republics and regions, the gap between GDP per capita of the most developed (Slovenia) and the least developed (Kosovo) actually widened, from 5:1 in 1955 to 8:1 in 1989.[40] There were other mechanisms of redistribution of income: budgetary transfers through the fiscal system; loans from the National Bank of Yugoslavia extended at preferential terms to specific administrative entities or special recipients (e.g. exporters, farmers); and the clearing system of payments in foreign trade with the CMEA countries, which favoured exporters and penalized importers. These mechanisms of redistribution provoked a long-lasting controversy over who was 'exploiting' whom.[41] The more developed republics – Slovenia and Croatia – felt exploited because of the obligatory transfer of resources to the Federal Development Fund, which usually remained outside their direct control, or other policies to their disadvantage, such as the retention of foreign currency earnings from exports and tourism. The less-developed republics felt exploited because of the unfavourable terms of trade deriving from the structure of their economies, namely a large share of basic industries, primarily agriculture, characterized by low efficiency and/or high capital-output ratios, in combination with distortions in relative prices due to more widespread price controls on basic than on manufacturing products, which in general implied lower prices for the former. The debate lasted for decades and was revived in the 1980s by the severe economic crisis, further stimulated by political disputes and the resurgence of nationalism.

On the eve of the transition to a market economy, in the late 1980s, the Yugoslav economy was therefore facing serious economic problems which had been accumulating for several decades. Although at that time there were wide differences regarding economic indicators of Yugoslavia's six republics (GDP per capita, unemployment, export orientation), they essentially had almost identical systemic features.

The Yugoslav republics in 1989 shared some important systemic advantages in comparison with other countries in Central and Eastern Europe (CEE). First, the continuous market-orientated economic reforms meant that many institutional changes – regarding prices, the banking system, taxation, foreign trade – had already

[39] Uvalic, *Serbia's Transition – Towards a Better Future*.
[40] Milica Uvalic, 'The Disintegration of Yugoslavia: Its Costs and Benefits' (1993) 5(3) *Communist Economies & Economic Transformation* 273–93.
[41] Milica Uvalic, 'The Disintegration of Yugoslavia: Its Costs and Benefits'.

been implemented. Second, Yugoslavia had a longer experience with macroeconomic stabilization policies, given that the government had aready had to combat unemployment and inflation from the mid-1960s. Finally, greater openness towards the West brought important advantages at both the macro and the microeconomic level, since trade orientation primarily towards Western economies enabled imports of modern technology and direct business contacts between enterprises. Therefore, in 1989, the Yugoslav government had a shorter reform agenda in comparison with CEE countries which had to start many economic reforms from scratch.

The Yugoslav economic system also had some disadvantages. Firstly, the ambiguous system of 'social property' hampered enterprise privatization. Given that no-one was officially the owner of enterprise property, who was to take the decision on privatization – the enterprise, enterprise workers, or the state? And to whom would the proceeds from privatization go: to the enterprise, its workers, the government? Secondly, there was greater resistance to radical economic reforms in Yugoslavia in comparison with other socialist countries, due to the population's major acceptance of the economic (and political) regime which, in some cases, slowed down more radical systemic changes.[42] Thirdly, the most serious disadvantage of the Yugoslav model in 1989 were the regional disparities stressed earlier, which greatly contributed to the political crisis which started to develop after Tito's death in May 1980. The political crisis was stimulated by the revival of the debate about 'unfair' economic arrangements within the federation, the resurgence of nationalism, rising social unrest and the tightening of relations among the republics due to the lack of compromise on how to reform the Yugoslav federation. The crisis culminated with the proclamation of Slovenia's and Croatia's political independence in June 1991 (though postponed until October 1991 upon request of the European Community), when Yugoslavia effectively disintegrated into five independent states: Bosnia and Herzegovina, Croatia, Macedonia, the Federal Republic of Yugoslavia (Serbia and Montenegro) and Slovenia.

V What happened to the Yugoslav model?

The fall of the Berlin Wall in November 1989, which officially marked the beginning of the transition to market economy and multiparty democracy in Eastern Europe, coincided with the first radical political and economic changes in Yugoslavia. The legislative acts announced by the Yugoslav governments in 1988–89 marked the beginning of the economic transition, which was to eliminate the main features of both the socialist economic system – party control of the economy, planning instruments, social property – and the system of self-management, although most of these processes were not immediate. The change in the political regime followed soon after, in 1990 (see below).

---

[42] The greater resistance to radical economic reforms and the preference for the *status quo* clearly emerged from the multiparty elections in some republics; for example, in Serbia, Slobodan Milošević won the first presidential elections in December 1990 because he was essentially promising continuity with respect to the previous political and economic regime (see Uvalic, *Serbia's Transition – Towards a Better Future*).

After a decade of Yugoslavia's sharply deteriorating economic performance and rising political unrest, which directly contributed to the country's break-up in 1991, each of the Yugoslav successor states implemented transition-related economic reforms according to their own national interests, at variable speeds and with very different strategies.

Initial systemic reforms

A decisive change in the official attitude towards the existing economic system took place in Yugoslavia after late 1988, when the government adopted thirty-nine amendments to the Yugoslav Constitution (on 25 November 1988) and twenty specific laws (between 1988 and 1990). These legislative changes announced the first radical economic reforms, away from the socialist self-management model towards private ownership and a mixed market economy.[43] Although the 1988 constitutional amendments did not put into question some of the key features of the Yugoslav economic system – including social planning, self-management, organizations of associated labour – some amendments did anticipate important changes of the property regime, in the direction of the expansion of the private sector. They introduced the possibility for citizens to invest personal resources into firms (Amendment X), abolished the limits on the number of workers that could be employed in private firms (Amendments XXI), allowed foreign persons to invest in firms, banks and other organizations (Amendment XV) and raised the limits on individual holdings in agriculture from 10 to 30 hectares per household (Amendment XXIII). The Foreign Direct Investment Law (December 1988) went in the same direction: it offered major protection of foreign investors ownership and management rights, eliminated existing limits on the foreign partner's capital share, announced specific incentives and tax benefits for foreign investors and permitted investments by foreign banks.

Two further laws were fundamental for dismantling the socialist and self-managed features of the Yugoslav economy: the Company Law (December 1988); and the Law on the Disposal and Circulation of Social Capital (December 1989) which was replaced by the Law on Social Capital (August 1990).[44]

The 1988 Company Law diversified property forms by adding mixed property (a combination of social and private property) to the already existing property forms (social, private and cooperative), introduced the commercialization of enterprises and new legal forms of enterprise, to include joint-stock companies, limited liability companies, limited partnerships, public enterprises etc. The law had important implications for self-management, since it announced the replacement of collective responsibility of workers by individual responsibility of managers and new capital owners, which would take place along with the privatization of socially owned enterprises. All enterprises were obliged to organize themselves in conformity with the new provisions of the Company Law by 31 December 1989.

---

[43] Uvalic, *Investment and Property Rights in Yugoslavia*, 182–84.
[44] It is interesting to note that the word 'privatization' was not mentioned in either the first or the second version of the law.

The Law on the Disposal and Circulation of Social Capital, adopted by the Yugoslav Prime Minister Ante Marković's government in December 1989, announced economy-wide privatization. However, since the law implicitly recognized that the real owner of enterprises' social capital was the state,[45] by June 1990 no privatizations were initiated.[46] The law had to be revised in August 1990, offering major incentives to firms to start privatization. According to the new Law on Social Capital, a firm could be sold at a discount of 30 per cent to workers, citizens and pension funds, but present and former workers had the right to an additional 1 per cent discount for each year of employment, up to a maximum of 70 per cent of the nominal value of shares, and could pay the shares within a period of ten years. Though several limits on share issues at a discount had to be respected, the law, in practice, offered extremely favourable conditions primarily to insiders – employed workers and managers.[47] Workers' shareholding was also promoted through the Law on Personal Incomes (August 1990) which envisaged that workers, in addition to basic wages, could receive a part of earnings in the form of enterprise shares.

Parallel with these decisive economic reforms, in December 1989 the federal government adopted a 'shock therapy' stabilization programme as a response to hyperinflation.[48] However, this was undermined in the second half of 1990. Most republican governments officially permitted wage increases and failed to respect their obligations regarding taxes, the financing of the federal budget and the monetary regulations of the National Bank of Yugoslavia.[49] The positive course taken during 1988–90 was interrupted by a series of disputes among the republics for both economic and political reasons.

Regarding political changes, the dissolution of the Central Committee of the League of Communist of Yugoslavia (LCY) on 20–22 January 1990 opened the doors to the first multiparty elections, which were held in the six Yugoslav republics during April–December 1990 (first in Slovenia, last in Serbia). However, elections at the federal level were not organized, nor was a popular referendum on Yugoslavia's future, which perhaps would have shown that the majority was not in favour of its disintegration; public opinion polls in Croatia suggested that, in 1990, only 15 per cent of ethnic Croats were for full and unconditional independence, while 64 per cent supported a confederative transformation of Yugoslavia.[50]

---

[45] The law envisaged the sale of social capital at public tenders. The decision to start privatization was to be taken by the workers' councils, but proceeds from sales were to go primarily to Development Funds, established by the republics and autonomous regions as public enterprises. A part of the proceeds could also be given to employed workers in the form of shares, but only up to a maximum value of six months' wages.

[46] Uvalic, *Investment and Property Rights in Yugoslavia*.

[47] Ibid at 185–6.

[48] The stabilization programme was based on the pegging of the dinar to the German mark, introduction of resident convertibility for current transactions, freezing of wages at their December 1989 level, stricter monetary control and liberalization of 75 per cent of prices and of 95 per cent of imports.

[49] Uvalic, *Investment and Property Rights in Yugoslavia*, p. 14.

[50] See Dejan Jović, *Rat i mit. Politika identiteta u suvremenoj Hrvatskoj* [in Croatian; *War and Myth. The Policy of Identities in Contemporary Croatia*] (Zagreb, 2018). Similar public opinion polls in the other republics would probably have indicated an even higher support of the population for a confederative transformation of Yugoslavia, considering the multi-ethnic composition of the population in all Yugoslav republics (except Slovenia).

Variable speed of transition in Yugoslavia's successor states

The five Yugoslav successor states in 1991 inherited similar institutional features from their former country, but thereafter followed different trajectories. Regarding the speed of economic reforms, Slovenia opted for a comparatively gradualist strategy of transition, in contrast to the 'shock therapy' approach implemented elsewhere in CEE. Nevertheless, Slovenia's transition strategy was faster than those in the other successor states of Yugoslavia, which can be explained by a number of factors. First, the events accompanying the break-up of Yugoslavia had a less profound impact on Slovenia than on the other countries. Although Slovenia was also affected by the loss of a common market and the disruption in trade flows, the effects were relatively quickly absorbed; moreover, the 1991 war on its territory was of very short duration. Second, Slovenia was at a relatively high level of economic development in 1991 (it had the highest GDP per capita among all CEE countries) which rendered it less dependent on foreign capital (international financial institutions assistance or foreign investors). Third, the Slovenian economy had excellent starting conditions in 1991: it faced minor internal and external imbalances, it had high-quality institutions and a strong export-orientated industry. Finally, Slovenia benefitted from early support of the European Union (EU), similar to the other CEE countries: it received financial assistance through the PHARE programme in 1992, and important trade concessions through the signing of an Association Agreement with the EU in 1996.

In the other successor states of Yugoslavia, transition-related economic reforms were interrupted or substantially delayed by military conflicts and major political instability. The particularly unfavourable political conditions in most countries strongly influenced unsatisfactory economic performance, delays in implementing economic reforms and the much-later arrival of EU support. The EU only changed its strategy towards the region in 2000 through the launch of the Stabilization and Association Process for the Western Balkans. This facilitated the gradual integration of these other successor states with the EU economy, but on a delayed schedule compared with Slovenia or the CEE countries.

In Croatia and Macedonia or the 'early reformers',[51] the most important political issues were resolved somewhat earlier, facilitating faster progress with some economic reforms. One-digit inflation was achieved in Croatia in 1994 and in Macedonia in 1995, and both countries adopted new privatization laws soon after independence which permitted progress with property reforms. Bosnia and Herzegovina and the Federal Republic of Yugoslavia (FRY) or the 'late reformers',[52] for different reasons, faced much greater political instability during the 1990s.

In Bosnia and Herzegovina, the four-year war (1992–95) caused not only extreme loss of human lives, displacement of the population, massive emigration and the destruction of a large part of productive capacity and infrastructure, but it also inevitably blocked all economic reforms. The dramatic consequences of the war and the institutional arrangements imposed by the Dayton Peace Accords have seriously

[51] Will Bartlett, *Europe's Troubled Region. Economic Development, Institutional Reform and Social Welfare in the Western Balkans* (London and New York, 2008).
[52] Ibid.

impeded faster progress in many areas for a long time, leaving deeply rooted constitutional problems which are still responsible today for the dysfunctional features of the state apparatus and limited progress with many economic reforms.

In FR Yugoslavia economic transition was also greatly delayed by extreme political and economic instability throughout the 1990s.[53] The UN sanctions during most of the decade (except in 1996–97), the Kosovo crisis which led to the NATO bombing in 1999, and the international isolation of the country, were accompanied by extreme economic problems, including 15-digit hyperinflation in 1992–93.[54] Only in October 2000, after the fall of the Milošević regime, were reforms of the economic system given top priority. Although until 2006, Montenegro and Serbia were part of the same country, their economic policies were already different during the 1990s. Particularly after 1997, when Milo Đukanović was elected president, Montenegro decided to implement its own monetary, fiscal and foreign trade policies, which also led to the unilateral adoption of the Euro in 2002. In Serbia, a strong acceleration of economic reforms took place primarily after 2001, when the hyper-liberal model based of fast liberalization and privatization seemed to be the safest strategy to compensate for the delays in economic reforms incurred in the 1990s. In the meantime, the country disintegrated further, following Montenegro's referendum that led to its separation from Serbia in June 2006, and Kosovo's unilateral declaration of independence in February 2008.

Contents of systemic reforms in the Yugoslav successor states

In addition to the variable speed of transition, the contents of economic reforms have also been very different across the Yugoslav successor states.

Among the successor states of the former Yugoslavia, Slovenia is the only country that could be said to have retained vestiges of some institutional features of the previous economic model. As a result of the 1993 Slovenian privatization law, which enabled substantial sales or transfers to employed workers and managers, 'red' managers remained in charge of many Slovenian firms.[55] The Slovenian government adopted a Codetermination Law in 1993, which provides for workers' representation on company boards in all larger firms, consistent – in part –with the spirit of self-management. A system of profit-sharing, that allows workers to receive bonuses linked to enterprise profits, is also legally permitted in Slovenian company law, again respecting the spirit of labour-managed firms in former Yugoslavia (thought this is not institutionalized but is implemented on a voluntary basis).[56] Slovenia also maintained a strong welfare state, characterized by high public expenditure (one of the highest among the EU Member States), which provides for practically free health care and education and a generous

---

[53] Uvalic, *Serbia's Transition – Towards a Better Future*.

[54] Ibid.

[55] Jože Mencinger, 'Formulating a Sustainable Growth Agenda. Experience of Slovenia', Paper prepared for the Friedrich Ebert Stiftung, Zagreb office, 2017.

[56] See Jens Lowitzsch, ed., The PEPPER III Report: Promotion of Employee Participation in Profits and Enterprise Results in the New Member and Candidate Countries of the European Union, Inter-University Centre Split/Berlin, Institute for Eastern European Studies, Free University of Berlin, 2006.

pensions system. Slovenia also has strong trade unions, a high rate of workers' unionization and an effective system of collective bargaining – contrary to the other countries of former Yugoslavia or the vast majority of CEE countries who have adopted the more liberal model of the welfare state.[57] Slovenia, therefore, chose a degree of continuity in many areas of economic policies and related reforms, rather than a radical break from the past.

The other Yugoslav successor states relied much less on the former Yugoslav economic model in devising their transition-related economic reforms. In most cases, the dismantling of the socialist economic system was not accompanied by the introduction of institutional arrangements which resembled the old economic model, but rather by a radical break from the past, especially countries who implemented economic reforms later. There was one main exception, however, with regard to privatization.

The initial privatization laws adopted after independence by the Yugoslav successor states were also (as in Slovenia) deeply rooted in the self-management tradition, since they also envisaged privileged conditions for sales or transfers of shares to employed workers and managers to provide incentives for the conversion of self-management into property rights.[58] Privatization was implemented using a variety of methods and imposing various limits on share issues to insiders, which crucially determined whether majority or minority employee ownership would be established after privatization.[59] The process of privatization also implied the elimination of not only social property but also of self-management, since with the start of privatization workers councils were formally abolished and replaced by supervisory boards representing the new shareholders.[60] In order to facilitate privatization, all countries (except Serbia) decided to first re-nationalize at least a part of social property by transferring it to government funds, to be sold at a later stage to interested buyers.

Although employee ownership of enterprises was, therefore, a frequent outcome of the initial privatizations of economies of the successor states of Yugoslavia, the ownership structure changed substantially in the meantime. Many small shareholders sold their shares to managers or outside owners, leading to more concentrated ownership. In the 2000s, the new provisions for privatization put major emphasis on the method of sales with the intention of attracting FDI, so many firms were sold to foreign companies. A further concentration of ownership also took place in the hands of the domestic owners, often tycoon capitalists. All countries have retained substantial government ownership shares in certain enterprises, since it was not possible to find interested buyers for all the privatizing enterprises.

Only in Serbia did social property and self-management survive somewhat longer. During the 1990s, privatization was left to the voluntary initiative of the enterprise,

[57] Nuti, Domenico Mario Nuti, 'Did We Go about Transition in the Right Way?' in Hare, P and Turley, G (eds) *Handbook of the Economics and Political Economy of Transition* (London and New York, 2014), pp 46–58.

[58] The only exception was Bosnia and Herzegovina where privatization was substantially delayed.

[59] See Milica Uvalic, 'Privatization in the Yugoslav Successor States: Converting Self-management into Property Rights', in M Uvalic and D Vaughan-Whitehead (eds), *Privatization Surprises in Transition Economies – Employee Ownership in Central and Eastern Europe* (Cheltenham, 1997), pp 267–301.

[60] Workers' decision-making rights were practically abolished under the provisions of the 1988 Yugoslav Company Law and thereafter under the company laws adopted by the newly created states.

which resulted in its very slow implementation. Although the government often maintained control of firms through the appointment of supervisory board members, and had also renationalized some socially owned enterprises by transferring them into public enterprises, the provisions of the 1997 Company Law still ensured workers some decision-making rights, at least formally.[61] After the political changes in October 2000, the implementation of the new privatization law based on sales was also slow, so by 2010, many socially owned enterprises had still not been privatized. Moreover, the 1990 Serbian Constitution continued to guarantee social property as one of the property forms, until these provisions were finally changed in the new Constitution adopted in 2006.[62] Despite slow legislative changes, the self-managed model in Serbia was, in practice, gradually extinguished: a 2013 survey in 69 Serbian firms suggested that owners were for the most part the exclusive decision makers; the position of workers seemed to be weak, particularly regarding their right to be informed, to make proposals and to participate in decision making, while traditional workers' rights (unionization, collective bargaining etc.) were largely absent.[63]

Other transition-related economic reforms in the Yugoslav successor states were country-specific, but with some common features. In most countries (except Slovenia), many economic reforms applied in the 2000s have had features of the typical liberal model: very fast foreign trade liberalization, restrictive monetary and fiscal policies, massive sales of the banking sector to foreign-owned banks and rapid financial liberalization. The liberal model of transition and slim government budgets have also strongly influenced reforms of the welfare state. Despite differences across countries, a general feature has been the reduction in public expenditure on health, education and pensions, along with the introduction of private provision of various services. All countries have seen the mushrooming of new trade unions, but their influence has remained weak throughout the region, as evidenced by the highly ineffective systems of wage bargaining, insufficient protection of workers' basic rights and virtual absence of social dialogue. Most of the successor states still have some way to go to implement important complementary reforms to ensure enforcement of laws, efficient collection of taxes, proper supervision of the financial sector, a more efficient judiciary and fight against corruption.

One of the most devastating consequences of delayed economic transition in most successor states of former Yugoslavia is their present low level of economic development. Due to a poor growth record during most of the last three decades – except in 2001–08 – the level of economic development of most countries of former Yugoslavia remains low in comparison with the more developed EU Member States or the EU28 average (Figure 8.2).[64]

---

[61] Uvalic, 'Privatization in the Yugoslav Successor States: Converting Self-management into Property Rights', p. 278. The 1997 Company Law envisaged that in mixed-property firms, decisions were to be taken jointly by the new private shareholders proportional to their capital stakes, and by current employees proportional to the share of social capital.

[62] See Uvalic, *Serbia's Transition – Towards a Better Future*.

[63] See Božidar Cerović, Jan Svejnar and Milica Uvalic, 'Workers Participation in a Former Labor-managed Economy: The Case of Serbian Transition' (2015) LX/205 *Economic Annals* 7–29.

[64] There is no official data for Kosovo that has the lowest GDP per capita (PPS), in 2016 probably not higher than 25 per cent of the EU average.

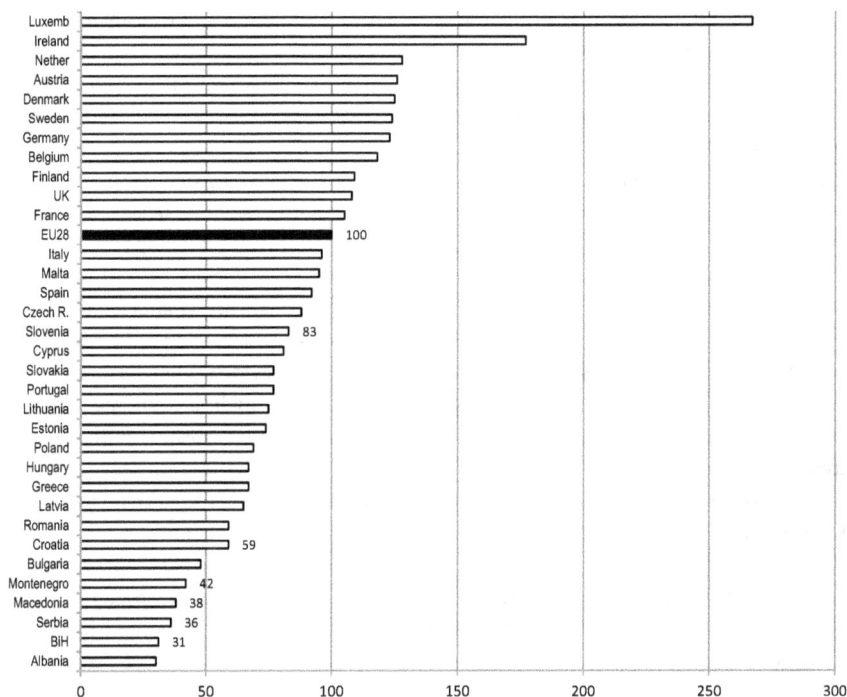

Figure 8.2 Gross domestic product per capita in purchasing power standards (PPS) in EU member states, countries of former Yugoslavia and EU candidates, 2016. *Source:* Prepared on the basis of Eurostat statistics, available online.

Croatia and Slovenia, who joined the EU in 2004 and 2013 respectively, are much more developed than the other countries in the former Yugoslavia, but they were already more developed at the time of Yugoslavia's disintegration. The other countries are among the poorest in Europe today, which also renders them strongly dependent on foreign capital (remittances, FDI, support of international financial institutions, donors' assistance), probably much more than Yugoslavia was in 1989.

VI Concluding remarks

The model of self-managed market socialism has vanished rapidly starting in 1989 with the first systemic reforms in Yugoslavia, the disintegration of the Yugoslav federation, multiple military conflicts that accompanied it and the intention of all countries to implement the transition to a capitalist market economy. Due to different political and economic conditions in the individual countries, the transition process has proceeded at variable speed, the contents of economic reforms have been country specific, and the overall results have also differed widely.

In retrospect, Slovenia has been among the most successful cases of transition, not only among the countries of former Yugoslavia but, arguably, also in a wider context of CEE. It implemented a model of transition based on gradualism and continuity, maintaining and building on previous systemic features of former Yugoslavia, rather than making a radical break with the past. In its institutional design of the capitalist model, Slovenia introduced, in various areas of reform, changes that were based on continuities, rather than discontinuities, with the previous economic legacy. However, Slovenia had a big advantage with respect to the other countries emerging from former Yugoslavia: it had political stability throughout more than a quarter of century of its post-independence history. In the absence of major external shocks after Yugoslavia's break-up, Slovenia was able to secure continuity in the implementation of its economic reforms and also preserve some of the advantages of the previous economic model.

The post-Yugoslav experience suggests that relative stability in a country's political environment is probably the most important precondition for positive outcomes of transition-related economic reforms. This is what was much less present, or even missing, for a whole decade, in most successor states of Yugoslavia (other than Slovenia). During the first ten years, all countries were involved in military conflicts[65] that were often accompanied by international sanctions and isolation of large parts of the region.

In concluding, an important question to be raised and tentatively answered is what was the most important positive legacy from former Yugoslavia inherited by all its successor states? An answer to this question cannot be based only on the economic aspects, but must consider a wider multi-dimensional perspective that takes into account political, social, cultural and other aspects. Probably the single most important feature of Yugoslavia that has benefitted most (if not all) of its citizens was the high degree of openness of the country to the outside world (both East and West) at the outset – which facilitated the cross-border flow of goods, services, people, technology, knowledge, communications, ideas, cultural and social values. Thanks to this fundamental feature of openness, Yugoslavia's population was probably able to learn and grasp some general benefits from the outside world more quickly than citizens in most other socialist countries.

The advantage of having an internationally open country was, however, interrupted immediately after Yugoslavia's disintegration for most successor states, when borders were closed and visas were introduced by EU Member States for citizens of most successor states of Yugoslavia.[66] Only in December 2009, almost twenty years later, was a visa-free regime of travel to Schengen countries again granted to citizens from Macedonia, Montenegro and Serbia,[67] and in December 2010 to those of Bosnia and Herzegovina. Some of the positive attributes of the Yugoslav model have been too easily forgotten in its successor states by the priority given to the main political objectives of sovereignty and building of nation-states. The expected benefits of the

---

[65] The armed conflicts took place, in chronological order, in Croatia (1991–95), Bosnia and Herzegovina (1992–95), FR Yugoslavia (1998–99) and Macedonia (2001).

[66] After the international recognition of the successor states of Yugoslavia, only Slovenia and Croatia were able to maintain the visa-free regime to travel to most EU Member States.

[67] Uvalic, *Serbia's Transition – Towards a Better Future*, 242.

capitalist economic system have been overestimated, as they were largely offset by the high economic costs of rising income inequality, slow economic development and limited increase in living standards in most countries.[68] Perhaps some lessons could still be learned from the Yugoslav experiment to guide future reforms in the direction of more inclusive and more equitable political and economic systems.

References

Bajt, Aleksandar. 'Property in Capital and in the Means of Production in Socialist Economies' (1968) 11 *Journal of Law and Economics*, pp. 1–4.

Bajt, Aleksandar. 'Economic Growth and Factor Substitution: What Happened to the Yugoslav Miracle?: Some Comments' (1986) 96 *The Economic Journal*, pp. 1084–88.

Bartlett, Will. 'Western Balkans' in David Lane and Martin Myant (eds) *Varieties of Capitalism in the post-Communist Countries* (London: Palgrave, 2007), pp 201–20.

Bartlett, Will. *Europe's Troubled Region. Economic Development, Institutional Reform and Social Welfare in the Western Balkans* (London and New York: Routledge, 2008).

Bartlett, Will and Milica Uvalić. 'Labour-managed Firms, Employee Participation and Profit-sharing: Theoretical Perspectives and European Experience' (1986) 12(4) Special Issue of *Management Bibliographies and Reviews*, pp. 3–66.

Cerović, Božidar, Jan Svejnar and Milica Uvalic. 'Workers Participation in a Former Labor-managed Economy: The Case of Serbian Transition' (2015) LX/205 *Economic Annals*, pp. 9–29.

Domar, Evsey. 'The Soviet Collective Farm as a Producer Co-operative' (1966) *American Economic Review*, pp. 734–57.

Dimitrijević, Branislav. *Potrošeni socijalizam. Kultura, konzumerizam i društvena imaginacija u Jugoslaviji (1950–1974)* [in Serbian; *Consumed Socialism. Culture, Consumerism and Social Immagination in Yugoslavia (1950–1974)*] (Beograd: Fabrika knjiga Peščanik, 2016).

Estrin, Saul. *Self-management: Economic Theory and Yugoslav Practice* (Cambridge: Cambridge University Press, 1983).

Estrin, Saul and Milica Uvalić. 'From Illyria towards Capitalism: Did Labour-Management Theory Teach Us Anything about Yugoslavia and Transition in Its Successor States?', 50th Anniversary Essay, (2008) 50 *Comparative Economic Studies*, pp. 663–96.

Estrin, Saul, Derek Jones and Jan Svejnar. 'The Productivity Effects of Worker Participation: Producer Cooperatives in Western Economies' (1987) 11 *Journal of Comparative Economics*, pp. 40–61.

Furubotn, Eirik and Steve Pejovich. 'Property Rights and the Behaviour of the Firm in a Socialist State – The Example of Yugoslavia' (1970) 30 *Zeitschrift fur Nationalökonomie*, pp. 431–54.

Horvat, Branko. 'A Contribution to the Theory of the Yugoslav Firm' (1967) (1)(1–2) *Economic Analysis*, pp. 288–93.

Horvat, Branko. *The Political Economy of Socialism* (Armonk, New York: ME Sharpe, 1982).

---

[68] See Branko Milanovic, 'For Whom the Wall Fell? A Balance Sheet of the Transition to Capitalism', *The Globalist, Rethinking Globalization,* 7 November 2014.

Jović, Dejan. *Rat i mit. Politika identiteta u suvremenoj Hrvatskoj* [in Croatian; *War and Myth. The Policy of Identities in Contemporary Croatia*], 2nd edn (Zagreb: Fraktura, 2018).

Kornai, Janos. *Economics of Shortage* (Amsterdam: North Holland, 1980).

Lavigne, Marie. *The Economics of Transition. From Socialist Economy to Market Economy*, 2nd edn (Basingstoke and London: Macmillan Press Limited, 1999).

Lowitzsch, Jens, (ed), (2006), *The PEPPER III Report: Promotion of Employee Participation in Profits and Enterprise Results in the New Member and Candidate Countries of the European Union*, Inter-University Centre Split/Berlin, Institute for Eastern European Studies, Free University of Berlin.

Meade, James. 'The Theory of Labour-managed Firms and of Profit-sharing' (1972) 82 *Economic Journal*, pp. 402–28.

Mencinger, Jože. 'Formulating a Sustainable Growth Agenda. Experience of Slovenia', Paper prepared for the Friedrich Ebert Stiftung, Zagreb office, 2017.

Milanovic, Branko. 'For Whom the Wall Fell? A Balance Sheet of the Transition to Capitalism', *The Globalist, Rethinking Globalization,* 7 November 2014.

Nuti, Domenico Mario. 'On Traditional Cooperatives and James Meade's Labor-Capital Discriminating Partnerships' (1992) 4 *Advances in the Economic Analysis of Participatory and Labor-Managed Firms*, pp. 1–26.

Nuti, Domenico Mario. 'Did We Go about Transition in the Right Way?' in Hare, P. and Turley, G. (eds) *Handbook of the Economics and Political Economy of Transition* (Abingdon and New York: Routledge, Taylor & Francis, 2014), pp. 46–58.

Sapir, André. 'Economic Growth and Factor Substitution: What Happened to the Yugoslav Miracle?' (1980) 90 (358) *The Economic Journal*, pp. 294–313.

Savezni zavod za statistiku. *Statistički godišnjak Jugoslavije 1991* (Beograd, 1991).

Svejnar, Jan. 'On the Theory of a Participatory Firm' (1982) 27(2) *Journal of Economic Theory*, pp. 313–30.

Uvalic, Milica. *Investment and Property Rights in Yugoslavia. The Long Transition to a Market Economy* (Cambridge: Cambridge University Press, 1992) Reprinted in paperback in 2009.

Uvalic, Milica. 'The Disintegration of Yugoslavia: Its Costs and Benefits' (1993) 5(3) *Communist Economies & Economic Transformation*, pp. 273–93.

Uvalic, Milica. 'Privatization in the Yugoslav Successor States: Converting Self-management into Property Rights' in Uvalic, M. and Vaughan-Whitehead, D. (eds), *Privatization Surprises in Transition Economies – Employee Ownership in Central and Eastern Europe* (Budapest, International Labour Office and Cheltenham: Edward Elgar, 1997), pp. 267–301.

Uvalic, Milica. *Serbia's Transition – Towards a Better Future* (Basingstoke, Palgrave Macmillan and New York: St Martin's Press, 2010). Expanded edition in Serbian: *Tranzicija u Srbiji – Ka boljoj budućnosti* (Belgrade: Zavod za udžbenike, 2012).

Uvalic, Milica. *The Rise and Fall of Market Socialism in Yugoslavia*, Berlin: Dialogue of Civilizations (DOC) Research Institute, Special Report, 27 March 2018.

Vanek, Jaroslav. *The General Theory of Labor-managed Market Economies* (Ithaca, NY: Cornell University Press, 1970).

Ward, Benjamin. 'The Firm in Illyria – Market Syndicalism' (1958) 48(4) *American Economic Review*, pp. 566–89.

9

Are Yugoslav Successor States on the Path to Sustainable Market Economies?

Jakov Milatović and Peter Sanfey
European Bank for Reconstruction and Development

I Introduction[1]

More than a quarter century after the break-up of Yugoslavia, most of the successor states still faced difficult economic circumstances. GDP per capita (adjusted for purchasing power standards) was less than half of the EU average in five of the seven countries.[2] Economic growth rates at the time had been positive for a number of years but not sufficient to have a noticeable beneficial impact on people's lives. Unemployment and poverty were still rife in many parts of former Yugoslavia and large numbers of (mostly) young and able people had voted with their feet and emigrated to other countries in search of a better life. For those who remained, there was often a sense of disappointment and missed opportunities.

In the late 1980s, Yugoslavia appeared to be at the forefront among socialist countries with market-orientated reforms, as outlined elsewhere in this volume.[3] The country had been famous for promoting a 'third path', between Soviet central planning socialism and Western market capitalism. Its relatively liberal economic and social policies, including a degree of private ownership and the freedom to live and work abroad, had been the envy of many in the communist bloc in Eastern Europe and the Soviet Union. At the same time, however, macroeconomic conditions had deteriorated alarmingly during the 1980s, with the economy being increasingly propped up by a

---

[1] Paper prepared for an edited volume on 'Revisiting Yugoslavia in the Shadow of the Present: Continuities and Discontinuities.' We thank the editors – Othon Anastasakis, Adam Bennett, David Madden and Adis Merdžanović – for helpful comments and suggestions, and Milan Lakićević for general research assistance. We have benefitted from the discussion among participants in a one-day seminar on the topic at St Antony's College, Oxford University, on 23 November 2017. The views expressed in this chaper are those of the authors only and not of the EBRD.

[2] See the estimates from Eurostat. Available at: http://ec.europa.eu/eurostat/tgm/table.do?tab=table& init=1&language=en&pcode=tec00114&plugin=1. Note that Kosovo is not included in this table but is estimated (by the IMF and others) to have a GDP per capita below that of all other ex-Yugoslav countries.

[3] See Bennett (Chapter 7) and Uvalic (Chapter 8).

combination of state subsidies (combined with soft budget constraints), foreign lending and remittances from Yugoslavs living abroad. The combination of growing economic problems and rising nationalist sentiment culminated in the violent disintegration of the former Yugoslavia in the early 1990s, with consequences that were still being felt two and a half decades later.[4]

This chapter draws on a range of information, including surveys conducted jointly by the EBRD and World Bank, to assess how far, twenty five years after the break-up of the country, the successor states of former Yugoslavia (Bosnia and Herzegovina, Croatia, Kosovo, Montenegro, North Macedonia, Serbia and Slovenia – henceforth, the YU-7) were from being sustainable market economies. The question immediately leads to others, such as: What do we mean by a sustainable market economy? How great were the differences among the seven new countries in terms of progress towards this end state? Where did these countries stand against their peers in Central and Eastern Europe? To what extent were the unique features of the Yugoslav model helping or hindering the achievement of economic goals?

We argue that the continued heavy state presence, a weak business environment, and pervasive corruption were among the main reasons for the relatively slow progress and poor economic performance of much of ex-Yugoslavia. Such problems were common across many countries in Central and Eastern Europe. But there are issues specific to the former Yugoslavia that made reforms towards a sustainable market economy particularly challenging. We provide evidence that many people in the successor states still believed – after a quarter of a century of transition – that jobs in the public sector were more desirable than those in the private sector and that political connections were the way to get ahead in life. These two features, in particular, distinguish this region from others in the ex-socialist bloc.

It is common to talk of nostalgia in this region for the socialist era, and the Yugoslav welfare state, harkening back to 'better days'. Despite transition, many people in ex-Yugoslav countries were still dissatisfied with life and pessimistic about the future. But, at the same time, there is little evidence that the citizens of the successor states wanted to return to a planned economy under a non-democratic government. People may have desired public sector jobs and connections but at the same time the support for democracy and the market economy expressed in surveys (as discussed in more detail below) was similar to the level in non-Yugoslav EU members from Central and Eastern Europe.

II Measuring progress towards a sustainable market economy

All countries in Central and Eastern Europe were in transition from socialism to some form of market economy over the three decades since the fall of the Berlin Wall.

---

[4] For a valuable guide to the politics, economics, demography and culture of former Yugoslavia, see John Allcock, *Explaining Yugoslavia*, London, Hurst & Co., 2000. A good discussion of the reasons for the break-up of Yugoslavia and the subsequent division into 'early' and 'late' reformers is in William Bartlett, *Europe's Troubled Region: Economic Development, Institutional Reform, and Social Welfare in the Western Balkans*, Routledge, 2007.

Measuring the extent of this transition and the degree to which the YU-7 countries had become more competitive is an inherently difficult task. There is a wide range of indicators to assist in this task, each of which has its own strengths and weaknesses.[5] For the purposes of this chapter we will draw on a methodological framework developed and refined over many years within the EBRD for tracking a country's progress towards a well-functioning and sustainable market economy.[6]

In the early days of transition, most of the focus among transition countries was on 'early stage' reforms such as price liberalization, small-scale privatization and openness to foreign trade and investment. In this regard, Yugoslavia had a significant head start over others. The reformist government of Ante Markovic, appointed in March 1989, introduced new business legislation allowing private ownership of businesses. This was one of twenty-four new laws proposed by the government to encourage market forces. In addition, price controls were removed on 85 per cent of commodities. The only exceptions were essential categories such as electricity, fuels, medicine, raw metals and minerals, and rail, postal, and telephone services, which remained under government control. Also, the 'new dinar', worth 10,000 old dinars, was introduced and pegged to the German mark, and made convertible with all Western currencies, which helped to bring down the rapid inflation rate, although it also triggered a deep recession (see Chapter 7).

These reforms were reflected in Yugoslavia's initially promising score on the EBRD's transition indicators (Chart 9.1). These annual indicators, first developed in 1994 and subsequently backdated to 1989, covered six aspects of a market economy: (1) large-scale privatization, (2) small-scale privatization, (3) governance and enterprise restructuring, (4) price liberalization, (5) trade and foreign exchange system, and (6) competition policy. The scale goes from 1 to 4+, where 1 represents a centrally planned economy while 4+ is awarded when standards on the particular indicator have reached those of a well-functioning market economy. In 1989, Yugoslavia averaged close to 2, while other Central and Eastern European countries (the EU-9) scored 1 in virtually all categories.[7]

Before long, however, most countries in the EBRD region,[8] and EU-9 countries in particular, had surpassed the average among the now ex-Yugoslav countries (Chart 2). Markovic's reforms, while welcome as far as they went, did little either to alter the dire

---

[5] The relative strengths and weaknesses of different measures of competitiveness are analysed in: Peter Sanfey and Simone Zeh, 'Making Sense of Competitiveness Indicators in South-Eastern Europe', Chapter 2 of *Defining a New Reform Agenda: Paths to Sustainable Convergence in South East Europe* (eds O Anastasakis, P Sanfey and M Watson), pp 25–50; South East European Studies at Oxford, St Antony's College, Oxford University, 2013.

[6] For an explanation of this methodology and how it has evolved over the years, see the annual EBRD *Transition Report*, various years, all available (since 2009) at: http://2017.tr-ebrd.com/.

[7] EU-9 includes Estonia, Lithuania, Latvia, Poland, Hungary, Czech Republic, Slovak Republic, Bulgaria and Romania.

[8] The EBRD region is predominantly comprised of the former socialist countries in Central and Eastern Europe and the former Soviet Union. However, the EBRD has also expanded into new countries such as Mongolia (in 2006), Turkey (2009), Jordan, Tunisia, Morocco, Egypt and Kosovo (in 2012), Cyprus (2014), Greece (2015) and Lebanon (2017). The Czech Republic is the only member to have 'graduated' from the EBRD and, as of 2007, is no longer eligible for EBRD investments.

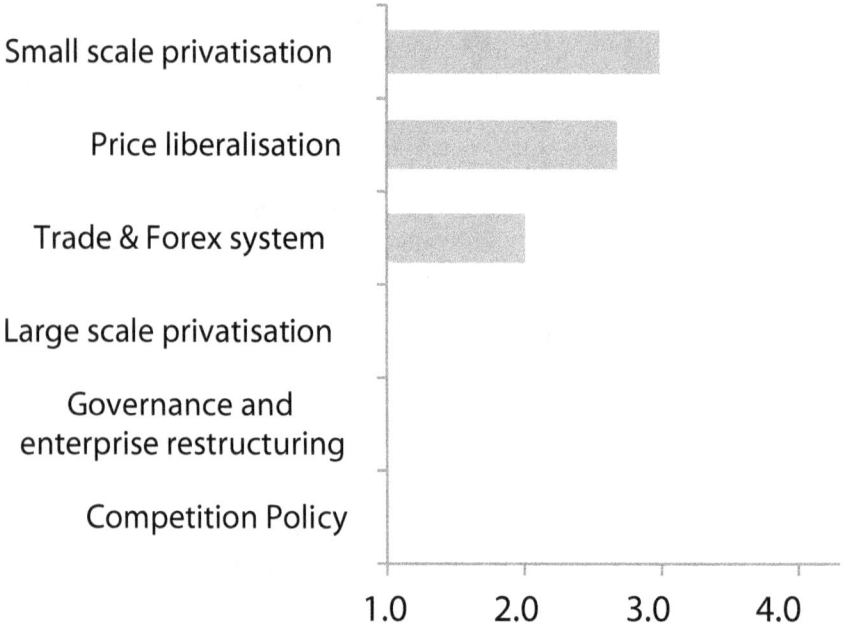

Chart 9.1 Transition indicators for SFR Yugoslavia in 1989. Source: EBRD. Note: Transition scores are based on a scale from 1 to 4.3, where 1 represents little or no progress in transition, and 4.3 is the standard of an advanced market economy.

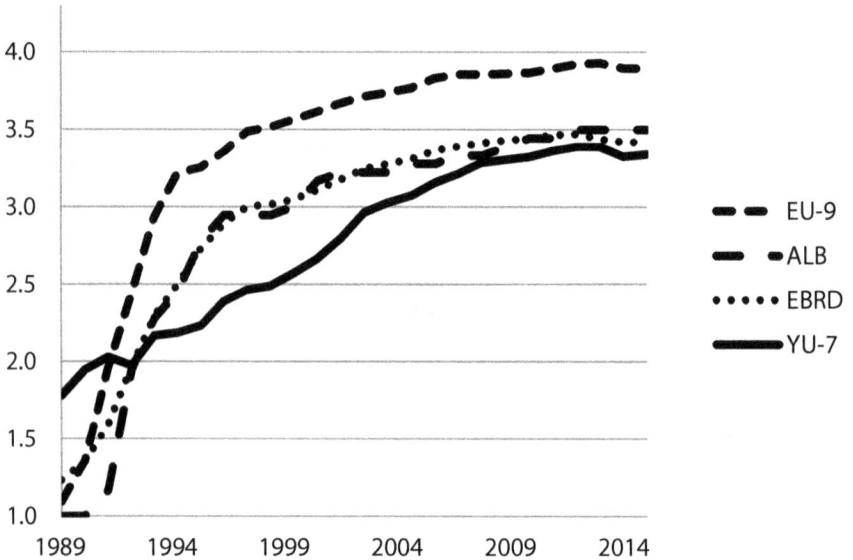

Chart 9.2 Country-level transition indicators. Source: EBRD. The scores in Chart 2 are a simple average of the six transition indicators in Chart 1.

state of the economy or to head off the dissolution of the country. The break-up of Yugoslavia and subsequent conflicts brought reforms in much of the YU-7 to a standstill while others forged ahead, especially in Central Europe and the Baltic states. This was the main reason why parts of the region lost up to ten years of transition time. By 2014, when these indicators were discontinued, the average transition score among the YU-7 was still below the overall EBRD regional average, with a score that the EU-9 had on average already reached in the mid-1990s.

The transition indicators went through various refinements and modifications over time. For several years the EBRD complemented the original measures with a set of sector-based transition indicators. In 2016, however, the EBRD revamped completely its approach to measuring transition, recasting the notion of a sustainable market economy in terms of six desirable 'qualities' that would characterize all successful market-orientated sustainable economies. The six qualities are: competitive, well-governed, green, inclusive, resilient, and integrated. Conceptually, some of these qualities overlap with the previous transition indicators whereas others, such as green and inclusive, reflect a growing recognition of the importance of environmental issues and the need to ensure that all groups of society can potentially enjoy the benefits of the market economy.

The new transition concept has a number of advantages, not least in terms of drawing together different but related concepts into a coherent framework. But measuring where each country stands on the six qualities is a challenging task. In 2017, the EBRD developed a methodology under which each quality is calibrated on a scale of 1 to 10. The scores and the underlying approach were unveiled for the first time in the EBRD *Transition Report 2017/18*. Table 9.1 shows the scores for the YU-7 countries and contrasts them with those for the EU-9.

Table 9.1 Assessment of transition qualities, 2017

	Competitive	Well-governed	Green	Inclusive	Resilient	Integrated	Average
Kosovo	2.5	3.7	3.8	4.7	5.1	4.9	4.1
Albania	4.8	4.0	4.3	4.9	5.1	4.9	4.7
BiH	4.2	3.7	4.8	4.8	5.3	5.5	4.7
FYR Macedonia	4.7	5.2	4.9	4.7	5.3	6.0	5.1
Serbia	4.2	4.4	5.8	5.2	5.6	6.4	5.2
Montenegro	4.3	5.1	5.2	5.6	5.9	5.6	5.3
EBRD	4.4	4.8	5.4	5.4	5.7	6.0	5.3
YU-7	**4.5**	**4.7**	**5.3**	**5.4**	**5.9**	**6.1**	**5.3**
Croatia	5.5	5.1	6.0	6.0	6.6	6.9	6.0
EU-9	6.6	6.0	5.8	6.4	6.3	7.4	6.4
Slovenia	6.4	5.7	6.7	7.0	7.4	7.6	6.8
United States	9.3	8.6	6.1	6.6	8.9	7.4	7.8
Germany	8.5	8.7	7.4	7.3	8.4	8.2	8.1

Source: EBRD.

Note: the scores for each quality are derived from a range of quantitative indicators and range from 1 to 10, with 1 representing the least advanced and 10 the most advanced.

Not surprisingly, ex-Yugoslav countries, on average, fell short once again vis-à-vis the EU-9, which not only had a higher score in the overall average, but also a higher average score for each quality. However, there was significant variation among the YU-7. Slovenia typically scored highest and was above the EU-9 average in four of the six qualities, with the two exceptions being competitive and well-governed. As the country where the Yugoslav conflict started first and lasted the shortest length of time, it is not surprising to see that Slovenia was the most advanced of the YU-7 on its path towards a sustainable market economy. After a ten-day war, the country proclaimed its independence in 1991 and embarked on its transition path, catching up quickly with the other EU-9 countries, and becoming an EU Member State in May 2004, together with seven other former socialist central European and Baltic countries (plus Cyprus and Malta).

Croatia was next highest, assessed as being greener and more resilient than the EU-9 average, but lagging behind in the other four qualities, particularly competitive and well governed (as in the case of Slovenia). The benefits of EU preparation, which Croatia began as a candidate in 2005, and membership (achieved in July 2013) are evident in these higher scores relative to the remaining YU-7 countries.

There was a fairly big gap between these two front runners, Slovenia and Croatia, down to Montenegro, the highest ranked among the non-EU members of YU-7. Kosovo brought up the rear with the lowest score (jointly or exclusively) in all six cases. Interestingly, however, despite the differences among the seven ex-YU countries, all of them shared a common legacy of weak competitiveness and poor governance, reminiscent of the old Yugoslav model. We explore this further in the next section.

III Weak competitiveness and poor governance: Shadows of the past

Countries of the former Yugoslavia have had only mixed success in terms of creating a market-orientated economy, and most fall some way short of the new EU members from Central and Eastern Europe. Two major problems of the former Yugoslav countries, according to the EBRD transition assessment methodology described above, are inadequate competitiveness and weak governance, where the scores were generally the lowest and where the overall difference vis-à-vis the EU-9 counterparts was the highest. These results chimed well with the findings of the World Economic Forum's Global Competitive Index (Chart 9.3) and the World Bank's Governance Indicators (Chart 9.4), where all YU-7 countries except Slovenia lagged behind the EU-9 average.[9]

The lack of competitiveness and good-governance is related to several fundamental features common in 2017–18 across most or all YU-7 countries. The state retained a heavy presence in the economy, through high spending and taxation and often through

---

[9] The WEF scores are available at: www.weforum.org/reports/the-global-competitveness-report-2018, and the World Bank's governance scores are at: https://info.worldbank.org/governance/wgi/#home.

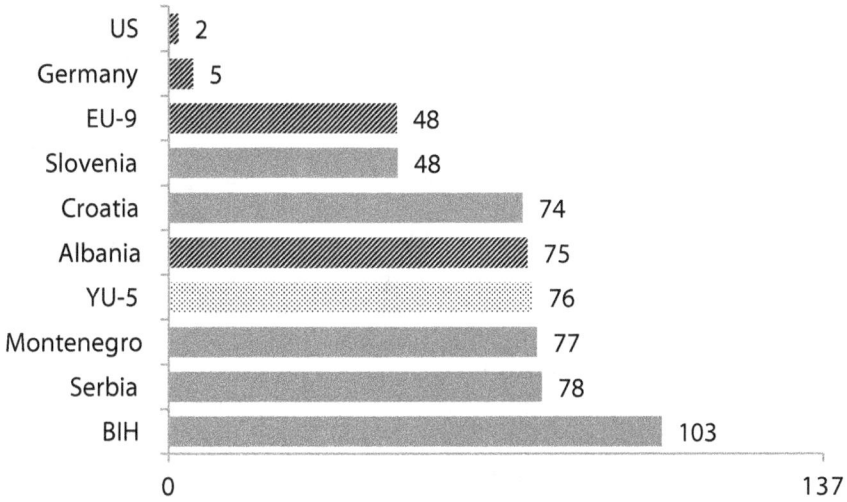

Chart 9.3 Global Competitiveness Index (ranking out of 137 countries). Source: WEF Global Competitiveness Report 2017–18. Note: The ranking does not cover Kosovo, and the 2017-18 ranking also does not include North Macedonia.

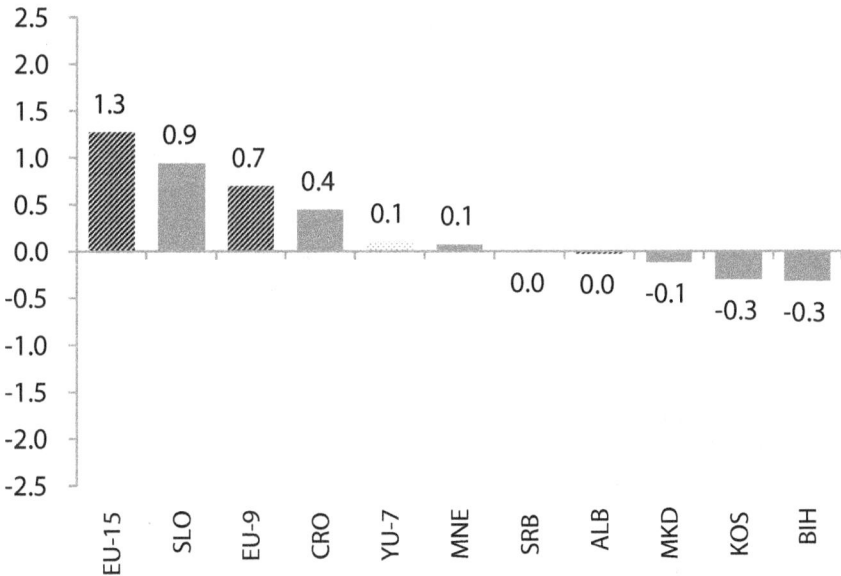

Chart 9.4 Governance indicators (average of six categories). Source: The World Bank's Worldwide Governance Indicators database. Note: the scores range from −2.5 (lowest) to 2.5 (highest).

ownership of, or extensive influence in, large companies. Private businesses faced a range of obstacles if they tried to engage in doing legitimate business. Efforts to promote better standards of governance were hindered by pervasive cronyism and corruption. We will examine each of these in turn.

State spending as a share of GDP was higher in most ex-Yugoslav countries than the EU-9 average, according to IMF cross-country data, albeit lower than in the EU-15. This finding reflects a number of ways in which countries in this region differed from other ex-socialist countries from Central and Eastern Europe. First, governments had retained many aspects of the old health and pension systems, which often involved high, inefficient, non-targeted levels of benefits. Second, privatization was more hesitant in this part of the world than elsewhere. In five of the seven countries – Bosnia and Herzegovina, Croatia, Kosovo, Serbia and Slovenia – many companies were still state-owned, either partially or completely. A privatization agenda was supposedly in place in all cases, but the appetite of policy makers for delivering results in this area was limited. IMF and EBRD research published in 2018–19 showed that many state-owned enterprises (SOEs) in some of these countries were highly indebted and suffered from weak corporate governance.[10]

Life was often made difficult by the authorities for those who had an entrepreneurial spirit and wished to set up a private sector company on their own. Even though private enterprise was more tolerated in the old Yugoslavia than elsewhere in the socialist bloc, modern companies in the YU-7 on average faced a greater range and severity of obstacles in their day-to-day business than those in the EU-9 did. One way to see this is to glance at the rankings in the World Bank's *Ease of Doing Business 2018* scores (Charts 9.5 and 9.6). All YU-7 countries except North Macedonia (ranked 11th) lagged behind the peer EU-9 average ranking. The high score of North Macedonia was the fruit of the country's sustained focus over a number of years on revamping its laws and regulations to bring them in line with best practice as perceived by the World Bank. The lowest ranking in the region was for Bosnia and Herzegovina, in 86th position. This country's complex constitutional structure was and remains a fundamental constraint on reforms and private sector activity, which is also reflected in a poor business environment. The remaining five countries were ranked similarly, between 37 and 51. On average, YU-7 countries scored most favourably in trading across borders, while getting electricity and dealing with construction permits were the most problematic areas of doing business in the region, according to this analysis. The region's average ranking was lower than its peers in the EU-9 region in seven out of ten areas, with a better performance only with respect to resolving insolvency, protecting minority investors and starting a business.

Since doing legitimate business was difficult, many companies resorted to what is euphemistically known as 'informal' activity, namely, tax evasion, under- or non-payment of social contributions and failure to obtain necessary permits. The size of the informal economy is difficult to assess precisely but, at the time, was usually estimated at around one quarter to one third of the total economy, and up to 50 per cent in the

---

[10] See the IMF report on SOEs (IMF, 2019) and the EBRD Regional Economic Prospects, May 2017, and Box 3 therein: 'Deeply indebted: Corporate over-indebtedness and potential consequences in Croatia, Serbia and Slovenia'. Available at: www.ebrd.com/cs/Satellite?c=Content&cid=13952364977 10&d=Mobile&pagename=EBRD%2FContent%2FContentLayout.

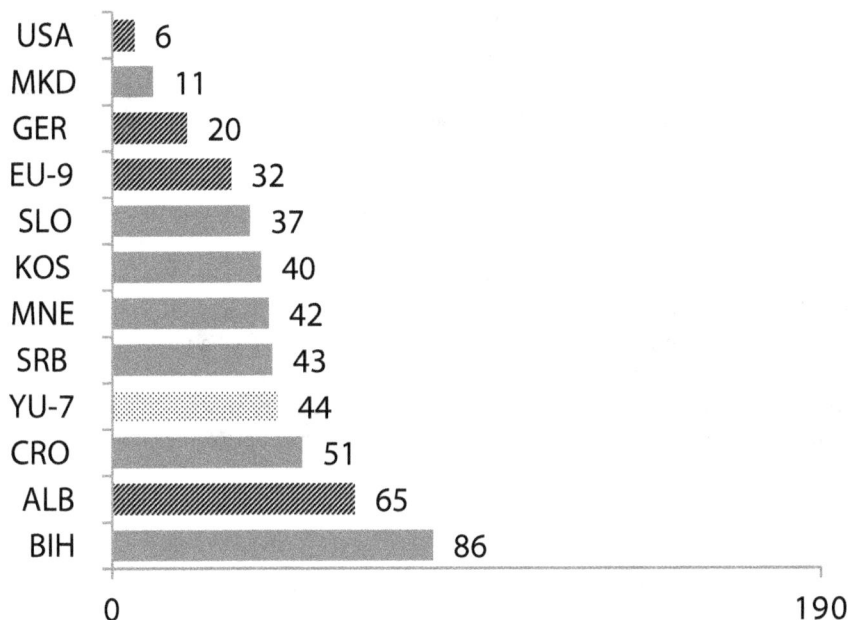

Chart 9.5 Ease of doing business, 2018. Source: World Bank Doing Business Report 2018.

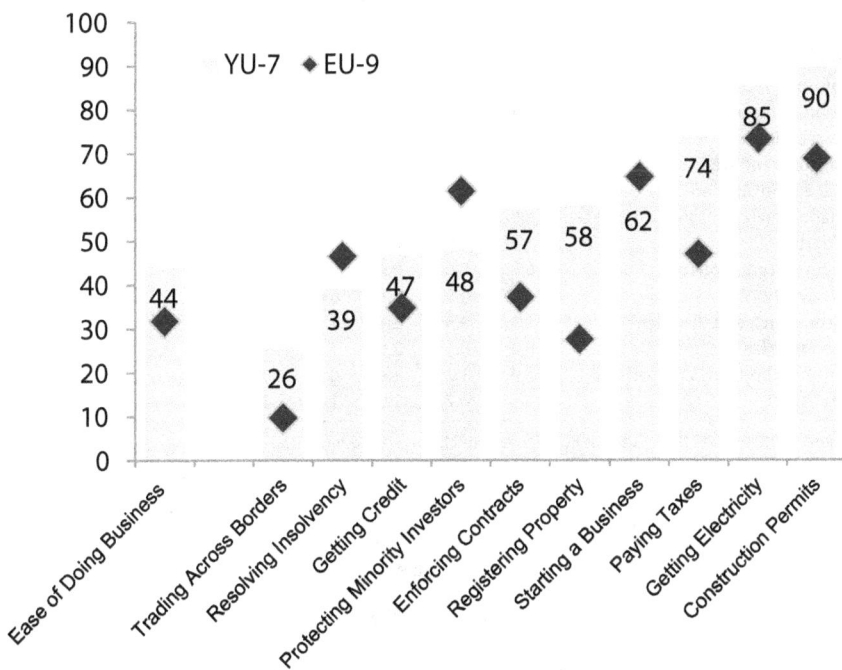

Chart 9.6 Areas of ease of doing business, 2018. Source: World Bank Doing Business Report 2018.

case of Bosnia and Herzegovina.[11] What is striking about YU-7 countries is the extent to which owners and senior managers of private companies found unfair competition from the informal economy to be a serious problem for their day-to-day operations. In the fifth round of the EBRD/World Bank Business Environment and Enterprise Performance Survey (BEEPS), on average 15.2 per cent of respondents in the YU-7 said that, out of a menu of 15 potential obstacles, this was the biggest one they faced (Table 9.2).[12] In a separate but related question, on average 23 per cent described it as a major or very severe problem.

Even if enterprise owners could circumvent the problems described above, good employees were often hard to find. An interesting finding from polls in ex-Yugoslav countries (excluding Slovenia) is that people typically preferred a public, rather than private, sector job.[13] The percentages who preferred private sector jobs ranged from just 2 per cent in Kosovo to 16 per cent in Croatia and North Macedonia. The large majority of respondents, more than 70 per cent in all cases, preferred employment in the public sector or in publicly-owned companies.

Table 9.2 Biggest obstacle to doing business, percentage vote

	BIH	CRO	KOS	MKD	MNE	SRB	SLO	YU-7 average
Tax rates	8.2	28.3	5.5	8.7	38.0	16.1	19.6	17.8
Access to finance	15.5	21.6	16.3	21.5	9.1	9.7	18.2	16.0
Practices of competitors in the informal sector	4.3	10.5	26.0	30.1	18.0	10.6	7.1	15.2
Political instability	31.4	8.7	4.0	10.2	6.9	28.7	16.0	15.1
Corruption	8.1	4.5	10.9	1.6	1.2	11.7	4.3	6.1
Customs and trade regulations	7.9	3.2	9.4	2.0	9.1	3.3	0.0	5.0
Tax administration	1.3	3.2	4.3	2.7	2.6	5.2	12.1	4.5
Inadequately educated workforce	2.0	3.5	7.0	6.8	2.7	6.1	0.9	4.1
Courts	3.4	4.9	1.5	5.1	0.2	4.5	6.3	3.7
Labour regulations	6.8	5.6	0.4	0.7	4.3	0.1	6.6	3.5
Electricity	1.6	0.5	7.8	6.6	2.6	0.2	0.9	2.9
Crime, theft and disorder	1.9	3.5	2.4	1.1	2.5	1.3	0.2	1.9
Access to land	0.9	0.1	2.0	1.3	1.2	0.9	5.7	1.7
Business licensing and permits	3.9	1.2	1.4	0.4	0.4	1.3	0.8	1.3
Transport	2.9	0.7	1.0	1.2	1.0	0.4	1.3	1.2

Source: EBRD/World Bank Business Environment and Enterprise Performance Survey.

[11] See European Commission, Country Progress Reports from November 2016. For an overview of informal economies and their measurement around the world, see Leandro Medina and Friedrich Schneider, 'Shadow Economies Around the World: What Did We Learn Over the Last 20 Years?' IMF Working Paper WP/18/17.

[12] Kresic et al. (2017) examine this issue in some detail. They show that the burden of unfair competition from the informal sector tends to fall disproportionately on smaller manufacturing firms with a local, rather than international, market.

[13] These findings are from the Balkan Barometer 2017, Public Opinion Survey. Available at: www.rcc.int/pubs/53/balkan-barometer-2017-public-opinion-survey.

Why did people in YU-7 countries want to work in the public sector in such overwhelming numbers? Job security and better working conditions (i.e. less overtime and lower workload) were the main reasons for this, as confirmed by Balkan Barometer, a public opinion survey. Also, this may be related to the fact that in all seven countries, as demonstrated by World Bank research, the public/private net wage ratio (in percentage terms) was above 100 (with an average ratio of 112), while it was marginally below 100 on average in the EU-9 (at 97) and EU-15 (at 99). When one adds the extra benefits that typically come with jobs in the public sector, the survey findings are perhaps not surprising. One can think of all these reasons as part of the legacy of the old Yugoslav system of high public welfare and job security.

Another way in which YU-7 countries stood out was the widespread belief that political connections were important for success in life. In other words, to get a cushy job in the public administration or a state-owned company – a sign of 'success' in the eyes of many – it was seen as helpful to know the right person. The point can be seen from Chart 7, which draws on the third round of the EBRD/World Bank Life in Transition Survey (LiTS III), carried out in 2016. In this survey, interviewees were asked the following question: '*In your opinion, which of the following factors is the most important to succeed in life in our country now?*' On average, more than one-third of people in the former Yugoslav countries rated political connections as more important than either effort and hard work, or intelligence and skills, as the key to success in life. The numbers ranged from 26 per cent in Slovenia to 45 per cent in North Macedonia. Notwithstanding this variation, the former Yugoslav countries stood out among all countries where the EBRD is operating, highlighting the frequent absence of meritocratic job selection and prevalence of clientelism and vested interests. In addition, there was an increase between 2010 (the time of the second round of the survey) and 2016 of respondents who put political connections as the number one

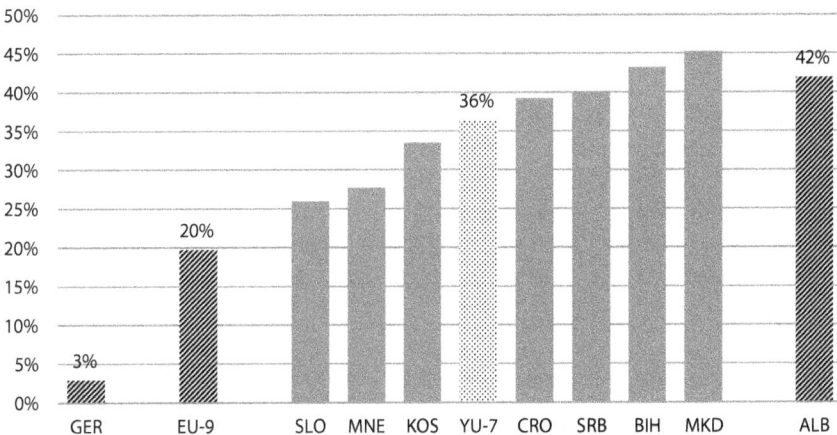

Chart 9.7 Percentage seeing political connections as the main factor behind success.
Source: EBRD/World Bank Life in Transition Survey.

factor for succeeding in life, suggesting that the problem was, if anything, getting worse. Clearly, this is also part of the Yugoslav legacy.

Such results were troubling because they highlight the challenges associated with promoting better governance and higher-quality institutions. Corruption is another area where the YU-7 countries scored poorly. Further insights into the how corruption affected the daily lives of ordinary individuals and households can be gleaned from the LiTS. One question was the following: '*In your opinion, how often is it necessary for people like you to have to make unofficial payments/gifts in these situations?*' offering answers which range from 1 (Never) to 5 (Always). The respondents answered this question for eight different situations.[14] On average, 6 per cent of ex-YU countries' residents believed that bribes were necessary for dealings with the public sector and the authorities, marginally higher than the average of 5 per cent of respondents in EU-9. However, perceived corruption was still twice as large as in the benchmark countries of Western Europe. Among the YU-7, citizens of Serbia and Bosnia and Herzegovina were the most inclined to believe in the necessity of bribes. According to this survey, the health care sector was on average seen as the most corrupted; in all cases perceived corruption in this sector was higher than overall perceived corruption.

IV Happiness and nostalgia: harkening back to 'better' days?

Life has been difficult during the transition for many people in the YU-7, whether they work, own and run a business, or rely on the creaking welfare system. Many people talk fondly of the 'old days' and Yugoslavia's distinctive brand of socialism. In the first round of the Life in Transition Survey, interviewees were asked whether they agreed or disagreed with the assertion that 'the economic situation in this country is better today than around 1989.' With the exception of Slovenia, where the numbers for and against were evenly split, the overwhelming majority in YU-7 countries (excluding Kosovo which was not included in LiTS I) disagreed with this view. The same survey showed that life dissatisfaction was widespread in the region. But twenty-five years into transition, were people still unhappy about their lives, and had they lost faith in the ideas of democracy and the market economy? The Life in Transition survey can also provide insights into these questions.

The three rounds of the LiTS showed that people in countries of former Yugoslavia on average tended to be less happy than in Western European countries, and at a similar (though slightly lower) level of happiness as in other Central and Eastern European countries. Chart 9.8 shows the percentages of respondents who agreed or strongly agreed with the statement: '*All things considered, I am satisfied with my life now*' in 2006,

---

[14] (1) interact with the road police; (2) request official documents; (3) go to court for a civil matter; (4) receive medical treatment in a public health system; (5) request unemployment benefits; (6) request social benefits; (7) receive public education (primary, secondary); (8) receive public education (vocation). Note: LiTS I (2006) asks about public education in general, and has an additional question for dealing with police other than road police. This question is not included in the LiTS II (2010) and LiTS III (2016), but is included in the average for LiTS I (2006)

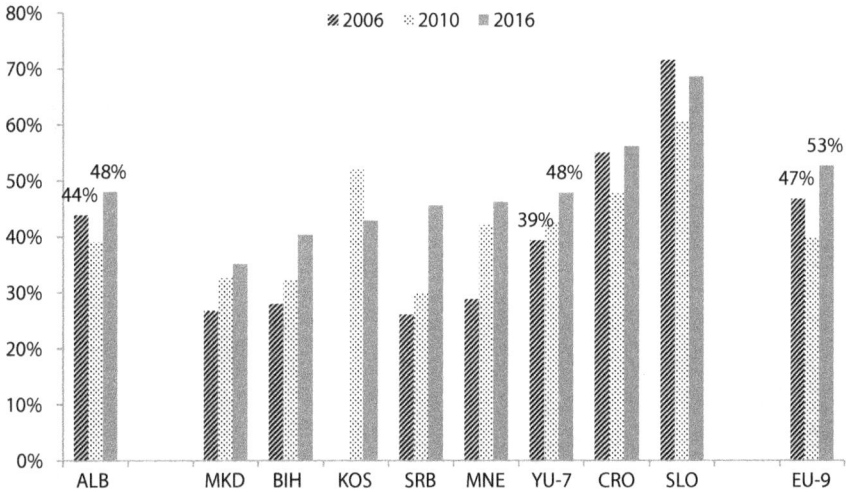

Chart 9.8 Level of life satisfaction in 2006, 2010, and 2016. Source: LiTS.

2010, and 2016. The results show a great degree of variation among the seven countries, with only Slovenians declaring a level of life satisfaction comparable to Western Europe (about 70 per cent of respondents). Higher life satisfaction in Slovenia was certainly connected with higher income level in the country. Moreover, low life happiness in the region can also be explained by the consequences of the additional turbulence in these countries brought about by the conflicts, as well as the reduced access to free public goods available in the former Yugoslavia.[15] The good news is that, generally speaking, life satisfaction rebounded in 2016, having experienced a drop in 2010 in the countries where the economic crisis hit harder, such as Croatia and Slovenia. This is consistent with EBRD analysis which showed that countries in transition had caught up with advanced market economies in terms of life satisfaction.[16]

Will life be better for future generations? All three rounds of LiTS presented respondents with a statement that reads '*Children who are born now will have a better life than my generation*' and asked them the extent to which they agree with it, ranging from 1 ('strongly disagree') to 5 ('strongly agree'). On average, YU-7 countries, apart from Kosovo, reported lower levels of optimism compared to Albanian, Baltic and Polish respondents, and similar levels to other EU-9 countries (Chart 9.9). In contrast to results cited above on life satisfaction, it was Slovenes who were least optimistic, while Kosovars were the most optimistic ones. Perhaps this is not a surprise: Slovenia is a relatively prosperous country, with a strong welfare system, and many of its citizens maybe felt fearful for the future, while for those in Kosovo, it may have been be a case of thinking that things could only get better.

---

[15] See '25 years of the EBRD – The people's view on transition' for further insights. Available at: www.ebrd.com/cs/Satellite?c=Content&cid=1395250149303&d=Mobile&pagename=EBRD%2FContent%2FContentLayout.

[16] See EBRD (2016).

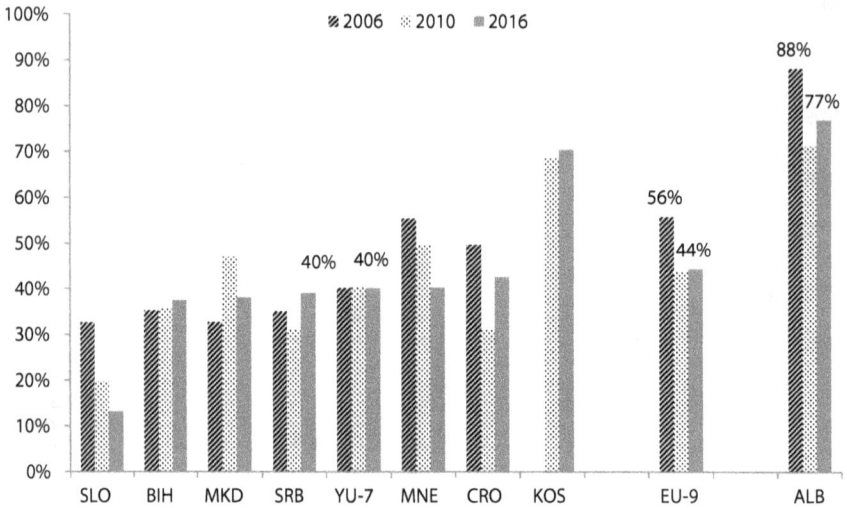

Chart 9.9 Level of optimism in 2006, 2010, and 2016. Source: LiTS.

Despite all the problems people face, support for the notion of a market economy in YU-7 countries was, on average, no different from that in the EU-9. In the LiTS, respondents were asked about their preferable economic system: specifically, they are asked to choose one of the following three scenarios: (1) *a market economy is preferable to any other form of economic system*, (2) *under some circumstances, a planned economy may be preferable to a market economy*, and (3) *for people like me, it does not matter whether the economic system is organized as a market economy or as a planned economy*. On average, support for markets increased in YU-7 over the ten years from 2006 through 2016, mainly due to a sizeable increase in support in Kosovo and FYR Macedonia (Chart 9.10). There was a noticeable drop in 2010 following the financial crisis and its aftermath, but there was a recovery in 2016. However, in Serbia and Croatia the majority of respondents reported that they did not care whether the economic system is organized as a market economy or as a planned economy.

A similar picture emerges with regard to support for the concept of democracy. In an analogously worded question to that for markets versus planned economy, the majority of respondents in all countries supported democracy over authoritarianism, but in some cases there was a significant proportion of those who were indifferent between the two (Chart 9.11). It should be noted that support for democracy was also hit by the financial and economic crisis, since in most countries respondents report declining levels of support to democracy over the three rounds of the LiTS survey. This was especially evident in the YU-7. Although respondents on average report less support to authoritarian governance, the trend was increasing, unlike in the comparison countries of Eastern Europe. The percentage of respondents who were indifferent between the two types of governance ranged from 14 per cent and 15 per cent in North Macedonia and Kosovo respectively, to 39 per cent in Serbia, the country with the

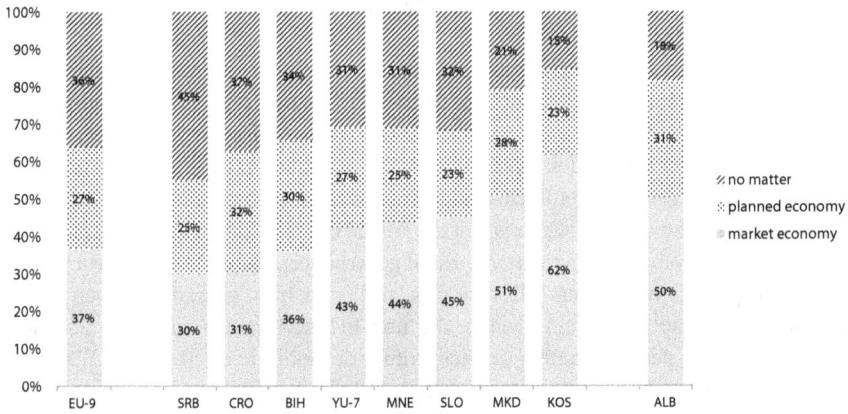

Chart 9.10 Level of support to market economy. Source: LiTS.

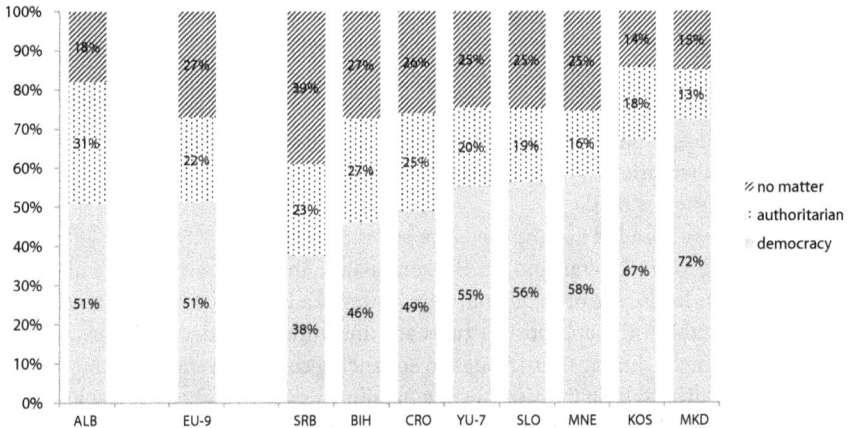

Chart 9.11 Level of support of democracy. Source: LiTS.

highest percentage of respondents indifferent between democracy and an authoritarian regime.

How should one interpret these results? Previous researchers have found a close link between support for democracy and support for the market economy, with some arguing for a causal relationship from the former to the latter.[17] The recent rise in support for authoritarianism therefore suggests that one should not be complacent about a market-oriented economy continuing to be favoured by the population. And even if liberalized market reforms remain intact in the short term, the experience of countries such as Hungary and Poland in recent years, both of which have had reversals to more authoritarian systems, shows that such gains cannot be taken for granted.[18]

[17] See Grosjean and Senik (2011).
[18] See Djankov (2016) for a useful discussion of this issue.

V Conclusion

In this chapter we have arrived at a number of conclusions about the state of the economies of the successor states of Yugoslavia after a quarter century of transition. Our main argument is that all of them fell short of being considered well-functioning sustainable market economies. Even the two EU members, Croatia and Slovenia, still faced significant structural problems. As for the rest, the path ahead to prosperity was still a long one. Our analysis suggests that the crucial issues holding back the region were lack of competitiveness and weak standards of governance. Addressing these problems is an urgent priority but success will take time and is far from guaranteed. Even under reasonable assumptions about growth, the non-EU ex-Yugoslav countries will take several decades – perhaps another quarter century or more – to catch up with EU living standards. However, EU accession remains their main anchor for comprehensive reforms, including in the areas required for a well-functioning sustainable market economy.

We have also argued that there are some important adverse continuities between the economic situation 25 years into the transition and the Yugoslav model that prevailed until the end of the 1980s. The failure of the successor states to be significantly more competitive and their poor governance, including the pervasiveness of corruption and cronyism, have not dropped onto these countries by accident. Rather, they reflect some of the problems of the previous model to which many people still remain attached, including the heavy presence of the state in the economy, preference for public rather than private sector employment, and belief in political connections as a factor behind success in life.

It is perhaps a paradox that the successor states of a country – Yugoslavia – that was seen as being more liberal and market-orientated than other Eastern European countries at the beginning of transition, were slower to adopt transformational reforms that would establish the appropriate rules and institutions needed for a sustainable market economy, including those related to enhancing competitiveness and improving governance. But, as our analysis shows, the paradox disappears when one looks more closely at the true legacy of the old Yugoslavia and the burden it placed on politicians who may want to reform.

Survey findings have suggested a deep unhappiness among much of the population and a pessimistic outlook for the future. At the same time, there is little evidence that people really wanted to return to the past, notwithstanding the nostalgic views often heard expressed in the region. The market economy and democracy were chosen as preferred economic and political systems by a majority of survey respondents. The past continues to cast a shadow on the present in the successor states of Yugoslavia, but it may be that, finally, people are willing to move on to a better economic future.

References

Allcock, John *Explaining Yugoslavia* (London, Hurst & Co, 2000).
Bartlett, William, *Europe's Troubled Region: Economic Development, Institutional Reform, and Social Welfare in the Western Balkans* (London and New York, Routledge, 2007).

Djankov, Simeon, *The Divergent Postcommunist Paths to Democracy and Economic Freedom*, Discussion Paper No 758, LSE, (2016).

EBRD, *Transition Report* (annual, various issues; London, EBRD).

EBRD, *Transition for All: Equal Opportunities in an Unequal World* (London, EBRD, 2016).

Grosjean, Pauline and Claudia Senik, 'Democracy, Market Liberalization, and Political Preferences', *Review of Economics and Statistics*, 93(1), pp. 365–81 (2011).

IMF, *Reassessing the Role of State-Owned Enterprises in Central, Eastern, and Southeastern Europe*, IMF Departmental Paper No 19/11 (2019).

Kresic, Ana, Jakov Milatovic and Peter Sanfey, 'Firm Performance and Obstacles to Doing Business in the Western Balkans: Evidence from the BEEPS', EBRD Working Paper No 200 (2017).

Medina, Leandro and Friedrich Schneider, 'Shadow Economies Around the World: What Did We Learn Over the Last 20 Years?' IMF Working Paper WP/18/17 (2018).

Sanfey, Peter and Simone Zeh, 'Making Sense of Competitiveness Indicators in South-Eastern Europe', in *Defining a New Reform Agenda: Paths to Sustainable Convergence in South East Europe* (eds O Anastasakis, P Sanfey and M Watson), pp. 25–50 (St Antony's College, Oxford University, 2013).

10

Conclusion: Yugoslavia, Lost in Transition?

Othon Anastasakis, Adam Bennett, David Madden
and Adis Merdzanovic
University of Oxford/Zurich University of Applied Sciences

After three score years and ten, Yugoslavia ceased to exist. True to its character as the multi-faceted country it once was, its process of disintegration took various forms, ranging from violent wars characterized by horrendous atrocities and ethnic cleansing, to smaller violent skirmishes lasting only a few days or weeks and producing few casualties, to mostly or completely peaceful secession by political acts and agreements. Some three decades after the disintegration process started in the 1990s, the landscape of the former Yugoslav region looks radically different from what it once was.

With the collapse of communism, it seemed as if Yugoslavia, having been the most liberal and outward-looking of the former communist countries, would surpass all the other transition countries in terms of adapting to the new international environment and sailing through to membership of the European Union (EU). Yet, as it turned out, with the exception of Slovenia and much later Croatia (and Slovenes and Croats had often tended to see themselves as 'different' and more 'Western' than other South Slavs), all the other successor countries are still struggling with their transitions and their accession to the EU. For all these new states, the goal of disintegration from Yugoslavia took over from the goal of integration with the EU.

Our central question in this book was whether countries like Yugoslavia, which left such a big mark on the international scene during the long Cold War period, and whose continuation was fought against by its own constituent republics and provinces, truly disappear after they cease to exist officially. In answering this question, we sought to challenge the easy generalization that the transition from communism to Western-style liberalism in Yugoslavia through the road of ethnic strife, divisive elite politics, and violent disintegration into seven new states, eradicated the Yugoslav past completely. Instead, we asked whether the complex multiple transitions in the former Yugoslav space had led to something totally new; or whether we see the continuation of the old, albeit in completely different clothes; or, indeed, whether there is a mixture of both.

In this volume, we have sought to reflect on the state of play in the region. We argue that one should not see the contemporary challenges in the Western Balkans as distinct from the past: by which we mean both the most recent past of disintegration, and also the longer-term legacy that living together in a state for seventy years has produced.

While there exist important discontinuities between Yugoslavia and the successor states, especially in terms of political economy and the values and realities of the new political and social systems, there are also important continuities which determine not only how the current state is perceived, but also what characteristics it possesses. The chapters in this volume support this original hypothesis, and should act as a stimulus for further research on the relevance of Yugoslavia in the present day.

On 19 December 2018, the municipal authorities in Podgorica, Montenegro, unveiled a statue of the Yugoslav leader Tito, who died in 1980 and is still revered by some, on the anniversary of the city's liberation from Nazi Germany by Tito's partisans in 1944. During the unveiling, Tito admirers and veterans waved Yugoslav flags. Whether this was a sign of 'Yugonostalgia', a homage to an anti-fascist past, or political manoeuvring, is a question to be debated; but it is worth noting that a 2016 Gallup poll – 25 years after the start of the dissolution of Yugoslavia – showed that 65% of Montenegrins believed that the dissolution of Yugoslavia was not beneficial to their country (Table 1).[1] Next door in Serbia, the Vučić government did not miss out on opportunities to compare his own leadership with the achievements in Tito's social and foreign policies. But the memory of Tito, one of the iconic leaders of the twentieth century, does not resonate so favourably in every part of former Yugoslavia – in Zagreb, for example, the city assembly voted in September 2017 to rename the 'Marshall Tito Square' as the 'Square of the Republic of Croatia'. Moreover, in other parts of the Western Balkan region, such as in Kosovo, there are very few Kosovo Albanians who regret the dissolution of Yugoslavia.

Beyond these manifestations of continuity or rejection, and the variety of collective memories of the recent, or not so recent past, the actual legacy of Yugoslavia still confuses people and produces a lot of scepticism. Some consider the country an original socio-economic experiment, others see it as a symbol of anti-fascist and anti-Stalinist struggle, others as an example of a doomed ethnic coexistence suppressing national identities, and others as an impossible combination of a totalitarian polity with some tolerance for a liberal opposition. People cannot even decide whether seventy years was a long or a short period for the life of a country.

Table 10.1 In general, did the break-up of Yugoslavia benefit or harm this country?

	Benefit (%)	Harm (%)	Don't know/refuse (%)
Serbia	4	81	8
Bosnia and Herzegovina	6	77	7
Montenegro	15	65	9
Macedonia	12	61	21
Slovenia (2014)	41	45	10
Croatia	55	23	9
Kosovo	75	10	10

Source: Gallup World Poll, 2016

---

[1] Elizabeth Keating and Zacc Ritter, 'Many in Balkans Still See More Harm From Yugoslavia Breakup', *Gallup.* Available at: https://news.gallup.com/poll/210866/balkans-harm-yugoslavia-breakup.aspx.

Faced with this controversial legacy, we attempted in this book to define some continuities with the Yugoslav past, thirty years after the beginning of its collapse. While some chapters considered the impact of imperial legacies in the region, as well as some of the defining economic features of the monarchic Yugoslavia that existed before the Second World War, most chapters have focused their attention on the immediate past, meaning the legacy of socialist Yugoslavia. In this respect, most of the discussion of continuities in the literature has focused on the notion of 'Yugo-nostalgia' which, in the most meaningful way, can be found in the social sphere. As Catherine Baker's contribution in our book shows, there exists a deep sociocultural nostalgia, or a longing for the olden days, which also expresses itself in the mass appeal of music and media throughout the region. Such continuity, however, has to be qualified, for it seems to be counterbalanced by other equally important factors. According to Baker, 'Yugo'-nostalgia is supplemented or tempered by an ethnocentric nostalgia for different ethnonational phenomena which are connected to the nation-building processes of the 1990s and for which the wars acted as important catalysts. These two forms of nostalgia, while clearly distinct, coexist in the contemporary post-Yugoslav space.

In this volume we have gone beyond the idea of Yugoslav continuity as only a psychological or cultural phenomenon. We propose that there are other legacies, which have continued to affect the present in the fields of politics, economics, and international relations. Adis Merdzanovic's chapter argues that the social liberal elements of Yugoslavia's socialist system produced not only significant benefits for the people, but also acted as a substitute for political and economic legitimacy, which was otherwise mostly lacking. As such, they formed a durable foundation for how political power and political, economic, and social outputs were and still are assessed. As a consequence, the genuinely liberal concepts of legitimising political rule fell short when applied to the post-Yugoslav context, since the foundations of Yugoslav politics were more social than political. The particular form of political and economic liberalism furthermore means that the post-Yugoslav system of liberal democracy, a teleological fixture for all states in the Balkans, has indeed the potentiality to be adopted, even if it currently lacks sound prescriptions for social justice.

There are tensions between the old system and the new, not only theoretically and in terms of the magnitude of changes necessary to complete the transition from one to the other, but also as a matter of practicalities, where the transition operates against different push and pull dynamics. The situation of civil society actors, discussed in the chapter by Sokolic, Kostovicova and Fagan, outlines this tension quite well. Seen as the backbone of liberal democracy, civil society actors are perceived as an important factor for the successful democratization of socialist systems. But as the case studies of Serbia and Croatia demonstrate, while some civil society actors did indeed contribute to the democratization of society, others exerted pressure in the opposite direction. Similarly, some rather powerful civil society actors happened to hold quite close connections with the governing parties and thus enjoyed important privileges, while others suffered from fragmentation and were ignored as a result of their critical stance towards the ruling elites. So, while the civil society activism that started in Yugoslavia with timid protests against the regime in the form of demonstrations or artistic criticism has indeed blossomed under the post-Yugoslav conditions, this development does not seem to be necessarily conducive to the larger goals of democratization.

At the same time, the act of protest, performed by members of the civil society in order to show discontent with the ruling structures or the elites, seems to constitute a particular continuity between Yugoslavia and the successor states. While the right to protest was, of course, not fully established in communist times, there were challenges to the rule of the political elites, e.g. the student movement of 1968 and the mass mobilization movement in Croatia. The Yugoslavs took to the streets en masse. In contemporary times, and within the framework of democracy, protests have become a natural right of the citizens and civil society seems to have rediscovered the street as a central battleground in the fight for political influence against the elites. Slovenia, Croatia, Bosnia and Herzegovina, Serbia and North Macedonia have all witnessed large-scale public demonstrations against the ruling elites. While the outcomes of these protests vary and some of them are still continuing, they may be seen in part as a Yugoslav legacy.

Turning to discontinuity, one of the most significant areas is to be found in the economic dimension. The end of the special Yugoslav system of worker self-management in enterprises and the introduction of privatization and shareholder business models represents the largest rift with the past. Since the 1970s there were concerns over whether the Yugoslav system of self-management was compatible with macroeconomic stability. Adam Bennett argues in his chapter that the two concepts presented an 'impossible marriage', because wage pressures and wasteful investment created the need for large-scale borrowing. The effect of efforts to finance these loans was chronic inflation and then hyperinflation, which ultimately undermined the credibility of the Federal government. The reforms undertaken by the end of the 1980s proved to be too late, leaving them to be fully implemented only in the successor states. Nevertheless, as Milica Uvalic points out in her chapter, Yugoslavia's economic system presented a mix of socialist and liberal elements that did rely on market mechanisms which enabled the country to function more effectively than its centrally planned neighbours. Among the most important achievements of the old model were rapid economic growth for most of the period which permitted industrialization, urbanization, and an increase in living standards. It did, however, create high levels of unemployment, regional disparities in economic development, and an unsustainable level of external debt that eventually halted the country's growth rate.

The transition to market economies in the successor states proceeded at variable speeds due to the different political and economic conditions in the individual countries, as discussed in these two chapters. Uvalic highlights the relative economic success of Slovenia which transitioned more gradually than the other successor states. However, as both Bennett and Uvalic point out, Slovenia enjoyed an important advantage in the transition process because it relied on a stable political system and managed to secede without war. It thus could proceed with the implementation of economic reforms without any major post-Yugoslav shocks. Uvalic notes that the 'spirit' of parts of the old worker-self management system can still be seen in Slovenia's reformed arrangements for worker representation on corporate boards, similar to those in Germany. The influence of Germany during transition was also evident in Croatia's use of the German *Treuhand* model for restructuring and privatization. Bennett observes that privatization did not always deliver the desired transformative results (at least initially), as in North Macedonia where sales to insiders left the same 'self-managers' (and their old habits) in charge of enterprises. Nevertheless, growth in the region overall (albeit interrupted by the Great Financial Crisis in 2008) has been respectable since the turn of the century and inflation is low – in marked contrast to the final decade of Yugoslavia.

The success and failure of transition should not, however, be judged only in terms of economic growth and other macroeconomic metrics but ought also take account of the larger socio-economic and political context, as explored in the chapter by Milatović and Sanfey. As they explain, there is a widely held belief that 'jobs in the public sector are more desirable than those in the private sector and that political connections are the way to get ahead in life'. The new economic systems seem to have left a lot of people disappointed with their situation, which helps partly explain the rather diffuse concept of nostalgia for the past.

In the international arena it is much harder to detect continuities given that the change in 1989 signified the defeat of the communist bloc and the victory of the capitalist one. For Yugoslavia and the successor states, this had an enormous impact. As Spaskovska argues, from an engaged international actor which played a significant role in various global initiatives, the post-Yugoslav region retreated, first into a conflict zone that required solutions itself, and eventually into a vulnerable geopolitical periphery. The notion of legacy may be more relevant here, in the sense that the international significance of Yugoslavia has been used as a point of reference, with positive as well as negative connotations. Because Yugoslavia had placed itself in the middle of the two superpowers and developed relations with all countries and blocs, a Titoist legacy of an 'equidistance in foreign policy' may be visible in some instances of the foreign policies of the new states. Othon Anastasakis' chapter shows exactly how the post-Yugoslav elites, despite their transatlantic orientation, have been developing close links with third countries beyond the EU, including Russia and Turkey. A neo-Titoist approach to foreign policy has been visible in most of the successor countries which, despite their much smaller size in the international arena, still rely a lot on external relations to sustain their internal agendas. This is most visible in the case of Serbian diplomacy which at times deliberately claims a degree of continuity with Yugoslavia's foreign policy for internal purposes: many of Yugoslavia's former non-aligned allies, for instance, are still refusing to recognize Kosovo. A less ideological and more pragmatic foreign policy has been helpful for the nation building process in the successor states of Yugoslavia. While some states such as Serbia and Slovenia chose to refer to the continuity of the Yugoslav third way in foreign policy and others like Croatia or Kosovo chose to break the links with the past, as Spaskovska shows, there is a tendency to revisit its merits as a synonym for active foreign policy with a global impact.

The more paradoxical legacy of Yugoslavia lies in the internal borders of the country between republics, which with the disintegration became external borders of the successor states and which have become important points of contestation between the states of the region from the Slovenian north to the Kosovo south. It is ironic, as James Ker-Lindsay argues, that in the transition from border irrelevance within Yugoslavia to (supposed) border irrelevance within the EU, the successor Yugoslav states have to go through the delimitation of their national borders with each other, contesting each other's land and sea border sovereignties as a reflection of intra-regional competition and nationalism.

These different chapters have presented us with a series of connected, inter-disciplinary snapshots addressing the question of *legacy* from different perspectives. For the purposes of this volume, we defined legacies as the persistent relevance of historical periods, developments, or personalities for the present. Structures and experiences from the past exert influence long after the breaking point between past and present has effectively occurred. This relevance persists through the survival and/or replication of, or as the reaction to, particular events, practices, conditions and institutions. While legacies as *analytical lenses* take the form of continuities and ruptures, the past which they depict and its consequences are variously perceived and evaluated, interconnecting the concept of legacy with other social and epistemological concepts such as memories and nostalgia. Personal, institutional, or state-created *memories* try to and do shape how legacies – and also historical periods, developments, or personalities – are assessed and remembered. Memories are thus both personal and collective. When they are superimposed on particular ruptures which make the past appear more desirable than the present, *nostalgia* in the form of a longing for the past may occur. As an analytical lens, legacy thus offers us an insight into the creation, utilization, and instrumentalization of both memories and nostalgia. As the chapters in this volume have shown, these are quite different aspects of a convoluted nexus of historical development which once again emphasizes the need for a deeper understanding of how the past influences the present and the present is shaped by the past on a personal, but also on a structural, level.

As is natural for a collected volume, the contributions in this book have focused on certain aspects while leaving others aside. In terms of societal legacy, for example, it would be interesting to look at the legacies of processes such as modernization or urbanization; or at how the understanding of gender and family roles changed due to transition. In terms of politics, further research could address the treatment of nationalities and national minorities in Yugoslavia and the successor states, which would include the very important question of the status of minority rights. Finally, the legacies of empires which are mentioned in the chapter dedicated to Russia and Turkey could be expanded to a more systematic comparison, both in a temporal and geographical sense. We sincerely hope that our volume has provided some starting points for further research into these areas – research which should, and we hope will, be taken up by others.

Nevertheless, in their totality, the different chapters in our volume have allowed us to build up a matrix of continuities and discontinuities, putting our focus on where practices, institutions, or experiences of Yugoslavia disappeared and on where they are still prevalent. As we have discussed, one end of the spectrum locates the *survival* of various structural and behavioural characteristics of the former state. Even in the economic area, old mentalities of state interference in the functionalities of markets and close ties between the economic community and the political elites have proved quite resilient. In the cultural sphere, television shows and music still manage to unite populations transcending political borders. In the political sphere, where much has changed, there still exists a particular notion of social justice which determines how the current systems are perceived and, if necessary, how they are challenged. In international affairs, the continuity of the old Yugoslav third-way policy is at times still employed as a diplomatic means when it best suits the interests of the successor states.

At the other end of the spectrum are the discontinuities, which occurred either as a result of large-scale developments or as conscious *reactions to the past*, meaning that a break was deliberately sought. The consequences of the destruction wrought by war and violence, which not only affected so many lives but also many successor states' infrastructures, certainly fuelled the drive for separate futures and a genuine rupture with the past. New political, social, and economic logics have been introduced into the region that make continuity with the past either politically undesirable, as in the cases of Yugoslav multilateralism and the legacy of camaraderie between the peoples, or practically impossible, as with the end of worker self-management.

Then, in the middle of the spectrum, there are some phenomena, which exhibit both continuities and discontinuities, and are characterized by the particularly problematic ambiguity which also remains closely connected to the Yugoslav state. When administrative boundaries within the common state metamorphosed into state borders they produced a number of challenges to the now international relations between the successor states. While membership of the European Union may seem a panacea due to the decreased importance of borders between member states, the dispute between Croatia and Slovenia may serve as a cautionary tale in this respect. Similarly, we are confronted with a particular continuity in assessing the relationship between the region and countries such as Russia and Turkey, which not only can build on a history of engagement in the region (particularly Turkey), but also through their authoritarian systems offer modes of political rule and legitimacy different to the liberal democratic systems on which the EU insists.

The fact that such questions fall in the middle of our spectrum means that the successor states still have not yet fully decided whether and to what degree they want to 'keep the past' and to what degree they want to break with it. In a way, they are 'lost in transition', for their systems have only partially adapted to the new paradigms. The dawn of the successor states started with the break from the old system, which is often portrayed as a new beginning. Yet for a number of years now, the Modern Balkans landscape has been characterized by states in a permanent state of 'transitocracy', i.e. moving neither forward nor backward on democratic consolidation.[2] In recent years, we may even observe a gradual democratic decline and the emergence of 'competitive authoritarianism'.[3] The final outcome of Yugoslavia's disintegration is still unclear.

---

[2] Ilir Kalemaj, 'Challenges and Opportunities in the Western Balkans: Albania in the Crossroad of Regionalization and European Integration', SSRN Scholarly Paper (Rochester, NY: Social Science Research Network, 2016). Available at: https://papers.ssrn.com/abstract=2785689.

[3] Florian Bieber, 'Patterns of Competitive Authoritarianism in the Western Balkans' (2018) 34(3) *East European Politics* 337–54.

What this volume has made clear, however, is that just as the present cannot be understood without reference to the past and the past exerts significant influence on the present, the states in the Western Balkans will one day have to deal not only with the legacies of Yugoslavia but also with the legacies of its disintegration.

References

Bieber, Florian. 'Patterns of Competitive Authoritarianism in the Western Balkans' (2018) 34(3) *East European Politics*, pp. 337–54.

Kalemaj, Ilir. 'Challenges and Opportunities in the Western Balkans: Albania in the Crossroad of Regionalization and European Integration'. SSRN Scholarly Paper. Rochester, NY: Social Science Research Network, 2016. Available at: https://papers.ssrn.com/abstract=2785689.

Keating, Elizabeth and Zacc Ritter. 'Many in Balkans Still See More Harm From Yugoslavia Breakup', *Gallup*. Available at: https://news.gallup.com/poll/210866/balkans-harm-yugoslavia-breakup.aspx.

Index

Diagrams, graphs and tables are given in italics.

Adria (label) 65
Africa 89–91, 93
Africa Research Institute *see* Institute for Development and International Relations (IRMO)
Agency for Restructuring and Privatization (Slovenia) 162
agriculture 142, 161, 170–71, 179, 181
Ahtisaari, Martti 106
Albania,
    exceptionalism of 2
    Gülenist educational institutions in 132
    and Kosovo 42, 63–64, 106
    resistance to post-Stalinist Soviet influence 121
    Turkey as one of its biggest investors 129
Albanosphere 64
Algeria 92–93
Algerian Museum of Modern and Contemporary Art 93
Algerian National Liberation Front (FLN) 93
Alliance for the Future of Kosovo (AAK) 111
Alliance of Socialist Youth 22
Alliance of Trade Unions 22
Anastasakis, Othon 9, 213
Andjelić, Neven 26, 29
Arab Spring 132
Army of Yugoslavia (VJ) 64
Article IV Consultation 149
Asian Crisis (1990s) 148
'Assassination of Croatia' (publication) 49
Associated Labour Act (1976) 172
Association of Students 'St Justin the Philosopher' 53

Austria 129, 134
Austria-Hungary 3
Avramović, Dragoslav 84

Badinter Commission 106
Badinter, Robert 102
Bajt, Aleksandar 175–76
Baker, Catherine 8, 211
Balkanika (tv channel) 66
Balkan Media Awards 66
Balkan Music Awards 66
Balkan (nomenclature) 65–66
Balkan Pact (1953) 121, 123
Ban Ki-moon 86–87
Basic Organizations of Associated Labour (BOALs) 173
Bay of Piran 9, 99, 101, 104–5
Bay of Savudrija *see* Bay of Piran
Belgrade declaration (1955) 121
Belgrade Museum of Yugoslavia 91
Bennett, Adam 9, 212
Bernama (Malaysian national news agency) 91
Bijelo Dugme (rock band) 62
Blaškić, Tihomir 74
Blum, Emerik 84
Bosnia-Herzegovina,
    and commemoration of Armed Forces Day 75
    and creation of Republic of Yugoslavia 101
    and the ekavica variant (language) 66
    end of war in 106
    establishment of state institutions 33
    and fight for political influence against elites 212
    Gülenist educational institutions in 132
    IMF support for reforms 163–64

introduction of visa-free regime
  (December 2010) 188
and MTV Adria franchise 65
multi-national republic 27
and NAM summits 87
NATO military intervention in 126
newly composed folk songs in 60
one of the late reformers 183
Peace Implementation Council in 125
and privatization in 185, 185n.58
and references to pre-independence
  past 90
and Stabilization Force (SFOR) 124
strategies of the elites 33
sustainable market economy progress
  in 192–93, *194–95*, 195–96, *197*,
  198, *199–201*, 200–206, *203–5*
and Turkey 125, 128–29
Yugoslav partisan tradition in 63–64
Bosnian-Croat Federation post-war army
  125
Brena, Lepa 68–71
Bretton Woods system 149
Brijuni Island 94
Bulgaria 119, 121, 130

capitalism 26–27, 169
Ceca 71, 71n.49
Čekuolis, Dalius 88
Cem, Ismail 128
Central Committee of the League of
  Communists of Yugoslavia (LCY)
  182
Central and Eastern Europe countries
  (CEE) 15, 34, 179–80, 183, 185, 187
Centre for Peace (human rights NGO) 47
Centre for Peace Studies (human rights
  NGO) 47
Cerar, Miro 105
China 109
Christian Orthodox communities 117–18
Civic Committee for Human Rights
  (human rights NGO) 47
civil society,
  in Communist Yugoslavia 41–46
  conclusions 54–55
  in Croatia 46–50, 54
  governance in Serbia 51–54
  introduction 39–41

civil society organizations (CSOs) 51–53,
  55
Club of Rome 84
Coca-Cola 62
Cockta (soft drink) 174
Codetermination Law 1993 (Slovenia)
  184
Cohen, Lenard J. 16
Cold War,
  cool economic relations between
    Soviet Union and Yugoslavia
    122
  and last Non-Aligned summit 86
  limits of external influence of Turkey
    and Russia 133, 135
  and new geo-political realignments 81
  and the non-aligned movement 7, 87, 92
  third way politics in 5
  Turkish foreign policy during 122–23
  Yugoslavia during 88, 118, 121, 123, 209
Colombia 87
Cominform 3, 21, 120, 142, 173
Commission on Security and Cooperation
  in Europe (CSCE) 87
Communism,
  collapse of 39, 123–24, 209
  cultural memories of regimes 61
  dissent in Kosovo (1981) 43–44
  ideology in Soviet Union 42
  Yugoslav brand of 7, 22, 41–42,
    54, 65
Company Law (1988) 181
Company Law (1997) 186, 186n.61
Complex Organization of Associated
  Labour (COAL) 173
Conference on International Economic
  Cooperation (CIEC) 84
Constitution (1953) 172
Copenhagen summit (1993) 31–32, 34
Corfu Declaration (1917) 3
Council of Mutual Economic Assistance
  (CMEA) 174, 179
*Council for the Norms of the Croatian
  Standard Language* 48
Crimea 131
Crimean Tatars 61
Croat Defence Council (HVO) 74–75
Croatia,
  breaking of links with the past 214

candidacy for UN Security Council
87–88
civil society in 46–50, 54
and creation of Republic of Yugoslavia
101
Croatian Spring (1971) 24, 24n.39, 27,
42, 121, 121n.15
cultural policy 75–76
delayed accession to EU 130
dispute over Bay of Piran 9, 99, 104–5,
112, 215
effect of war on economy 163
and the ekavica variant (language) 66
and the Eurovision Song Contest 70
favoured confederative transformation
of Yugoslavia 182, 182n.50
fighting the Bosniaks 125
and fight for political influence against
elites 212
and Franjo Tuđman 33, 63
higher level of development in 179,
187, 209
independence of (June 1991) 3, 64, 180
liberal ideas within 20
limited interest in non-alignment 94
mass mobilization movement in 212
and MTV Adria franchise 65
and musicians' performances 68
and NAM summits 90
nostalgia in 71
one of the early reformers 183
one of first republics to break away
101–2
participation in the Homeland War 71,
73–75
Russian volunteers fought with Serbs
in 124
strength of civil society in 45
sustainable market economy progress
in 192–93, *194–95*, 195–96, *197*,
198, *199–201*, 200–206, *203–5*
and 'turbo-folk' 71
Turkey's consultation mechanisms in
128
Croatian Academy of Sciences and Arts
(HAZU) 48
Croatian Communist Party 42
Croatian Democratic Union (HDZ)
46–47, 73

Croatian Football Association (HNS)
74–75
Croatian Helsinki Committee (human
rights NGO) 47
*Croatian Memorial and Documentation
Centre for the Homeland War* 48–50
Croatian Privatization Fund 163
crony-capitalism 148
Cuba 87
Cyprus 103, 134
Czechoslovakia 121

Danube, River 114
Davutoglu, Ahmet 128
Dayton Peace Agreement (1995) 63, 103,
183–84
Demirel, Suleyman 128
Democratic Party of Kosovo (PDK) 111
Democratic Party of Serbia 127
Development Fund (Slovenia) 162
Diamond Palace Casino, Zagreb 69
Djilas, Milovan 27–28
Djindjić, Zoran 54
Djukanović, Milo 131
*Documenta–Centre of Dealing with the
Past* (human rights NGO) 47–50
Dodik, Milorad 127
Domar, Evsey 175
Dragović, Doris 69
Đukanović, Milo 184
Dumančič, Marko 71
Dutch Art Institute 92

Ease of Doing Business 2018 scores (World
Bank) 198
Ecevit, Bulent 128
Egypt 3, 83, 92, 174
Ekiert, Grzegorz 40
electrocracy 39
Enhanced Structural Adjustment Facility
165
Enhanced Surveillance (ES) 149, 154,
154n.20
enterprise self-management 150–51,
150n.13, 160, 166, *see also*
labour-managed firms, worker-
managed enterprises, and workers'
self-management
Erdogan, Recep Tayyip 131–32

Estrin, Saul 175
European Bank for Reconstruction and
    Development (EBRD) 192–93,
    193n.9, 196
European Commission 105–6, 110
European Community (EC) 30
European Court of Justice (ECJ) 105, 113
European Economic Community (EEC),
    economic interconnectedness with
        25–26
    Yugoslavia's privileged relations with
        174
European External Action Service 114
European Union (EU),
    accession of Serbia 51
    accession of Slovenia 103–6
    biggest investor in the Balkans 2
    and border dispute between Kosovo
        and Montenegro 110–12
    and border elimination 9
    a central role in post-conflict
        reconstruction 126
    characterized by free movement policy
        100, 100n.3
    and Croatia's bid to join 99
    and CSOs in Serbia 53
    early support of Slovenia 183
    engagement with Yugoslavia 7, 30–32
    and enlargement fatigue 135
    growth comparison with Yugoslavian
        successor states 186, 186n.64, 196,
        198–203
    and independence of Kosovo 107–8,
        113–14
    insistence on economic liberalism
        33–34
    principle of territorial integrity 102–3
    and Serbia's accession 114
    slowing down of Turkey's accession
        talks 132
    visas for Yugoslavian successor states
        188, 188n.66
    weakening influence during Eurozone
        crisis 130
    Western Balkans' integration into
        15–16, 113
EU-Turkey refugee agreement (2016) 133

façade democracy 39

Fagan, Adam 8, 211
Federal Development Fund 179
Federal Republic of Yugoslavia (FRY)
    183
'Firm in Illyria' (Ward) 174
First World War 100, 119
Five-Year Plan (1946–51) 142–43
Foreign Direct Investment law (1988)
    181
Former Yugoslav Republic of Macedonia
    see Macedonia
France 20
Friedman, Milton 26, 156
Fund for the Development of the Less
    Developed Republics and Regions
    171
Furubotn, Eirik 175

G-77 84–87
Galeb (ship) 94
Gazprom 127
General Agreement on Tariffs and Trade
    (GATT) 27, 174
General Investment Funds 171
genocide 130
Germany 3, 61, 92, 108, 114, 120, 134, 147,
    163, 213
Gligorov, Vladimir 20
global citizenship,
    conclusions 95
    introduction 81–83
    non-alignment after Yugoslavia
        86–91
    re-imagined 91–95
    Yugoslav socialist 83–86
global financial crisis 2007–8 (GFC) 74,
    160–66
Goli otok prison camp 94
Grabar-Kitarović, Kolinda 74–75
Grašo, Petar 67
Great Depression (1931–32) 142
'Greater Serbian Aggression' (publication)
    49
Great Financial Crisis (2008) 213
Greece,
    competition with Turkey 134
    dispute with Macedonia 63, 103
    heavy investment in Balkans banking
        sector 129

June 2018 agreement with Macedonia 132

non-aggression Balkan Entente with Turkey 122

and the Prespa agreement 4

and the Treaty of Alliance (1954) 123

Group of Eminent Persons 84

Gul, Abdullah 130

Gülen movement 132

Hajduk Split 69

Haradinaj, Ramush 111–12

'Hej, Balkano' (Šuput) 70

Helsinki Process/the establishment of the Conference for Security and Cooperation in Europe (CSCE) 83

Historical Witnesses: Stevan Labudovic (exhibition) 93

Hofman, Ana 66

Homeland War (1991–95) 60, 73–74

Horvat, Branko 175

Hotel Jugoslavija 66–68

'Hotel Jugoslavija' (Saša Kapor) 66–68

Huljić, Tonči 70

human rights advocacy groups (HRGs) 51, 53

Hungary 54, 121, 205

hyperinflation 145, 157–58, 165, 182, 184, 212

Implementation Force (IFOR) 124

Independent Commission on International Development Issues 84, 84n.13

India 3, 83, 87, 89–90, 174

Indonesia 90, 92

Institute for the Croatian Language and Linguistics (IHJJ) 48

Institute for Development and International Relations (IRMO) 89

Institute for International Relations 89

interest rate policy 151–52, 152n.15

International Centre for Promotion of Enterprises (ICPE) 89, 89n.35

International Civilian Office (ICO) 109

International Commission for the Study of Communication Problems *see* MacBride Commission

International Court of Arbitration 113

International Court of Justice (ICJ) 107

International Criminal Tribunal for the former Yugoslavia (ICTY) 47–48

International Monetary Fund (IMF), agreement of 1988 29

and concessions to developing countries 85

introduction 7

reforms focused on setting up central banks 159–60

stand-by Arrangement with Croatia (1994) 163

stand-by arrangement with Serbia (2001) 164

supporting Yugoslavia's stability programmes 9, 141

support for reforms of Bosnia and Herzegovina 163–64

Yugoslavia a founding member of 173

Iron Curtain 31, 169

Italy 3, 104, 134, 147

Janša, Janez 43

Jansen, Stef 83

JAT (Yugoslav airline) 174

Jeremić, Vuk 88, 90

Jordanova, Liudmilla 88

'Josip Broz Tito on Brijuni' (exhibition) 94

Judah, Tim 60

'Jugoslovenka' (song) 68

Justice and Development Party (AKP) 128

Kant, Immanuel 19

Kapor, Saša 66

Karađorđević Alexander, King 3

Kardelj, Edvard 22

Kaunda, Kenneth 90

Ker-Lindsay, James 9, 90, 214

Kesovija, Tereza 69

Khrushchev, Nikita 121

Kiossev, Alexander 70

Kornai, Janos 176

Kosovo,

and 1999 NATO bombing 184

and Albanian cultural and linguistic rights 63–64

Albanian demonstrations in (1981) 42–43

border dispute with Montenegro 99,
108, 112
breaking of links with the past 214
contested territorial issues of 9
end of military campaign in 126
and future recognitions lobbying 82
Gülenist educational institutions in
132, 132n.60
and high unemployment rates in 178
independence of 1–2, 90, 99, 184
introduction 9
least developed area 179
never as exposed to the GFC 164
and NGOs 52
placed under UN administration 103
recognition of 213
and Russia 124, 127, 136
and Serbia 131, 164
support for dissolution of Yugoslavia
210, *210*
sustainable market economy progress
in 192–93, *194–95*, 195–96, *197*,
198, *199–201*, 200–206, *203–5*
and Turkey 125–26, 129, 130
Kosovo Energy Corporation 129
Kosovo Liberation Army (KLA) 64, 106
Kostovicova, Denisa 8, 211
Kostunica, Vojislav 127
Kouaci, Mohamed 93
Krajina Serb community 47
Krolo, Krešimir 71
Kubik, Jan 40
Kurds 135
Kurtović, Larisa 33
Kusturica, Emir 75

labour-managed firms (LMFs) 170,
174–76, *see also* enterprise
self-management, worker-managed
enterprises and workers'
self-management
Labudović, Stevan 93
Lampe, John R. 16
Law on Disposal and Circulation of Social
Capital (1989) 181–82, 182n.45
Law on Ownership Transformation 1992
(Slovenia) 162
Law on Personal Incomes (1990) 182
Law on Social Capital (1990) 181

Law on Transformation of Social Capital
1993 (Macedonia) 165
Law on Transformation of Socially Owned
Enterprises 1991 (Croatia) 163
League of Communists of Yugoslavia
(LCY) 22
*Les photographes de guerre: les djonouds du
noir et blanc* (exhibition) 93
Let's not drown Belgrade (protest
movement) 53
Liberal Democratic Party (LDP) 109
liberalism,
economic 18–19, 25–30
introduction 7–8
political 18, 21–25, 32–33
social 18–19, 27–29, 31–32
Yugoslav model 16–17, 19–21, 34
Life in Transition Survey (LiTS) 200–205
'Lijepa li si' (song) 74
Lisbon Treaty 105, 113
Lončar, Budimir 88

MacBride Commission 85
MacBride, Sean 85
Macedonia,
and border delimitation 9
border issues with Serbia 109
and creation of Republic of Yugoslavia
101
and IMF financial arrangements 165
and June 2018 agreement with Greece
132
last to bear term 'Yugoslav' 4
and Ohrid agreement (2001) 126
one of the early reformers 183
peaceful secession of 63–64, 103
Turkish investment in 129
very high unemployment rates in 178
visa-free regime (December 2009)
188
Maclean, Fitzroy 94
macroeconomic stability,
conclusion 165–66
IMF and the World Bank 149–59,
149nn.9–11, *151*, 154n.22, *155–59*,
155n.23, 156n.25, 157nn.28–9
introduction 141–42, 141n.1
Money and Inflation in Yugoslavia
(1987–89) 167–68

transition of successor states 159–65, *161*, 162n.35–6
underlying break-up factors 144–45, *145–46*, 147–49, *148*, 149n.8
Yugoslavian political economy 142–44, *143*
Many Voices One World: Communication and Society Today and Tomorrow (MacBride) 85
market mechanism 171–72
Marković, Ante 157–58, 160, 182, 193, 195
Marxism 21–22, 121
MASPOK 42
Mastnak, Tomaž 43
Matica Hrvatska 48
Meade, James 175
media/culture,
    beyond Yugonostalgia 71–75
    conclusions 75–76
    introduction 59–60
    post-socialist nostalgia 61–65, 61n.8, 62n.15
    Post-Yugoslav cultural spaces 65–68
    return performances 68–71, 68nn.36–7,40
Merdzanović, Adis 8
Mesić, Stjepan 88
Mikulić, Branko 29, 156–57, 160
Milatović, Jakov 10, 213
Milošević, Slobodan,
    departure from most understandings of Yugoslavism 63–64
    downfall of regime 126, 184
    illiberal politics of 54
    politics after 51
    pop-folk associations with 71
    and the Socialist party of Serbia 127
    Turkish opposition to brutality of regime 126
Mirković, Dragana 71
Mišina, Dalibor 71–72
Mogherini, Federica 111
Montenegro,
    and border delimitation 9, 99, 110, 112
    and creation of Republic of Yugoslavia 101
    Croatian musicians performing in 68
    decision to implement own policies 184

and the ekavica variant (language) 66
formerly under Austro-Hungarian rule 100
growth rate accelerated in 2006 164
and the JNA siege of Dubrovnik 69
and NAM summits 87, 90
and Russia 127, 127n.40, 131–32, 134
and State Union with Serbia 103
strength of Yugoslavia in 63–64
sustainable market economy progress in 192–93, *194–95*, 195–96, *197*, 198, *199–201*, 200–206, *203–5*
unpopularity of dissolution of Yugoslavia 210
visa-free regime (December 2009) 188
MTV 65
Multi Year Rescheduling Agreement (MYRA) 149, 153–54
Museum of African Art, Belgrade 81
Muslims 64, 117, 119, 123, 125–26, 129, 130

Namibia 89
NAM News Network (NNN) 91
Narodni pokret initiative 54
'narodnjaci' (music) 71
Nasser, Gamal Abdel 93
National Bank of Yugoslavia 152, 178–79, 182
nationalism 34
NATO,
    bombing of rump-Yugoslavia 130
    and Croatia 74
    military campaign against Serbia 106
    military campaign in Serbia 126
    policy towards Western Balkans 131
    and Russia 131, 134
    and Soviet Union 120
    and Turkey 122–23, 126
NATO-Russia Founding Act (1997) 124
Nazis 3
Nazor, Ante 48–50
ne da(vi)mo Beograd (CSO) 51
Negotiating Committee on Establishment of Global System of Trade Preferences (GSTP) 85–86
neoliberalism 26, 62
Netsa Art Village, Addis Ababa 92

new Constitution (1974) 172
New International Economic Order
    (NIEO) 83, 85
New World Information and
    Communication Order (NWICO)
    85
Nikolic, Tomislav 127, 127n.39
Nkrumah, Kwame 93
Non-Aligned Movement (NAM),
    and 16th summit (2012) 87
    and 17th summit (2016) 86–87
    50th anniversary message 82
    and Belgrade Summit (1961) 91–92
    and Cartagena summit (1995) 87
    establishment of 3–4
    and North/South inequality 83–84
    self-reliance one of the axes of 85
    and Venezuela Summit 90–91
    and Yugoslavia 23, 83, 120, 121,
        174
Non-Aligned News Agencies Pool
    (NANAP) 85, 90
non-governmental organisations (NGOs)
    47, 51–53, 55
North Macedonia,
    and fight for political influence against
        elites 212
    sustainable market economy progress
        in 192–93, *194–95*, 195–96, *197*,
        198, *199–201*, 200–206, *203–5*
    territorial issues in 109–10
North–South dialogue 83, 86
nostalgia 59–60, 75, 91
Nuti, Mario 175

OECD Development Assistance
    Committee 90
Ohrid agreement (2001) 126
Open Broadcasting Network (OBN) 65
Organization of Associated Labour (OAL)
    173
Organization for Economic Cooperation
    and Development (OECD) 174
Organization for Security and
    Co-operation in Europe (OSCE)
    87, 124
Osolnik, Bogdan 85
Ostalgie 61
Otpor! (coalition) 52, 54

Ottoman Empire,
    and the Armenian massacres 130
    heritage of 69, 118
    and millet system 119, 119n.5
    Serbs' persecution under 64
    and Turkey's dogma of non-
        interference 122
*Our Great Songbook: The Great Yugoslav
    Songbook* (Pisarovic) 70
Ozal, Turgut 125

Pan-Slavism 118
parallel trajectories,
    age of the empires 118–20
    Cold War geopolitics 120–23
    conclusions 133–36
    era of US hegemony 123–26
    global multipolarity 126–33
    introduction 117–18
Parekh, Bhikhu 83
Paris Club 153–54, 154n.19
Patriotic Movement Dignity 53
Pejovich, Steve 175
People's Liberation Front (PLF) 21
Permanent Court of Arbitration (PCA)
    104–6, 111
Petrov, Ana 66–67
Petrović, Tanja 91
PHARE programme (1992) 183
Pisarović, Vesna 70
Plenković, Andrej 75
Poland 54, 205
Post and Telecommunications of Kosovo
    129
post-Yugoslav Croatian football team
    73–74
Praxis group 23–24, 23n.37
Presevo Valley 108
Presley, Elvis 174
'Prijatelji' (Friends) veterans' movement
    74
privatization 185–86, 212–13
property regime 170
Putin, Vladimir 126–27, 131

Radical Party 127
Radić, Stjepan 3
Ramet, Sabrina 19–20
Rašković, Slaven 50

Ražnatović, Ceca 70
real exchange rate rules 141, 152–53,
    152n.16, *153*
Republic of Serb Krajina (RSK) 60
Republika Srpska 75, 127
Romania 121–22, 130
Russia,
    accused of obstructing Montenegro's
        NATO membership 131
    annexation of Crimea 61, 61n.8
    approach towards liberal
        interventionist international order
        126
    close relations with Republika Srpska
        127
    energy hegemony of 126–27
    increased influence in Balkans 131–32
    influence of 9, 117–18, 133–36
    multilateralism in 123–25
    objection to secession of Kosovo 126
    and post-Yugoslav elites 213
    and the Russian-Turkish war (1877)
        119
    support for Serbia 107, 109, 124, 133
    support for unity of Yugoslavia 125
    sustaining dynamic engagement in the
        Balkans 130

Sandžak region 128
Sanfey, Peter 10, 213
Sapir, André 175–76
Saudi Arabia 147
Schengen countries 188
Schmitter, Philippe 45
Second World War,
    creation of Kingdom of Yugoslavia 100
    partisans' victory in 21
    people's liberation struggle in 22
    post-war Yugoslavia 142
    and Slovenia 94
    and strategic importance of Yugoslavia
        120
self-censorship 23
self-reliance 85
Serbia,
    acceleration of economic reforms in 184
    aggression of 46
    autonomous provinces in 27
    border issues with Macedonia 109–10

civil society in 51–54
contested territorial issues of 9
and continuity with Yugoslav past
    63–64, 88, 90, 214
and creation of Republic of Yugoslavia
    101
and the ekavica variant (language) 66
and fight for political influence against
    elites 212
formerly under Austro-Hungarian rule
    100
guarantee of social property in 186
liberal ideas within 20
and memory of Tito 210
musicians performing in 68–69
and the NAM 87, 90, 93
NATO military campaign in 126
newly composed folk songs 60
normalization agreement with Kosovo
    131
ousting of Miloševic 33
poor relations with Soviet Union 122
resistance to reform of enterprise
    self-management 158
right to secession 102
and Russia 124–25, 127, 132, 134, 136
and the Russian-Turkish war (1877) 119
sense of historical continuity of 94
slowest to reform 164, 164n.38
and State Union with Montenegro 103
strength of civil society in 45
survival of social property and
    self-management in 186
sustainable market economy progress
    in 192–93, *194–95*, 195–96, *197*,
    198, *199–201*, 200–206, *203–5*
and *Travelling Communiqué*
    (exhibition) 91–92
and Turkey 126, 128, 129–30
visa-free regime (December 2009) 188
Serbian Assembly 'Doorway 53
Serbian Association of Writers 44
Serbian Karadjordjevic dynasty 120
Serbian Orthodox Church 53
Skopje earthquake 91
Slav communities 117
Slovenia,
    among the most successful in
        transition 187, 189, 209

and Bay of Piran dispute 9, 99, 104–5,
    112, 215
cultural policy 75
declaration of independence of 2
difficulty in emerging from post GFC
    recession 163
and fight for political influence against
    elites 212
and ICPE 89–90
independence of (June 1991) 180
membership of European Union
    (2004) 103
and MTV Adria franchise 65
and NAM summits 87
one of first republics to break away 101
one of the more developed republics
    162–63, 178–79
opted for gradualist strategy of
    transition 183
and references to pre-independence
    past 90
reformed arrangements for worker
    representation 212–13
retention of vestiges of previous
    economic model 184–85
significant role for worker
    representation 160, 160n.32
sustainable market economy progress
    in 192–93, *194–95*, 195–96, *197*,
    198, *199–201*, 200–206, *203–5*
worker representation in 160,
    160n.32
and Yugoslavia 63, 94, 101, 214
Smith, Adam 19
socialism 29–35, 170
Socialist Alliance of Working People 22
Socialist Civil Society (Mastnak) 43
Socialist party of Serbia 127
social property system 180
Sokolić, Ivor 8, 211
South Stream project 127, 131
Soviet Union,
    and the Balkan Pact (1953) 121
    breakup of 124
    Communism within 42, 119
    disintegration of 125
    envious of Yugoslavia 191
    fear of Yugoslav spillover 120–22,
        122n.15

fragmented along state socialist
    internal boundaries 61
introduction 3
normalization of relations with
    Yugoslavia (in 1988) 122
system of centralized planning 170
and the Treaty of Alliance (1954) 123
Yugoslavia's break with 22, 83, 158
Yugoslavia's relations with 25, 27–28
Spaskovska, Ljubica 8, 213–14
Stabilization and Association Process
    (SAP) 32, 157, 182–83, 182n.48
Stalin, Josef 3, 21–22, 25, 61, 121
Stand-by Arrangements 153–59, 154,
    154n.21, 158
Stanovnik, Janez 86
State Union of Serbia and Montenegro 4
Stinchcombe, Arthur 5
student uprisings (1968) 24, 24n.38
Šuput, Maja 70, 70n.47
Sustainable Development Agenda 87
Svejnar, Jan 175

Taconis, Kryn 93
TANJUG (Yugoslav news agency) 85, 90
territorial disputes,
    break-up of Yugoslavia 100–103,
        102n.7
    conclusions 112–14
    introduction 99–100
    Kosovo and Montenegro 109–13,
        109n.37
    Serbia and Kosovo 106–9, 108n.33,
        112–14
    Slovenia and Croatia 103–6, 113
Thaci, Hashim 108
Thessaloniki Summit (2003) 32, 130
Thompson, Marko Perković 73–74,
    73n.58
Ti & To company 94
Tito in Africa – Picturing Solidarity
    (exhibition) 91
Tito, Marshal Josip Broz,
    and break with Russia 120, 125
    and centrality of the UN 83
    and cottage industry of mementoes 63
    death of 4, 22, 180, 209
    effective use of Soviet threat 121
    and equidistance in foreign policy 213

fought on the side of Allied power 120, 120n.11
legacy of 135–36
and meeting with Kenneth Kaunda 90
and Migration Treaty with Menderes 123
a new kind of European 91
and Non-Aligned Movement 25, 81, 93–94
and popular culture 60
reforms impossible under his watch 166
rule of 3, 100–101
a unifying force 5
and Yugonostalgia 65
Tito – a Yugoslav Icon (exhibition) 93
tourism 26, 65, 127, 164, 178–79
Trans-National Corporations (TNCs) 84, 87
Travelling Communiqué (exhibition) 91–92
Treaty of Alliance (1954) 123
Treaty of Sevres 120, 120n.8
Tuđman, Franjo 60, 63, 69, 74–75
'turbo-folk' 71
Turkey,
    accession talks with EU 132
    anti-austerity mobilizations 54
    foreign policy during Cold War 122–23, 123n.25
    increased influence in Balkans at EU expense 131
    influence of 9, 117–18
    a key destination for Bosniak refugees 125
    limits of external influence 133–36
    and Muslim solidarity 125–26
    and neo-Ottomanism 127–30, 129n.49
    obstacle to EU accessions 103
    policy of engagement with Western Balkans 132–33
    and post-Yugoslav elites 213
    and the Sevres syndrome 119–20
    sustaining dynamic engagement in the Balkans 130
    and the Treaty of Alliance (1954) 123
Turkish Cooperation and Coordination Agency (TIKA) 129

U Ime Obitelji (human rights NGO) 48
Ukraine 127, 131

UN Centre on TNCs 84–85
UN Conference on Trade and Development (UNCTAD) 85
UN Council for Namibia 89
UNCTAD VI 85
UN Economic and Social Council 84
UN Educational, Scientific and Cultural Organization (UNESCO) 85, 108
Unfinished Modernisations: Between Utopia and Pragmatism (exhibition) 91
UN General Assembly 84, 88, 107, 132
UN Global Compact 87
UN Human Rights Council 87
Union of Fighters of the National-Liberation Struggle 22
United Kingdom 63, 147
United Nations 88, 90, 103, 108, 127
United Nations Charter 102
United States 20, 25, 108, 121, 123–26, 135
UN Security Council (SC),
    and independence for Kosovo 107, 136
    Resolution 1244 83, 126, 126n.36
    Yugoslavia a non-permanent elected member 83
Up Close and Personal with Tito (exhibition) 93–94
USSR *see* Soviet Union
uti possidetis juris 102
Uvalic, Milica 9, 176, 212
'Uvijek vjerni tebi' (song) 73

Vanek, Jaroslav 175
Versailles State 3
Vetevendosje (self-Determination) 110–11
Vienna Initiative 164
Višegrad 75
Vojvodina province 101
Volčič, Zala 62
Volcker, Paul 148
Vucić, Aleksandar 51, 108, 210
Vučković, Severina 70

Ward, Benjamin 174
Warsaw Pact 3, 174
War veterans' associations 47–48
Washington consensus 81

Western Balkans,
  and border disputes 105–6, 112–13
  contemporary challenges in 99–100,
    209
  and European Union 15, 101, 130–31
  further enlargement of 109
  history of strong social liberalism
    31–32
  influence of Russia and Turkey on
    117
  introduction 6
  liberalization of 34
  policy of NATO 131
  and Russia 131
  and Stabilization and Association
    Process (SAP) 183
  states in a permanent state of
    'transitocracy' 215–16
  and Turkey 128–29, 132, 134, 134n.63
  uniqueness of 133
women's emancipation project 43
Woodward, Susan L. 144
worker-managed enterprises 25–27,
    142–43, 212, *see also* enterprise
    self-management, labour-managed
    firms, and workers'
    self-management'

workers councils 185, 185n.60
workers' self-management 172–73, *see also*
    enterprise self-management,
    labour-managed firms, and
    worker-managed enterprises
World Bank 165, 173, 192, 198, 201

X Factor franchise 65, 65n.27

Yugonostalgia 8, 62, 65, 75, 210–11
Yugoslav Constitution 181
Yugoslav economic model,
    achievements and failures of 177–80,
      177n.33, *178*, 180n.4
    conclusions 187–89
    controversies about 174–77, 174n.9
    end of 180–87, 181n.44, *187*
    introduction 169–70
    main features of 170–74, 171n.4
Yugoslav People's Army (JNA) 43, 60–61,
    69, 101
Yugosphere 59–60, 64

zabavna (music) 69–70
Zagreb je NAŠ! 52
Zimmer frei (rooms available) schemes 26
Zvezde Granda (TV Pink) 65

www.ingramcontent.com/pod-product-compliance
Lightning Source LLC
Chambersburg PA
CBHW050427280326
41932CB00013BA/2013